Traitors

Traitors

Suspicion, Intimacy,
and the Ethics of State-Building

Edited by
Sharika Thiranagama
and
Tobias Kelly

PENN

UNIVERSITY OF PENNSYLVANIA PRESS

PHILADELPHIA

Published by
University of Pennsylvania Press
Philadelphia, Pennsylvania 19104-4112

Printed in the United States of America on acid-free paper
10 9 8 7 6 5 4 3 2 1

Library of Congress Cataloging-in-Publication Data

Traitors : suspicion, intimacy, and the ethics of state-building / edited by Sharika Thiranagama and Tobias Kelly.
    p. cm.
  Includes bibliographical references and index.
  ISBN 978-0-8122-4213-3 (alk. paper)
  1. Treason—Cross-cultural studies.   2. Treason—Moral and ethical aspects.
3. Traitors—Cross-cultural studies.   I. Thiranagama, Sharika.   II. Kelly, Tobias.
JC328.T73   2009
364.1'31—dc22   2009018800

Contents

Introduction: Specters of Treason

Tobias Kelly and Sharika Thiranagama

The English novelist E. M. Forster once wrote that "if I had to choose between betraying my country and betraying my friend I hope I should have the guts to betray my country" (1972, 66). Forster's claim seems particularly provocative, given that it was written in 1939, on the eve of World War II, a time when accusations of treason could have deadly implications. Yet for Forster personal bonds of love and friendship were to take priority over the demands of state and nation. At a personal level, Forster's claim should almost certainly be read in terms of the criminalization of homosexuality in early twentieth-century Britain. It cannot be surprising if loyalty to lovers and confidantes overrides allegiance to a discriminatory legal regime. However, at the same time, Forster also recognized that the demands of one's country can be hard to resist. It is not clear if the courage he asks for is bravery in the face of the coercive power of the state or moral fortitude to make an ultimately difficult ethical decision.

The tension among intimate personal relationships, the demands of states, and the hard moral choices that these produce are at the heart of this book. Traitors are rarely, if ever, simply venal or self-interested, and accusations of treachery are seldom self-evident. Rather, treason is a product of often contradictory social and political obligations. As Forster reminds us, we are never simply citizens or friends but always and necessarily both at the same time. As we try to negotiate our multiple allegiances, we must balance competing demands on our loyalty. In this context, any act of treachery can also be a potential act of loyalty to another cause. The guilt or innocence of traitors is, therefore, never clear-cut, as competing moral values make often-conflicting demands. Treachery is reproduced in the "gray zones" of political life, destabilizing the rigid moral binaries of victim and persecutor, friend and enemy.

Despite or even because of the ethical ambiguity of treason, accusations of treachery often attract the most vehement, sometimes violent, condemnation. Treason was the last crime to attract the death penalty in the United Kingdom, and elsewhere is subject to the most brutal forms of punishment. The violence of accusations of treason can perhaps be explained by the fact that acts of treason seem to threaten and destabilize the fragile moral and social relationships that hold us together and bind us to the perhaps otherwise abstract notions of nation, people, or community. Furthermore, and perhaps most important, traitors arguably attract a particular aversion because they are not a distant "other" but the enemy within. They are a source of internal transgression, and as such, they call into question the moral and political commitments of those who seem to be closest to us. McCarthyism, Stalinist purges, and even medieval witch crazes did not focus on distant strangers but tried to root out internal subversion. In this context, accusations of treason try to define who is inside and who is out, laying claim to moral and political certainty in the face of uncertainty.

Treason has often been treated as a pathology or a distortion of political life. Its importance has, therefore, been sidelined in social and political analysis. However, one of the central propositions of this volume is that, far from being pathological, the identification and prosecution of treason are constant, essential, and "normal" parts of the processes by which attempts are made to reproduce social and political order. Placing treason at the heart of our attempts to understand the ways in which political regimes are made and unmade helps us raise important questions about categories of belonging, about their moral, political, and economic foundations, and about the often contradictory choices faced by modern political subjects. The bond between the state and its citizens is never complete, as it is mediated by a host of contradictory affiliations to kin and social groups and can be overruled by wider ethical obligations. The specter of treason is thus embedded within notions of the loyal citizen. Citizenship is itself fraught with risk. The fidelity of even those who appear to have the greatest allegiance can never be assured. Betrayal is always a possibility.[1] It is not just the stranger that is feared and suspected but also the seemingly faithful citizen. Therefore, political conflict should not be understood as just the marking of difference or the delineation of boundaries but as the product of a tension inherent in the state-citizen relationship. Both states and their citizen/subjects are prone to the moral and social unease produced by fundamentally incomplete forms of loyalty and legitimacy. Antagonism is produced not only between the citizen and the one who appears to be different but among those who seem to be the same, those who, at first glance, seem to share the most intense sense of solidarity. Intimacy is not the antithesis of fear but can be at its core.

In asking how traitors, both as an abstract category and as concrete persons, are reproduced in the context of local histories, contributors to this volume address larger theoretical questions about the nature of shifts in (postcolonial) citizenship. They explore how the historically specific dimensions of the relationship between citizens/subjects and those who speak in the name of the state create particular configurations of trust, suspicion, and belonging. As such, three key themes run through the volume. The first is the relationship between treason and the fragile nature of state-building processes. All modern states are built on betrayal, and continuing acts of treasons are central to their development. In a context where states depend on the multiple and often contradictory intimate relationships of kinship, ethnicity, and class to extend their reach, claims of treason help map the moral boundaries of the state and the people in whose name they speak. The second theme is the forms of suspicion and fear that are inherent in social and political relationships. We suggest that the possibility of betrayal is the ever-present dark side of intimacy, taking on new and ever more frightening forms in the context of state-building. The third and final theme is the ethical nature of treason. Acts of treason are produced through the contradictory loyalties and fears produced by rapid social change, creating particular configurations of accountability and responsibility.

State-Building

Treason is at the heart of the processes through which modern states are made. The declaration of American independence, the formation of Communist China, or the creation of the states that emerged from the break up of the Soviet Union, to name but a few examples, all saw old ties of loyalty severed in favor of new. Such acts of betrayal can be found at the birth of perhaps all new nations and states. However, these betrayals of the old regime continue to haunt their successors, serving as a constant reminder of the fragility of power. Accusations of treason have, therefore, historically played a central role in the attempt to maintain social order and political authority. To make an accusation of treason is to make a claim to power, to try to police the boundaries of permissible politics, and to exert authority in the face of constantly shifting affiliations. As new states are brought into being, they must not only build on but also try to transcend already existing social and political relationships. States and loyal citizens never exist solely in the abstract but are grounded in the intimate relationships of kinship, ethnicity, religion, and class. As such, state-building projects must manage multiple loyalties and allegiances and rephrase these as loyalty and belonging to the state and the new nation.

As states expand and contract, as new factions and classes take control, new forms of loyalty are demanded, and new forms of treason are defined. States, social groups, and kin constantly transform themselves around new sets of allegiances as they navigate ever-changing realities. At the same time, the same agents can shift among acting in the name of the state, nation, or personal affiliation. As such, treason is never given once and for all: its content changes alongside fluctuations in power and authority. The shifting nature of treason is perhaps shown most clearly in the history of royal privilege in medieval Europe. From the twelfth century onward in France and England, we see a continuous expansion of state power through ever-new amendments to treason statutes. Definitions of treason moved from a focus on injury to the person of the king toward an emphasis on words and activities against the Crown (Lemon 2006; Cutler 1982). Treason was no longer a form of personal betrayal but an act of disloyalty to the political order. Early medieval concepts of treason were linked to breaches of faith against others, primarily conducted through vassal and liege relationships. However, this was a very weak concept, as loyalty was seen as voluntary, and the withdrawal of fidelity was a prescripted and acceptable declaration of enmity that could not easily be converted to "treason." The development of the law of treason was, therefore, part of a larger attempt by the Crown to convert "vassal into subject" (Cutler 1981). In this process, Roman law concepts of *lèse majesté*—injury to the dignity or person of the divine king/emperor—became increasingly significant in French legal statutes. The Crown transcended the particular king; therefore, an act of treason not only attacked the specific king but the moral and sacred Crown, the union of king and kingdom itself. Treachery was an increasingly impersonal and grand crime against a divine emperor/king. In this process, not only did the object of loyalty change but also the texture and content of that allegiance. As treason became an offense against the foundation of power itself, "the prosecution of treason could be construed not as a personal vengeance but as a necessary measure to maintain public order" (Cutler 1981, 14). We have here a shift from a personal fidelity to the king toward a more diffuse loyalty to the institution of the Crown.

The prosecution of treason has practical consequences for the expansion of political control. Instead of demonstrating an already stable hold on power, an accusation of treason is an attempt to make that claim more concrete or to extend the reach of power still further. The redefinition of treason in medieval Europe, for example, was linked to attempts by the Crown to exert power over competing forms of authority. The barons and the church had until this time exercised considerable alternative claims of loyalty. The Crown, however, sought to become the ultimate object of allegiance. Treason as a crime against the

Crown was exclusively prosecuted by the king and the officers he nominated and most often involved the confiscation of large estates. This meant the Crown could press exclusive jurisdictional authority over municipal and ecclesiastical courts and garner resources for increasing its power and patronage. Such processes encouraged the French and English crowns to identify as wide a scope as possible for treasonous activity. This did not mean, however, that such activity went unquestioned. Counterfeiting, seditious texts, secret meetings, and possible intentions were never self-evidently treasonous and had to be made to seem so. The attribution of treason is always first and foremost an *interpretive* act. The burden of proof always lay lies with the prosecuting authority to make treason tangible and meaningful. Crucially, in giving treason a concrete presence, those who make claims to treachery also simultaneously give their own claims to power tangibility.

There are, of course, historically and culturally specific modes of regulating obedience and loyalty. In his analysis of medieval Christianity in Europe, Talal Asad (1993) argues that there was a shift from religious devotion being a matter of the correct performance of ritual to a focus on belief and internal convictions. The church, therefore, became concerned not simply with regulating and controlling observable acts of devotion but also the internal thoughts of Christians. While Asad's argument is concerned with the particular history of the medieval Christianity, his broad argument helps us make a distinction between treasonous acts and treasonous beliefs. This is not a once-and-for-all transition but a tension that runs through attempts at political and social control. Some regimes attempt to penetrate/colonize the intimate thoughts and dreams of their people (Arendt 1999). This patrolling of inner life creates fears and suspicions over the very thoughts that people hold. Mere emotions can be a source of betrayal and are constantly monitored. Other regimes are interested in regulating only the public behavior and publicly demonstrated loyalties of their citizens (Žižek 1997). Such regimes are not interested in whether their citizens believe in them as long as the people act "as if" they do (Wedeen 1999). Treason here is linked to concrete acts, not merely thoughts. The implications of this distinction between treasonous behavior and treacherous beliefs are played out through the ways in which regimes seek to control their citizen/subjects and the manner in which notions of the private, public, self-censorship, and dissent are articulated.

The brief discussion above of early modern Europe displays one of the most important continuities between premodern and modern discussions of treason: namely, that treason and sovereignty can be mutually constitutive. However, we also argue in this volume that there is a crucial disjuncture between premodern and modern notions of treason.

Central to this disjuncture is the move to notions of popular sovereignty, where states claim to act in the name of the people. The people are a crucially intangible presence, making the object of loyalty ever more diffuse and the accusation of treason an ever more potent vehicle of the assertion of sovereign power. The French historian and philosopher Claude Lefort writes that the shift from the monarchic to the democratic state saw a fundamental realignment in the symbolization of power. For Lefort, democracy evacuated the locus of power, turning the place of power from a definite substantial figure embodied by the king into an empty place occupied by "the people" (1988, 17). This new, empty place of power as residing with the people can never be entirely occupied by any one government or group, as no one can entirely subsume the claim to speak in the people's name. As such, "power becomes and remains democratic when it proves to belong to no-one" (27). The people are both the condition of the democratic revolution and at the same time fundamentally irrepresentable, as they can never be given a concrete location or held in one place. As a result, the claim to act in the name of the people is never self-evident but needs constantly to be grounded and remade. Lefort asserts that debates about legitimacy are institutionalized at the heart of democracy, as the people are always in a state of becoming, never to be finished (16). Democracy opens up a question that can never be fully answered and frees up a space of power that can never be completely filled.

Ernesto Laclau takes Lefort's work on the symbolization of power under democracy a step further. For Laclau, the democratic imaginary is less to do with the emergence of liberal institutions and is more concerned with the ways in which popular sovereignty has become the organizing force of the modern state and modern political imaginaries (2005, 166–68). Laclau argues that the emptiness that Lefort identifies at the place of power is "a type of identity, not a structural location" and is always potentially irrepresentably full and thus potent (105). For Laclau, such empty signifiers are fundamental to the ways in which political subjectivity is created. The emptiness of the signifiers makes it possible for a people to be constructed out of a heterogeneous political and social terrain. He stresses, against classical theories of political representation, that the people are a political category, not a pre-given collective that comes to be represented (163). Crucially, however, the instability of popular subjectivity is constitutive, not pathological. *When* the people are *named*, they are called into existence. In this volume, we suggest the modern state and nation are unified around a central empty signifier par excellence—the name of the people, constantly irrepresentable, empty but full. As the people have come to be named continually in political struggles, empty signifiers have come to unify and make coherent all kinds of unconnected demands.

One of the problems for scholars working on political theory and state formation in the non-Western world is that our primary theoretical inspirations are still founded in reference to what remains a largely Euro-American history. The history of treason in European monarchies clearly cannot be universalized. We need to pay careful attention to the cultural specificity of treachery. However, while traitors are always products of particular histories, they can be fitted into more general specters that haunt the nation-state and are, therefore, ripe for cross-cultural and historical analysis. Although the democratic imaginary arguably has its roots in the history of Europe and North America, it is now a globalized idea that is fundamental to the modern state and politics. Postcolonial states, whether liberal democratic or not, widely claim to speak in the name of the people. In his contribution to this volume, Richard Whitecross offers a specific political and historical trajectory as he explores the distinctive forms of loyalty in Bhutanese history. Whitecross's detailed examination of the kingdom of Bhutan shows the ways in which royal power had to perform continually in the face of a ghostly theocratic Buddhist power that was only imperfectly contained by the Crown. His essay considers the implications of the emerging notion of the people of Bhutan for forms of loyalty, allegiance, and betrayal. As Whitecross argues, the placing of the people as the symbolic heart of the Bhutanese state has had fundamental and irreversibly concrete consequences for the newly created citizens (and noncitizens) of the region. Ethnic and religious markers have increasingly come to divide those who are seen as loyal citizens in need of protections and those seen as potentially subversive and dangerous aliens.

In the context of postcolonial anxieties, accusations of treason give the people a more definite presence. The accusation of treachery is socially productive in that it calls the people into being despite, or even because of their historical absence. Many of the contributions to this volume describe new states emerging from colonial pasts where the institutions of state power are in place but the process of people-making has only just begun. The colonial state was characterized by the construction of state and governmental infrastructure but was also fundamentally marked by the nonidentity of the ruled and the ruler. The emergence of the postcolonial nation fundamentally changed this opposition. Popular sovereignty suggests a symbolic identity between rulers and ruled—government of the people by the people. Yet the people remain diffuse and undefined. They had to be formed out of an array of religious, economic, ethnic, and familial affiliations that often had little to do with the formal boundaries of the new states. Accusations of treason allow popular sovereignty to be produced out of the often highly fragmented and disparate raw material upon which postcolonial states are built. They help to mark out the boundaries of acceptable behavior and stake claims to ultimate authority. In this volume, Lars Buur examines the attempt of the Mozambican state to unify a highly diverse and fractured social body into a new nation-state. The new Mozambican state sought both to act in the name of and to impose an ever elusive nontribal, socialist "New Man." In this process, the cartoon figure Xiconhoca, unifying a host of negative social, political, and moral attitudes, came to stand for all that the new state had to overcome. Ironically, Xiconhoca remained far more recognizable than the abstract Mozambican citizens that the state was trying to reproduce, testifying to the ubiquitous presence of potential betrayal. Similarly, as Nayanika Mookherjee argues in her chapter, left-wing intellectuals in contemporary Bangladesh attempt to cut through the complex webs of complicity and violence that marked the Bangladesh War of 1971 by portraying bearded Islamists as the archetypal traitor. As Mookherjee shows, such claims have to be seen in the context of the desire for a socialist secular state that has never been born.

Accusations of treachery, then, are central to attempts to concretize the empty signifier of "the people." The allegation of treason allows popular sovereignty to take on a corporeal form. However, in doing so, these accusations also reveal the fragility of any claim to act in the name of the people. Despite Laclau's claim in *On Populist Reason* to offer a catchall theory of politics, he, like many other social theorists, does not deal with treason and the problem of the traitor. For Laclau, the materialization of a common enemy is fundamental to the constitution of the antagonistic frontiers around which otherwise unconnected demands are made equivalent (2005, 83–93). However, while he sees this frontier as unstable, he never fully considers its potential transgression. The fear of oneself and of one's own kind constantly flickers within boundaries of "the people." Laclau, therefore, neglects the fundamental instability of the people as they appear *to themselves*. We build upon and move beyond Laclau's arguments about popular sovereignty by pointing to the neglected underside of contemporary political practice—a discourse about the people that is shot through with shame and fear. This fear is not of some distant other but is an anxiety about yourself and those seemingly closest to you, a suspicion that even the most apparently loyal can potentially turn on you and that any claimed unity is always in doubt. It is no coincidence that the French Revolution, an event that is often seen as the birth of modern democracy and as the herald of new concepts of popular sovereignty and rights, was also accompanied by the mass bloodletting of *le terreur*. Up to 40,000 suspected collaborators, spies, and enemies of the people were purged and sentenced under the catchall notion of "crimes against liberty," as enemies of the people were found in ever increasing numbers. We argue, therefore, that, although the crime of treason may have its roots in medieval monarchy, the instability of popular sovereignty sees the problem of treason recreated in ever more intense forms.

The traitor lies not so much at the margins or beyond the nation but at its heart. She or he is not the stranger, the common enemy, but is in fact always potentially one of us. This specific and potent significance of the figure of the traitor has been ignored in larger political theory; traitors come to give the people their identity not by being different but by being perversely the same. James Siegel begins his monograph *A New Criminal Type in Jakarta* with the sentence: "most peoples of the world kill those they want to consider other than themselves. . . . There is another type of massacre, however, in which one kills those in one's own image" (1998, 1). Siegel describes three major purges that have marked Indonesian postcolonial history: the nationalist and communist combat in 1948, the 1965 massacres of Indonesian communists, and the 1980s killings of "criminals." These purges, he points out, are all the mass killings of Indonesians by Indonesians. Siegel particularly focuses on the killing of thousands of criminals under the New Order government. The criminal is portrayed as being "on the edge of Indonesian society but never outside it, never the foreigner" (1998, 3). The criminal

is an Indonesian, a member of the same nation to which those who killed him belong or who, often enough, applauded his murder. He is a version of oneself. . . . Precisely because he is not different from oneself, what is his is potentially one's own. One can imagine standing in his place, as the forces of the Indonesian state do. (1998, 7)

Siegel's analysis resonates with the problematic that we identify as a central issue for all nationalist enterprises: the problem of sameness.

It is an old adage in social theory that the same is familiar, safe but sterile, while the other is dangerous yet fertile and productive. The problem of how "the other" is conceived and made visible has become one of the raisons d'être of social science writing on issues of nationalism, citizenship, and the state (see, for example, Balibar 2003). Almost all contemporary studies of violence, state making, and citizenship have focused on the violent "othering" within political and social life and/or the treatment of marginality. However, this has ignored an equally strong interpretive, political, and social anxiety about the problem of sameness, specifically *perverted sameness.* States and communities are as much concerned with defining and reproducing those who are within their embrace as they are with identifying those who are outside. This is as equally significant and often as violent an enterprise as othering. It is not strangers who represent the abiding concern of many political projects but those who are known and close by. Intimates cause the most anxiety. The traitor holds a particular place in this fear of the same, as he or she presents a distorted, even perverted image of the self, creating a particularly visceral form of hatred. The traitor holds up a mirror to society of all that it most fears about itself, revealing the contingency of political affiliation and the fragility of loyalty. We could, if we are not careful, become the traitor ourselves: the traitor is a continual potential self.

The figure of the traitor exposes the complexity of the contradictory affiliations for those who are meant to be "inside." Loyal citizens emerge out of conditions where individuals are constituted by multiple and dense and often contradictory attachments and out of histories in which the violent creation of difference takes place in a context of radical sameness. The problem of unbearable similarity is explored at length in Julia Strauss's chapter in this volume through her comparison of the People's Republic of China and the Republic of China in Taiwan. Strauss points out that the centrality of the prosecution of treason for both regimes was rooted in the simultaneous presence of nationalist, communist, and collaborationist regimes under Japanese occupation. These regimes had fluctuating and porous geographical and political alliances at both macro- and microlevels. The legacy of these historical intimacies was an obsession with traitors at the heart of both regimes' attempts to create new nations out of the same people. The people were, therefore, simultaneously to be protected but also feared as potential enemies.

Violence seems to play a central role whenever fears about treachery arise. The genocidal killings in the former Yugoslavia and the African Great Lakes region, to name but two examples, were not carried out by strangers but by neighbors, friends, and colleagues. Such events remind us that those seemingly closest to us, those supposedly most like us, can be the object of the most intense hatred. In contexts of deep uncertainty, nothing is more certain than violence, and nothing differentiates more than bloodshed (Appadurai 1998). Such violence can be politically productive: it allows those who speak in the name of the state to demonstrate their power and brutally cuts people off from claims to intimacy. Few things mark distance more clearly than the failure of empathy seen in violence. However, the violent punishment of those accused of treason can create its own kinds of uncertainty (Kelly 2006). The prosecution of treason has a tendency to spiral out of control. Siegel points out that the more the Indonesian New Order government founded its legitimacy on its violent massacres and its power over criminals, the more it found itself rooted in relations to criminals (1998). Furthermore, if the otherwise intangible people become visible through acts of violence, the same violence can also raise its own specters. What if the accusation of treachery reveals not the presence of a venal traitor but the absence of any concrete basis for the people? Claims of treachery therefore play an immensely ambiguous role in attempts to consolidate power. On the one hand, the identification and elimination of traitors help to make claims to power tangible; on the other hand, the elimination of traitors reveals the constant fragility of the social body and a seemingly subterranean world of multiple loyalties.

Intimacy

Hitherto, we have placed treason as a problem for those who speak in the name of the state or the people. However, a concern with treachery is not simply a top-down process. Recent revelations from the Soviet and East German state archives, for example, make us aware of the important role that ordinary people played in maintaining suspicions and claims about treachery. Histories of nation- and state-building never simply take place in the abstract but are also intimate histories of kinship, sexuality, and friendship. In this process, the practices of state penetrate into the most intimate aspects of life and demand that people view these relationships through the prism of the state. As such, neighbors, friends, family, and conationals, those who are like us, are also always potentially enemies or traitors to the state. This constant movement between the abstract state that stands apart and the state as bound up in our everyday hopes and fears gives state-building projects their strength but also serves as one of their greatest weaknesses. This tension is not a one-time event, a transitional stage on the way to stability, but rather is part of the larger inherent fragility that always informs political life.

The punitive policing of sexuality provides a particularly powerful lens through which claims of treason are refracted, as the national and the intimate are conjoined. In his poem "Punishment," the Irish poet Seamus Heaney (1998b) utilizes the figure of the ancient Windeby Bog girl sacrificed for unknown crimes to reflect upon the Irish women in Derry and Belfast who were tarred, their heads shorn by Irish nationalists for associating with British soldiers. The poem addresses her as "my poor scapegoat", seeing in her "tar black face" the lineaments of a sparse beauty before punishment. Gazing at her shorn head "like a stubble of black corn," Heaney cannot absolve himself of the revenge. He himself recalls how he has "stood dumb" when

> your betraying sisters
> cauled in tar
> wept by the railings,

Heaney explores his own relationship to such violence—he abhors the brutal scapegoating but also recognizes the attractions of such intimate revenge. He admits that he himself

> . . . would have cast, I know,
> the stones of silence.
> I am the artful voyeur
> . . . .
> who would connive
> in civilized outrage
> yet understand the exact
> and tribal, intimate revenge.

Heaney's poem demonstrates the ways in which ideas about treason and betrayal knot together the intimate—familial and sexual—and the national. As Begona Aretxaga argues, in her own analysis of the poem, women's sexuality in Northern Ireland has become "a material and symbolic arena of political demarcation and a political battleground itself" (1997, 153). Ambiguous political boundaries are policed through sexual and domestic borders. Such a reading alludes to the unpredictable and ambiguous way in which women are made the repositories for complex, potent, and often violent ideas about betrayal and national belonging.

The invocation of the tar-cauled women in Northern Ireland immediately recalls the thousands of women publicly punished for collaboration across postwar Europe. Fabrice Virgili has estimated that between 1943 and 1946 around 20,000 French women had their heads publicly shaved. Although Nazi occupation necessitated treason as a series of everyday acts committed at all levels by both genders, cleansing was particularly directed at women. The forms of collaboration that women were accused of varied from economic profiteering to political support for the Nazis to being from an ethnic group associated with the Germans (2002, 11). However, the image of the shorn "horizontal collaborator," shaved because of her sexual betrayal of the nation, has lingered in popular and cultural imaginations. Sexual relations reproduce the boundary for group and corporate identities, turning sexual intimacy inside out. It is, of course, not just in Europe that the honor of women came to stand for the honor of the people. The 1947 partition of India and Pakistan saw the writing of new national boundaries onto female bodies, as Hindu and Muslim women were subject to horrific communal sexualized violence. Women were killed by men of the other community as well as by those from their own, in order to preserve the "honor" and "shame" of their families (Butalia 2000; Menon and Bhasin 1998; Das 1995).

Treason is a unique crime not simply because it is considered a crime against the king, the Crown, the state, or the people, but rather because it reaches across boundaries of state and citizen, transgressing the distinctions of public and private. Accusations of treason are powerful because they are at least partly produced in the dark side of our intimate lives with others. Thus, it is important to understand the dynamics and distinctions between treason as a legal norm and treachery as a moral category. The movement between the two is immensely productive for both the accused and the accuser. The legal prosecution of treason builds on the moral objection to treachery, allowing it to run free from the limitations of personal animosity.[2]

The extensive body of work on witchcraft accusations provides the most important parallel here to our own investigation of modern treachery. Witchcraft trials can be understood as a response to fears about the dangers that threaten social bodies from *within*. Furthermore, and equally important, witchcraft accusations take place in the same context of suspicion and aversion among intimates. Robin Brigg's (2002) now seminal *Witches and Neighbours* highlights the emotional intensity of early modern communities. While we like to idealize the premodern world and the closeness of neighbors and communities, Briggs's work reveals "a world dominated less by values of sharing and collectivity than by murderous antagonisms where the absence of privacy afforded no protection against extremes of emotional intensity" (Roper 1998, 266). Fantasies about potential harm to one and fears about others circulated constantly. The intimacy of the premodern world was responsible for the virulence of the witchcraft craze, running counter to our assumptions about the amicable and intrinsically peaceful core of neighborliness as a value in itself. Simon Turner's chapter in this volume highlights how, among Burundian Hutu and Tutsi, fear and the suspicion of treachery are products of intimacy. Turner focuses on the suspicion caused by everyday interactions in households, schools, and families. The particular mixture of intimacy and violence creates two related discourses on treachery. Does apparent friendship mean that one is a traitor to one's ethnic loyalties, or does violence mean one is a traitor to the values of neighborliness?

The "dark side of intimacy," to paraphrase Peter Geschiere (1997), is often downplayed by our idealization of neighbors and kin as caring, supportive, and free from jealousy. However, intimate relationships create vulnerability and anxiety as well as friendship and support. The very people we think we know best and with whom we share the most can do the most damage and turn unexpectedly (Klein 1967). Our inherent sociality opens us up to hurt and damage from other people. Knowledge about the most private aspects of people's lives can produce a sense of responsibility and care (Jamieson 1998). Yet this shared sociality also increases the stakes of disappointment. As Hannah Arendt argues, human beings are inherently unpredictable, and the "impossibility of relying upon the future is the price they pay for plurality and reality, for the joy of inhabiting the world together" (1999, 244). We depend on others for our most basic needs and wants, yet the fragility of communication means that we can never be entirely sure what other people are going to do (Simmel 1972). How much do we really know about those who seem to be closest to us? How do we understand what they are thinking and what they want? Closeness does not lessen these anxieties and uncertainties but amplifies them. The more we know about people, the more we are aware of the layers of significance and meaning that inform their actions, and the more difficult they become to read. Ironically, both knowing too little and knowing too much have their own dangers. Knowing too little can be worrying, as we can never predict what people will do. Yet too much knowledge of other people's inner desires and aspirations can make us all too aware of their potential to turn on us. Knowledge about what other people have done or are likely to do can be too much to bear. Ignorance really can be bliss. Trust, after all, is built on the lack of knowledge and, therefore, always assumes that betrayal is a possibility. We trust precisely because we are not certain. Because of this, disproving betrayal becomes doubly difficult. The initial act of betrayal proves that someone cannot be entirely trusted, making it almost impossible to create the stable ground upon which loyalty can be proved once more. The fear of betrayal is an anxiety over the self and raises important issues about our own commitments, weaknesses, and responsibilities. We do not trust others because we know what we ourselves are capable of.

The seemingly more abstracted, clinical, and reified politics of the modern state does not necessarily offer a refuge from the suspicions of intimacy but emerges merely as a new dimension. As states become larger and more disembedded from intimate everyday interactions, the necessity of generalized trust increases and, therefore, so does the presence of mistrust. The institutions of accountability and transparency that are supposed to make betrayal more difficult can actually increase the fear of betrayal. With the creation of bureaucracies, parliaments, courts, and security services, issues of loyalty and betrayal are partly dispersed into institutions rather than rooted entirely in personal relationship. However, there is a dark side to the institutions of the modern state as well. The search for transparency can produce its own forms of opaqueness, and as Comaroff and Comaroff argue, "changing patterns of illumination cast new shadows and, with them, new domains of darkness beyond their arcs of light" (2003, 288; see also Sanders and West 2003). The archives of totalitarian regimes across the world, for example, show us that attempts to uncover treachery can lead to more suspicion, as "winks upon winks" are read to ever-increasing degrees of subtlety. Purges have the habit of turning in on themselves, as ever more layers of information are uncovered, amid accusations and counteraccusation about what is known or what is being hidden. Modern forms of surveillance increase not only the sense of what can be known but also the sense of what is not known, amplifying the feeling of suspicion and the impression that betrayal is always possible.

A focus on the fears, anxieties, and hatreds of intimacy illuminates what is often presented as a perennial paradox in contemporary work on violence and conflict—why it is that people who seem to live peacefully side by side can turn on each other brutally. The suggestion made here is that intimacy does not stand in opposition to violence but can lie at its foundation. In his study of violence in civil war, the political scientist Stathis Kalyvas (2006) argues that intimacy is essential, not incidental, to civil war, but not because people are inherently violent as Hobbesian perspectives might suggest. Rather, because, in ordinary life, we avoid conflict and fear to do violence to each other, in times of conflict, we are relieved when another supralocal actor performs his violence against those with whom we have disputes. While intimate life may be fractious and complex, civil war and the heightened possibility of violence turns "common dispute" into "lethal violence."

Supralocal political actors offer people the possibility of turning personal rivalries into conflicts. Robin Briggs points out that "when people had little chance of acting out their fantasies or suppositions on a public stage these would have tended to remain private and shadowy" (1996, 1). The onset of witchcraft trials "added a powerful new element, moving witchcraft out into public view, and legitimating open discussion" (1996, 1). When the state, legal systems, and church legitimized and provided a forum in which antagonisms, rivalries, and fears about injuries were tabulated and prosecuted, things took a different and unpredictable turn. Because of this, states and supralocal actors, even as they expand their power through accusations and prosecutions of treason, run the risk of making the dark side of familial and community life into a legitimate instrument of violent sovereignty (Fitzpatrick and Gellately 1997). The Gestapo, as Vandana Joshi points out, may have "derived its strength from the co-operation of the masses, [but] clearly, the masses did not do it with the sole intention of rooting out the enemies of the state" (2003, 9). Once they initiate these processes "by exchanging violence for denunciation, political actors assume considerable moral and practical costs of ridding people of their personal enemies" (Kalyvas 2006, 339). As such, Kalyvas argues that intimate violence is not so much a "politicization of individual life" but a "pervasive privatization of politics" and less "a transgression of social ties and more their full, though perverse expression" (2006, 363–64). By grounding its legal and policing capacities within intimate personal relations, the state opens itself up to the fear and uncertainty that mark the dark side of intimacy. While, as Fitzpatrick and Gellately point out, denunciatory practices exist in some form in all organized societies and communities, the willingness of the state to utilize them creates new political spaces.

There are very specific political and historical contexts around which the prosecution of treason becomes a central feature of political sovereignty. Ideas of betrayal may be integral to treason, but not all betrayals are considered treasonous. Betrayal, as contributors in this volume and authors such as Gabriella Turnaturi (2007) point out, is a commonplace and everyday feature of life with others, but it takes the intervention of the state to turn betrayal into treason. We suggest, therefore, a multilayered perspective on betrayal and treason, one that opens up consideration of betrayal as a productive and everyday social interaction upon which accusations of treason build in the particular and often violent contexts of state building, occupation, or civil war. Thus, it is important to make distinctions between legal and moral notions of treachery, as well as to understand how the latter makes the former potent. We argue that while betrayal is ubiquitous and fundamental, there is something specific about regimes and periods where the fear of traitors assumes violent form. The category of treason grows out of the fundamental anxiety of betrayal built into the fragilities of intimate life by giving these anxieties institutional and political form.

Fears of treason and betrayal can, of course, be highly corrosive to social relationships. As Veena Das argues, the apprehension of violence can lead to a "withdrawal of trust" from even the most mundane and seemingly ordinary practice (1998b). In this volume, Sharika Thiranagama examines how an increasingly violent and authoritarian Liberation Tigers of Tamil Eelam (LTTE) has become obsessed with violently rooting out "traitors" as it seeks to assert its moral and political sovereignty over the Sri Lankan Tamil community. The result is the dismemberment of the networks of trust, as not only the fear of the traitor but also fear of the LTTE becomes overwhelming. Yet Thiranagama also describes how the fear of treachery can be the basis of new forms of less malignant sociality. Because the shared secrets that people hold, the things that people know but cannot say ultimately bind people together, intimacy is rebuilt, not necessarily through kinship but around a shared sense of complicity and vulnerability. Intimacy is created by the profound sense of trust formed through the ability to speak to each other, while violence rages all around.

As such, we argue that suspicion, rather than trust, is the default condition of social and political life. However, at the same time, as we attempt to overcome suspicions over the motives and desires of those closest to us, we can build relationships of trust. Trust and suspicion are, therefore, not opposed but are bound up in one another. The fear of betrayal is at the productive core of social and political interaction. Through the attempt to overcome suspicion, or at least put it to one side, the possibility for a more benign form of sociality is created. In his 1995 Nobel lecture, Seamus Heaney (1998a) describes an incident in July 1976 in Northern Ireland where a minibus of workers was stopped by armed actors; the passengers were told to line up on the road. The masked men asked the Catholics to step forward; all those gathered assumed that these were paramilitaries targeting Catholics. As the only Catholic among the workers made a motion to step forward, he felt the Protestant worker next to him squeeze his hand to hold him back, as if to say that he should not step forward and that his friends would protect him. However, he did step forward, only to find that the masked men were members of the Provisional IRA. The Protestants were executed. Heaney reflects on this incident with both despair and the belief that "the birth of the future we desire is surely in the contraction which that terrified Catholic felt on the roadside when another hand gripped his hand, not in the gunfire that followed, so absolute and so desolate, if also so much a part of the music of what happens" (1998, 457).

Ethics and History

Acts of treason attract a particularly vehement form of legal and moral condemnation. Treachery is often seen as an ethical perversion, a venal act of self-serving duplicity. The liberal philosopher Judith Shklar famously includes betrayal as one of her "ordinary vices" (1984), implying that it is a corrupting moral defect. However, despite widespread denigration, treason and betrayal are rarely, if ever, ethically straightforward. People are more often than not faced with multiple and conflicting pressures, producing particular mixtures of complicity and ambiguity. It is, therefore, essential to examine the difficult dilemmas and choices faced by the accused as they grapple with often contradictory ethical demands. Far from being ethically absolute, treachery is inherently ambiguous. Indeed, although often seen as morally pathological, treachery can have a positive moral charge of its own. Judas Iscariot, for example, the first traitor in Christianity, can be seen as a duplicitous and self-interested scoundrel or as a necessary instrument in a divine plan. Machiavelli famously turned treachery into a virtue, as part of his wider instrumental political ethics. The writer Rebecca West similarly thought that traitors can play an essential, positive role by introducing necessary change (1985). It should be remembered that the term "collaboration," one of the dominant forms of treachery running through this volume, has both positive and negative meanings, referring to both cooperation and complicity. The notion of "informing" similarly contains a sense of providing benign information, as well as of spying. Acts of denunciation also retain considerable moral ambiguity. A distinction between good and bad forms of denunciation is often maintained; in French, this distinction is poised between "public-spirited" *denonciation* and self-interested, malicious *delation* (Fitzpatrick and Gellately 1997; Lucas 1997). One can see denunciation as a duty to authority or as a betrayal of friends and neighbors. In this volume, Steffen Jensen explores the contradictory ethics of collaboration for "Cape Coloureds" in South Africa and how, in the new democratic South Africa, the residents of a township have been forced to renegotiate the relationship between moralized notions of motherhood and masculinity, crime and citizenship, as they form new communities. Should a raped woman, for example, turn to the police for help or rely on local gang-based notions of justice? In this context, for many of the residents of the township, it remains an open question as to whether calling on the state for help or refusing to inform on known criminals is the greater act of treason.

Acts of treachery and loyalty can overlap. The multiple forms of commitment and affiliation within which people are bound create varied forms of ethical duty and responsibility. Here, the distinction between betrayal and loyalty can become blurred. Many of the puppet regimes of Second World War Europe, for example, argued that they did not betray their people by seeking accommodation with Nazi Germany, but instead attempted to protect them from the worst ravages of the German occupation (Deak 2000b). On the other hand, opposition and resistance can have potentially disastrous consequences for those the resisters seek to protect. A strong, if contestable, argument can be made that "if Hungary had maintained its position as a political ally of Germany rather than engaging in attempts to make diplomatic connections with allies, the German invasion could have been avoided, and the Jews of Hungary might have survived the war relatively unscathed" (2000b, 61). The point here is not a moral relativist one, but rather that, in situations of extreme violence and political pressure, there exists what Primo Levi has famously called a "grey zone" (1986), where the line between victim and perpetrator is far from absolute. As Levi argues, it would be a mistake to think that oppression sanctifies its victims. Indeed, he claims that the harsher the oppression, the more willing people are to collaborate. A straightforward condemnation of such acts would be to gloss over the difficult moral choices that people can face in extreme circumstances. Under extraordinary pressure, people can commit both acts of utmost

brutality and of compassion. Those accused of treachery are often neither pathological perpetrators nor innocent victims, but rather complex
agents attempting to negotiate their way through contradictory ethical
and political demands.

Social analysis has traditionally been reluctant to explore the motivations of traitors, informers, and impostors, focusing instead on the
accuser rather than the accused. Literature, however, has not been so
coy, and the dilemmas faced by traitors and betrayers run through the
work of Shakespeare, Harold Pinter, Luigi Pirandello, and many others.
Sebastian Barry's novel *A Long Long Way* (2005), for one, tells the story
of Willie Dunn, a man who attempts to make choices based on loyalty
and duty but who finds himself unwittingly accused of treason. Willie
joins the Irish Fusiliers at the age of seventeen to fight in World War I.
Many of his fellow soldiers believe that, by helping to defeat the Germans, they will eventually pave the way to Home Rule in Ireland. Willie's
motivations are much more down to earth—under six feet tall, he cannot join the police force, and in an effort to please his staunchly Union-
ist father, he joins the army instead. However, while Willie is fighting on
mainland Europe, the Irish Republican Brotherhood launches the Eas-
ter Uprising of 1916 against British rule. The brutal response of the British army results in the rise of Republican sentiment across Ireland.
When Willie returns on leave from the front, he is no longer regarded
as a hero but is greeted with jeers wherever he goes, as a traitor fighting
for the occupying British army. Willie is torn between ethical commitments to his family, his fellow soldiers, and his country. Although, at
each point, he has tried to "do the right thing," he eventually stands
accused of betrayal by all those around him. His behavior is condemned
not due to any deliberate decision that he has made but because the
political ground has changed. The unpredictable course of history has
overwhelmed him.

The ethical structure of treachery is perhaps best seen as one of tragedy. There is no pure ethical moment, as not all moral duties can be
reconciled. The very dependency of the state on kinship or ethnic
groups, for example, may in itself create forms of affiliation that conflict
with the state's demand for absolute acquiescence. Thus, the attempt to
force clear moral distinctions and to make people commit in regular
and clear ways is constantly undermined by the shifting nature of personal affiliations. Sophocles' *Antigone*, perhaps provides one of the most
vivid examples of the tension between conflicting ethical commitments.
From Jacques Lacan to Judith Butler, the figure of Antigone has been a
recurring subject in much philosophical and historical writing, showing
the salience of its themes. The play centers on Antigone's attempts to
secure a respectable burial for her brother Polynices, who has been

declared a traitor to kingdom of Thebes. Creon, the king of Thebes, initially refuses to allow the funeral, and Antigone commits suicide, unaware that Creon has changed his mind. The play ends with Creon's own wife and son also committing suicide, unable to come to terms with what the king has done. In her analysis of the play, Martha Nussbaum argues that Creon tried to create a world where good and bad are defined in terms of being good and bad for the city, whereas, for Antigone, friend or enemy is simply a function of family relationships (2001). The tragedy is that Creon cannot see that any attempt to make the city the supreme good fails to appreciate the values of the individuals and families that constitute it, whereas Antigone fails to see that family and religious life are only possible within the framework of civic institutions. Following Antigone's death, Creon is eventually forced to abandon his simplistic ethics in favor of a more complicated, deliberative world.

In the context of the ethical conflicts of treachery, actions that on their own may seem innocent or insignificant can, in the long term, have immense importance. Short-term ethical decisions can have long-term implications that are morally corrosive. As such, the unforeseen course of social and political life produces reluctant or unpredictable traitors. As in the case of Willie Dunn, people do not change, but history alters around them. Positions that at one moment seemed the epitome of patriotism and loyalty can be transformed to be seen as disloyal and duplicitous, as historical conditions create new frames of evaluation. As Tobias Kelly argues in his chapter, for West Bank Palestinians, complicity with the Israeli state runs through the most seemingly mundane activity, due to the entrenchment of Israeli occupation. However, the second intifada in 2000 created new alignments of collaboration and opposition and forced Palestinians to renegotiate the historically shifting boundaries of permissible complicity with the Israeli state. In this context, collaboration is not a one-off event but can be the product of many small-scale treacheries forced on people as they try to feed their children or provide for their families. As the French diplomat Talleyrand famously remarked, "treason is a matter of dates."

The moral frameworks through which those accused of treachery and betrayal are evaluated are also framed by wider historical narratives. Immediately after the fall of Vichy France, the majority of the French population did not want Marshall Pétain tried for collaborating with Germany, seeing him as the "shield" that protected the French people from Nazism (Burton 2001). The German occupation was seen as a fait accompli, and many French people saw accommodation as the only way in which they could protect France from the same fate as Poland and Czechoslovakia (Gross 2000, 30). Indeed, the first major French figure to be charged with treason was Édouard Daladier, the socialist prime minister of France in the run up to the German invasion. The Vichy regime convicted Daladier on the grounds that he was directly responsible for the French defeat. It was only in the decades following World War II, as the French attempted to come to terms with their collective complicity, that Pétain came widely to be seen as a traitor to France (Deak 2000a, 3). Similarly, Subhas Chandra Bose, the former president of the Indian National Congress and leader of the Japanese-allied Indian National Army, can be seen either as a patriotic hero of Indian independence or a collaborationist quisling. Impatient with Gandhi's campaign of nonviolence and angered by the British declaration of war on Germany on India's behalf, Bose turned to the Japanese as the only way to guarantee Indian independence. The defeat of the Japanese and the eventual independence of India in 1947 make it easier to portray Bose's behavior as an act of betrayal; but, to many Indians, his actions at that time seemed to be a pragmatic response to the demands of Indian freedom, and Bose is still venerated by many as a freedom fighter and national hero.

Traitors, then, are not given once and for all but created by history, as new frames of interpretation are opened up, allowing a sense that it could have been different, that there were other possible forms of engagement. Only by exploring the complex ethical terrain through which acts of treason are judged and evaluated can we begin to understand why some people are violently punished for acts of betrayal, while others are either forgiven or ignored. Writers and intellectuals and, as we highlighted above, low-level female collaborators were particularly singled out for punishment after the fall of Vichy France, whereas economic collaborators and administrators, for several decades at least, remained relatively uncensored (Burton 2001, 260). François Mitterrand, for example, was able to become president of France despite having been a mid-level Vichy official. Contradictory ethics of commitment can produce equally contradictory ethics of accountability. In this volume, Kamran Rastegar, through a focus on the popular Iranian film *The Glass Agency*, explores the process through which veterans of the Iran-Iraq War gradually moved from heroes to maligned traitors. Even twenty-five years later, the sacrifices made and demanded as part of the Iran-Iraq War remain a central trope through which contemporary politics is assessed, and the veterans of the war act as ciphers for a commentary on the demands of modern Iran. Rastegar examines how, while the commitments of the veterans have remained unchanged, the demands of the state within which they live have evolved, rendering their own demands for recognition of their heroic acts of commitment in danger of being seen as treason.

If treason takes the form of tragedy, the lesson of tragedy is not that ethics is impossible or that all ethical choices are equally valid; rather, ethical choices come at high costs (Eagleton 2002). As Primo Levi argued, although it is important to recognize the shared humanity of even the most brutal oppressor, it is still necessary to insist on ethical notions of guilt and innocence (1986). The moral tensions of treason therefore raise important questions for how historians and anthropologists write about such cases. On the one hand, there is a widespread desire, in both anthropology and history, to express empathy with those we study. On the other hand, we are also ethical persons with our own moral evaluations, which should not and cannot be ignored. Many acts of treasons seem truly reprehensible, as do the brutal forms of punishment that are meted out, and these cannot be glossed over. There is surely a difference between a man who works in an Israeli settlement in order to feed his children and someone complicit with the genocide in Bangladesh. Throughout this century, we have also seen authoritarian regimes and groups label dissidents and activists "traitors" as a precursor to a targeted terror strategy against them. How then, can we avoid seeking shelter in the false refuge of ethical neutrality and moral relativism, while at the same time not falling into the trap of easy condemnation? Part of the answer is through providing fine-grained descriptions of the dilemmas and choices faced by people who are accused of acts of treason. However, this is only part of the answer. The very act of description risks participating in the flow of denunciations and counterdenunciation, a flow that, by its very nature, is produced through rumor and fantasy. If, as T. Min-Ha Trinh argues, anthropology is a form of scientific gossip (1989), then the ways in which we write about acts of apparent treachery are intractably bound up with the flow of accusation and counteraccusation.

Although, there may be no hard ethical core to treason, we still need to find a language through which to talk about such morally charged categories. In his contribution to this volume, István Rév explores the accusation that the celebrated Hungarian filmmaker István Szabó informed for the Communist regime during and after the Hungarian uprising of 1956. Amid claim and counterclaim, as well as debate about the particular political responsibilities of the artist, Szabó argued that he was forced to inform and that, in doing, so he actually saved some of his colleagues from greater retribution from the Soviets. Rév asks how the historian can evaluate such claims, advocating the use of "thick" moral concepts, which hover close to the ground and are rooted in a particular set of historical possibilities and dilemmas. Through the use of such ethical concepts, we can understand the use of an ethical category at a particular historical juncture and gain an imaginative grasp of its evaluative point, without necessarily sharing all its values. In writing about treason, we need to avoid abstract moralizing but also recognize that we cannot write about such ethical issues in a neutral and disinterested manner. As such, nearly all the contributors to the volume straddle the middle ground between a narrowly positivist stance that simply seeks to describe what is and a more morally charged sense of what ought to be. In doing so, they avoid predetermining the ethics of treason by rooting their analysis in the context of particular historical and social constraints.

Chapter 1

Xiconhoca: Mozambique's Ubiquitous Post-Independence Traitor

Lars Buur

> A nation can survive its fools, even the ambitious ones. But it cannot survive treason from within. An enemy at the gates is less formidable, for he is known and carries his banner openly. But the traitor moves amongst those within the gate freely, his sly whispers rustling through all the alleys, heard in the very halls of government itself. For the traitor appears not a traitor; he speaks in accents familiar to his victims, and he wears their face and their arguments; he appeals to the baseness that lies deep in the hearts of all men. He rots the soul of a nation; he works secretly and unknown in the night to undermine the pillars of the city; he infects the body politic so that it can no longer resist. A murderer is less to fear. The traitor is the plague.
> —Marcus Tullius Cicero, *The Enemy Within*, 45 B.C.E.

> There exist many Xiconhocas infiltrated in the midst of us.
> —*Tempo 303*, 1976, 2

In 2005, a few months after Mozambican president Armando Guebuza had been elected, I met "João" in Mavago, in Niassa Province.[1] Visibly nervous and unsettled, João was on his way back to Maputo after spending more than twenty years in Mavago. In 1983, he had been forcibly rounded up during Operation Production for not having all the required identity papers or official confirmation of employment. Within twenty-four hours, he had been sent to a work camp outside Mavago—in the direction of the Tanzanian border, close to Msiwise and Base Central, where the Liberation Front of Mozambique's (Frelimo, from its Portuguese title Frente de Libertação de Moçambique) first "liberated zones" were established in the 1960s—without any subsequent contact with his family in Maputo. He had survived the sixteen years of internal war between the Resistência Nacional Moçambicana (Renamo) and the government of Frelimo, although he had been forced to move several times and went on to marry a local woman after the Peace Accord in 1992. "The authorities" (the Frelimo secretary and district state officials) had approached him after Guebuza's election victory in December 2004 and told him, "You are going back now; the president has pardoned you." Guebuza had been in charge of the (in)famous Operation Production[2]; the decision to return all former victims of the campaign to their homes seemed to be a sign of clemency and goodwill designed to lay to rest the (still volatile) issue of Guebuza's involvement in the operation. At the local level, neither state nor Frelimo officials could tell exactly who had made the decision or who was in charge of the return. They knew only that it was the *chefes grandes* (senior leadership) who had made the decision and put resources behind the plan.[3] João had been told that a small "one-off pension" would be paid out when he returned to Maputo if he did not "make any trouble." He struggled to find words for the new situation; he could only say, "I am no longer an *inimigo interno* (internal enemy)."

I had read about Operation Production, but I had so far never met people who were ready to identify themselves with the campaign as either office bearer or target, even though most families in Maputo and other larger cities knew about *somebody* who had been "sent away up north." Exactly how many had been "sent away" is not known, but estimates range from 30,000 to 50,000 people. For Frelimo, which was in charge and the only party allowed between 1977 and 1992, Operation Production serves as an unfortunate specter of the socialist period in postsocialist Mozambique. Operation Production undoubtedly warrants further attention, not least in light of Guebuza's election as president. However, my interest in this chapter is, rather, to explore the wider ideological and symbolic terrain of betrayal and treachery underpinning the construction and production of "internal enemies" that made Operation Production possible and, moreover, an obvious consequence of the attempt to establish the new Mozambican nation-state after independence in 1975.

Mozambique's independence came in 1975 after the Portuguese Carnation Revolution (Revolução dos Cravos) of 25 April 1974. Political power was handed over to Frelimo without elections. Since then, Frelimo has been in government, first as a liberation front; then, after 1977, as a one-party government structured along Marxist-Leninist lines; and, after the peace agreement in 1992 between Frelimo and Renamo, within a multiparty system. During the first fifteen years of Frelimo rule, societal forces were permitted to organize through the party only, according to a principle of "democratic centralism" that was "inscribed by law into the structures of non-party organisations" (Hall and Young 1997, 70).

At the end of the 1970s, a devastating civil war slowly but steadily absorbed the new nation-state, as Renamo emerged with increasing force. Renamo was set up and supported by the Rhodesian government and, after 1980, had the backing of the South African government (Vines 1991). However, Renamo capitalized on a wide range of local grievances after 1977 related to the Frelimo government (see Schafer 2001).The tragic death of Mozambique's first president, Samora Machel, happened in 1986 at a time when the Mozambican economy was close to collapsing and Renamo was threatening to overthrow Frelimo by force. However, reforms guided by the World Bank and International Monetary Fund were accepted (Hanlon 1991), resulting in the 1990 Constitution that allowed for multiparty elections. The shift to a liberal economic policy and democracy, enacted by the selfsame leaders who for two decades had openly pursued a planned economy and used Lenin-Stalinist or Maoist-style campaigns and mobilization, generated its own ambiguity. Since independence, when the new nation-state found itself under siege by racist neighbors, a political ethos of monism and national unity had been the supreme values of the Frelimo government. This ethos not only distinguished sharply between the *political* distinction of "friends" and "enemies"—between those who endorsed it and those who did not—but also made the urge to identify new internal enemies and purge them an ongoing feature of the Mozambican nation-state.[4]

This chapter will analyze the role played by the ambiguous cartoon figure Xiconhoca after Mozambique's independence, when the figure became "institutionalised suspicion" (Harrison 1998, 587); the embodiment par excellence of negative social, political, and moral attitudes; the intense and sublime object of techniques of government; and the ever-present and all-embracing internal enemy. The cartoon character came to stand for a host of negative figures undermining the new state and nation through ideological and moral decay, "types" that the new nation-state needed to contain, transform, and, if necessary, ultimately purge in order to present itself as one people. In the ethos of the new nation-state, even the most innocent action could be considered a sign of defiance, quite literally as venomous opposition, leading to correction at "people's tribunals" that could grant or deny the right to belong to the moral and political community of the new polity. As the sublime object of political and ethical betrayal, Xiconhoca unified a host of political and moral messages. In Frelimo's attempts to produce the new order, Xiconhoca represented everything that the party's equally elusive, modern, and rational "New Man" (*Homen Novo*) must reject. Thus, these two antithetical abstractions were set up in opposition to each other. Because of the postcolonial state's weakness, it had to rely on informal political and economic practices that would be ferociously denied even though such practices secured the survival of the regime. Xiconhoca, the personification of evil, was used to give these denials a concrete, vivid form that could reach people at all levels of literacy.

As such, the figures of the New Man and Xiconhoca were a "floating signifier" (Lévi-Strauss 1950)—a stable figure or form with a fluid content—in the Mozambican nation-state's attempt at establishing a coherent cosmology and symbolic order for the new society. In this sense, the internal enemy figure was not unlike the Maussian Mana, an expression of a surplus of meaning, the content of which could crystallize into a range of specific figures, inversely mirroring the New Man. Despite efforts to mold him from the ruins of the ideological and symbolic order of the colonial state, this new socialist man remained stable in his unachievability; the internal enemy, by contrast, fictionalized in the cartoon figure Xiconhoca, took specific forms that could be acted upon. As with all Xiconhoca's treacheries, the key problem was how to go from "everyone" to "someone" or "some *body*" in the different contexts that the figure appeared.

One of the most important instantiations of Xiconhoca was the informal trader. During the liberation war, informal trading by Africans was celebrated as one form of resistance against the colonial regime, undermining the regime's resource base and hierarchies. This was reversed, however, within the postcolonial, centralized, socialist nation-state project, over two decades of economic and political hardship and sacrifice. Now, informal traders came to represent the ever-expanding ranks of enemies of party, state, and nation, providing an antagonist against whom to focus rallying calls for unity. I suggest that, right from the emergence of the independent Mozambican state, informal trade exposed the economic limits of the Frelimo centralized state project. The informal trader figure was, therefore, constructed as an enemy that needed to be repelled and fought with all available means to protect the *patria*, an *inimigo interno* of the state and nation. To put this another way, the capacity to feed the nation, extract in a reasonable manner the products of the nation, distribute and redistribute and so forth became everyday signs of the well-being (or otherwise) of the project. The informal trader challenged the centralized post-independence planning state and became an everyday embodiment of the regime's incapacity to feed and provide for the people. When it failed in these basic aims, the Frelimo state reasoned that its failure must be the result of sabotage and wilful actions orchestrated by the state's enemies.

Thus, the Xiconhoca figure and its concrete instantiations, like the informal trader, came to be constructed as a radical figure in the sense that treason is the ultimate betrayal of one's nation, which in the Mozambican context was betrayal of the Frelimo party-state. Cultural, social, and economic activities, however innocent, could in this way come to be seen as conspiracies to overthrow the government, even if neither a foreign country nor any larger group of people was involved.[5] The "traitor" category could result in dire consequences for those subjects who came to be identified with "wrongful" activities, as we saw with João, who paid with a twenty-year sentence, and is still paying, for not having his papers in order. The chapter discusses first the position of the internal enemy and traitor in the context of fragmented, postcolonial, nation-state building. Next, it explores the Frelimo government's attempt at producing a unified new society, in which Xiconhoca played a prominent role as the society's internal enemy. This is followed by an analysis of the figure of Xiconhoca in the context of the symbolic and ideological terrain of the new society. Finally, the chapter discusses the informal trader in greater detail as one of the most important instantiations of Xiconhoca. This figure not only made possible the movement from the abstract to the concrete and from the ideological to the everyday but also reveals many of the inherent contradictions that structured Xiconhoca's position in the new society.

The People and the Notion of the Internal Enemy

As the Introduction to this book suggests, the figure of the traitor is a universal one, at the heart of politics. As the quote from Cicero opening this chapter so vividly conveys, traitors are frightening because they can be anywhere, even within the best-guarded fortress. The depiction of the traitor as a mirage or fantasy indicates the enormous energy generated by the awareness of the presence of enemies within: every whisper travels, creating uncertainty; no utterance, even in one's own ideological language, can be taken at face value. As Cicero suggests, when some *body* first becomes "aware" of the enemy within—that is, loses one's innocence and begins to live with and through the doubt and fear—the power of the traitor blossoms and "the soul" of the body politic can rot or become infected, undermining even the most energetic and sound ideological course. This is all so *real* in its unreal presence, in that the effects are material, yet the cause is a mere mirage. This chapter is as such a first attempt at accounting for the processes that take place for the fantasy to become a concrete embodiment, an identifiable "enemy within," in the form of those who are taken captive by it.

Nearly all the most powerful southern African governments today are constituted by former liberation movements, none of which, despite protracted struggles, ever won a war through straightforward military victory. Negotiated settlements bringing liberation movements or fronts to power have been the rule, and in each one, the fear of the internal enemy seems to structure the very texture of the current governments. All the movements or fronts coming into power have experienced internal struggles in which leaders have been killed. In Mozambique, the first and second leaders of the front and later party were killed during internal struggles over the direction Frelimo was to take, while the third leader, Joaquim Chissano, managed to survive the liberating force itself. In the same way, identifying and punishing traitors in the body politic may be the externalization of internal party struggles, written large and extended to the body politic through the violence and fear that form part of such struggles.

Another implication of negotiated political settlements is that the nation-states and "their people" (in whose name liberation was fought) have already been fractured. The new state was never able to constitute the people in a totally new image. From the outset, it was a losing battle because the emergence of this unified image depended on the very forms of politics and economics that the state claimed to have moved beyond. It not only had to straddle multiple loyalties and allegiances but also to work with and through what Giorgio Agamben has suggested is the inherent ambiguity at the core of the political concept of "people" and popular sovereignty. As he argues, "what we call people was actually not a unitary subject but rather a dialectical oscillation between two opposite poles: on the one hand, the *People* as a whole and as an integral body politic and, on the other hand, the *people* as a subset and a fragmentary multiplicity of the needy and excluded bodies" (2000, 30). In all attempts at establishing a unified polity, then, the concept of "people" is structured along a constitutive fracture, a "pure source of identity [which has yet] to be redefined and [which purifies] itself continuously according to exclusion, language, blood, and territory" (Agamben 2000, 31). In this ambivalent ideological and symbolic terrain, the new nation-states still had to deal with the relationship between what already is and what has yet to be realized: the liberated and those that "still" need to be liberated, the backward and the enlightened, the trusted and the untrustworthy—in other words, the subject aspiring to become the citizen of the new polity. The quest for a collective identity among the multiplicity of particular social forces has not vanished, and new nation-states often confront the labor of unification with physical and symbolic violence.[6]

An interesting aspect of this continuous labor has been the techniques of labeling related to internal enemies usually perceived to be confronting and undermining the idealized "new man" the new regime aimed for. In order to fashion one united "People" (*Povo* is often capitalized in official Mozambican documents), the attempt was made to create a new society with access to education and health, political training, local governance, and so forth in the areas that Frelimo controlled during the war against the Portuguese. A myth was created that idealized these "liberated zones." As Samora Machel described the liberated zones, "everything is directed towards liberating man, serving the people . . . there is nothing to divide us" (Machel 1981, 43). Even though limited in extent (covering only certain areas in two of the ten provinces), this vision of the liberated zones nonetheless came to shape the "strategic politico-moral map" of the country after 1975 (Hall and Young 1997, 54; Henriksen 1978, 448). The liberated zone and the idea of the liberation war were based on a military imaginary in which Frelimo was constantly under siege and surrounded by enemies (Hall and Young 1997, 55). But the territory had also to be liberated internally, not only from capitalist exploitation but also from all elements of the old society, in order that there be "no tribes, no regions, no races, no religious belief . . . to divide us" (Machel 1981, 43). The people occupying the territory were, therefore, as Hall and Young suggest, seen as "possessing the potential to develop" (1997, 65). The liberation on the ground meant that all parts of the territory that had not been liberated were "regarded as enemy terrain" (1997, 55). This made the list of possible enemies and enemy territories rather long. Each element was vested with multiple layers of meaning, as I will illustrate in the following sections, because producing the "new, pure and healthy society" was like chasing shadows.[7] It also made the assertion of the *Homen Novo* an elusive goal outside the liberated zones, although even there, the best cadre and "new man" could be corrupted, with the possible exception of the vanguard leadership, with the least likely being Samora Machel.

I suggest that the universality of the figure of the traitor within, along with the perpetual fear it continues to produce, cannot be understood outside the continuous political labor of nation-state formation. The work of defining who belongs to the nation-state and what characterizes its members is often achieved by way of a negative procedure, that is, through the creation of an exemplary Other. At the core of any such externalizations—and often missing from such a meta-account—are the important specificities and histories of what constitutes treason and which internal enemy was defined as the traitor par excellence. If the traitor figure is deployed to rearrange multiple loyalties and allegiances in order to rephrase and regulate the multiplicity and fluidity of the "people," then othering is merely a by-product of the more basic attempt at creating a collective identity or sameness (see the Introduction to this volume). In other words, at the heart of labeling certain deeds treason and treachery are attempts at (positively) producing obedience and belonging to the new nation and state.

Laboring to Become One People

The traitor that defined the new society's feared self had a markedly *political* nature in Mozambique. Independence in 1975, after ten years of protracted liberation war against the colonial Portuguese, was followed by a devastating sixteen-year civil war. The people in whose name Frelimo had been fighting the liberation struggle were crosscut by ethnic, racial, economic, social, cultural, and political differences. Hardly any aspect of the new societal being would, over the first ten years, be left untouched in the attempt to define, mold, and purify the new society of its own dirt and excesses. At the core of the Frelimo project was "Unity." As they stated just before they came to power, "To form the true personality of our People, it is necessary to create conditions to unify the habits, customs and traditions and to give them a revolutionary dimension" (Frelimo 1975, quoted in Hall and Young 1997, 36). Besides seemingly endless lists of commissions and committees aimed at defining what should be done in every imaginable aspect of life, at the core of this labor was a constantly changing identification of internal enemies, as the content of the category changed with the forms of power and authority the regime claimed or lost control over. The figure that could capture all these shifting meanings and at the same time remain stable and easily identifiable was Xiconhoca, a creation of Frelimo's Maputo Departamento de Informaçao e Propaganda da Frelimo (Office of Mass Communications).[8]

The "enemy within" figure first appeared publicly on 25 July 1976, just a year after the achievement of independence, when the department presented Xiconhoca (*Tempo 303*, 1976, 2). The figure was soon to become familiar in radio messages, murals, cartoons, public speeches, posters, newspaper features, theater plays, and songs. The caricature was ideal for multimedia presentation. Skillfully designed to convey and represent its social, political, and ideological message, the cartoon figure was intended to encourage communication with and among the nonliterate population.

The name Xiconhoca was drawn from two words: Xico and Nhoca. Xico-Feio was a famous and despised agent of the dreaded colonial secret police, Polícia Internacional e de Defesa do Estado (PIDE), and its successor, Direcção-Geral de Segurança (DGS). *Nhoca* is the name in nearly all Mozambican dialects for "cobra" or snake. Xiconhoca, English "Chico the Snake," is thus a combination of the conqueror's spy with folklore imagery of stealth, poison, and lurking danger. As

Informaçao e Propaganda da Frelimo explained, "We know that in whatever *modo de vida* (way of life) of a snake, it uses tricks when it wants to attack a person." Like snakes, "Xiconhocas have infiltrated our family [midst, core, breast], they live with us" (*Tempo 303*, 1976, 2).

The list of possible fifth-column or treacherous deeds for which one should look out was long from the outset, ranging from the promotion of ethnicity and racism to everyday antisocial behavior and economic exploitation. But, just as people in a specific area can distinguish dangerous from harmless snakes according to their specific characteristics, so were Mozambicans expected to identify local incarnations of Xiconhoca. In short, the figure

represents all we are fighting [and can be identified because] he has the mouth of a drunkard, the tongue of a rumor-monger, hands like a racketeer and speculator, eyes like a racist, a nose like a tribalist, the teeth of a regionalist, and the legs of someone who spreads confusion. Xiconhoca is a figure that represents all the bad things left behind from colonialism, against which the People are fighting. . . . [He is] the individual . . . the parasite that doesn't want to work or participate in collective production. (*Tempo 303*, 1976, 2)

It is worth dwelling on what Xiconhoca embodies because, for each depiction, this list presents a specific aspect that could be enacted and displayed graphically and metaphorically as the new society's feared self. Xiconhoca was thus not empty of meaning, but rather an overloaded "floating signifier" that could take specific meanings that, in turn, could, as I will illustrate below, be transferred to subjects or take subjects.[9] It was directly aimed at teaching the nation what not to be, providing a universal point of reference that enabled people to pinpoint local incarnations of all that did not qualify to belong to the People.[10]

Tribalism and Regionalism: Splitting the Nation-State

Xiconhoca in his literal and graphic presence embodied (real and/or imagined) forces that attempted to splinter the new nation-state. One of his key features was that he "sought to rally popular support by appealing . . . to exclusive identities, such as racism, regionalism or tribalism" or to "mystifying ideologies" like liberalism, populism, or ultraleftism (Dinerman 2006, 70). The critique of racism was expressed in his hard, snake-like eyes. However, this critique was fraught with contradiction because, while Frelimo was antiracist, there was also criticism of the *assimilados*, *índianos*, and *brancos* who, due to their access to education and willingness to flirt with Marxism, came to play a prominent role in the Frelimo movement after independence. For this reason, the party-state apparatus had to be fiercely vigilant against deviance and double-talk within its ranks because the state, with the party at the helm, was seen as the driving force for societal transformation and unity building. As Machel put it in 1980,

The [enemy's] head is outside! Here we merely have the body, but the head is outside! The ones here are simply carrying out orders. They are mere tools. They are lackeys cut off from the exterior, abandoned children, bastard children. . . . the enemy has begun to operate at two levels: from abroad, particularly through criminal attacks by the racist Rhodesian regime and by infiltration of armed bandits; internally, through its agents and lackeys, with the aim of sabotaging from within the objectives laid down by the [Party]. Their fundamental target internally is the state apparatus, the structures designed to insure implementation of the [Party's program]. Their mission is to disorganize our party and our people's state.

Thus, the internal enemy could be anywhere, taking almost any form, often without even knowing it, so that even though "born of the people [they could and inevitably did] betray the people" (Ottaway and Ottaway 1981, 77–78). The fact that they were "anti-national," as Dinerman (2006, 70) has suggested, meant that the fallen could be redeemed, for example, through education and physical labor, even though this could be a long drawn-out process, as João's case illustrates. Xiconhoca's "nose like a tribalist" and "teeth of a regionalist" also refers to division: the nose alludes to tribes who supported the Portuguese and from which the Portuguese military drew many of its Mozambican troops (and, later, the core of armed resistance to the Frelimo government). The reference to teeth invokes the snake's sharp fangs; they are separate, full of poison, representing in the most extreme sense separation and disunity.

The images linking tribalism and division are inscribed on the uniforms of the community authorities that were recognized in 2002.[11] Authorities emerging from postcolonial Frelimo governance, the *secretaries*, got three stripes close to each other on the sleeves of their uniform, indicating that they worked for the unity of the People. By contrast, and as a way of marking continuing suspicion, the traditional leaders that were recognized by the state in 2002 got three distinctly separate stripes on the sleeves of their uniform. According to state officials in Niassa Province, this denotes the separate tribes to which they are supposed to belong and which they are to represent in the state.

Culture and Tradition: Reforming Backward People

Even before Frelimo came to power, it had initiated the task of defining the new society's cultural manifestations: "the Party must create a committee at the national level to gather and analyse all cultural manifestations, such as habits, sport etc.—rejecting whatever divides us and gathering together all the common factors of our lives" (Frelimo 1975, quoted in Hall and Young 1997, 36). Immediately after coming to power, the Frelimo government tried from 1977 on to reform the colonial institutions that linked state and population in order to build a single-party state along Marxist-Leninist lines.[12] For example, traditional authorities were excluded from positions in the new Frelimo state or, more precisely, formally banned from governance and replaced by "dynamizing groups" (*grupos dinamizadores*) led by party secretaries elected by the *Povo*—in other words, individuals trusted by the party. Adhering to the modernist perspective that predominated, the government branded the rule of traditional authorities detrimental to modernization and national unity (Artur and Weimer 1998, 4); they were portrayed as collaborators of the colonial state (O'Laughlin 2000, 26–30; see also Kyed and Buur 2006; Buur and Kyed 2006). However, this does not mean that certain aspects of local culture were not to be celebrated in the new society, in fact, quite the reverse. Frelimo—and President Samora Machel, in particular—celebrated an authentic, pristine, and true culture that stressed origin and was unspoiled by the colonial past, as expressed in traditional dances and precolonial war heroes.

In one famous depiction of a disreputable Xiconhoca, an ever-present bottle of liquor dangles from his pocket as he converses with a member of the Portuguese regime or with a South African or Rhodesian Boer in characteristic long, wool socks and khakis. In the background, a group of well-trained, smiling African "warriors" are dancing with spears and shields. Xiconhoca says: "Culture, this? This is the dance of wild men. True culture is European culture. Nothing else" (DTIPF 1979). What had been disturbed by the colonial regime must be eradicated. For example, a yearly dance festival was organized at district, provincial, and national levels where authentic and unspoiled culture could be presented as part of a program of national unity. The pure image of the precolonial warrior could be promoted, in the same way that, in addition to the *maçaroca* (corncob), Frelimo used a *batuque* (traditional drum) in the party flag. But those types of cultural and traditional expressions whose modus operandi came from the exterior—colonialism and later ethnicity promoted by the Rhodesian and the apartheid regime—were considered to be the work and expressions of enemies of the state and party.

Thus, what was promoted was the authentic will and spirit of the people that existed and could be drawn on by everyone but interpreted only by Frelimo.[13] For example, traditional spiritual rites to promote rain and fertility were branded as "feudal," "tribalist," and harmful not only to the modernization of society but to the production of national unity (O'Laughlin 2000, 26–30; West and Kloeck-Jenson 1999, 456; Alexander

1997, 2). Not only traditional authorities who had been employed by the colonial state but also large sections of the general population were thus disqualified from being proper members of the polity. The negative procedure for defining the right way of being or "the true personality of our People" extended to apparently neutral issues such as the use of *soruma* (cannabis), which was said to make the rural population docile and unproductive. All instances of Xiconhoca featured a long "flower" with three long leaves held in his hand or sticking up from the back pocket of a pair of dirty trousers. However, the allusion to soruma was also a reference to the backwardness of the central areas of Mozambique, which were not only known for soruma production but were also regions where Frelimo encountered strong resistance during the liberation war and where the party never really managed to take control.[14]

However, social institutions based on kinship and hereditary succession continued to exist, and many local state officials relied unofficially on day-to-day collaboration with chiefs (O'Laughlin 2000; Alexander 1997) or even used chiefs to organize agricultural production (Dinerman 2006, 82). West and Kloeck-Jenson (1999, 458) illustrate the attempt by Frelimo to shore up control over local state/party structures by nationalizing all land in 1979, pointing out that the party did not put the necessary resources behind collectivized and cooperative forms of agricultural production. This, in turn, meant neglect of the mundane yet important issue of who was to cultivate which parcels of land. As a consequence, land tenure in large parts of the rural areas continued to be rooted in kin-based networks and overseen by local elders. Kin-based institutions also continued to resolve land conflicts and disputes related to marriage, divorce, and witchcraft, along with counseling on everyday aspects of life. Because cultural manifestations continued to be important, they gained in influence and power as they went underground, becoming more significant in their official absence: what you cannot "see" can potentially be everywhere doing its work in "clandestinity and parallelism" (Baptista Lundin quoted in Dinerman 2006, 68). The party-state embraced a fear of the clandestine; suspicion became institutionalized so that neighbors and rural villagers were instructed to report on those who spoke positively about the new society's enemies. To be reported and declared an "enemy" or "Xiconhoca" could have dire consequences, going as far as a reeducation camp or even disappearance (Harrison 1998, 587ff).

The Xiconhoca figure supported Frelimo's revolutionary project because it was "through the public condemnation and repression of deviance" that the regime "legitimated itself" (Macamo 2003, 7). Such condemnation extended to traditional modes of production and settlement patterns and aimed to "alter completely the way the rural people occupy the territory—the existing rural settlement pattern" (Coelho 1993, 16). At the core of this pattern was ways of living classified as traditional and at odds with modern collective living. Frelimo's rural strategy for proper living and being was *aldeias comunais* (communal villages) based on collective forms of production and cooperative organization as a substitute for both rural family settlement patterns and colonial *aldeamentos* (protected villages). Through the nucleation that formed collective villages, services could be provided (agricultural, health, educational, ideological, etc). This would make it possible for the peasantry to shed backward practices—the "traditional-feudal society" (Dinerman 2006)—and alter the relations of production as a means to cultivate and prepare for the "great leap forward" as part of the transition to socialism.

The aim was, in other words, the production of the New Man modelled on "embryonic political and administrative organization" from the liberated zones (Hall and Young 1997, 32), with economic and productive activities collectivized and health and education services provided.[15] Peasants had been denied access to modern production with its superior, scientifically developed technology by the colonial regime; now, following the experiences of the liberated zones, they could be educated and learn to become proper members of society and the people. But the communal villages were a problematic project because they resembled the colonial "protected villages," which had been established largely for the same practical reasons. This was made more ambiguous by Frelimo propaganda, which referred to such villages as concentration camps (Coelho 1993, 22), bequeathing a somewhat twisted image to collective villages. Where peasants and rural residents had, with independence, begun to leave the despised protected villages to return to their old homesteads close to their ancestral land, Frelimo's collectivization created great hostility and resistance.

Even though the permanent enemy of the new Mozambican people was the colonial, imperialist, and capitalist world system (an abstract permanence), concrete enemies were increasingly decoded and identified locally and thus potentially everywhere (Hall and Young 1997, 48). Even the smallest deviance from the planned reality of collective villages could be seen as a sign of obstruction or resistance. This made nearly everyone in the rural areas outside the former liberated zones a potential suspect, a possible internal enemy. Such enemies were constructed as hostile, backward, and/or obstructive, deploying rumors, conspiracy, or outright sabotage to undermine the Frelimo government. After the initial euphoria of the arrival of Frelimo cadres and liberty, the attempt to gain control over these ubiquitous forces, undercover or not, came to dominate Frelimo's perception of rural populations.

From the General to the Specific: The Case of the Informal Trader

Both as a liberation front and (after 1977) as a party, Frelimo's political analysis of enemies followed Marxist-Leninist lines and vocabulary (Dinerman 2006). As such, the various instantiations of Xiconhoca were class-based and emanated from a critique of "the exploitation of man by man" and of a wider ideological universe, expressed in rather incoherent and overlapping references to "colonialism," "capitalism," "colonial capitalism," "imperialism," "liberalism," "petty bourgeoisie," "democratic bourgeoisie," "social-democratic bourgeoisie," and so on, through a seemingly endless list of ideological mutations (Hall and Young 1997, 89). "Culture," "tradition," "tribalism," "regionalism," and so forth simply joined the list, as they could also be articulated as "class ideological enemies" such as "reactionaries" or "anti-revolutionary" forces. In an African postcolonial context, such predominantly ideological references gained their strength from being linked to potent vernacular discourses of power and morality that were moored, in many cases, to long-running and constantly evolving dialectics of accommodation and struggle. Mozambique's fear of its neighbors was not unwarranted, as the military power of the Rhodesian regime (at least until 1980 when Zimbabwe became a reality) and the apartheid regime was indeed concrete. But international boycotts and misrecognition of Mozambique, due to its alignment to the East bloc, also played a prominent role in sustaining and giving force to the ideological battle Mozambique found itself part of. The intricate play between the general and the specific could also render such potent constructions of enemies latent and even hollow.

From 1975, Samora Machel placed a strong emphasis on the moral regeneration of the population, as Macamo (2003) has suggested.[16] Central to this project was the promulgation of a new ethical person—*Homen Novo*—as a counterweight to the degeneration of values, culture, and human ways of being under the Portuguese colonial regime: "In nearly all the speeches he delivered on his triumphal journey from the North to the South of Mozambique to proclaim the independence of the country in 1975, it is not so much capitalist exploitation that worries him, but rather moral degeneration in urban areas" (Macamo 2003, 7; see also Harrison 1999, 540). Xiconhoca's ever-present bottle of alcohol was the most concrete symbol of the moral degeneration that destroyed the rural man when he came to town. Xiconhoca's ubiquitous bottle dramatized the critique of excessive drinking and of a man's neglect of his community and family responsibilities in the pursuit of his own pleasure. This wastrel figure was set up in opposition to its positive mirror image, that of *Homen Novo*, the self-denying man from the liberated areas who worked his plot for family consumption and, far more importantly, produced collectively to support the revolution and to feed the army, in adherence to the "watchwords of 'Unity, Work and Vigilance'" (Henriksen 1978, 455). In the cities, the New Man was the worker and public servant or state and party functionary who put public service before his own needs and enjoyment. Text and speeches would reiterate in detail how the new modern man could enjoy one or two beers but would never engage in excessive drinking (*Noticias* 13 August 1976, 9). Embodying the consumption related to the degenerated man was the figure of the prostitute accompanying Xiconhoca and living off his treacherous acts and scheming. Xiconhoca's woman was contrasted to the figure of a decently dressed woman who turned away from his excesses, expressing her disapproval with body language.

Rumors, Racketeering, and Speculation

It has been suggested that it was not "capitalist exploitation" in a strict sense that worried Samora Machel as such (see Macamo 2003). I think this is largely correct, but as Hall and Young suggest, underpinning the political order was the attempt to mold a "new kind of economy" as part of developing the new society (1997, 89). As Machel himself asserted, "Marxism-Leninism does not concern itself with garages . . . with selling eggs in the market [it] concerns itself with major economic development" (Machel quoted in Hall and Young 1997, 95). However, Frelimo lacked detail, so this project was formulated and implemented in an ad hoc fashion. It was also based on what were formulated as socialist experiences, with party-state-driven and centrally formulated collective production from the liberated zones.

I will suggest that the most important aspects of Xiconhoca's public life were intimately related to the economic life of the new nation-state. It was not only the abstract or generalized exploitation related to the various "isms" but the more mundane, concrete, everyday aspects of economic life that were vigorously and persistently addressed. When the figure of Xiconhoca first appeared in *Tempo*, it was as a "rumor-monger" (*boateiro*) with a subtitle explaining that "rumour is the weapon of the enemy" (*boato e' arma do inimgo*) (*Tempo* 303, 1976, 2). The depiction of Xiconhoca with the "tongue of a rumor-monger [and] hands like a racketeer and speculator" referred to a whole series of cartoons in which the well-fed figure sits on sacks of beans, rice, and corn or inside the characteristic small grocery stall with plenty of products for sale (DTIPF 1979). There was an easy movement from the abstract to the concrete and from the general to the specific, and these references to everyday economic issues should not be overlooked.

From early 1976, the Frelimo-controlled media circulated in-depth discussions about some of the many constraints the government encountered with regard to securing food and essential commodities for the people.[17] The media particularly highlighted the rampant abuse of the fixed-price system by speculators who hoarded or siphoned *produtos alimentares* and sold them outside formal markets and price codes at the *candonga* (informal or black market) (Chingono 1996, 37). This created an "exasperate speculation . . . where small traders mushroomed . . . on the margin of legality . . . [and] where people sold goods on any small street corner" (*Tempo 303*, 1976, 17). This soon spread to formal shops, which also began to engage in speculation and racketeering, and to sell products at much higher prices through "straw men" on the street (*Tempo 303*, 1976, 18). By avoiding tax authorities, these traders were siphoning off money that belonged to *o Povo* and putting it to their own uses, thus undermining the Frelimo government's goal of being the sublime provider for its people. With the party controlling import and export via parastatals, many state and Frelimo officials also became deeply involved in siphoning and speculation. Ironically, the emergence of these parallel markets allowed the official regime to survive and carry out its basic functions and later structured the war economy (Chingono 1996, 79–82; Harrison 1999, 541).

Who was to blame? Not the Frelimo government. Rather, the state media suggested, the situation was triggered by the Portuguese colonial regime. Negative associations became linked to informal traders and speculation during the extended period of insecurity after the Portuguese carnation revolution, as the colonial system of urban control slowly deteriorated and "an authentic proliferation of traders . . . emerged all over the country" (*Tempo 303*, 1976, 20). In concert with this, the party's dynamizing groups and cadres began to organize people to ensure that goods were available in the official, nationalized outlets of *lojas do povo* (people's shops) that had been set up to counter black market speculation (see *Noticias* No. 1 Especial, 1976, 24).

Like the ideal New Man, the people's shops were based on ideas from the liberated zones in Niassa and Capo Delgado, where abandoned rural shops had been taken over by the front and nominally collectively run and renamed (Hall and Young 1997, 22). But these were constantly undermined by speculators who withheld or siphoned off the official import and distribution networks and spread rumors about where to find particular products without needing to stand in long *bichas* (queues). An iconic image of that period was the long line of people waiting for products, some of which did not exist, at least not in the official shops. One cartoon illustrated such a scene with Xiconhoca standing in front of such a long queue, clearly impatient. As the caption explained, all the others in the queue were Xiconhoca's family members trying to spread "false ideas" about the government's incapacity to supply its population (DTIPF 1979). Here, one "real" image—the queue—was countered with a cartoon image displaying irresponsibility (rumor-mongers), thus suggesting that what appeared as "real" (the long *bichas*) was not real.

In other words, I suggest that, right from the first day of independence, the new regime encountered problems of legitimacy relating to everyday economic issues and relationships and that it was within this domain of social reality that Xiconhoca's more intimate and domestic life was to be revealed. The revolutionary project had to legitimate itself on a daily basis with regard to providing food and other everyday necessities, and here it struggled from the outset.[18] To a large extent, the regime had to depict the economic hardship as a moral struggle that the party-state and people had to embark on together. As falling industrial and agricultural production put pressure on the new regime, the "racketeer and speculator's unspoiled hands" became the metonymical expression of a petty- or neo-bourgeois lazy and indulgent lifestyle, a vivid symbol of the person who lived well without laboring, making a good living out of speculation and racketeering by exploiting structural weaknesses. While other aspects and body parts of Xiconhoca had deep resonance as old foes or enemies of the revolution—"an enemy of the People is an individual who has the same life as the enemy, the reactionary, the enemy of independence and the sovereignty of Mozambicans" (*Tempo 310*, 1976)—it was rumor-mongering, racketeering, and economic speculation that dominated. In these guises, Xiconhoca encapsulated everyday immorality where illicit transactions were flourishing, where "all the undisciplined, the corrupt, the bandits, assassins, thieves, diversionists, regionalists, racists etc." became apparent.

It is striking that depictions of Xiconhoca were juxtaposed at times with photographs of lorries full of fresh products for sale informally or illegally at the *candonga* or of marketplace women on a lorry or in a stall selling products that were scarce or simply unavailable in the official people's shops (see *Tempo 303*, 1976, 17–20).[19] In other instances, text explaining the work of Xiconhoca was accompanied by photographs of and interviews with informal traders. The easy slippage from the fiction of the cartoon figure to the modernist reality of the photographic image and text created its own dissimulations. While the cartoon figures continued to circulate as the internal enemies par excellence, they also formed an important basis for real actions against those who failed to qualify as the *Homen Novo* of the new nation-state.

Eradicating the Ambiguous and Its Return

Right from the outset, the public life of Xiconhoca was accompanied by attempts to eradicate its real-life manifestations as informal trader, speculator, and racketeer. A new "tax code for consumer goods" and a "National Emergency Plan" based on and built around a national system of "people's shops" were enacted in 1976 (*Tempo 305*, 1976, 5; 27). The intent was to "create a simple form of control" that would let the provisional and immoral vanish without much struggle (*Tempo 305*, 1976, 5, 26). The simplicity lay in the fact that the emergency plan directly outlawed all other forms of trading and retail by individuals; these were termed "economic sabotage" and "speculation crimes," serious matters punishable by public flogging or even death (Chingono 1996, 37). It was hoped that this would frighten and thus deter people from operating outside the law. The plan would be monitored by members of the new governance system of *grupos dinamizadores* led by party secretaries and the new enforcement agency "People's Brigades for Taxation" (*Tempo 401*, 1976, 27).

In keeping with Frelimo's past as a liberation movement, the new legislation was coined in military jargon: "Know and Fight (or Combat) different types of 'Xiconhoca,'" it is an "offensive against speculation," we need to "fight speculators in defence of the People," we should form "brigades" and create an "offensive" against the "internal enemy."[20] The official outlawing of even the most innocent actions was more than merely legislating against greed or everyday livelihood strategies; it meant that everyday economic activities came to be interpreted as expressions of political dissent designed to convey opposition to the policies of the Frelimo government. The party reacted to dissidence by increasing suppression, reintroducing corporal punishment, introducing capital punishment and public flogging, and increasing prison terms for the economic and political crimes for which Xiconhoca stood (see Amnesty International 1983 and 1984; Chingono 1996, 37). The fact that the military and security forces were allowed free rein to deal with opponents of the new regime is evidence that these problems were there from the start of the postcolonial era. According to Amnesty International, "between 1975 and 1978, inmates of 're-education camps' reported that torture, beatings and corporal punishment were used extensively, particularly against suspected opponents of the Frelimo" (Amnesty International 1985, 2–6). The Servicio Nacional de Seguranca Popular (SNASP), the new national intelligence created in 1975 (Decreto-Lei No. 21/75, *Boletin da Republica* de 11 Outubro), was able to hold suspects indefinitely and incommunicado, without charge or trial.

Particularly after 1977 and the Third Party Congress, when the Marxist-Leninist line gained prominence (see Coelho 2004) and the front became a party, the connection between everyday transgressions and perceived affirmations of "bourgeois values"—a drive toward individual or private accumulation, which was detrimental to the goals of the new society (Hanlon 1984; Saul 1985)—created a strong link between everyday livelihood strategies and expressions of political dissent. This blurring between wider ideological frameworks and everyday acts that made people vulnerable to being labeled traitors was accelerated to the point where, as Hall and Young suggest, "almost everyone was suspect, including the peasantry outside the liberated zones" (1997, 48). From then on, the "institutionalised suspicion, which was present from the early days of independence, became more developed and militarised" (Harrison 1998, 587).

SNASP's activities were initially directed at settling old scores within the party and with old enemies from the transitional period, but the camps filled rapidly with ordinary suspects, the majority of them *inimigo internos* involved in everyday forms of transgression and deviance: "prostitution," "decadence," "drug consumption," "religious belief," "economic sabotage" (informal trade), "dissidence within Frelimo," "agitators and lawbreakers," and those unwilling to "produce and work," which was becoming the new societal mantra (see *Noticias* No. 1 Especial, 1976, 102; DTIPF 1979; *Tempo 303*, 1976, 2; Hall and Young 1997, 46–48). It is generally acknowledged that detention without trial, along with the worst excesses in the camps, came to an end in 1978 when the Frelimo government took more direct control; by the early 1980s, most camps had closed. However, this respite would be short-lived, and the camps would soon return in an even more frightening form.

To understand the reemergence of repression, one must understand the emergence of Xiconhoca within society and the public sector. Explanations for the government's failure to secure everyday products and to organize the new society were structural in two main ways. First, problems were conceived as economic and therefore primarily technical. They were related, for example, to sanctions imposed by neighboring countries and destabilization and sabotage by powerful neighbors, primarily apartheid South Africa and Rhodesia, valid factors indeed. Added to these constraints were the limited availability of transport, poorly developed colonial infrastructure, excessive and immature bureaucracy, low productivity, and so forth, all issues to which purely technical solutions could be found.

Secondary and related problems were attributed to the party's structural role in society, more precisely, to the failure of the People's party to take its proper role. Flamboyant "neo-bourgeois" tendencies were seen as a result of the party's far-too-relaxed approach to its leadership role during what Coelho (2004) describes as "the liberal period." The problems Mozambique encountered were, according to this interpretation, caused by lack of control and discipline. By the time the party held its Fourth Congress in 1983, the economic situation has so worsened and the black market had grown so large that the leadership felt illicit trading threatened state control over the economy. Addressing this was potentially as important as the war against Renamo. In this context, today's president, Armando Guebuza, was put in charge of implementing the now notorious Operation Production. At the time, when first formulated by Samora Machel, the operation was carried out by local authorities without any clear idea about how to identify the enemies it targeted (Hall and Young 1997, 81; Chingono 1996, 38).

While one could argue, as Robinson does, that "this was a programme born out of the sheer desperation caused by war and economic crisis," I would counter that in the wider history of postcolonial rhetoric, discourse, and practices of *o inimigo interno*, Operation Production inscribed itself, in the most extreme fashion, in the history of Xiconhoca (*Noticias* 10 April 1984). A type of forced labor, the operation aimed to get rid of all subversive elements in the cities: the "parasites" and "unproductive" people, the moral decadents who consumed the scarce resources of the People (Hall and Young 1997, 104). It targeted the urban unemployed, which included those working with informal traders, single women accused of being prostitutes, any people who did not pay their rent, and, like João, youth lacking the appropriate papers. In other words, any*body* could be targeted or branded as one of the multifarious forms of the composite enemy, Xiconhoca. The solution, in this operation, was the forced removal from the cities of all "surplus." Army, police, and militia groups rounded up thousands of people in house-to-house searches. They were all sent to the rural areas, with the majority flown to Niassa, where they were meant to produce food for the country and become real members of the polity.

Since economic and political crimes were so interlinked and equally associated with the corrosion of the ideals of the New Man, nearly everything could be seen as an act of Xiconhoca: not only economic activities but also ways of walking and talking (or not walking and talking) could trigger a transfer of meaning through metaphoric and metonymic extension. Here, apparently innocent activities came to *stand in* for—a phrase that, we should not forget, derives etymologically from sacrifice (see Olsen 1993)—powerful ideological landscapes and/or to take on a concrete form of what the people should not be. A person with unauthorized dollar notes, for example, could be assumed to have loyalties to ideologies such as "evil capitalism," while a South African rand could be interpreted as allegiance to the racist South Africa or Ian Smith's Rhodesia. Metonymical and metaphorical extension and transferral of meaning in this sense were not necessarily moored to any verifiable treasonous action in the literal sense, such as the selling of classified information or wilful sabotage. Rather, holding a dollar note or selling everyday commodities such as rice or vegetables could be a traitorous action that betrayed the nation and implied that a person—*somebody* who could be identified and named—had somehow collaborated with an enemy in the act of feeding the nation.

In this sense, apparently innocent actions became more than just questions of "bourgeois greed," and everyday livelihood strategies became more than just a way of surviving economic hardship. Instead, they became expressions of political dissent "designed" (a priori or retrospectively) to undermine the Frelimo government by exposing the limits of its control and/or displaying dissatisfaction with or opposition to its policies. In fact, one could say that the Frelimo government created the dissent against itself by acting against livelihood strategies as though they were dissent strategies. In the context of newly independent Mozambique, surrounded as it was by enemies and steeped in military discourses, such "dissent," constructed as treason, justified an extreme set of responses to protect the "freedoms" of the revolution. As with all Xiconhoca's treacheries, the key problem was how to go from "everyone" to "someone" or "*somebody*." Since everyone relied, potentially and actually, on speculation and hoarding, everyone was potentially an internal enemy. Whether one became a captive to the category was something that depended on the civility and ethical discretion of the police and other authoritative formations, who had now become the clearest instantiation of the sovereign power of the People.

The postcolonial representation of the informal trader (and associated economic livelihood strategies) as traitor, as with other aspects of Xiconhoca's identity, was inherently ambiguous. To a large extent, what became classified after independence as racketeering and speculation was actually encouraged as a form of resistance during the struggle against colonialism. Then, noncompliance with or evasion of taxation regimes, official trade markets, forced labor, and shared-crops schemes was seen as an effective means to deprive the colonial regime of labor and resources (see Isaacman 1982). While these forms of resistance did not amount to sabotage, they had a considerable impact on the colonial regime's fiscal capacity and on the various companies running parts of Mozambique. Furthermore, they became an important source of insecurity through the very fact that, despite the colonial government's continuous attempts to counter these practices with reforms, new laws, and, in some instances, direct violence, they seemed unstoppable. On top of this, informal traders who were circumventing the rules of the colonial state provided the Frelimo liberation front with important underground networks for the distribution of military supplies and internal communication.

In a nutshell, during the liberation war, the trader's informal African economic livelihood strategies were celebrated as one form of resistance against the colonial regime, undermining the latter's resource base and hierarchies. The figure of the informal trader has, therefore, always been contested, the intense and sublime object of techniques of government, from the Portuguese colonial regime through the post-independence Frelimo party state to today's *democracia*. As a transhistorical figure, then, it has always been the object of policing, social control, health regimes, economic policies, party ideology, promotion, and, even at times, celebration. From Mozambique's independence in 1975 through the 1980s, informal traders became the antagonists, standing for the ever-expanding enemy ranks against whom the state called for unity during economic and political hardship and sacrifice.

In a circumscribed fashion, the memory of the ambivalence of the informal trader lives on in Niassa today. High-ranking state and party officials speak about "the spirit of Samora" when they complain about unpaid taxes and the continuation of informal trade between Tanzania, Malawi, and Mozambique. As one very senior state official put it to me in 2006, "I know it could get me into trouble, but it is Samora's fault, maybe his biggest mistake. It was he who told the people not to pay tax and to trade as they wanted. The spirit of Samora is with us today." Thus, the spirit of Samora has turned into a ghost that the present Frelimo state is still hunting down and haunted by, just as it did after independence.

Conclusion

In the contested ideological and symbolic terrain of nation-state formation, Mozambique had to deal with the relationship between what is and what has yet to be realized. The quest for a collective identity among the multiplicity of particular social forces required a unifying political message, one that could function as the rallying call for cohesion against the enemies of state and nation. The cartoon figure of Xiconhoca emerged in multiple forms. In any and all shapes, Xiconhoca's moral conduct was considered capable of undermining the whole project of social transformation. As an intense object of techniques of government, the figure can usefully be analyzed as a "floating signifier," its polyvalent meanings and figures all functioning as the reverse image of the New Man propagated by the new regime.

The chapter has illustrated how the designation of traitor could result in dire consequences for those identified with activities associated with Xiconhoca, the ever-present internal enemy, the "traitor of the people," a "fifth columnist" working clandestinely to undermine the revolutionary gains of the people's party. In light of this, the chapter has argued that the epithet or label of traitor is first of all political in two important ways. First, activities of Xiconhoca referred to a whole range of everyday activities and struggles related to nearly all domains of the cultural, social, economic, and political life of the new polity. Second, this type of politics should not be confused with what has been referred to as *the political* or the "high points of politics . . . the moments in which the enemy is, in concrete clarity, recognized as the enemy" (Schmitt 1996, 67; Mouffe 2005). Rather, this type of politics points toward the threshold that articulates most clearly what is rational for one political group to do in order to preserve itself (see Schmitt 1996). The content of the category *the political* cannot be rationally and universally defined for each and every political system, group, or nation-state. It is, in other words, open. Nonetheless, friend/enemy schemas structure and undercut other political concerns. As such, *the political*, or high politics, inscribes itself in the history of the political concept of the people, in the attempts at establishing a unified polity despite the constitutive fractures that characterize nation-state formation. It is, in other words, concerned with the aspirations of postindependent Mozambique. I have suggested that the key problem that all political formations encounter is how to go from everyone to someone or some *body*, since everyone is potentially a traitor.

Immediately after independence, the figure of Xiconhoca was first of all a convenient caricature or a straw man (Macamo 2003) that functioned as the antithesis of the equally ideal New Man whom the regime wanted not only to promote but actually to impose. The chapter has suggested that while the figure of Xiconhoca embodied all the most general and abstract political evils, one should not overlook the fact that socioeconomic struggles had acquired bona fide contours in public life far earlier than suggested by sympathetic historians of the Mozambican revolution. In light of these developments and representations, all of which gloss over certain things and contain their own modes of forgetting, I suggest that, with the emergence of the independent Mozambican state, Xiconhoca in the form of the informal trader became both a symbol of disloyalty to the new polity and someone who must be harnessed if he or she was to give true allegiance to the new sovereign: *o Povo* and the party-state leading the people. Here, the act of selling goods lawfully implied devotion and reverence to the new sovereign, while "illicit" or informal sales became acts not only of deviance and criminal behavior but also of treason.

Has the public life of the internal enemy, Xiconhoca, disappeared with the shift to *democracia?* Recent developments in Mozambique suggest otherwise. In April 2007, President Guebuza suggested that "The lack of a habit of hard work is perpetuating hunger and poverty. We have to work more and harder. . . . There are many lazy-bones in Mozambique. We have to admit we don't work much. [These are people who] relax without having done anything, and then become tired [from] so much relaxing" (Hanlon 2007). According to the respected journalist and head of Agencia de Informação de Moçambique Gustavo Mavie, President Guebuza hinted that it might be necessary to resort to "persuasion" (Hanlon 2007), a possible indication that Operation Production, which Guebuza led against "unproductive" people in 1983, might once again show its ugly face.

Chapter 2
Denunciatory Practices and the Constitutive Role of Collaboration in the Bangladesh War

Nayanika Mookherjee

> On the screen flashed scenes of the Liberation Fighters shooting the Pakistani army. As I watched the film *Orunodoyer Ognishakhi* (1972) (Pledge to a New Dawn) sitting in the Projection Room of the National Museum, the crowd started cheering from the packed auditorium below me, and a deafening applause followed. In the next scene as the Liberation Fighters gunned down the collaborators, the crowd cheered wildly with incessant shrill whistles, hooting and applause, which carried on for quite sometime. I could even see silhouetted images of people from among the audience standing up as they cheered the death of the Razakars (what collaborators are referred to as in Bangladesh) in the movie.
>
> —*fieldwork diary*

This brief extract from my fieldwork diary relives the celebration of Victory Day in Dhaka on 16 December 1997. Victory Day commemorates the formation of Bangladesh after nine months of a liberation war against Pakistan. To mark the occasion, the National Museum in Dhaka was screening for free the film *Orunodoyer Ognishakhi*, one of the first films made in 1972 after the war. Because it was a national holiday, the auditorium was packed with people and was constituted mainly of Dhaka University students, poor and lower-middle-class families, their children, and garment workers who had a day off, a very different audience from the middle class and left-liberal intellectuals who normally frequent the premier shows at the National Museum. I had waited in the queue for over an hour to be told that the National Museum auditorium was packed and that people were also sitting on the floor and stairs. My research and "foreigner" (i.e., Indian) credentials proved to be fruitful at this moment: I was ushered in to see the film from the projection room of the National Museum.

The film focuses on the personal trauma of a film actor Altaf who does not take part in the liberation war and eventually takes refuge in Calcutta. The woman he loves is taken away by the army; his family is gunned down in front of him, and he manages to flee by joining the refugees in India. The film shows the intensive fighting and valor of the liberation fighters who get the better of the Pakistani army and the Razakars (local collaborators). Seen in 1997, the film seems to elicit a certain collective response, centered around the issue of punishing Razakars. The need to punish Razakars and to bring them to trial for their wartime collaboration is a pivotal issue in contemporary Bangladesh and impinges on the formation of the state and its various political communities.

The term *Razakar*, which has come to mean 'collaborator' in Bangladesh, primarily refers to those local Bengalis and Biharis who collaborated with the West Pakistani army in the Bangladesh war of 1971, leading to the death of three million civilians, around fifty intellectuals,[1] and the rape of 200,000 women (these are official—but contested—numbers).[2] The term, which literarily means "volunteer" or "helper" in Persian and Urdu, is used in contemporary Bangladesh as a verbal abuse like the terms *Judas* in Europe or *Mirjafar* in West Bengal.[3] One would call an individual a Razakar or *Razakarer bachcha*—child of a Razakar—to highlight that this person is bound to betray, is scheming, has malicious intentions, and is untrustworthy. Numbering up to 50,000 in 1971, Razakars were mainly comprised of Bihari Muslims (who spoke in Urdu and came to Bangladesh during the 1947 partition) and religious reactionary parties like Jamaat-e-Islami (JMI) (Salek 1977), Al Badr, and Al Shams, which formed "Peace Committees" all over Bangladesh. Thirty-eight years after independence, the Razakars have not been tried in Bangladesh for the killings of intellectuals and rape of women. Some of them have even become cabinet ministers in the Bangladeshi government.

This chapter is based on my decade-long research on the public memories of sexual violence during the Bangladesh war of 1971 (Mookherjee 2006, 2008, forthcoming 2011). Here, I explore ethnographically how collaborators are perceived among the left-liberal activist community in Dhaka (the capital of Bangladesh) and in Enayetpur, a village in western Bangladesh where I did part of my fieldwork. The left-liberal activist community are part of the political and cultural elite, but they are not necessarily homogeneous, and disagreements exist among them. The feminist networks, in particular, were critical about the leading male intellectuals. However, on the issue of the war, a certain consensus exists. Similarly, varied hierarchies exist in Enayetpur. I juxtapose the perception of Razakars among the left-liberal community in Dhaka and among all classes in Enayetpur, not to cater to a subaltern checklist but to highlight the various emotions and interests that generate these perceptions. This juxtaposition can be comprehended best through Nancy Lindisfarne's words:

anthropology from below works only if it includes looking up. And ethnographies only become gripping and relevant to the anthropologist's own life, when they include a commitment to make sense of ethnographic data in terms of explicit, coherent theories about regional and national elites, and their relation to all other players in the global political economy. (2002, 420)

As such, I map the relationship among the collaborators, left-liberal intellectuals in Dhaka, and inhabitants of Enayetpur through an exploration of the practices of denunciation. Writing about modern Europe, Sheila Fitzpatrick and Robert Gellately define denunciation as "spontaneous communications from individual citizens to the state containing accusations of wrongdoing by other citizens or officials and implicitly or explicitly calling for punishment" (1996, 747). According to Fitzpatrick and Gellately, denunciations have widely been delivered in private to authorities. Any personal interest is denied on the part of the denunciators as they claim they are fulfilling their duty to the state or public good. In comparison, denunciatory practices toward the Razakars, rather than being delivered privately, are primarily performed and staged at the national and local level in Bangladesh. The presence of such perceived collaborators in Bangladesh is considered by the left-liberal activists as a sign of weakness in the Bangladeshi nation and an attack on the sovereignty of Bangladeshi nation-state. Denunciatory practices become, therefore, a language of state accountability. Indeed, denunciations could be considered the only morally righteous language of accountability available to left-liberal activists and the villagers in Enayetpur, as they try to hold the powerful to account. In the process, denunciation calls into question the failure of the state to fulfill its promises to the Bangladeshi nation. However, to consider denunciation only as a language of resistance and accountability would fail to capture the morally ambiguous terrain in which it is evoked. Instead, I would argue that denunciatory practices provide a lens through which a fractured picture of the constitution of collaboration during and after 1971 can be comprehended.

Razakars and the Political Trajectory of Bangladesh

The political and social trajectory of Bangladesh is a history of fractured and multiple pasts and identities: from being a part of colonial British

India to being a part of Pakistan after the partition of India in 1947 and, finally, to becoming an independent nation in 1971. In 1947, the independence of India from British colonial rule resulted in the creation of a new homeland for India's Muslims by carving out the eastern and northwestern corners of the country, which became known as East and West Pakistan respectively. In the formation of Pakistan, Islam was the sole principle of nationhood unifying two widely disparate units, separated not only geographically but also by sharp cultural and linguistic differences. West Pakistani authorities considered the Bengali Muslims of East Pakistan, with their focus on literature, music, and dance, as too "Bengali" (perceived as Indianized/Hinduized) and their practice of Islam as "inferior and impure" (Roy 1983, 1996; Ahmed 1988). This made the East Pakistanis unreliable coreligionists (Ali 1983). This insight can be contrasted with the contemporary perceptions of Indians about the "Muslimness" of Bangladeshis. Reluctant to rely on religious allegiance alone, successive governments in Pakistan embarked on a strategy of forcible cultural assimilation toward the Bengalis. Over the years, various impositions, as well as West Pakistani administrative, military, linguistic, civil, and economic control, led to the nine-month-long liberation war in 1971, which resulted in the formation of Bangladesh. It is important to note that the political and cultural elite in Bangladesh who espoused the position of a Muslim East Pakistan in 1947 were also the propagators of a Bengali Muslim Bangladesh as distinct from West Pakistan twenty-five years later in 1971.

The new nation of Bangladesh was faced with the staggering number of three million dead and 200,000 women raped in a span of nine months in 1971 by the Pakistani army and Razakars. The liberation of Bangladesh was led by the left-liberal, secular Awami League party and its charismatic leader Sheikh Mujibur Rehman, who became the first prime minister of Bangladesh and is considered by some as the father of the nation. The Bangladeshi constitution was based on the four principles of democracy, secularism, socialism, and nationalism. Sheikh Mujib was assassinated in 1975, and his death was followed by fifteen years of military rule under General Ziaur Rahman (General Zia) and General Hussain Muhammad Ershad. Democratic elections were first held in 1990, and General Ziaur Rahman's widow, Khaleda Zia, who was also the leader of the Bangladesh National Party (BNP)—considered to be more aligned to the military, Islamicist politics and Bangladeshi nationalism (which emphasized the Islamic identity over the Bengali identity of the Bengali Muslims in Bangladesh)—was victorious. In the 1996 elections, the assassinated Mujib's daughter Sheikh Hasina Wazed, leader of the left-liberal Awami League, came to power. In 2001, the BNP government under Khaleda Zia again formed the government. However, the military took over power in January 2007 and promised elections around the end of 2008. During this period, both female leaders were in jail as part of the anticorruption drive instituted by the military-backed caretaker government. In December 2008, Sheikh Hasina overwhelmingly won the elections and promised to address the issue of trying the collaborators in a war-crimes tribunal.

It is clear that the Bengali Muslim identity upon which Bangladesh was formed in 1971 is embedded in a fraught history and a contested discourse (Mookherjee 2007). This is apparent in the character of the postcolonial party politics in which the Awami League and the Bangladesh National Party have opposed each other. Since Bangladesh secured its independence under the aegis of the Awami League, the celebration of a secular Bengali identity has become rooted in several factors: a literary and left-liberal tradition, the focus on the civilian role during the Bangladesh War of 1971, support for Hindu minorities, and a pro-Indian geopolitical position. As a result, left-liberal activists and intellectuals tend to be supporters of the Awami League. In contrast, the BNP formed in 1975 spearheaded quite different constitutional changes—replacing secularism with the Islamic Republic of Bangladesh and changing the identity of the citizens from Bengali to Bangladeshi. This is to distinguish the Bengali-speaking population of Bangladesh from the Hindu Bengalis of India.[4] A large number of collaborators who had supported and aided the Pakistani army in committing the killings and rapes during the war in 1971 were politically rehabilitated under the BNP. In contrast to the Awami League, the BNP is associated with upholding right-wing values related to Islam and the military. The party is predominantly perceived to be less sympathetic to Hindu minorities and is deemed to be anti-Indian and pro-Pakistani in its policies.

In this political trajectory, the role of the Islamicist party Jamaat-e-Islami (JMI), which was led by known collaborators like Gholam Azum, has been central to political calculations and alliances. In January 1972 a Collaborator Law was passed, and Sheikh Mujib's government formulated the International Crimes (Tribunal) Act in 1973. On 13 November 1972, a Dr. Malek was tried under this law (*Banglar Bani* 11 November 1972, and on 19 November, he was given life imprisonment. By this time 37,000 collaborators had been identified (*Bhorer Kagoj* 2 May 2002). This process was, however, stalled with the granting of the infamous *shadharon khoma* (general amnesty) by Mujib on 30 November 1973, which foreclosed any possibility of trial.[5] The reason cited by those in the Awami League for this general amnesty was an attempt by Mujib to seek peace rather than retribution in a postconflict independent Bangladesh. Out of the 37,000 collaborators, 33,000 (who were alleged to be members of JMI) were released without trial and investigation, while "thousands of supporters of left wing parties languished in prison" (Khan 2000,582). Until July 1972, there were deemed to be 500 war criminals. Afterward, this number was reduced to 200 and various documents are alleged to have disappeared.[6]

This process of absolving collaborators initiated by Mujib was institutionalized under General Zia's government. Through amendments made to the constitution, it was possible politically to reinstate Islamist parties such as the JMI and their allies, as well as Shah Azizur Rahman and Gholam Azum who had openly collaborated with the Pakistani Army in 1971. All remaining collaborators were released from prison under Zia. The literary accounts in the 1980s and 1990s show how the collaborators of the war changed sides after 1971 and became socially and politically reinstituted without any redress. In the last scene of famous playwright Syed Shamsul Huq's *Paer Aoaj Paoa Jai* (Footsteps Can Be Heard, 1976), the collaborator changes his position as soon as the liberation fighters come into the village after the war:

Let me show you where, when, what,
In what danger people lived
When the tyrant was in power . . .
Those who were with them. (author's translation)

After Zia's assassination, the collaborators were further reinstated politically under General Ershad, with prominent Razakars becoming the law minister and vice-president. By this time, through various constitutional amendments introduced during the military rule, Bangladesh had adopted a full-fledged free market economy, Bengali nationalism had become Bangladeshi nationalism, and secularism had given way to Islam being declared as the state religion. Lamenting the rehabilitation of Razakars, Allauddin Alazad notes in his poem written in the late 1970s:

Thirty Lakh murders,
Three lakh and fifty rapes,
Fifty Thousand Arsons,
But Collaborators only 195? (*Ghatok 195*, late 1970s; author's translation)

It is important to note that alliances with the JMI have been pivotal in the formation of both the Awami League and BNP governments. In the last BNP government, in particular, well-known collaborators and JMI members were cabinet ministers. In this context, the JMI holds the strings through which government is formed by both political parties. However, the left-liberal activist community has continued to demand the trial of collaborators. The significant role of the left-liberal activists needs to be comprehended in the contexts of the killings of the fifty intellectuals on the eve of independence. The martyred intellectuals were considered to be the cultural guardians and repositories of Bengali Muslim identity through their contribution to ideas, art, literature, poems, and songs, which form the central plank of this identity. Thus, their killings are considered to be an attempt to weaken Bengali nationalism. To the left-liberal community in Bangladesh, their deaths and the assassination of Sheikh Mujib in 1975 represent the loss of the possibility of a particular kind of nation building, centered on secular and socialist nationalism. Also, many of the left-liberal activists are related to the families of the martyred intellectuals and have suffered violent, personal losses in the war through the death of their fathers, brothers and uncles. The very fact that 14 December is officially and annually commemorated as the "Martyred Intellectual Killing Day" (Mookherjee 2007) highlights the significant role intellectuals play for the Bengali Muslim identity in Bangladesh.

The demand for the trial of collaborators was first brought to a head in 1992 in the Gono Adalat (People's Court). After the war, Gholam Azum, the best-known Razakar and head of JMI fled to Pakistan, and the Bangladesh government revoked his citizenship.[7] However, after the 1991 elections, when the BNP came to power in alliance with the JMI, Gholam Azum finally reapplied for a Bangladeshi citizenship, rekindling a growing surge of anger against the increasing role of Razakars in the political landscape of Bangladesh. In this context, the Gono Adalat took place on 26 March 1992 led by the left-liberal cultural elites and "civil society" in Dhaka demanding the trial of Gholam Azum. The court was held under the organizational structure of the Ghatok Dalal Nirmul Committee (Committee for the Eradication of Collaborators and Assassins of 1971)—an organization that is also engaged in documenting the names of collaborators all over Bangladesh—and was led by Jahanara Imam and renowned poets, historians, writers, journalists, and lawyers.[8] Shahriar Kobir, a renowned journalist and writer who is a leading member of the organizing committee, told me that after the BNP government demolished the stage that had been built by the organizers and disconnected electricity, the organizers used two big lorries to serve as a stage in the middle of the huge Ramna Park in Dhaka. From atop the lorries, various testimonies of affected individuals—those who had lost their father, brother, or son—were narrated. Alongside these accounts was the "visual testimony" (they did not speak, but their very presence was deemed as testimony against Gholam Azum) of three *birangonas*—Rohima, Kajoli and Moyna—landless women (from a village in western Bangladesh where I did some of my fieldwork). *Birangonas* is a term propagated by the Bangladeshi government to refer to all women raped as a result of the war in 1971.

While watching the video of Gono Adalat, shot by Kawser Chowdhury, I saw that Jahanara Imam read out charges against Gholam Azum: "Three hundred thousand mothers and sisters have been dishonored; three million martyrs have been killed. All this is the work of Gholam Azum for which he should be given a death sentence. The government should carry out the verdict within a month." The video showed that, by 10:30 a.m., the park was teeming with people, including leading liberation fighters, politicians, lawyers, wheelchair-bound veterans, families of martyrs, garment workers, heads of nongovernmental organizations (NGO), journalists, students, and young children. A disabled liberation fighter asserted, "We want to defeat them again. It is a stigma that more Razakars are sitting on the throne than liberation fighters." Lawyers and NGO heads felt that this event would instill the spirit of the liberation war among the younger generation and, hence, restore independence to Bangladesh.

The event was designed by the leftist intellectuals to communicate to the younger generation the "real" events of 1971 in order to correct the "doctored" history put forward by the fifteen years of military rule and the Islamicist state under the BNP. It also highlighted the growing influence of collaborators in Bangladesh. For the left-liberal intellectuals, Bangladesh's unacknowledged "genocidal" birth represented the unresolved, unreconciled history of the nation. For many of these intellectuals, the importance of the Gono Adalat was further magnified by the increase of fatwas against women and NGO workers at this juncture. These fatwas were attributed to the collaborators by feminists and various poor women interviewed in the documentary film *Eclipse* (1999):

The present rise of rapes and violence against women in society is only a continuation of the violence against women committed during 1971. This is because the fundamentalist forces and those giving fatwas endanger women's liberty of movement and activity. These are the same forces whose war crimes during 1971 were not tried. (*Doinik Jonokontho* 12 December 1997)[9]

The significance of the Gono Adalat and the demand for the trial of collaborators need to be located within the images of the Bangladeshi nation that circulate within and outside the country. Around the early 1990s, Bangladesh attracted international press coverage when it banned the well-known feminist writer Taslima Nasrin's 1993 novel *Lojja* (Shame). In this novel, the author portrays the nightmare that befalls a Hindu (Duttas) family, in Bangladesh in the context of a backlash against minority Hindu communities. The violence is perpetrated by the Muslim majority in response to the demolition of Babri Masjid at Ayodhya in India and the resultant massacre of minority Muslim communities in India. *Lojja* ends with the Duttas leaving Bangladesh for India. When the book was banned in 1993, Nasrin had to flee Bangladesh and went into exile in Sweden. In India, Nasrin's work was appropriated by the right-wing Hindu nationalist party Bharatiya Janata Party (BJP), whose supporters had been instrumental in the demolition of Babri Masjid and the consequent communal carnage. It was rumored that the BJP was selling pirated copies of *Lojja* that included BJP propaganda about "Muslim violence" against Hindus. Nasrin's writings made Bangladeshis feel wrongly portrayed within the subcontinent and beyond as fundamentalists. Paradoxically, Taslima's novels *Nirbachito Column* and *Lojja* strengthened already existing negative stereotypes in West Bengal and India about the Muslims of Bangladesh. In the post-9/11 Islamophobic world, Bangladesh is seen to be a hotbed of Islamic extremists, even though the U.S. administration considers it to be "moderate."

The Biharis as Foreign Collaborators

The partition of 1947 not only metamorphosed the ethnoscape of subcontinental migrancy but also spawned multiple identities (Ghosh 1998, 232). The Biharis, notable among the collaborators, stand out as an ethnic group deemed to be foreigners in Bangladesh.[10] Moving to Bangladesh during the partition of India in 1947, they are identified through speaking Urdu and speaking Bengali with an Urdu accent and are often referred to as "stranded Pakistanis," "Biharis," "Bangladeshi/Pakistani Biharis," or "Bihari Muslims."

Biharis are widely thought to have been behind the killing of the fifty intellectuals mentioned above. These leading intellectuals comprised doctors, engineers, lawyers, litterateurs, academics, and journalists, as well as top bureaucrats and business elites. They were both Hindus and Muslims and included one female journalist, Selina Parveen. Their bodies were found in a brick kiln in Rayerbajar, in Dhaka, lying face down, blindfolded, hands tied behind their backs with red pieces of cloth, their bodies submerged in water. To commemorate the loss of the intellectuals, two memorials in Mirpur and Rayerbajar have been built (Mookherjee 2007). Significantly, the memorials are located in a predominantly lower-middle-class and poor neighborhoods where Biharis reside. These neighborhoods are primarily perceived by the left-liberal activist communities to be religiously conservative, extreme Islamicist localities and are alleged to have collaborated with the Pakistani army in 1971. Adding to Mirpur's collaborator reputation, human bones were discovered in a mosque in Mirpur a few years ago. This site has now become a mass grave memorial.

The huge Geneva Camp run by the Red Cross and housing thousands of Biharis is located in Mirpur next to these war memorials. Since 1971,

Biharis have been left stranded in deplorable conditions in the Geneva Camp and occupy a liminal space, with neither the Bangladeshi nor the Pakistani government accepting them as citizens. Stigmatized as collaborators in Bangladesh, only 118,866 out of 534,792 Biharis were granted repatriation by the Pakistan government. The Stranded Pakistanis General Repatriation Committee, formed in 1977, deployed the language of refugees with the UN and of Muslim refugees with Islamic heads of state. In the 1980s, the Committee idealized Bihar as the Bihari homeland and blamed the Muslim League of Pakistan for dislodging them twice over, in 1947 and 1971. At the same time, the Committee seems to have kept alive its allegiance to Pakistan. Before the elections of January 2007, the BNP government, hoping to secure votes from Biharis living in the Geneva Camp, proposed that they be added to the electoral list. In response, some of these Biharis held a press conference with pictures of Pakistani presidents behind them and announced that they did not want to be on any of the voters' list in Bangladesh because they wanted to go back to Pakistan, whose citizens they are. Only in May 2008 were they granted Bangladeshi citizenship. These events show the shifting allegiances that this liminal community have to keep alive, making them seem an untrustworthy group and potential collaborators to many Bengali Bangladeshis.

Denunciatory Practices and Fractured Understandings of Razakars

Through his denunciation during the Gono Adalat, Gholam Azum stands for the wider figure of the collaborator. Such denunciations need to be comprehended through an understanding of the historical role of the martyred intellectuals within the Bengali Muslim identity of Bangladesh. In the video *Gono Adalat,* various university students talk with passion about the build up to the events of the day. The forms of justice against collaborators ranged from the humiliating idiom of slapping Azum's effigy with slippers, the juridical nature of the "public" court, and the right of violence through the "public" death sentence given to Azum's effigy, a scene that was accompanied by cheering jubilation from the crowds. The poster in Figure 2.1 highlights this juridical framework and also mark's Gholam Azum's allegiance to Islam (shown by his beard and cap) and Pakistan (shown by the moon and crescent on the cap). The 1996 poster (Figure 2.2) warns about the rise of the JMI and its student wing Shibir and also highlights their historical roots. Showing the groups to be as dangerous as snakes, the poster indicates that Jamaat (as represented by Azum in the middle, with his beard, star, crescent cap, and menacing look with his tongue out) has allegiance to Islam, Pakistan, and the military. This is underscored through the Pakistani

Figure 2.1. Poster announcing the Gono Adalat and the trial of the leader of the collaborators of 1971 and JMI, Gholam Azum. Ekattorer Ghatok Dalal Nirmul Committee, February 1992. International Institute of Social History.

generals A. K. Niazi on the right and Zia-ul-Haq on the left—the patrons of Jamaat and Shibir. On a closer look at the poster, the trio represents an octopus with quivering tentacles. Those tentacles are coupled with the sharp nails and the teeth of demons and monsters. The poster indicates that the Islamic and militaristic forces linked to Pakistan are seeking to infiltrate and prey on Bangladeshis.

The denunciatory practices in the Gono Adalat brought together a large number of citizens, with the aim of directing attention to the acts of collaboration by the Razakars. More widely, the aim of the Gono Adalat was to create a political community among the younger generation. It provided a theatrical space for private pain to move into the public realm. A staged, performative denunciation, where Gholam Azum was sentenced to death in absentia, these enactments ensured the continuation of the environment of death. The posters, which could be found all over Dhaka to advertise the event, served to provide a visual, preview of the process of denunciation. The Gono Adalat pronounced a public verdict and punishment of collaborators for their collaboration in 1971. Through these practices, the left-liberal activists simultaneously sought to appeal to an imagined court of public opinion and to mobilize the

একাত্তরের ঘাতকরা আবারও হত্যায় মেতেছে
স্বৈরাচার ও তার দোসর
সশস্ত্র জামাত-শিবিরকে ঐক্যবদ্ধভাবে
প্রতিরোধ কর

COLL IISG

পাঁচ দল

Figure 2.2. Resist autocracy and its collaborator the armed Jamat-Shibir (the student wing of Jamaat) unitedly, Joint council of Panch Dol (five parties), 1996. International Institute of Social History.

public. At the same time, this public denunciation was directed to the BNP government and the state that is seen to be attempting to protect the collaborators. The local authorities sought to disrupt the event by disconnecting the electricity in order to disable the use of microphones for the huge gathering. This act itself generated an added fervor to the event, as Shazzad, a Dhaka University student said to me: "We could not hear what was being said and could only see from a distance. But we knew we had to be there precisely because we could not see or hear clearly."

In 2005, various Islamist parties were allegedly linked with multiple bomb blasts and suicide bombings that killed and injured top Awami League politicians and liberation fighters. In this context, various forms of denunciation against the collaborators continued in Bangladesh. In

Figure 2.3. The Dhikkar Stombho (Monument of Reprimand) at the Dhaka University Student Union (DACSU) Cafeteria. Courtesy Saydia Kamal, June 2008.

December 2007, ad hoc memorials were set up all over Bangladesh to remind communities that collaborators are living among them. These are called *dhikkar stombho* or monuments of rapprochement/reprimand, and communities place garlands of shoes on these structures to show their derision for local collaborators. Such a monument can be seen in the Dhaka University Student Union (DACSU) cafeteria—a black pillar with the names of various groups of collaborators written in white paint along with the sign of the crescent and moon. Here, the message is that not only is it important to indict individual enemies, but a collective purging is necessary.

However, ridding the country of Razakars faces social and political obstacles since many of the collaborators are entrenched in Bangladeshi politics. As a result of electoral alliances, the JMI, widely thought of as a party dominated by collaborators, has become central to Bangladeshi politics. The anger at the presence of the JMI in mainstream politics should, therefore, also be seen as a criticism of the party politics of both the BNP and Awami League. Denunciation does not emerge in this instance out of a loyalty for the state. Instead, denouncing the Razakars is a critique of the historical and political trajectory of Bangladesh: it is a critique of the government in power, of the political machinations of the two parties. It provides a morally righteous language through which the state can be made accountable and through which a vision of a future state based on the values of the liberation war can be put forward.

This language of accountability is itself rife with moral ambiguity. While those who are collaborators are partly identified through their relationship with Pakistan and Islam, language itself, particularly fluency in Urdu, is also deemed to be a signifier of one's closeness to Pakistan. As such, Biharis are predominantly marked off by their Bengali accent tinged with Hindi. Some well-off Bengali families who were in Pakistan before 1971 would often speak Urdu at home. Though these individuals would not be referred to as collaborators, they would be deemed to have Razakar tendencies, that is, to be biased toward Pakistan. It is also often asserted that many self-proclaimed liberation fighters were actually collaborators during the war. There exists intense contestation among liberation fighters about the claims made by other fighters. Questions are raised as to where one was during the war, what one might have done, and what feats of valor one is claiming in the present. Finally, the role of intellectuals is also ambiguous. Intellectuals are revered, and their work is seen to support the secular Bengali Muslim identity in Bangladesh. However, many who were supporters of the BNP (as well as critical supporters of the Awami League) pointed out to me that intellectuals have "prostituted" themselves and changed alliances with changing governments. This allegation was particularly targeted at intellectuals who are NGO heads. Others claimed that I would get to know nothing from intellectuals as they were blind followers of the Awami League. Referring to the intellectuals' intricate familial and professional interconnections, some journalists advised me to obtain their biographies before interviewing them. Although the significance of the role of the intellectuals might be based on an exaggerated sense of self-importance, they nonetheless comprise a significant collective whose perspectives are deeply interwoven with Bangladesh's Bengali Muslim identity.

Perhaps most importantly, the retelling of Bangladesh's genocidal birth has not addressed the killing of Biharis and rape of Bihari women by Bengalis. The untold story of the atrocities on the Bihari community ruptures this nationalist narrative based on loss, pain, and valor. Increasingly, this history is being highlighted in contemporary Bangladesh through photographs, films, and oral histories.

"If One Tried to Clear the Bristles of a Blanket, There Would Be Nothing Left of It"

The ambiguities of collaboration and denunciation are not found among just left-wing intellectuals. During my fieldwork, villagers would often use Sheikh Mujib's quote "if one tried to clear the bristles of a blanket, there would be nothing left of it" to refer to the blurred boundaries between the liberation fighters and collaborators in Enayetpur.[11] In Enayetpur, everyone everywhere had a story of *gondogoler bochor* (the year of chaos, that is, the war of 1971).[12] The local events of the war, the role of liberation fighters, military training, stories of valor, arson, killings, bombings, ambushes, everyday travails of survival, displacement, floods, hardships, and food scarcity were all vividly and spontaneously narrated. In rural Bangladesh, the war of 1971 is often referred to as "chaos," instead of independence. In the following paragraphs, I contrast the link made by left-liberal activists in Dhaka between collaboration and political Islam and the complicated picture in Enayetpur, where accusations of collaboration have an intricate entanglement with local political machinations.

Interviews with liberation fighters in Enayetpur produced detailed descriptions of training in India, operations against the Pakistani army, the role of local Razakars, the names of associates and weapons used, and, overall, a reflection of the postwar and contemporary situation in Bangladesh. It was also obvious that the role of the collaborators had clear hierarchies in Enayetpur. The dominant force in the village is the Munshibari, the Munshi household. Bhulen "Master" (a retired teacher in the local school) was one of the most prominent members of the Munshibari and was the best-known liberation fighter of the village, but he was also considered to be extremely arrogant. In contrast, Muzaam, a poor, low-level weaver, and Shamsuddin, a local youth, who are both dead, are widely cited in the village as the main Razakars in Enayetpur. However, one day, when I sat chatting about the war events with a group of villagers, one of them commented that I could only know about Razakars by inquiring in Munshibari. Probing further, I was told that Bhulen's cousins Manik and Hiru were the main Razakars of the area. They hung around with the Pakistani army, brought the soldiers to Enayetpur, and entertained them in Munshibari's *kacharighar* (front quarters). Others told me that, although Manik and Hiru's aim in bringing in the military to the village was to protect Enayetpur, the military ran amuck. The aforementioned Muzaam did only what Manik asked him to do; but after the war, Muzaam was the one who was brutally killed (through application of electric shocks to his genitals) by the liberation fighters, while Manik, as Bhulen's cousin, went scot-free. Similarly, Shamsuddin, who was killed after the war by liberation fighters for raping a fleeing Hindu refugee's daughter, is easily labeled a Razakar (though not "technically" so), but this glosses over the role of his accomplices (Chandu and Fazlu) in the rape. Being linked to powerful families, Chandu and Fazlu were exonerated and continue to live in Enayetpur. Villagers would also criticize Bhulen and mention that they are aware of what he did in the years of the war. They would suggestively add that they know which liberation fighter was "hiding and sleeping in boats" and which was fighting during the war. After the war, according to these villagers, those who had the loudest voice could become liberation fighters—that is how Bhulen has earned his fame. In an interview, Manik, a man characterized by urban sensibilities, stated that Enayetpur was totally unaffected by the war, that there was no loss and no food scarcity, and that he moved freely. In fact to him, Bangladesh should have remained with Pakistan. Here, Manik ideologically fits the image of the collaborator held by the left-liberal activists in Dhaka, though he has none of the Islamic markers of beard and cap. Similarly, villagers refer to *Jolas* or the weaver communities as Razakars, as they stayed in Enayetpur in 1971, accompanied the Pakistani military, and provided them food and assistance. Villagers refer to them as *Molla* type (fundamentalist), alluding to their staunch Islamic beliefs.

The position of the Munshi family as the most powerful household in Enayetpur owed to its rich liberation fighter credentials. However, as I mentioned earlier, the same family is also known as Razakars. This was highlighted further by Alom (son of one of the women raped during the war and who had testified at the Gono Adalat) during a conversation I had with him while watching a cricket match. In January 1998, the Pepsi Independence Cup was played in Dhaka among India, Pakistan, and Bangladesh. The final, played between India and Pakistan, ended with a nail-biting finish, and India won. Alom said that most of Enayetpur supported Pakistan, but he supported India. He told me that " 'What else would Razakars support? Only if what happened to us [referring to his mother's rape] had happened to them, then I would see whether they could support Pakistan."

The collaborationist characteristics of the supposed liberation fighters are further highlighted by the villager's narration and criticism of the transactions and alliances set up between liberation fighters and Razakars after 1971. Such alliances served as a "reinforcement of horizontal division" (Gilsenan 1977, 182), whereby dominant groups of shared class position crystallize and consolidate themselves and ensure the dependence of favor seekers. Further evidence of this is the support by liberation fighters of known collaborators in local elections, the usurpation of land and jewelry by Bhulen of Hindus who have gone off to India, and the behavior of other liberation fighters who were known for taking refugees to the river (the village is located on one of the largest rivers of Bangladesh, one of the main routes of fleeing to India) in 1971 and then seizing their jewelry and possessions.

Many of these denunciations take the shape of what Fitzpatrick and Gellately (1996, 757) have referred to as "manipulative denunciation," whereby everyday hostilities take violent forms in the context of wars. However, these criticisms also allow denunciations to be made against those in power by citizens from a less powerful position. That everyday competitiveness among neighbors can assume lethal forms during wars is evident in an exhibit in the Bangladesh Liberation War Museum—a letter to the secretary of the local Peace Committee written on 7 June 1971 by an M Joynal Abedin, stating that he had been forced to flee his house because the liberation fighters had "attempted to arrest and kill" him. Abedin notes that he was a "supporter of the Muslim League and worked in favor of the same during the last general election" and then asks whether he could move into a house, the particulars of which he lists as

Owner: Kumar Dhirendranath Chakrabarty, s/o late Monoranjan Chakrabarty (Manik babu), Village Ulipur (Jotder Para), one south facing tin shed, measuring 20 x 10$^{1}/_{2}$ and two bamboo houses.

The details of the "south facing" tin shed found within this letter show how, during wars, everyday familiarity can turn into complicity and jealousy. The looting in 1971 of wooden doors, tin roofs, and kitchen utensils within the neighborhood was widespread. Everyday neighbors become the sources for amassing material resources, however minimal or substantial.

While villagers critique the alliances between elite liberation fighters and Razakars, the reasons for poor and illiterate people to be Razakars were often very nuanced. Many became a Razakar in order to prevent torture, to relieve economic need, or to prevent reprisals against their family. When I visited the home of a man who was known to be a collaborator, I found that he and his wife readily acknowledged that he worked as a Razakar during the war. He added that there was no work and that they had to eat, so he hung around with the military and guarded bridges. Similarly, a Hindu fisherman told me that Muslim families had to be on both sides to save their skins. So, in one family, there would be both Razakars and liberation fighters in order to ensure security. Stories of torture by liberation fighters of Biharis in Kushtia were also common.

A man in Bhashkhal who was critiquing Awami League's policies said he should not talk about this as he would be easily termed a Razakar since he is known as a Bihari rather than through his family name.

Today, the active politicking in the local liberation fighters' council is characterized by the formulation of endless new lists with the change of governments and with varied political factions of liberation fighters taking over at different times. Some poor liberation fighters would lament how young men make speeches as liberation fighters today though they would have been children during 1971. There are also the *false* liberation fighters known as the "16th squadron," people who did not fight but picked up weapons on 16 December when Bangladesh became independent and claimed to be liberation fighters (though they might have been Razakars). The symbolic power of the liberation fighters and local leaders is thereby contested by highlighting the disjunctions between their contradictory moral position as liberation fighters and their local actions of corruption and powermongering.

Along with manipulative denunciations, the narrations in Enayetpur redefine the nature of collaboration and show the permeable boundaries between some collaborators and liberation fighters. The positions taken against the local liberation fighter also allow denunciations to be made by the weak against those in power, based on everyday grievance and local politics. To follow Mujib's quote, there was no point in trying to clear the bristles of the blanket as everyone had been in various instances of complicity and collaboration during the war.

Conclusion

In M. A. Saber's 1991 novel *Sotero Bochor Pore* (Seventeen Years Later), the character BD, a Razakar, visits Bangladesh after seventeen years and finds that all those who had been defeated in 1971 are in power and the liberation fighters are powerless. Even individuals who had been actively involved in the supply and trafficking of women to the Pakistani army are hosting and making speeches in commemorative programs on the war. Similarly, in Saber's earlier *Pathor Somoy* (Difficult Times, 1981), a young man, Mahmud, is made aware about the "distortions of history" when he learns from his uncle that his father was involved in supplying women and collaborating with the Pakistani army. Such portrayals of Razakars in the late 1980s emphasize the varied social complicities of collaborators and the complex and varied subject positions they occupied. However, the characterization of the collaborator as a criminal aiming to accumulate money gave way to more bounded constructions of Razakars from the early 1990s. With the onset of parliamentary democracy in the 1990s, left-liberal intellectuals sought to institutionalize their discourse of history. The Razakar image fits a stereotypical image of a devout fanatical Muslim with a cap and beard. The alliance of the Razakars with Pakistan, Islam, and their continued political influence are seen by liberal intellectuals as undermining the possibility of a secular nationalism. This construction of the collaborator is distinct from literary accounts of the 1980s that highlight their complicity, contradictions, and economic self-interest.

The roles of the left-liberal activist community and the martyred intellectuals are pivotal to this construction of collaboration. The birth and independence of Bangladesh corresponded with the loss of these intellectuals and the ideals they stood for—a secularist nationalism based on a Bengali Muslim identity. The left-liberal community seeks to remind the country of the ideals lost through the killing of the intellectuals in order to make these ideals constitutive of the political configuration of Bangladesh. The dead intellectuals not only remind Bangladesh about this loss but are also configured as a moral compass for the nation. By highlighting the Islamic and Pakistani affiliations of the Razakar, the left-liberal activists show that the genocidal birth of Bangladesh continues to be unacknowledged and that the secular nationalism that the formation of Bangladesh promised is yet to be achieved. This, nonetheless, does not address the ways in which many of these same activists supported Islamic Pakistan in 1947 and a Bengali Muslim identity twenty-five years later during the formation of Bangladesh against Islamic West Pakistan. Also unaddressed is the current decrepit, liminal conditions occupied by the Biharis and the rape of Bihari women in 1971.

When juxtaposed with the absoluteness of left-liberal denunciation, the ethnographic accounts in Enayetpur highlight the blurred boundaries between collaborators and liberation fighters. The accumulation of money, votes, and land becomes a means through which Razakars and liberation fighters are brought together. The liberation fighter and collaborator are fused in their economic and moral interests. Collaboration seems to have little to do with Islamic politics but is instead intertwined with the webs of economic and political complicity.

These formulations of the left-liberal community highlight the unresolved injustices surrounding the collaborator. However, characterizing collaborators through their repetitive links to Islam and Pakistan shows how the Razakars have been made in order to be found. The lack of acknowledgment of rape, killings, and Bangladesh's "genocidal" birth represents to the left-liberals the unresolved, unreconciled history of the nation, the wound of the nation still raw, gaping and unhealed in the present. This, thus, necessitates the need for an "epic culture" of heroes and villains, the need for identifying the Islamicist collaborator all over Bangladesh. This epic culture maybe necessary if we follow Žižek's

(1989, 127) analysis of how "the block" is projected onto the figure of the "Jew." He shows how society is prevented from achieving its full identity by its own antagonistic nature, by its own immanent blockage, and in this case by its own denunciations.[13] Through the block or obstacle of the Islamicist collaborator, the fantasy of the full Bangladeshi identity is sustained as this identity is yet to be. Accusations of collaboration help to map out not only the boundaries of the collective subject: they also lay claim to moral and political certainty in the face of uncertainty in Bangladesh.

Chapter 3

Intimacy, Loyalty, and State Formation: The Specter of the "Anti-National"

Richard W. Whitecross

On 19 April 1998, the Tiger's Nest temple, in Taktshang, near Paro in western Bhutan, caught fire and was substantially destroyed. The destruction of this major Buddhist pilgrimage site was attributed, though never publicly established, to be the work of "anti-nationals" or "traitors." Commencing fieldwork the following summer, I found the so-called anti-national was an ever-present entity. Each evening, I would watch as Senge made offerings to placate those spirits that cause illness, and for a long time, the anti-national felt equally intangible. Conversations would touch on their presence in the community, and I was advised on several occasions about places and people to avoid. At the same time, I was slowly learning about *thadamtshi*—the concept of loyalty and respect. I became increasingly aware that this concept had been transformed in recent years as the Bhutanese state sought to protect Bhutan cultural identity and political sovereignty.

In this chapter, the first section illustrates how loyalty and its counterpart treason were, until recently, based on intimate personal relations rather than on abstract notions of the nation. However, as part of the modernization of Bhutan commenced in the late 1950s, this traditional view of loyalty based on direct social relations was transformed and extended to include new concepts of the "Country" and the "People." The Bhutanese subject/citizen was now held to be loyal to the "Three Roots." The next section outlines the emergence in Bhutan of a legitimate state—a state backed by something called a "nation" and able to speak in the "name of the people"—and specifically the production of a national ethnos (Appadurai 2006).

Central to the process of creating the nation-state in Bhutan was the promotion of an official vision that presented Bhutan as a homogeneous country with shared values, culture, and history. However, this image of Bhutan presents selected fragments of Bhutanese history that emphasizes unity while, both by omission and conscious choice, excluding those who do not conform to this image. The production of a nation as ideal, I argue, destabilized relations between different groups, creating a homogenized majority, the northern Bhutanese—Buddhist in religion and with languages falling within the Tibeto-Burman language group—and a minority, the Lhotshampa (Bhutanese-Nepalese), a hyphenated group whose language, customs, and histories do not fit the national ideal. I outline the escalation of tensions between the royal government and members of the Lhotshampa community during the late 1980s, culminating in the outbreak of violence in 1990–91. As a result, approximately 100,000 Lhotshampa left Bhutan and were settled in refugee camps in eastern Nepal. I argue that, following the flight of these refugees, the politically active Lhotshampa who remained, as well as those who had fled, were presented in the Bhutanese media as "anti-nationals." By 1999, when I began my fieldwork, the "anti-national" had become a spectral form that threatened not only the Bhutanese state but the whole country, a situation created by the presentation of this group and the reports of their crimes in the media. As a result, a rhetoric of loyalty to the nation emerged and soon conflated the remaining Lhotshampa with the spectral shadow of the anti-national.

Through a series of mundane processes, just as national identities are created and embedded in people's consciousness, the anti-national was transformed into a banal, social fact (Billig 1995). The specter of the anti-national, I argue, has filtered into the Bhutanese consciousness, resulting in a subtle "vilification and targeting of others" (Gorringe 2006, 257). The final section of this chapter presents a more general reflection on the role of the traitor and its capacity to serve as an important point of entry to critique the self-proclaimed sovereignty of the nation-state.

Thadamtshi: Loyalty and Rebellion

We had an instance of a rebellion, successful for some time before it was suppressed, which cost but few lives and only one of them could be called an execution, the zempin of Wandepore. (Turner 1800)

To understand the relationship between the emergent modern nation-state of Bhutan and the concept of the anti-national, I outline an alternative understanding of loyalty and treason, based on semifeudal, religious notions of devotion. Drawing from Bhutanese history, I look at instances of, on the one hand, insurgency and, on the other, of personal loyalty (again, *thadamtshi*). I argue that the notion of loyalty to the state was absent in Bhutan prior to 1950. Rather, loyalty and treachery, its corollary, were seen in terms of intimate personal relationships and hierarchically structured bonds of allegiance. This section provides the context for the discussion in section II of a new political concept, the Tsa Wa Sum (Thee Roots), and the creation of a new juridical category, the anti-national in Bhutan.

Insurgency, Charisma, and Devotion: Loyalty to the "Lord on High"

The two British missions sent north to Tibet in 1774 and 1783 coincided with insurrections in Bhutan in support of the ousted secular ruler Zhidar. Zhidar was appointed *desi* (secular ruler) in 1768 and subsequently ousted from power in 1773 by clerical forces concerned about his influence over the very young reincarnate *zhabdrung*, the symbolic head of the Drukpa state.[1] When the insurrection crumbled in 1774 and the rebels sought shelter in a nearby fortress, villages adjacent to it, loyal to the ousted *desi*, were destroyed by the government (Teltscher 2006). At the time of the second insurrection in 1783, Zhidar had been executed yet appears to have retained, even in death, the loyalty of a number of lay and ecclesiastical figures, as evidenced by Turner's comment above that the governor (*sic* zempin) of Wangduephodrang (*sic* Wangdepore) was executed, and through those individuals secured the support of various villages throughout central Bhutan (Turner 1800, 117–18). This loyalty, even in death, is an important and recurring feature in Bhutan. Loyalty was personal, based on relations and ties established between the lord and his followers—the villages that were destroyed were probably bound in a reciprocal fashion with Zhidar's followers.

The importance of personal loyalty is illustrated in the "Ballad of Pema Tshewang Tashi," composed in the mid-nineteenth century, which recalls the tale of its eponymous doomed hero, the lay chamberlain of the governor of Wangduephodrang *dzong* (fortress/monastery) (Aris 1987; Ura 1996).[2] At the request of the governor of Jakar dzong for military assistance to deal with the Tongsa governor, the central government decided that the obligation of military service should fall on men conscripted from the regions of Wangduephodrang and Dagana. Tshewang Tashi's loyalty is not expressed to the nation or the state. In his parting words to his friends among the lay officials of Wangduephodrang, he advises them that, until he returns, if he returns, they should

> First, do service to the lord on high.
> Second, see to the welfare of the subjects beneath
> Third, make yourselves successful in between. (Aris 1987, 157)

Throughout the ballad, there are two key themes. The first is the subtle criticism of the reckless use of power and the indifference of the powerful to the lives lost and suffering caused. The second is the strong sense of personal loyalty expressed by Tshewang Tashi. Raised in the service of Andruk Nyima, Tshewang Tashi manifests *thadamtshi*, which in Dzongkha literally means "the ultimate vow."[3] His admonition to his friends encapsulates the ideal system of priorities governing rival claims on personal loyalty that form the main theme of the ballad. The welfare of the people is secondary to providing "service to the lord." The term used for lord—*gong ma*—carries powerful religious overtones that highlight the intertwining of religious and secular values under the system of government established by the zhabdrung. Although it is unclear to what extent the ballad is about a historical figure and not merely a literary form, its underlying themes reflect the importance in mid-nineteenth-century Bhutanese society of personal ties and the very intimate nature of political power.

The Zhabdrung and the Monarch: Competing Loyalties

Perhaps the most dramatic story and one that continues to resonate in Bhutan was the murder of the last officially recognized reincarnation of the zhabdrung in November 1931. The first Zzhabdrung, Ngawang Namgyal, created Bhutan by a process of expansion in the early seventeenth century. When he died in 1651, his death was kept secret for approximately fifty years to allow the theocracy created by him to secure its power. Over the next two centuries, the reincarnates of the zhabdrung were politically powerless, yet the prestige of the zhabdrung never diminished. It was only in 1907 that the monarchy was established after an extended period of civil war between competing warlords. In 1930, the monarchy was less than a quarter of a century old, and the second king faced continued opposition, notably from the family of the most recent incarnation of the zhabdrung, Jigme Dorji. It is thought that, in the spring of 1931, the zhabdrung's brother, Chokyi Gyeltsen, sought Mahatma Gandhi's support for the restoration of the zhabdrung's temporal powers. This came to the attention of the king and his advisers who sought an explanation from the zhabdrung who was confined to Talo dzong. Three sets of troops under the command of followers of the king besieged Talo dzong and, on the express instructions of the second king entered the *dzong* and murdered the zhabdrung, Jigme Dorji.

In a letter to the British political officer, Lt. Col. Weir, in Sikkim sent the day after the murder of Jigme Dorji, the king claimed that "the Zhabdrung Rimpoche had been performing ceremonies calculated to do me harm, and had been invoking deadly maledictions upon me"

(Aris 1998, 122). To these charges of black magic, which remains a criminal offense in Bhutan, was to be added that of treason. The only Bhutanese chronicle that deals with the matter says: "Saddened by the deeds he had committed from listening to the plots of these evil persons the Zhabdrung died on the first day of the tenth month" (Aris 1998, 122).[4] Lt. Col. Weir, reporting the zhabdrung's death to Delhi, states, "The cause of the Zhabdrung's death is still a mystery. By the death of Zhabdrung Rimpoche a chapter of Bhutanese history, fraught with potential danger to the existing rule, may be considered closed" (3 December 1931, cited in Aris 1998, 122).

The murder of Jigme Dorji, as with the execution of Zhidar, removed a potent figurehead for opponents of the king and the monarchy. The second king's followers who carried out the murder were, as with Tshewang Tashi, doing service to their "lord on high," underlining the importance of personal loyalty and ties during the early years of the Bhutanese monarchy.

Because of the reverence for the zhabdrung, the monarchy would never have been able to take precedence; as a result, it was necessary to eliminate this potent rival. Since 1931, there has been no official incarnation of the zhabdrung recognized and installed. There are rumors that two possible incarnations were both murdered and that the Indian authorities rescued another from Tawang as the Chinese forces entered Tibet.[5] Rather, the figure of the founding zhabdrung, as opposed to his physical embodiment, "presides over the monarchy and nation as the ultimate source of all spiritual value, power and legitimacy" (Aris 1998, 124). Yet while the shade of the zhabdrung acts as a reminder of the origins of Bhutan as a religious estate rather than as a nation, there has arguably been an increasing sacralization of the monarchy.

The marriage in 1989 of the fourth king to four of the great nieces of the murdered zhabdrung, Jigmi Dorji, was viewed as reconciling the two families. More recently, the religious head of the country issued a prayer dedicated to the fourth king, and photographs of the monarch seated below an appliqué image of the zhabdrung appear in many private households. This intertwining of the imagery of the zhabdrung with the monarch has served to enhance the prestige of the monarchy. Arguably, the contractual nature of the monarchy established in 1907 was transformed during the late twentieth century with the monarch's assuming a quasi-religious role in the popular imagination, a role promoted by the state-sponsored Monk Body. The monarchy has, in part at least, successfully created an imagined bond between king and subjects. Yet many Bhutanese remain equally loyal to the zhabdrung and his physical incarnations. Although the Bhutanese state prevented the last incarnation from entering Bhutan, the state chose not to prevent Bhutanese from making pilgrimages to Manali where he resided, nor even for wealthier Bhutanese to provide financial support to the zhabdrung. These actions were accepted because they did not directly threaten state control. However, as I outline below, the language of this personal bond (*thadamtshi*) has been transformed in the process of modernization and the emergence of Bhutanese nationalism in the second half of the twentieth century.

The Nation-State Under Threat: The Specter of the Anti-National

A defendant shall be guilty of the offence of treason, if the defendant commits a subversive act against the state within or without Bhutan. (National Security Act 1992, s4)

Traditional bonds of personal loyalty (*thadamtshi*) were transformed as the Bhutanese state encouraged devotion to the abstract ideal of the Bhutanese nation expressed in the modern political concept of the Tsa Wa Sum (Three Roots, or Three Foundations). Accompanying the political, social, and economic reforms introduced by the third king and commencing in the early 1950s, a new juridical category was created— the anti-national (*ngolop*). By the mid-1970s, the political emphasis was increasingly focused on promoting a vision of a homogenous national identity, rather than regional or local identities.[6] As a result, the "anti-national" emerged in the late 1980s and 1990s as the antithesis of the ideal, loyal Bhutanese citizen. At the same time that loyalty to the nation began to crystallize around the ideal Bhutanese citizen, concerns over the presence of Lhotshampa (Nepalese migrants and their descendants) began to increase.

By reading the National Assembly debates and examining the alteration of the citizenship legislation from the mid-1970s and particularly during the 1980s, it is possible, in my opinion, to trace the creation of the Lhotshampa as a visible minority that neither conformed nor could conform to the Bhutanese ideal. Following the outbreak in 1990–91 of violent clashes between members of the Lhotshampa minority and the royal government, approximately 100,000 Lhosthampa fled the country and currently reside in refugee camps in eastern Nepal. Arjun Appadurai, writing on the globalization of violence against minorities, notes that such violence "enacts a deep anxiety about the national project and its own ambiguous relationship to globalization" (2006, 44). His argument illuminates a great deal of what I have been attempting to express in my writing over the last few years—namely, that minorities "create uncertainties about the national self and national citizenship because of their mixed status" (2006, 44–45).[7]

In this section, I briefly outline the background to the conflict between the Bhutanese government and the Lhotshampa that broke out in the early 1990s. I discuss how changes to the legal requirements for Bhutanese citizenship were explicitly intertwined with the concept of the the Three Roots. Against this background, I illustrate how the figure of the anti-national was brought to life as a living, if spectral, threat to Bhutan during the 1990s and beyond. The anti-national became associated specifically with the Lhotshampa. As a consequence, those Lhotshampa who remain in Bhutan, on the face of it loyal citizens of the Bhutanese state, have in reality been transformed in the minds of the majority and, in particular, from the perspective of the government into a problematic minority—transformed from neighbors, colleagues, friends, even adoptive kin, into potential anti-nationals.

The Lhotshampa: Origins of a Crisis

Borders, frontiers, and their control are sensitive issues in Bhutan. Waves of Tibetan invaders during the seventeenth and eighteenth centuries threatened Bhutan's independence. The northern border with the Tibetan Autonomous Region remains undefined despite ongoing discussions with the Chinese over its demarcation. To the south, Bhutan historically extended beyond its current borders to include sections of Darjeeling and the plains immediately to the south of its mountains that form the northern edge of West Bengal. Following the Treaty of Sinchula in 1865 between the British and the Bhutanese, Nepalese migrants were encouraged by the British colonial authorities to move into the newly acquired Duars. In the late nineteenth century, Nepalese from the eastern hill tribes (notably from the Rai, Tamang, and Gurung), began to settle in Sikkim, Darjeeling, and further west in Assam. However, according to British colonial reports, few Nepalese settled in Bhutan for fear of antagonizing the Bhutanese.

The first wave of migration into Bhutan by Nepalese began in the late nineteenth century when permission was given for them to enter the southern border region of Bhutan. The Nepalese immigrants cleared and planted the fertile valleys that had previously been uncultivated, creating small farms and villages across the southwest of Bhutan. At this point in the late nineteenth and early twentieth century, these immigrants became known in Bhutan as Lhotshampa, the "people of the southern border."[8] After this initial wave, a second wave of immigrants entered and settled permanently during the 1950s and 1960s. The subsequent waves of immigration in the mid-twentieth century occurred as major social, economic, and political reforms were being introduced. More important, these waves of immigration coincided with the development of a conscious move toward creating a national identity that transcended local ethnic and linguistic identities and loyalties. In the 1960s, labor was required for the economic expansion set out in a series of five-year plans funded by the Indian government. Accordingly, inward migration was encouraged, and, as briefly outlined below, full citizenship was available provided qualifying periods of residency could be established.

Relations between the government and the Lhotshampa began to deteriorate gradually following the annexation of Sikkim by India. In 1980, a new marriage act restricted the right to marry non-Bhutanese nationals and introduced strict penalties. Anybody marrying a non-Bhutanese forfeited his or her right to participate in various agricultural programs as well as the possibility to receive land or cash loans from the government. Nor would he or she be eligible for foreign education or government assistance with education in Bhutan. Although the act was not retroactive in application, the Bhutanese government thought at the time that as many as 10,000 Lhotshampa had married outside Bhutan (Strawn 1994). In 1985, a new Citizenship Act (discussed below) was passed by the National Assembly.

As part of the implementation of the Citizenship Act, a census was held to validate claims to Bhutanese citizenship and the award of national identity cards. Specifically, the census focused on the Lhotshampa population, among whom the government suspected a large number of illegal immigrants.[9] Two prominent Lhotshampa, Tek Nath Rizal and B. P. Bhandari, drafted a petition to the king highlighting problems under both the Marriage Act and the Citizenship Act and submitted it on 9 April 1988. Rizal was arrested shortly afterward and charged with treason. Tensions between the government and the Lhotshampa were further increased in 1989 with the introduction of various cultural policies that appeared to undermine the Lhotshampa culture and heritage in favor of that of the majority northern Bhutanese. In 1990, forty-two people were arrested for "anti-national" activities, and the king, addressing the sixty-ninth session of the National Assembly, stated that "subversive elements" were trying to "disturb the minds of our people" (National Assembly of Bhutan 1990). Against this background, conflict between the government and the Lhotshampa broke out in 1990. This background provides the context for the remainder of the chapter.

Creating a Nation: Citizenship and the Tsa Wa Sum

Bhutan began the process of nation building from the 1950s. Abolishing serfdom and slavery, the third king, Jigme Dorji Wangchuck, began the reform of the political structures with the establishment of the National Assembly in 1953. Among the first formal pieces of legislation was the Nationality Act 1958.[10] The Nationality Act was a response to demands by Lhotshampa activists who established the Bhutan State Congress Party in the early 1950s. The Lhotshampa were encouraged by political changes underway in neighboring Nepal with the overthrow of the Rana regime and the brief introduction of multiparty democracy under King Tribhuvan in 1951.[11] Under the Nationality Act 1958, Bhutanese citizenship was to be granted to any person, irrespective of ethnicity, who had resided in Bhutan for ten years and owned agricultural land. Those applying for Bhutanese nationality had to have reached the age of majority (twenty-one) and were required to swear an oath of loyalty to the king once their application was accepted by the Home Ministry. Those who did not own land but satisfied the residency requirement and had worked for the government for at least five years also qualified.

From the ascension of the fourth king in 1972 onward, the debates of the National Assembly reveal a conservative shift in government policies.[12] China had suppressed Tibet after the March Uprising in 1959 and set about destroying its cultural heritage during the Cultural Revolution of the 1960s. To the west, the semi-independent kingdom of Sikkim was annexed by the Indian Republic following a major political crisis. From the perspective of the Bhutanese authorities, this was due to ethnic Nepalese in Sikkim pressing for merger with India. These events unsettled the Bhutanese authorities, who became increasingly concerned at the high numbers of Lhotshampa settled in the south, the most productive agricultural area in the country. These fears became intertwined with increasingly vocal concerns over perceived threats to Bhutanese independence and identity. As a result of these different factors, the government amended the criteria required for citizenship in 1977 (Whitecross, 2009).

In 1985, a new Citizenship Act was endorsed by the National Assembly. Once again, the grounds of eligibility were significantly altered. Under the 1985 act, both parents (unlike the provision in the 1958 act) must be Bhutanese for citizenship to be acquired by birth. Otherwise, an individual can be naturalized provided that he or she is twenty-one years old, or fifteen if either parent is Bhutanese. All applicants have to be able to demonstrate residency in Bhutan for between fifteen and twenty years. All such periods of residency have to had been registered prior to 31 December 1958 and appear in the records of the Department of Immigration and Census. Further conditions apply, including being mentally sound; being able to speak, read, and write Dzongkha proficiently (though no indication is given as to what would pass as proficiency in Dzongkha); possessing a good knowledge of the customs, traditions, and history of Bhutan; having no criminal record; and not having acted or spoken against the Tsa Wa Sum.

Central to the reforms commenced by the third king in the 1950s was the emergence of the concept of the Tsa Wa Sum. This new official trinity appears for the first time in the Supreme Law Code issued in 1957. The term has several levels of meaning. The tripartite nature of this concept mirrors the Buddhist trinity of Buddha, Dharma, and Sangha. It also can refer in terms of Himalayan Buddhism to the Guru, the Yidam (personal deity), and Dharma Protector. However, in the Supreme Law Code, the phrase does not refer to either of these Buddhist trinities; rather, it is understood to mean "Country, King, and Government" (RGOB, n.d, 136).[13]

Tsa Wa Sum appears to have not been actively promoted as a concept until it reemerged as a precondition for citizenship in 1977. Under the Citizenship Act 1977, an oath of loyalty to the Tsa Wa Sum was made a prerequisite for any award of citizenship. Over the next decade, Tsa Wa Sum became increasingly part of a nationalist vocabulary that stressed loyalty as a cornerstone of Bhutanese national identity. By the late 1980s, those held to be against the Tsa Wa Sum were branded as ngolop or anti-nationals. In the National Assembly in 1991, at the height of tensions with the Lhotshampa community, Tsa Wa Sum was defined as the "King, Country and People, united by a shared identity" (NAB 1991, 2). More generally, the government used the concept to promote—and it continues to do so—the idea of a united and homogenous Bhutanese populace. I would argue that the shift from "Government" to "People" is directly linked to the emergence of a "one–nation, one-people" policy in the mid-1980s.

The concept of Tsa Wa Sum was transformed as a result of the political and social violence of the early 1990s and has been described as a "mantra to excite patriotism and nationalism . . . a buzzword which encapsulated everything that is Bhutanese" (Phuntsho 2004, 576–77). Phuntsho's concern over the nationalistic and exclusionary aspects of this concept is well founded. Reading the National Assembly debates, the phrase Tsa Wa Sum can appear as "empty rhetoric" (ibid.). However, we should not dismiss so easily a concept that has gained currency with the majority of Bhutanese. For many Bhutanese interviewed during my fieldwork, its actual meaning is unclear precisely because it draws its power and deeper resonance in Bhutanese society from the blurring of the Three Roots of the nation with Buddhist concepts.

During the 1990s, the Tsa Wa Sum was invoked in the media, during National Assembly debates, and in state education. In June 2008, when the constitution was enacted, the concept of the Tsa Wa Sum was enshrined at its core. All Bhutanese are held to be loyal to the Tsa Wa

Sum, and any person seeking naturalization under article 6 must "have no record of having spoken or acted against the King, the Country or the People of Bhutan" (RGOB 2007, 8).[14] Loyalty to the Tsa Wa Sum became intimately intertwined with northern Bhutanese culture, history, and values. For the Lhotshampa, this presents a dilemma: to maintain their own customs, language, and practices is to challenge those of their northern countrymen—in effect, not to be truly loyal to the Tsa Wa Sum. In the following section, I illustrate why the Tsa Wa Sum is more than a rhetorical flourish.

The Anti-National Made Flesh: From Juridical Category to Physical Presence

On my first day of fieldwork, the front-page headline announced "Terrorists Killed." Harka Bahadur Subba and an accomplice died at the hands of "village volunteers" (*Kuensel,* 26 June 1999, 1).[15] The dead men were found holding a householder at gunpoint by a group of village volunteers who attacked and "fatally injur[ed]" them. Village volunteers were viewed as empowered to "safeguard the life and property of villagers." Harka, described as a "wanted terrorist," left Bhutan, according to the report, "in 1990 and registered himself as a Bhutanese refugee in Sector F-III, Hut No.67 in Khudunabrai camp in Nepal" (ibid.). A list of his other crimes included armed robbery and physically assaulting householders, all of whom were, incidentally, Lhotshampa. Yet what is striking is the choice of language: "Terrorists Killed." His crimes are transformed from serious crimes into the actions of a terrorist. The details of his residence in one of the refugee camps established by international aid agencies in eastern Nepal for the Lhotshampa refugees suggest the knowledge or ability of the Bhutanese authorities to track anti-nationals. Harka, as with other reports of convicted or killed "terrorists," represents the tangible manifestation of the anti-national. Anti-nationals became increasingly tangible immediately after the escalation of violence between the royal government and members of the Lhotshampa community between 1990 and 1991.

Throughout the 1990s, newspaper reports about anti-nationals appeared on a weekly basis in the only national newspaper, *Kuensel.*[16] In 1994, the High Court sentenced seven men to prison terms ranging from ten years to life imprisonment for "acts of treason and terrorist activities" (*Kuensel,* 14 May 1994, 1). The trial lasted for thirteen months and involved a full bench. From the limited available sources, it appears that the seven men faced a range of charges—rape, assault, looting, and involvement in organizing violent demonstrations against "the royal government and forcing members of the public to take part in these activities" (ibid.). One of those convicted was Ash Bahadur Samal, a former village elder of Gairigaon, who was charged with being the leader of the group and sentenced to life imprisonment. Described as a "block leader of the militant dissident organization, the Bhutan People's Party," Samal was accused of organizing guerrilla training and making personal contributions to the "anti-national movement." (ibid). The Bhutan People's Party was formed by refugee Lhotshampa in June 1990 and remains a prohibited political party in Bhutan. As a former village elder or head of the village block, Samal ought to have been loyal to the government. The report by implication suggests that he had been disingenuous, wearing a mask of loyalty while in reality harboring treasonous loyalties and intentions.

The depth of the concerns over the anti-national was brought home to me one evening. About four months into my fieldwork in the autumn of 1999, a young Bhutanese man came to my room to return my copy of that week's issue of *Kuensel.* Pema handed the tattered newspaper to me and apologized. Some friends had visited him and started to read the paper. One of his friends became excited when he read a report about a former school friend. The school friend, a Lhotshampa, was suspected of anti-national activities. A photograph of the accused appeared beside the report of his acts against Bhutan, including burning down a local official's office in one of the southern, mainly Lhotshampa, districts. Pema pointed to the photograph and apologized. "I know you keep these, so they should not have done this." He pointed to the obliterated face of the accused. "My friend was angry. He could not believe that this person could be a traitor. We really cannot trust these people."

"Which people?" I asked.

Pema pointed back to the photograph. "These . . . they are not Bhutanese. They deceive us. . . . You should be careful. Don't let them fool you."

Reflecting on this incident and other similar comments made to me by informants, I increasingly became aware that *Kuensel* reports created and maintained a social uncertainty about the remaining Lhotshampa. The banality of the reports served to raise doubts or associations in the minds of the majority about the loyalty of the minority. Appardurai convincingly writes that no "amount of politically induced panic and doctrinally induced conviction" will lead to extreme violence. However, if there is "a deep sort of social uncertainty" mixed with high levels of "doctrinal certainty," then it can explode into social violence (2006, 91).

Through the processes outlined above, the Bhutanese authorities have promoted a particular vision of Bhutanese identity while creating a visible, and apparently alien, Lhotshampa minority. In turn, this has increased social uncertainties that are in part media-driven and politically promoted. Yet, it reflects more than propaganda: it reflects other concerns and everyday jealousies that serve to reinforce the specter of the Lhotshampa "anti-national." In the National Assembly in 1992, calls to safeguard the Tsa Wa Sum were made by a number of delegates. According to Tandi, the local village leader of Bartsham village block, "I have been to southern Bhutan and seen the Lhotshampa enjoying a very good life. They have large land holdings, orange gardens and cardamom fields, and more schools, motor roads, health centres and other developmental facilities, and still *they rebelled!*" (*Kuensel*, 25 April 1992, 12). Tandi further declared that all able-bodied men in his village block were "ready to fight the anti-nationals." Among those I interviewed, there was a belief that the Lhotshampa were turning against the Tsa Wa Sum after "receiving larger development budgets and facilities from the government than people in other districts." Elsewhere, the Lhotshampa are referred to as recent immigrants, and one person states that "we are ready to leave aside all other work to fight and overcome the anti-nationals" and protect the country from harm caused by immigrants. We can see the conflation of Lhotshampa and anti-national and an underlying sense of distrust and fear borne by Tandi and his fellow villagers toward the Lhotshampa.

Within a short period of time after the violent clashes between the government and sections of the Lhotshampa community in the early 1990s, the vocabulary and imagery of the anti-national were established not only in the media but in the minds of ordinary Bhutanese. As a result, the remaining Lhotshampa came increasingly under suspicion. This sense of distrust was perhaps most pronounced during the 77th National Assembly in 1999 when it was decided that all Lhotshampa civil servants related to anti-nationals should be retired from their posts. During the debate on what should be done with the relatives of "anti-nationals" members of the National Assembly argued that, despite the king's "magnanimous gesture" that the relatives of ngolop should not be accused simply for being "relatives of anti-nationals" (*Kuensel* 18 September 1999, 17) that the Lhotshampa 'changed neither their behaviour nor their thinking. . . . Instead, they continuously provided sensitive information to their relatives living outside the country." In other words, the remaining Lhotshampa could not be trust and acted as spies for their "anti-national" relatives resident outside Bhutan.

During the same debate, the secretary of the Royal Civil Service Commission, noting that it was not in the national interest to employ relatives of anti-nationals in the civil service, submitted to the National Assembly that the former civil servants should be "allowed to continue working in the private sector, not just for their livelihood, but to also give them a chance to appreciate the opportunities they were receiving and develop

a sense of loyalty and dedication to the Three Roots (Tsa Wa Sum)"
(*Kuensel* 18 September 1999, 18). This statement reflects a widely held
view that I encountered time and time again during fieldwork. It
expresses a deep distrust of the Lhotshampa and a belief that they neither appreciate being "Bhutanese" nor possess, even though they have
not left Bhutan, a devotion to the Three Roots. Often, as in the debate
cited, the discussion revolved around those Lhotshampa who are related
to anti-nationals. What was unclear to me was who exactly were the "anti-
nationals" in question. Were they those who had engaged in political or
criminal activities or, more simply, those who resided in one of the refugee camps in eastern Nepal? This lack of clarity of who precisely was an
"anti-national" appeared to suggest that all remaining Lhotshampa
were under suspicion since almost all had relatives, including parents
and siblings, living in the camps.

There is one dimension that should be acknowledged—the transfer-
ring of anxieties about anti-nationals to the Lhotshampa implies the
denial that northern Bhutanese could be "traitors." The government
slogan introduced in the late 1980s of "One Nation, One People"
ignored the ethnic and linguistic diversity of the northern Bhutanese.[17]
In the mid-1990s, only a few years after the conflict between the government and the Lhotshampa escalated, the Druk National Congress party
attempted to challenge the Bhutanese state and sought to develop its
powerbase among the second largest minority group, the Sharchop.
After a swift military crackdown in 1997 in eastern Bhutan, public dissent or criticism of the king or government was effectively ended. Those
who had engaged in antigovernment activities were reported as criminals rather than as anti-nationals or traitors. It would appear that northern Bhutanese could not be anti-national. This may be a small
distinction, but it has significant consequences. The reluctance on the
part of the Bhutanese authorities to acknowledge dissent and the parallels between the demands of the Druk National Congress and the Lhotshampa underscores the process of "othering." To acknowledge the
possibility that members of the majority population could be traitors
would undermine the ideal of "One Nation, One People" united
behind the government. Instead, the Lhotshampa became both individually and communally the scapegoat on to which this fear was placed.
For a northern Bhutanese either individually or communally to act
against the Tsa Wa Sum was too unsettling, even if Bhutanese history
proves otherwise.[18]

Trial as Public Spectacle

The trial and reporting of anti-national cases and the more problematic
issue of the convicted's pardon and release are underscored by the

unprecedented crowds who attended the trial of forty anti-nationals at the High Court in May 1992 (*Kuensel*, 23 May 1992, 1). According to eyewitnesses, there were several thousand, mainly men, outside the court when the anti-nationals were brought for their hearing. I discussed the trial nine years later with a former member of the Royal Body-Guard who was present, and he recalled the anger of the crowd, something he had never previously experienced. He met with friends from the civil service who were particularly vehement in their animosity toward one of the accused, Dhan Kumar Rai.

Dhan Kumar Rai was the general secretary of the Bhutan People's Party and, it was claimed, the leader of its hard core wing, the Action Group. The list of charges prepared against him by the Home Ministry— this was before the creation of a separate prosecution service in 2000— included the kidnapping and murder of two local government officials whose severed heads were left near a police outpost. From sources present at the time, it appears that, as the charges were read out, Rai denied some and admitted others, including specifically inciting villagers to turn against the government or, rather, against the Tsa Wa Sum. When accused of being a terrorist and a traitor, Rai denied the charge and described himself to the court as a "freelance activist."

This major trial of a large number of anti-nationals began at the same time that another government official was killed in an ambush in the southern district of Geleyphug. The official, Chime Dorji, age 36, was described by the Royal Civil Service Commission as the victim of "yet another heinous act of terrorism by the anti-nationals" (*Kuensel* 23 May 1992, 1).The victim was described in the newspaper report as "one of the solid pillars of Bhutanese society for his strong commitment to the Tsa Wa Sum, especially since the start of the political problems in Southern Bhutan. Chimi had often told his friends that he was willing to sacrifice his own life to protect the nation." As if to emphasis Chimi's loyalty to the kingdom, the report informs the reader that the king granted a private audience to the family of the murdered official, and other members of the royal family and ministers visited the family at the Changlimithang temple in Thimphu before the body was transferred for cremation at Punakha. A small point, but one that should not be overlooked for its symbolism, is that Changlimithang was where the founder of the royal dynasty defeated his opponents. The cremation of Chimi, especially on this historic site, served to create a national hero or ideal martyr figure. Therefore, the direct association of the deceased with his willingness to die for the Tsa Wa Sum would not have been lost on those reading and listening to the report.

Pardoning Anti-Nationals: Tel Nath Rizal

In December 1999, to mark the twenty-fifth anniversary of his corona-tion, the king granted royal pardons to 200 prisoners on National Day. Only those who had committed murder or desecrated a sacred site were ineligible for pardon and of the 200 pardons, 40 had been convicted for "involvements which were harmful to the Tsa Wa Sum" (*Kuensel*, 18 December 1999, 1). Among those released was Tek Nath Rizal, a former Royal Advisory Councillor. Tek Nath Rizal was a prominent Lhotshampa leader who had opposed the 1987 Census. He was placed under deten-tion in June 1988 and pardoned by the king after signing a pledge (*genja*) not to undertake any activity that may harm the Tsa Wa Sum. However, he left Bhutan and set up a political movement in Nepal before being extradited/abducted in November 1989. Describing his experiences after being abducted, Rizal hoped that after "torturing me . . . it would surely release me from jail" (n.d).[19] Instead, he was informed that the king had commanded that he be taken to Lingshi prison (toward the northern border with the Tibetan Autonomous Region of the People's Republic of China). Hearing that he was not to stand trial, Rizal states that "the government had adopted even greater harshness [and] dealt a blow to my feelings for the Three Roots law, the king and the Wangchuck dynasty" (n.d.). After several years in various prisons, Tek Nath Rizal was placed on trial.

After a trial which lasted eleven months and during which he repre-sented himself, Rizal was found guilty on four charges of subversive and treasonable acts against the Three Roots. The judgment pronounced him guilty of instigating and leading the anti-nationals in a conspiracy and movement to subvert the Three Roots, establishing an organization that "gave birth to the terrorist organization, the Bhutan People's Party"; attempting to create discord between Bhutan and its two neigh-bors, Nepal and India; and finally, attempting to incite communal dis-cord in Bhutan.[20] He was sentenced to life imprisonment.

In an unprecedented move, the king issued a royal decree that stated that Tek Nath Rizal's subversion and treachery had caused "untold suf-fering on many Lhotshampa people and great losses to the government through the destruction of infrastructure and service facilities which had been established for the benefit of the people" (*Kuensel* 20 November 1993, 1). It is worth noting the implicit separation of the Lhotshampa from the more general "people" in the king's decree. The king indi-cated in the decree that he would pardon Rizal once the problem with the refugees living in camps in eastern Nepal was resolved; however, at the time of his pardon in 1999, the refugee issue remained unresolved.[21]

The then home minister, Lyonpo Thinley Gyamtaho, expressed a hope that Rizal and the other prisoners would appreciate the "magnanimity of His Majesty the King." In the National Assembly held in 2000, the citizens of Pemagatshel submitted a statement through their representative, indicating that ngolop who were involved in anti-national activities against the Tsa Wa Sum, once arrested, "should not be granted amnesty but must be punished strictly under the nation's laws."[22] Tek Nath Rizal left Bhutan and settled in Kathmandu, where he continues to lead the opposition. The attempt to rehabilitate convicted traitors was resisted by the majority of people, and the sense of unease and lack of trust reflects the depth to which many northern Bhutanese have come to distrust their Lhotshampa neighbors.

"Harming the National Interest": Synchronized Mass Trials

Eight months after a military campaign carried out in December 2003 against United Liberation Front of Assam (ULFA) and Bodo guerrillas settled in the jungles of southern Bhutan, *Kuensel* carried a report on the trials of "those who harmed the national interest." On the day the report was published, I accompanied Bhim, a young, educated Lhotshampa, on a hike in the mountains behind Thimphu. Stopping for lunch, Bhim reached into his backpack and pulled out that latest issue of *Kuensel.* At this time, it was the only national newspaper, published each Saturday. Bhim had purchased it on his way to collect me and was anxious to read the report of the recent trials of 111 Bhutanese under the National Security Act 1992. Pointing at the list of names, his eyes anxiously scanning down it, he said, "See, mainly Lhotshampa!"[23] I leaned across and began reading the list of those convicted.

The trials were conducted simultaneously in the district courts in Sarpang (33 accused), Samdrup Jongkhar (38), Pemagatshel (3), Geleyphug (27), Phuentsholing (4), and Thimphu (11). Based on the names of the convicted individuals, the majority of those sentenced in Sarpang and Geleyphu were Lhotshampa. The others had Drukpa names, though given that Samdrup Jongkhar is in the east, it is likely that the majority were Sharchop. What was striking was that Bhim focused on the Lhotshampa names that made up seventy of the 111. Two of those sentenced received life imprisonment, five were sentenced to between fifteen and eighteen years, and the rest from four to ten years. Their crimes under the National Security Act 1992 were related to providing assistance to ULFA and Bodo militants who had established camps in the south and southeastern districts during the 1990s. A court spokesman stated that those convicted had engaged in the "heinous crime of aiding and abetting the militants for personal gain and seriously harming the national interest is a crime against the state."[24]

In our discussions, Bhim spoke of his increasing sense of exclusion and suspicion. His own family had been affected by the events of the early 1990s when he was studying in southern India, sponsored by the government. He returned from his studies after being told to stay away by his parents only to find that his uncles and cousins had left Bhutan for Nepal. An older brother and his family had also left their home village in Tsirang. His parents remained, despite pressure from family members and local political leaders. Shortly after his return to Bhutan, Bhim entered government service and married. However, although he had been given employment by the government and was even sent for additional training in India, when he went to obtain a certificate of "no objection" from the police in Thimphu, he found that his name was on a list of individuals with dissident family members.

According to Bhim, the fact that his brother, uncles, and cousins were living outside Bhutan and were viewed by the Bhutanese authorities as anti-nationals had a direct effect on his life in Bhutan. He described feeling ill at ease with his employers, who would have seen his official papers and would be aware of his connection to anti-nationals. Bhim described feeling that he was overlooked for promotion specifically because of his relatives and indirectly because he is Lhotshampa. After twelve years of trying to persuade the Home Ministry that he was loyal, his records were amended, and the reference to his anti-national relatives removed from his data. For Bhim, this brought a sense of relief, yet he also felt that he was betraying his family by apparently siding with the authorities. However, he hoped that, in the long term, his relatives would be allowed to return and that, for his children's sake, his association with anti-nationals would not present an invisible barrier to education or employment in Bhutan.

Shortly after my walk with Bhim, I found myself at lunch with a family from central Bhutan. Sitting opposite a large framed poster of the fourth king, I recalled Bhim's recently voiced concerns. Listening to the conversation, I was struck by a number of remarks concerning the Lhotshampa communities in the south. My hosts were not wealthy, and the extended family I knew had pooled their resources to buy land in one of the southern districts with road access to India in order to develop a business. When I first met the family in 1999, the husband had referred to his "adopted mother," a Lhotshampa woman who had cared for him as a teenager. Gradually, over the space of a few years, it became clear to me that the former intimate relationship with this woman and her family had been severed. Karma, who had previously introduced me to his "adopted family," now sat and expressed his deep distrust of the

Lhotshampa. This encounter highlights both the powerful effect of othering and a fear that intimacy with an anti-national may be dangerous or contaminating. When asked about his adopted mother, Karma informed me that she was related to "known ngolop."

The accounts of Bhim and Karma are not unique. However, Karma's change in attitude toward his Lhotshampa "mother" and her family was echoed in other behavior. When I first met Karma in 2000, he would typically speak in Nepali when we were with a group of people some of whom were Lhotshampa. Yet several years later in similar circumstances, he spoke in Dzongkha or Sharchop, even if there were Lhotshampa present. When I commented on this change, he merely shrugged and advised me that the Lhotshampa should learn Bhutanese languages. This volte-face disturbed me. I became aware that social relations between my northern Bhutanese informants and the Lhotshampa had been altered, transformed by suspicion. Karma's comments and attitude demonstrate the corrosive effect on social relations that the discourse on anti-nationals and loyalty to the Tsa Wa Sum has had in Bhutan.

Conclusion

In his essay "Dead Certainty," Appadurai (1998) develops a detailed argument outlining the ways in which social uncertainty can drive ethnic cleansing. This social uncertainty is intimately connected to the mundane reality that ethnic minorities, such as the Lhotshampa, their movements, customs, and media representations "create doubts about who exactly are among the 'we' and who are among the 'they'" (Appadurai 2006, 5). In 1987, as tensions escalated, a national census—part of the modern technology of governance—sought to provide answers to the uncertainties presented by the presence of the Lhotshampa. The Lhotshampa are not simply an abstract "they" to use Appadurai's formula. Rather, as a result of the conflicts with the Bhutanese government over rights to land and over Lhotshampa cultural practices and identity, they came to embody the abstract category of the anti-national, both as individuals and as an ethnic group.

This can be illustrated by a recent online article in which the prodemocracy movements in Bhutan in the late 1980s are described as "led by ethnically Nepalese persons such as [Tek Nath] Rizal" (Phuntsho 2006). The rise of the prodemocracy movement in Bhutan is placed in the broader political context of the eastern Himalayas and presented as occurring simultaneously with other politically charged events: "[the] late King Birendra [was stripped] of power, Sikkim had Bhandari at its helm, and the Darjeeling hills were being turned into an autonomous Gorkhaland by Gisling." These events demonstrate that the "fervour of

Nepali dominion and nationalism was at its peak. From the perspective of the royal government in Thimphu, the demonstrations organized by Rizal's Bhutan People's Party were "never just non-violent protests by patriotic citizens. . . . Most dissidents were seen . . . to be more loyal to the Nepalese power abroad than to the Royal Government. As the demonstrations turned violent, Thimphu considered the movement as an armed rebellion to overthrow the ruling regime."[25] While the author notes that the fears about a pan-Nepalese state or Greater Gorkhaland may or may not be legitimate, he asserts that "Nepalese cultural expansion and demographic takeover was as serious as it could be."[26] Although the article seeks to present a balanced view of the Bhutanese refugee crisis, Phuntsho describes these clashes as a "sordid ethnic conflict" that affected all sides and presents the pro-democracy Lhotshampa movement as promoting Nepal and Nepalese interests over those of Bhutan. The description of Tek Nath Rizal as "Nepalese" rather than as Bhutanese—or, at the very least, Lhotshampa—demonstrates the coalescing of the discourses around the "anti-national" and the weakening, if not the actual severing, of social and communal ties. Addressing the demonstrations and violent clashes of the early 1990s, Phuntsho states that the protestors became viewed as and publicly described as "anti-nationals and terrorists" (2006). Of more general note, he highlights the polarization of relations between Nepal and Bhutan. I would go further than this and argue that the conflict of the early 1990s and the subsequent media and political discussions have extended the abstract idea of anti-national beyond those who actively engaged in opposition to the regime to include all members of the Lhotshampa community.

Lhotshampas who consider themselves loyal to Bhutan feel that, as a consequence of the conflicts of the early 1990s and the violent incidents that periodically remind ordinary Bhutanese of the specter of the anti-national, they are seen as traitors and untrustworthy (for example, *Kuensel*, 3 December, 2006). The former intimacy across ethnic boundaries has been ruptured and social relations between the Lhotshamapa and the northern Bhutanese made tense and problematic. For the Lhotshampa continuing to reside in Bhutan, they must live with a range of contradictory affiliations, including kin who reside in the refugee camps and who are viewed as not "genuine" Bhutanese by the Bhutanese authorities. While Phuntsho refers to the clashes as a 'sordid ethnic conflict" he is silent about the impact of the crisis on these remaining Lhotshampa and the damage done to the social fabric as a result of a sustained campaign illustrated in this chapter, a campaign that has transformed former friends, neighbors, and adopted kin into figures of mistrust and, for the foreseeable future, cast them in the role of the resident alien whose loyalties and moral character are suspect. Treason may be viewed as a radical break, but we should not overlook the banal aspects of treason, the tiny yet incremental treasons people engage in. Through these people, an alternative ideal, different from that presented by the current regime, can begin to be articulated. Equally, through other tiny yet incremental steps, people can start to embody the current regime's discourse and turn against those believed not to belong, the enemy within. I have argued that the figure of the traitor—or more specifically, the anti-national derives its emotive force from a contrast between those willing to belong (and conform) and those whose loyalties are perceived as lying elsewhere, often outside the national borders.

Chapter 4
Traitors, Terror, and Regime Consolidation on the Two Sides of the Taiwan Straits: "Revolutionaries" and "Reactionaries" from 1949 to 1956

Julia C. Strauss

The Case for Thinking Comparatively About China and Taiwan

In the post-Cold War twenty-first century, it is all too easy to forget that coercion, both real and implied, lies at the heart of the state. When we turn our gaze back to the early stages of the Cold War, particularly to the divided nations on opposite sides of that conflict (Germany, Korea, and China) in the late 1940s and early 1950s, we can see that the coercive core at the heart of the state lay close to the surface in a way that is hard to recapture today. Here was a situation in which the countries concerned had all undergone years of militarization, invasion, and either occupation or direct colonization. The ideological commitments and identities of individuals as well as the security of the state's borders were all uncertain. Each of these nations was divided between ideologically supercharged, mutually antagonistic regimes claiming legitimacy over the *entirety* of the nation. Sharp ideological and moral differentiation from the unimaginable "other" was imperative, as was its accompaniment: hysterical propaganda and didactic indoctrination of the population.

This was nowhere more true than in China. At midcentury, China had undergone nearly incessant political fragmentation, warlordism, civil war, and foreign invasion after the collapse of the Qing dynasty in 1911. This, in turn, led to the rise of the Guomindang (GMD) and the Chinese Communist Party (CCP) in the mid-1920s, when Sun Yat-sen's Guomindang (Nationalist Party) accepted Soviet advisors, military aid, Leninist principles of organization, and the inclusion of the then tiny Chinese Communist Party as a party fraction within the larger Guomindang. But significantly different ideological positions about whether the revolution should be defined to include violent class struggle led to deep mutual suspicion between Guomindang and Communists, and broke apart the alliance when the Guomindang unleashed a vicious White Terror on the Communists in 1927, just as their joint National Revolutionary Army was on the verge of nominally unifying the country. After the Nationalist government was established in 1927, it launched repeated military campaigns against Communist base areas; but in the end, the Communists managed to retreat and establish a base area in the far northwest, centered around Yan'an, from which it greatly expanded its de facto power and range into North China during the Sino-Japanese War (1937–45), before decisively winning the civil war and establishing the People's Republic of China in 1949. Chiang Kai-shek fled to the island of Taiwan with the Nationalist government's gold reserves, air force, and top military command. Thus, in 1949, there were two rival party-state regimes on opposite sides of the Taiwan Straits that had not only aligned with opposite sides of the deepening Cold War but had undergone over twenty years of mutual bloodletting. Each claimed to represent China and to speak for the whole. And each had reason to feel deeply insecure; the People's Republic of China (PRC) because of the hostility of the United States and its historic support for the Guomindang; the Republic of China on Taiwan (ROC) because in late 1949 and early 1950 the United States had made it clear that it would not intervene in support of the Guomindang should the PRC launch an expected amphibious invasion of Taiwan in the summer of 1950.

The outbreak of the Korean War in June 1950 hardened international and domestic positions. Internationally, it prompted an overnight recalibration of United States policy to include Taiwan within its defensive perimeter of containment. The dispatch of the U.S. Seventh Fleet to "neutralize" the Taiwan Straits prevented the People's Republic of China from invading Taiwan and concluding the Chinese civil war once and for all. Domestically, the regional insecurity generated by the Korean War created an immediate political environment in which it became credible for hard-liners in both China and Taiwan to launch campaigns of repressive terror against real and imagined enemies of the state, in turn clearing the ground of most social organization and institutions able to resist state programs.

With the salutary example of the Guomindang's signal failure to either secure its borders or entirely quell internal armed opposition between 1927 and 1949 still vivid, both regimes recognized that internal security was, along with protective external alliances, the cornerstone of the wider state-building project. Both the PRC and the ROC were regimes of military occupation with weak social bases and shallow roots in much, if not all, of the territory each controlled. The question of how traitorous and subversive activity was defined and treated was at the very heart of regime consolidation and state making. Fear of subversion on both sides of the Taiwan Straits in the 1950s was real and widespread, at least in part because it was so very difficult to differentiate "them" from "us." Intraparty bloodletting between Nationalists and Communists in the mid-1920s; protracted intelligence wars between Communist, Japanese collaborationist, and Nationalist regimes between 1937 and 1945; and the inherent murkiness of individual motives and actions after so many years of foreign invasion and civil war made it virtually impossible to clearly identify friends from enemies, supporters from betrayers, and simply getting along in difficult circumstances from collaborative activity and outright traitorous activity (Wakeman 2000).

At heart, this obsession with traitors and subversion was intimately wrapped up with each regime's attempt to define clear borders and generate moral legitimacy. The history of mutual closeness, collaboration, and betrayal between Communists and Nationalists meant that families split over which party was supported, individuals frequently changed sides, and clarity was often muddied. Each regime felt the urgency of drawing sharp moral, personal, and emotional boundaries in order to make clear differentiation between the pure and righteous "us" and the evil and unreconstructable "them." In this way, the shadowy figure of the traitor simultaneously embodied the weak Chinese state's recent failures *and* provided the justification for dramatically extending the coercive apparatus of the state and intensifying top-down "instruction" of the population to ensure its ideological commitment to the regime. The differences between these regimes were much less than their respective ideologies suggested for the very reason that it proved so difficult to delineate traitors and separate "them" from "us": both nascent partystates subscribed to a broadly similar state-building agenda and had undergone similar experiences of mobilization, militarization, and Leninist party (re)organization.[1]

I suggest that, despite the strong ideological antipathy between the two Chinas at the height of the Cold War in the early 1950s, a comparison of how traitors were identified and prosecuted reveals both unexpected similarities and significant differences in the agendas, ethos, and evolution of these two different variants on the modern Chinese state. After considering how traitors were defined and the approximate scale of anti-traitor campaigns in the early 1950s, I turn to three interrelated factors: (1) the broad similarities and consistency in state building *agendas*; (2) similarities and differences in the *packaging and tactics* of campaigns to suppress traitors and subversives; and (3) the increasing divergence in *process and prosecution* of anti-traitor campaigns over time. For both, the reasonable fear of traitors and subversion was put to great tactical use as part of an analogous state-building logic: to clear the ground of all meaningful social organizations, institutions, and individuals who could act as a brake on the expansion of state power and its reach into the most basic units of social and economic organization in city and countryside. In both cases, the suppression of traitors was implemented by a bureaucratic campaign. And, ultimately, the differences in the packaging and prosecution of these early campaigns suggested significant differences in terms of regime developmental trajectory, ending with two substantively different variants of the contemporary Chinese state.

Defining and Categorizing *Hanjian* (Traitors) Before and After 1949

Frederic Wakeman usefully reminds us that the Chinese term for traitor, *hanjian*, has long had three interconnected meanings: illicit crossing of boundaries, invitation of *luan* or chaos, and sexual excess (2002, 298–99). The very etymology of the term suggests that, as a matter of definition, one had to be Han Chinese in order to be categorized as *hanjian*, thus conflating political treason with ethnic transgression. The term *hanjian*, or, in Guomindang use on Taiwan, simply *jian*, was an emotive and evocative epithet to label the worst of all enemies (traitors to the Han Chinese race). It often coexisted with other dehumanizing terms that denoted the illegitimate "other": "clique" (*pai*), "counterrevolutionary element" (*fangeming fenzi*), and "Communist bandit" (*gongfei*). But transgression presumes that there are clear boundaries to cross, and the chronic militarization, civil war, foreign invasion, state weakness, and (for Taiwan) direct colonization that China experienced in the first half of the twentieth century resulted in a profound lack of clear boundaries.

The ongoing difficulties with boundary demarcation were the natural product of China's political fragmentation and militarization in the aftermath of the collapse of the late imperial state in 1911–12. The entirety of the Republican period (1912–49) can in many respects be best understood as an era in which aspiring political elites struggled with the problem of profoundly unclear individual, political, and military boundaries. The warlord-riven 1910s and 1920s produced many who claimed to speak for the nation but no clear politico-military winner. The partial successes of the centralizing Guomindang regime in the 1930s were reversed by the outbreak of the Sino-Japanese War in 1937.

The Sino-Japanese War produced three competing proto-regimes (Communist in the far northwest, Guomindang in the southwest, and Japanese collaborationist in the east); but none managed to establish its hegemony over the entirety of China, and the geographical, economic, and human boundaries between these different zones remained shifting and porous. Indeed, geographical and ideological boundaries only began to congeal visibly with the total military victory of the CCP, collapse of the Guomindang, and Guomindang subsequent retreat to the island in Taiwan in early 1949.

The Sino-Japanese War made it temporarily easier to denote the *hanjian*, as the chief lines of demarcation moved away from the tangle of personal, factional, and ideological alliances within a loosely defined set of Chinese political elites and toward those individuals who actively collaborated with a visible enemy. The Japanese military established, or attempted to establish, a variety of collaborationist regimes in North and East China, and those who served them were suddenly clear and visible traitors. But even here there were ambiguities: how to categorize the very large numbers of Chinese who lived under the collaborationist regimes of North and East China, where simply ensuring subsistence could lead to acts that could reasonably be construed as traitorous to those who had fled to the interior for the duration of the war.

Taiwan, meanwhile, had a population that was almost entirely ethnically Han Chinese but that had experienced an entirely separate political history from the rest of China in the first half of the twentieth century as a direct colony of Japan between 1895 and 1945. While this meant that Taiwanese Chinese were able to avoid the tangled web of accusation, betrayal, and fratricidal bloodletting that was such a defining feature on the mainland of China in this period, it also suggested collaboration on a very large scale. Indeed, when Taiwan was returned to China in late 1945, the only Taiwanese who could *not* logically be accused of being traitors or at least collaborators were the small minority of liberal intellectuals who actively engaged in resistance to Japanese rule. Ironically, these were the very people who were accused and prosecuted with vigor as traitors (*jian*) and subversives (*panluan*) by the Chiang Kai-shek government shortly after the island-wide uprising in the 2-28 Incident of 1947 and the subsequent White Terror of the early 1950s. By 1949, the combination of internecine squabbling, vicious civil war, foreign invasion, and, for Taiwan, direct colonization resulted in a situation in which very few families in either China or Taiwan could claim completely unblemished histories.

But even as clear geographical separation and the deepening Cold War helped to harden political and ideological identities and boundaries in the early 1950s, only a minority on either side of the Taiwan Straits were branded as traitors, subversives, or enemies of the state, despite widespread collaboration and accommodation to a range of "foreign" regimes in the very recent past. The larger, ultimately political question of how this minority of traitors/subversives/enemies of the state were delineated, targeted, and dispatched was one of the core projects in the early years of regime consolidation on both sides of the Taiwan Straits. How each emerging regime treated its own putative traitors and subversives became in microcosm an embodiment of its ethos and core ideology.

The Campaign to Suppress Counterrevolutionaries and the White Terror Compared: Issues of Background and Scale

Both the PRC and the ROC launched vicious and bloody campaigns against potential subversives and enemies of the state via the Campaign to Suppress Counterrevolutionaries (for the PRC) and the White Terror (for Taiwan) at roughly the same time—between 1950 and 1953—a critical early stage in regime consolidation. Although the Republic of China cranked up its engines of repression roughly a year earlier than did the People's Republic, both were unleashed in a context of deepening Cold War and were inseparable from the outbreak and unfolding of the Korean War. For both China and Taiwan leaderships, perception of fundamental geopolitical insecurity was filtered by the combination of the implacably hostile "Other" across the Taiwan Straits, the outbreak of the Korean War, and the overnight recasting of U.S. security policy in East Asia that guaranteed Taiwan's existence and prevented the natural conclusion of the Chinese civil war. This timing rendered hysteria against potential subversives and fifth columns plausible, in turn making it possible for each to mobilize the commitments of large numbers of repressors within the state and the acquiescence of society. Indeed, it is very difficult to imagine such vigorous prosecution of subversives without this wider regional background of Cold War turned hot. The Campaign to Suppress Counterrevolutionaries was almost exactly coterminous with China's involvement in the Korean War (autumn of 1950 through winding down in mid-1953). While there is disagreement on when the White Terror actually began, almost all sources concur that systematic suppression began roughly a year earlier than did the Campaign to Suppress Counterrevolutionaries, in autumn of 1949, but it, too, peaked in 1950–51, when the fighting in Korea was most intense.

Despite the Guomindang's reticence in publicizing the repression and its insistent packaging of repression as "order" under the terms of martial law, both the White Terror on Taiwan and the Campaign to Suppress Counterrevolutionaries on the mainland must be understood as bureaucratic campaigns—an extraordinary period in which the state intensified and amplified its insistence on the pursuit of particular policy outcomes (in this case, the ensuring of domestic security through the suppression of traitors and subversion). In addition, both blurred at the borders with other ongoing state campaigns, notably land reform and the Aid-Korea/Resist America campaign in the People's Republic and the Guomindang Party rectification in Taiwan.

The scale of the terror in each case is difficult to measure, as the statistics kept on each are a combination of inaccessible, inconsistent, and incomplete. But where we have numbers, there are some unexpected findings. In absolute terms, the terror was naturally greater in the People's Republic than in Taiwan because the PRC was roughly fifty times larger in population. Additionally, the sheer scale of the PRC and the distances between much of the far-flung hinterland and Beijing made it difficult to implement a campaign of suppression with any degree of uniformity. The original guidelines for the campaign held that the vast majority were not counterrevolutionary, that counterrevolutionaries comprised only a small minority of the population, and that the number of counterrevolutionaries with crimes so serious that they merited execution was smaller still at a mere .5–1 percent of the population. Official figures on the campaign released later in the 1950s varied but held that between 700,000 and two million had been dispatched.[2]

Recent work by Yang Kuisong revises these numbers upward, suggesting that, in aggregate, the execution rate was considerably higher than these general guidelines of .5–1 percent. There was considerable regional variation in how vigorously the campaign was prosecuted. The party's leadership in eastern China was initially very reluctant to go out and execute people, while in other areas, it proved to be quite difficult to get local cadres to stop the bloodletting. Big cities like Shanghai implemented the campaign according to the suggested target of .5–1 percent, but for much of the hinterland in the south and southwest, execution rates were concealed and underreported, falling anywhere between 1.5 and 2 percent of the population (Yang 2006).

Furthermore, those executed were but a minority of those sentenced to some lesser term. Even in relatively mild Shanghai and its immediate environs (population 5,400,000 in 1950) there were 14,391 officially sentenced counterrevolutionaries in 1951: of these, 2,916 (roughly one-fifth of the total) were sentenced to death.[3] From the central archives, recently revealed figures for the campaign suggest totals of 712,000 (1.24% of the population) executed, 1,290,000 (2.58%) imprisoned, 1,200,000 (2.54%) subjected to house arrest, and a further 380,000 guilty of minor crimes and let go after a brief period of reeducation (Yang 2006, 76). In sum, we now know that the sheer scale of the terror

was significantly higher than the CCP admitted to at the time (or probably originally intended), that execution rates were wildly variable
depending on location and how responsive local officials were to signals
from above, and that execution rates of those apprehended in visible
and well-reported locales like Shanghai were considerably lower than
was the case either in the interior or in the country at large.

Despite increasing interest in Taiwan in the White Terror period of
martial law, reliable statistics on the scale of the White Terror in the
1950s are even more problematic than those for the People's Republic
of China, where official propaganda in the early 1950s openly trumpeted the importance of suppressing counterrevolutionaries and the
current leadership of the PRC remains unembarrassed enough by this
bloody history to continue to include this campaign in the official
chronicles and histories that comprise the Chinese Communist Party's
master history of its own rise and consolidation of power. In contrast,
the leadership of the Guomindang party-state was consistently unwilling
to acknowledge publicly that there even *was* a "Terror," and for decades
either shunted aside embarrassing questions about the scale and type of
the repression or responded in terms of the maintenance of order and
the provisions of martial law. Inquiries into human rights abuses, unresolved cases, improper accusation, false imprisonment, and politically
motivated execution has, in Taiwan, been closely associated with the
coalescence of the political opposition of the Democratic Progressive
Party (DPP) in the late 1980s and early 1990s. Greater political clout on
the part of the DPP over the course of the 1990s has led to an explosion
of memoirs, the creation of a national archive, the establishment of a
committee for redress—the Foundation for Compensating Improper
Verdicts on Sedition and Espionage Cases During the Martial Law
Period—and the creation of public spaces and memorials commemorat-
ing the victims of the White Terror. But greater openness about the past
is itself the product of politics and subethnic sensitivities in the present.
Many still in or close to centers of political and administrative power
have little incentive to delve into these affairs and sort out chaotic and
unorganized records, much less make them publicly available.

The current political contestation and sensitivity of the topic, widespread loss or destruction of documents, and way the process of suppression was fragmented between different organizations in the 1950s have
resulted in contested, variable, and probably unresolvable numbers.
Activists' estimates of the scale of the White Terror at the high end run
to anywhere between 30,000 and 70,000, and claims have been made
that put the total numbers executed at around 15 percent of those
arrested, but these are unsubstantiated with hard evidence and cover the
entirety of the period between 1949 and 1987 (Monk 2002). The archi-

val statistics from the Ministry of Defense Internal Security Headquarters' own documents have been reprinted and are publicly available but are internally inconsistent as to the ways sedition was defined. Which of the five different organizations involved in the suppression of subversion was responsible for what shifted from year to year.[4] These official but partial statistics from late 1949 through 1954 suggest a lower number of 5,856 and an upper of 6565, but are likely to be an undercount. The real total may well surpass 11,000.[5] What does emerge from this range of estimates is that, in absolute (total numbers) and relative terms (percentage of the population), campaigns of internal suppression of subversion were considerably less severe in Taiwan than in China. When directly compared even to "mild" Shanghai, the Guomindang state on Taiwan "suppressed" between one-third and one-half fewer suspects in a population 28 percent larger.[6]

Numbers arrested and sentenced in either the total or proportional population is but one crude estimate for the scale of terror. Equally useful indicators would include severity in meting out punishment after detainment and prosecution of the degree of arbitrariness with which sentence was passed. When considered in this way, the White Terror on Taiwan in the early 1950s begins to seem much more like the campaigns against counterrevolutionaries and traitors in the People's Republic. In the greater Shanghai area, the death penalty in 1951 was meted out to an almost-even 20 percent of those apprehended and prosecuted. Percentages elsewhere in the country varied, in aggregate coming out at roughly one in four. The currently available sources in Taiwan that give figures on death sentences for the early 1950s are inconsistent and suggest percentages that are significantly lower (13.6 percent) or virtually identical to those in the greater Shanghai area (20 percent and 19 percent).[7] But when we look at particular *cases* in Taiwan, it is also apparent that there was considerable variation there as well. When the full force of government suppression was brought in, the percentage of death sentences could be very much in line with practice in the People's Republic at around 20 percent, as was the case in the vicious quashing of the Luku base area in 1952–53, when 35 of 165 (21 percent) were given the death penalty (Zhang and Gao 1998, 32). In other cases, the death penalty seems to have been variable as a function of timing, spatial distance from Taibei, and (perceived) relative importance of the target of suppression. In August 1949, a Communist network in Jilong was broken up with a death penalty of 18 percent (7 of 38) but the very next month, a similar group was suppressed in Gaoxiong, with only relatively light sentencing—most of the accused received a standard 5 five-year jail term, and there was no imposition of the death penalty at all.[8] On the other hand, the January 1950 suppression of the Taibei Working Committee saw 29 percent (15 of 51) executed[9] and the suppression of a network in the national Ministry of Social Affairs in May 1950 the highest of all at 57 percent (19 of 33).[10]

Thus, at a minimum, the Guomindang party-state could, when it chose, be at least as repressive as the Chinese Communist party-state. Despite its emphasis on law, procedure, and order, the ROC meted out the most stringent forms of violence to its perceived enemies in a manner nearly as terrifying as the mass campaigns of the People's Republic for the same reason: inherent unpredictability.

Core Agendas, Campaign Implementation, and the Extension of State Power

The ways in which the PRC and the ROC announced their respective targets and clamped down on subversion in the early 1950s suggest that these two Chinese regimes were substantively different. In some key respects, of course, they were. Rhetorical nomenclature was different even when the kinds of people referred to were surprisingly similar. The CCP prosecuted "counterrevolutionaries" (*fangeming*), of whom "traitors" (*hanjian*) were a distinct subset. Counterrevolutionaries were so designated on the basis of either their formal status as high-ranking Guomindang party, government, or military officials or their behavior in the present or the recent past: as "bullies," "bandits," and so on. The GMD also defined its enemies on the basis of some combination of ongoing activity and putative (although almost always secret) status as part of Communist networks of subversion. "Subversives" (*panluan*) and "Communist bandits" (*gongfei*) were, as a matter of definition, also "traitors" (*jian*).

The CCP and GMD also packaged and represented repression very differently. The CCP openly and proudly conducted its campaign against counterrevolutionaries and traitors between 1950 and 1953; to this day, it remains understood in the official master histories as one of the core successful, early mass campaigns of regime consolidation. The GMD insisted that it was merely implementing regular procedures and "law" in ridding the country of subversion and communism, and did not openly admit the scale of the suppression until well after the process of democratization was underway in the 1990s.

Nevertheless, despite these differences in rhetoric and packaging, the designation and prosecution of presumptive traitors in the two Chinas were remarkably similar in (1) the core state *agendas* pursued by each, (2) the method of bureaucratic *campaigns* of intensification to implement the suppression of traitors, which, in turn, led to some overlap in (3) shared *tactics*, although here there were also sharp divergences.

Finally, for both, the prosecution of traitors/subversives/counterrevolutionaries was surprisingly *successful*: political and social opposition was physically liquidated or cowed into submission and the coercive and reporting apparatus of the state enormously strengthened as a result of these campaigns.

The core state agenda—the raison d'être—for the suppression was in each case identical: both regimes sought to wipe out real and imagined *political* competitors, as well as to destroy disturbers of public *social* order. The vehicle by which these programs were implemented was the campaign, and although the rhetorical packaging was different (mass political campaign versus martial law), the suppression in each case hit at a surprisingly wide range of mirror image targets; potential political competitors (the mirror image of the "Other" across the Straits), as well as real and imagined sources of potential social and economic competition (counterfeiters, hoodlums, thieves, bullies, smugglers, and a wide range of other social undesirables). Despite its insistence on dry, legal formalism in comparison to the populist campaign mobilization of the PRC, the range of targets was as wide in Taiwan as in the PRC.

Both party-states cast very wide nets in their definitions of subversion, and both struggled with the age-old problem of how to define targets for arrest and repression with enough bureaucratic precision to hit hard at subversives but leave enough flexibility and interpretation for either harshness or lenience in individual cases. The background of Cold War hysteria made it possible for martial law rules and mass political campaigns to push through arrests and sentences with correspondingly lower levels of evidence and proof than would have been the case in normal times under civil courts. But whether justly led by martial law or legitimized by mass mobilization, each needed to be implemented by the bureaucratic organizations of the consolidating state, and here there are surprising similarities in how these institutions formulated categories and implemented repression. Both campaigns were begun with pronouncements from the very apex of the political system that indicated severity and crackdown against targets painted in the direst terms but whose characteristics were loosely defined and even more loosely applied in practice by the repressive organizations of the state.[11]

In the People's Republic, the "Double Ten Directive" (*shuangshi zhishi*) of 10 October 1950 moved away from what it characterized as the government's previously "excessive lenience" in favor of "combining suppression and lenience" (*zhenya kuanda jiehe*). Later explanatory circulars issued by the central government in the autumn of 1950 cranked up the campaign by referring to its goals as "executing some, imprisoning some, and confining some to house arrest" and exhorted local cadres to "not fear executing people, only to fear mistakenly executing people" (Double Ten Directive 1950/1994). In the People's Republic of China, those designated as counterrevolutionaries were a hodgepodge of the clearly bureaucratically definable, the criminal, and the socially undesirable. The regime's own guidelines included those who worked for security organizations or held high positions in vanquished Guomindang military, party, or the Youth Corps. Determining the status of these individuals was straightforward if time consuming; there were clear rules to follow and confirming paper trails to use as evidence.[12] More problematic were the much larger, amorphous social groups of counterrevolutionaries whose status was much less clear and amenable to bureaucratic rules. Determining who ought to be deemed bullies (*e'ba*), hardened bandits (*guaifei*), the leaders of counterrevolutionary sects (*fandong huimentou*), and traitors (*hanjian*) was a much more subjective process, particularly given the complete lack of guidelines on how "counterrevolutionary crime" ought to be separated from regular workaday "serious crime."

This was particularly the case in the countryside and peri-urban areas around Shanghai, where the Campaign to Suppress Counterrevolutionaries merged with the land reform campaign. As the highly commercialized and commodified area around Shanghai simply did not have enough bona fide landlords to go around, traitors (which in this context meant those who had taken up positions with local Japanese collaborationist regimes between 1937 and 1945), bullies, and counterrevolutionaries became the reservoir that supplied the usual suspects to fill informal campaign quotas. For example, in what was then Qingpu county, due west of Shanghai, only two-thirds (862 of 1,290) of the individuals subjected to struggle sessions in the land reform campaign of 1951 were landlords at all. The remaining third was divided between traitors (252) and bullies and counterrevolutionaries (176).[13] In fact, in many places, traitors were "struggled against" even when they were middle peasants, in absolute breach of CCP rules that forbade targeting middle peasants. In practice, the combination of a mass campaign mentality, de facto discretion, and significant pressure on local cadres to meet bureaucratic quotas made it next to impossible for local cadres consistently to distinguish local bullies from the merely disliked, "hardened bandits" from garden variety robbers, hated traitors from those embedded in village networks of mutuality, and the leaders of counterrevolutionary religious organizations from followers. As the levels of the campaign were respectively ratcheted up and dampened down from above, those entrusted with implementing the campaign often found themselves in real quandaries: one month admonished for being too soft and then next for not being accurate in distinguishing between regular crime and counterrevolutionary crime.[14]

The rhetoric and packaging surrounding the White Terror in Taiwan was quite different. Rather than proudly labeling its campaign as such (and doing its best to convince the population that this campaign was both necessary and desirable), the Guomindang regime conducted its campaign against subversion behind the closed doors of military trials, with their ostensible forms and processes of law. Guomindang rhetoric reified "order," and the state set itself up to exemplify order, procedure, and regularity through the promulgation of laws, regulations, amendments, and openly published directives. It also built on precedent by extending and adding sets of extraordinary regulations to the version of martial law brought in to Taiwan in the aftermath of the 2–28 Incident. This, in turn, referred back to the version of martial law promulgated during the Encirclement Campaigns against the Communists in the mid-1930s. In contrast to the PRC's loosely worded "Double Ten Directive," with its invigorating call to the masses to mobilize in support of the regime and stamp out counterrevolutionaries, the key documents of reference for the early years of the White Terror are dry, legalistic, and formal, and mass popular involvement was completely absent.[15]

Even a cursory glance at these texts shows that they were at best general guidelines for action on how to punish the already accused on the basis of putative severity of crime. The Rules on Rectifying Sedition, for example, state clearly a punishment of ten years to life for anyone belonging to a seditious organization or group (rule no. 5), a punishment of seven years to life for disseminating seditious printed or auditory material or harming public order (rule no. 6), and ten years to life for strike agitation or subverting either public order or public finance (rule no. 4, item 1, no. 10). The rules, however, give no hint as to how the burden of proof was determined and standards of evidence established. In terms of implementation, the rules were as loose and flexible as the campaign pronouncements for the suppression of counterrevolutionaries in the PRC. In effect, almost anyone was fair game: quite literally anyone who had been as much as handed a periodical mentioning Marxism could be taken in and deemed a communist.

Formal documents consistently make no distinction between the (presumptively) guilty and the merely suspect. Like the Chinese Communist Party, the Guomindang in Taiwan used the background atmosphere of insecurity and terror to stamp out the sorts of behavior that in more normal times would be considered either criminal, socially undesirable, or merely careless. Smuggling, counterfeiting, thievery, illicit entry into the country, and damage to state property all show up in a range of extraordinary regulations under martial law and often were prosecutable as instances of sedition. A set of regulations on "rectifying thieving bandits" (*zhengzhi zeifei tiaoli*), although not officially promulgated until June 1957, illustrates the tendency to conflate regular (indeed, petty) crime with "banditry" and subversion. The Internal Security Headquarters' own yearly reports from the early 1950s on the suppression of subversion prominently featured a standard section on suppressing hoodlums (*liumang*)—an equally prime target for the Chinese Communists in their suppression of counterrevolutionaries. For both, the boundaries between the pure "us" and the depraved "enemy" were redrawn to justify a harsh crackdown and imposition of a particular vision of order and, in so doing, to go for the soft targets of any law and order campaign: the small-time hoodlums, the local toughs, the urban lumpen hanging around on the street. Whether presented through legal formalism or the emotional call to arms of a society-wide mass mobilization, standards were vague, burdens of proof even vaguer, categories ill demarcated, and the boundaries between subversion, criminality, and social undesirability at best blurred.

In some ways, the terror in Taiwan, while significantly less bloody than the Campaign to Suppress Counterrevolutionaries in either absolute or proportional terms, was in the short term more terrifying. The Campaign to Suppress Counterrevolutionaries' targets were a mix of the obviously counterrevolutionary (those whose recent bureaucratic positions in the National Government, the Youth Corps, and the GMD military were, by definition, counterrevolutionary) and the socially undesirable (petty crooks, hoodlums, local toughs, and thieves). White-collar workers and regular workers were relatively immune, as long as they had not been part of GMD organizations at high levels, and members of the Chinese Communist Party and Youth League were entirely untouched by the campaign. In Taiwan, however, the targets of the White Terror included a significantly broader range of individuals: there were *no* social groups completely immune from being spirited off by the security forces. The Internal Security Bureau's own statistics confirm that the Guomindang party-state in Taiwan was an equal opportunity repressor: the White Terror was directed at both mainlander refugees and local Taiwanese. In 1952, the numbers of Taiwanese designated "bandit traitors" (870) was slightly more than twice as much as mainlanders (410).[16] More surprising is the occupational distribution: in the same year, there were more "subversives" from the ranks of civil servants (140) than professors and students combined (110). Workers (166) and farmers (166) comprised the two largest occupational groups, with shopkeepers and businessmen (114) coming in just after civil servants. Nor were soldiers immune (58), coming in right after the unemployed (65).[17]

Finally, in both the People's Republic and Taiwan, the suppression of putative subversion was deliberately used as a pretext for the state to extend and strengthen its powers and coercive presence into a range of new geographical and social spheres. The prosecution of counterrevolutionaries in Shanghai was directly linked to the state's "strengthening" of police and security organizations, and the campaign seems to have been as much aimed at toughening up the "overly merciful view" of local cadres and deploying that toughness in organizational form to first register, then to strike against counterrevolutionaries.[18] The Shanghai authorities mobilized the police in general through setting up work committees to take charge of the campaign. This general strengthening of police organization was taken a step further by requiring that state offices and state factories establish internal-security committees that reported to a municipal level internal-security committee.[19] In the spring of 1951, for example, the East China Military region began to send its own cadres to larger state-owned and private factories to supervise all aspects of the campaign, from producing exhortatory propaganda to helping local leaders run accusation meetings.[20] This was explicitly justified at the time in terms of grave security risk and the importance of strengthening the state. But once the campaign was over, these systems of internal security, monitoring, and reporting remained in place and provided a precedent for extension to other work places.

In Taiwan, something very similar happened. The state used the pretext of security work and the undercutting of subversion to extend its domination downward into society as well as inward—to the geographical hinterland of the high mountains. In early 1950, the Internal Security Bureau itself was beefed up. Sixteen special units to receive intelligence on spies were established, plus a special security group to monitor intelligence reports in the postal, educational, and overseas Chinese sectors. A combination of the regular and military police monitored port traffic and extended surveillance deep into society. All forms of social organization that were anything other than strictly controlled by the Guomindang were subject to surveillance and repression: universities and middle schools (to prevent the emergence of student protests), known democracy activists and members of liberal associations, workers' unions, and even seemingly innocuous organizations like native place associations.[21]

In an almost exact parallel with practice in the PRC, in early 1952, over fifty in-house security committees with reporting links to higher levels of the security apparatus were established in schools, universities, government offices, state-owned factories, and province-run enterprises.

The educational sector was at all levels particularly singled out for scrutiny, with the establishment of county-level Education and Society Security organizations, operating under the provincial Bureau of Education.[22] If anything, security work in Taiwan in the early 1950s was even more pervasive than was the case in the China at the time, although the People's Republic soon caught up and surpassed Taiwan in intensity of routine surveillance, informing, and dossier keeping on individual citizens. Although details are sketchy, it is clear that, in Taiwan, security organizations also set up networks of secret informants and snitches at the most basic levels of society; and monitoring of mail, telephone, and telegram traffic came to be pervasive and routine by the end of 1950.[23] We know little about the ways in which informal reporting, mutual surveillance, snitching, and personal vendettas and grievances accelerated the White Terror, as little of this comes through the final trial "decisions" (*panjue*) that are the main sources of record. But these were surely important factors. The state also deliberately linked the strengthening of internal security with the expansion of state presence through much tighter control of places where its hold was weak in the high mountains. In 1952, thirty small special-security groups were dispatched to mountainous communities to engage in a combination of "education" and rooting out of suspects.[24]

Packaging and Implementing Terror: Participatory Public Theater Versus Bureaucratic Atomization

Despite these similarities in timing, targets, and the expansion of state power, there was one fundamental difference in the way in which terror was implemented on the two sides of the Taiwan Straits in the 1950s. In the People's Republic, as soon as counterrevolutionaries were determined and incarcerated, they were put to another, equally important public heuristic use as the subjects of mass-accusation sessions (*kongsu hui*). The Chinese Communist Party deliberately mobilized urban society in support of its policies through these theatrical spectacles. This kind of participatory theater not only "hit hard" at counterrevolutionaries but garnered the emotional compliance and complicity of the public in support of state-led violence against targeted enemies. Counterrevolutionaries, landlords, traitors, and their crimes were punished in public in a manner that invited "the masses" to participate in the state's terror and collectively reaffirm the popular legitimacy of the regime.[25]

Here the implementation of terror oscillated unevenly between the party-state's genuine desire to mobilize the masses in support of state-sanctioned goals and the bureaucratic need to keep the spectacle on track and roughly according to script. At this still early stage of regime

consolidation, it is doubtful that the masses attending the public accusation meetings were aware that they were participating in a version of a
show trial; that would come later in the 1950s, when the culture of isolat-
ing and targeting enemies for verbal attack became closely associated
with an externally imposed cycle of political campaigns and modes of
power and domination within the confines of the work unit.

But even as early as 1951, the public accusation session was but the
visible dénouement of a show that had been many weeks in preparation.
Local cadres in most cases spent weeks in advance behind closed doors
in preparation for the public event. Materials against the accused were
gathered, the venue (typically in a public place like a park or a school-
yard) chosen, a rough script of the proceedings drafted, and hand-
picked "accusers" carefully coached before being strategically sprinkled
around the audience. At key moments in the proceedings, these accusers would be invited to quite literally "take the stage" and dramatically
accuse the offender of past wrongdoings. Typically, cadres singled out
the more visibly vulnerable members of society—the very young, the
very old, and women—as the best "speakers of bitterness" because they
would be the most likely to engage the emotions and stir up the crowd.
When the public-accusation meeting went off well, the crowd's emotions
were, in fact, engaged, the crowd wept freely, the accused were visibly
cowed (often through the expedient of a garrote discreetly placed
around the neck to enforce kneeling at key moments), and the event
concluded with public mass affirmation of support for the regime.

Inviting the crowd to participate in state sanctioned violence carried
two types of risks. Either the mass accusation meeting could fail to work
well due to insufficient "advance preparation," so that neither the leaders of the event nor the audience members quite knew why they were
there or what they were supposed to do; or, equally problematic, the
emotional manipulation worked so well that uncoached individuals in
the crowd spontaneously hurled new, unproven accusations, with the
event threatening to spiral the event out of control entirely. In both
cases, the admonishment was to "more thoroughly prepare," but overly
thorough preparation led to heavy-handed bureaucratic control that
would itself choke off exactly the sort of spontaneous public support
that the regime was hoping to mobilize.[26] The young People's Republic
of China was startling in its self-confidence in so openly resorting to this
kind of populism and its assumption that, given half a chance, the
masses would support the regime and its violence against designated
enemies. It was also caught in a bind characteristic of all populist
regimes: how to maintain control *and* whip up popular mobilization at
the same time.

This kind of publicly performed morality tale, with its willingness to

collectively invite in the mass urban public to participate in state violence against political undesirables, was completely unimaginable in Taiwan. Ironically, perhaps reflecting Chiang Ching-kuo's own murky
involvement with security forces and prior training in the Soviet Union,
the actual prosecution of real and imagined subversion in Taiwan in the
early 1950s was much more Stalinist than it was in the PRC regime across
the Straits and was then seeking to remake itself and society along
explicitly Stalinist lines. In both the Soviet Union and Taiwan, the range
of targets was broader than was the case in the PRC and included state
civil servants, the military, and no small number of regular people doing
nothing more than going about their lives. Fewer people were beyond
the possible reach of the terror in Taiwan. The public participation, dramatic theatricality, and public shows of support for the regime so commonly manifested through public accusation meetings in the PRC were
conspicuously absent. In Taiwan, as in Stalin's Soviet Union, terror was
conducted by faceless gray men and shadowy security organizations that
knocked on the door in the middle of the night and spirited one away.
Despite the regime's self-justification in terms of law, order, and procedure, both laws and procedures were full of such gaping holes that, in
practice, almost anyone could be accused of being a communist. Arrests
were not made public, family members did not have to be notified, and
it was common practice for the accused to be held for months or even
years. Lawyers, when appointed, were typically reluctant to do anything
more than attempt to plead for clemency and reduction of sentence
(Jian 1993, 43–44).

In this early stage of regime consolidation, both regimes effectively
mobilized power successfully to isolate and punish designated enemies
while extending the coercive apparatus of the state through the vehicle
of the bureaucratic campaign. There was also substantial overlap in the
kinds of people singled out as subversive and traitorous. On the other
hand, the PRC and Taiwan differed substantially in the ways in which
these campaigns were rhetorically justified, packaged, and carried out.
What was typically played out in public space through enthusiastic crowd
participation in public accusation meetings in the People's Republic was
implemented with secrecy, flawed processes of ostensible legality, and
near total public silence in Taiwan.

Post-Consolidation Legacies of Terror

In both the People's Republic of China and Taiwan, the antisubversion
campaigns prosecuted with such vigor were successful, but the medium-
term lessons drawn from those successes diverged sharply. In Taiwan,
the White Terror of the early 1950s did, likely with more collateral dam-

age than was necessary, accomplish what it set out to do. Not only were the obviously traitorous dispatched, the terror unleashed in so doing also "instructed" the people in which political and social boundaries could and could not be crossed. Once the obviously "Communist" networks were rolled up, the party and military purged of suspects and waverers, and the independence-minded (or simply liberally minded) remainder of a potential political opposition terrified into relative silence, the regime did not have to go to such extraordinary lengths again. A reminder here and there with the prosecution of a high-level political case was sufficient to keep society sufficiently atomized and quiescent, and with time, the prosecution of designated subversives seems to have become institutionalized and regularized, even if the much vaunted legal basis for all this remained vague and weak on basic protections for the accused.

This was not the case in the People's Republic. Although the Campaign to Suppress Counterrevolutionaries was publicly trumpeted as a great success, the leaders of the Chinese Communist Party remained in such thrall to the public and participatory methods behind its success that it proved quite unable to adapt when circumstances changed. The regime remained susceptible to paranoia about subversion and launched another next round of campaigns against counterrevolutionaries with the *sufan* ("Cleaning out counterrevolutionaries") campaign of 1955, as China was nationalizing urban enterprises as state work units. *Sufan* had an even wider and vaguer set of targets than the Campaign to Suppress Counterrevolutionaries, and its spatial locus shifted from out in public to more enclosed boundaries of the state's work unit, with the full complement of punishments and rewards that the workplace could proffer. In the summer of 1955, work unit leaders were enjoined to "stir up and unite with the masses." But apart from designated activists who had an interest prosecuting suspected counterrevolutionaries as a way of proving their credentials, a solid majority of "the masses"—those with official labels as "backward and middle elements"—did their best to keep their heads down and were "formalistic" in the campaign's unavoidable group discussions and accusation meetings. The guidelines for the campaign were so vague that anyone with "historical questions" (having served the previous Guomindang regime in any way), "complicated social relations" (a relative or close friend who had served the Guomindang), or even a quietist attitude was vulnerable. The campaign gave activists a rare opportunity to earn their spurs, but since there were strict quotas on the numbers of people who could be officially designated as activists, proactive participation in small group-discussion sessions could buy the nonactivist majority nothing but unwanted attention.[27] It was but a short step from the leftist excesses of *sufan* to the witch hunts of the Anti-Rightist campaign of 1957 and beyond.

There is little doubt that the Chinese Communist Party was normatively committed to the principle of mass mobilization in support of its campaigns. But this only worked when the targets were both visible and clearly distinguishable from the majority. In 1951, most of the "masses" were unaware that they were the extras, the chorus, in a show of violence put on by the state against designated targets. But people learned quickly. By 1955, most were keenly aware of the staging and manipulation and understood exactly where power and life chances lay. The minority of activists who did have something to gain from promoting the campaign made increasingly wild accusations for the same mixture of ideological and instrumental reasons common in other revolutionary and authoritarian regimes; and with successive campaigns, the revolution began to consume its own children (see, for example, Fitzpatrick and Gellately 1997, 15).

Even though the White Terror in Taiwan was initially wider ranging than was the Campaign to Suppress Counterrevolutionaries, its stress on law and the relatively limited goals of the regime (getting people to comply with new norms of acceptability for political and social behavior) and the very harshness of the early 1950s may have rendered the island safe and secure enough for the leadership to thereafter ease off on the terror, opening a space in which to concentrate on development and begin to try to appeal—at least materially—to the disaffected and disenfranchised. This was palpably not the case in the People's Republic. The early successes of the Campaign to Suppress Counterrevolutionaries— garnering the quick responsiveness of the bureaucracy, educating the urban population in the regime's position on counterrevolutionaries and subversion, and mobilizing the masses in public shows of support for the regime—could not be replicated in subsequent campaign cycles with anything like the same popular enthusiasm, but that did not prevent the leadership from making the attempt. Ironically, the CCP's later problems in mobilizing the masses were the product of the very successes in the early regime consolidation in which the Campaign to Suppress Counterrevolutionaries and land reform had played such a big part. In a very short period of time in the early to mid-1950s, the PRC brought about the fundamental transformation in how the economy was managed, society organized, and individual status determined. Once the PRC succeeded in locking up the majority of the population in nationalized work units, the targets became looser and vaguer, the standards of proof lower, the political and moral incentives to engage in accusation stronger, and the entire process more prone to "leftist excesses."

Both the PRC and the ROC cultivated an atmosphere of insecurity and terror in their concurrent early phases of regime consolidation. Both deliberately whipped up fears to strike at internal enemies, garner the compliance of the bureaucracy, and extend the coercive hand of the state further into society through permanent organizations of monitoring and reporting. In both cases, the regime was caught between its own bureaucratic rules for the management of terror and the ways in which it represented itself. In the PRC, this meant a tension between the state's representation of itself as a populist mass democracy implementing the people's will and the practical need for bureaucratic control over the proceedings. For Taiwan, it meant the looseness—indeed, meaninglessness—of its much touted and legitimating "law." The international context (the onset of the Korean War and the hardening of the Cold War) was identical and critical in both cases to each regime's credibility in whipping up an atmosphere of fear and insecurity and encouraging a culture of informing and snitching. The campaign reached its peak in both places in 1951. The types of targets sought out included a hard core of the usual suspects that, for both, easily blurred with social undesirables and petty criminals. The scale of the terror was by one set of standards (absolute and relative numbers of individuals "suppressed") worse in the PRC; by another (unpredictability due to a much broader range of targets), worse in Taiwan. And—critically—in both places, the regime deliberately used its campaigns against potential subversives to extend the power and coercive presence of the state itself to new arenas, both geographical and social. Yet the differences in the way in which terror was packaged and implemented illustrate different fundamental ambivalences in regime goals and tendencies, tendencies that would become manifested even more sharply in the years after regime consolidation on both sides of the Taiwan Straits.

Chapter 5
Betraying Trust and the Elusive Nature of Ethnicity in Burundi

Simon Turner

In the African Great Lakes region, Hutu and Tutsi for the most part live peacefully side by side, while at times they have committed genocide and other atrocities in the name of ethnicity. On the one hand, ethnicity is strong enough to mobilize hundreds of thousands of ordinary Hutu peasants in Rwanda to kill, maim, and molest their Tutsi neighbors and to have the Tutsi-dominated army in Burundi systematically and brutally kill more that 100 000 Hutu civilians. On the other hand, they have so much in common that it is strongly debated and heavily disputed whether one can in fact talk of ethnic groups in these two, small central African states. Much of the literature on the area claims that the conflicts are not about ethnicity at all: that ethnicity is constructed, instrumentalized, and manipulated by political elites in order to achieve certain goals and that the main issue is access to resources and/or political power. Others claim that the conflicts are less about the skillful manipulation of identities by greedy elites and more about genuine grievances among the common population.[1] Neither position explains in full, however, the ambiguity of ethnicity in the region—the fact that enemies become friends and friends become enemies almost overnight.

In this chapter, I explore the ambiguous nature of ethnicity through the figure of the traitor. The traitor transgresses the boundaries of ethnic belonging, thereby permitting the constant negotiation and policing of these boundaries. However, if we go beyond this obvious observation, we find that there are several kinds of traitors at play and that each kind of traitor figure presents a different kind of sociality. The first kind of traitor in popular imagination is the Hutu next door who used to interact freely with Tutsi and who suddenly turns into a dangerous ethnic "Other," killing Tutsi neighbors and friends indiscriminately. He may also be the schoolmate whose ethnic identity you did not know, basically because it did not matter, until you discover not only that he is Tutsi but that he has known your ethnicity all along and has been hatching secret plans against you. They are perceived as traitors in the sense that they break the faith and trust of their close friends and neighbors, betraying intimate relations (kin, friends, neighbors) due to a loyalty toward ethnic categories. In these constructions of the traitor in popular discourse, the traitor is believed to be created by an inner, demonic, and very real ethnic identity, and betrayal lies in pretending that ethnicity does not matter. There is a second kind of ethnic traitor, however, in Burundian narratives on ethnicity: people who choose to turn their backs on their "true" ethnic identity. This is especially a central narrative among the Hutu, who are concerned with Hutu individuals who try to become Tutsi for reasons of personal gain.[2] By marrying Tutsi women or accepting high positions in the Tutsi government or army, they are believed to be seeking personal advantages by turning their backs on their true ethnic identity. These stories of betrayal build on another notion of sociality, one that is based on ethnic loyalty. Based on concrete case studies of the various perceptions of treachery in Burundian ethnopolitics,[3] this chapter explores how these two apparently opposing modes of treachery relate to the ambiguous position of ethnicity, thereby contributing to ethnic violence in Burundi. While the first type of treason destroys inter-ethnic harmony and the second type blurs ethnic belonging, both kinds reveal an understanding of ethnicity as inescapable yet malleable. The traitor, on the one hand, illustrates the ability of individuals to manipulate and hide ethnic identities, while, on the other hand, the narratives point out that individuals cannot escape their inherent and deep-seated ethnic identities in the long run.

Intimacy, Knowledge, and Betrayal

It is commonly claimed in anthropological debates that violence has the effect of breaking down the social-symbolic order of everyday life, effacing social memory and questioning taken-for-granted meanings (Feldman 1995; Balibar 1998) and that, after large-scale violence, societies must reestablish meaning (Das 1995; Nordstrom and Robben 1995). Throughout my own fieldwork, whenever I discussed genocidal violence with Burundians, one of the central themes was their sense of being betrayed by people whom they had previously trusted, people whom they believed that they knew and who suddenly turned against them during these violent events. This betrayal shattered their previous assumptions about whom to trust and shook their knowledge about the world around them. In her book on *Moral Repair*, Margaret Urban Walker

(2006) claims that it is important to distinguish between "mere reliance" and trust. Trust is interpersonal and goes beyond predictability, linked as it is to moral norms: "In trusting one has *normative expectations* of others, expectations of others that they will do what they should and hence we are entitled to hold them to it" (80). Often trust is based on our knowledge and experience of a person whom we trust to act in certain ways in certain situations. However, for large parts of our lives, we also trust total strangers: the nurse, the bus driver, the policeman. This is what Walker terms "zones of default trust" (85), unreflected, impersonal, institutionalized trust in "the system." When default trust is violated, we tend to look for someone or some others to be held responsible "because trust implies responsibility" (86). Because trust is about more than simple predictability, because we do not simply trust someone due to our knowledge about him or her, with violations of trust—as in cases of ethnic violence—"it is not only the violated relationship that is shattered but a whole nexus of the injured person's beliefs about himself, his judgement, his understanding of a shared history and even the nature of 'people', 'the world', and 'right and wrong'" (Flanigan in Walker 2006, 90). In other words, when someone whom one trusted to act according to certain (moral) norms acts differently, one loses confidence not only in the person or persons who broke one's trust but also in one's own ability to assess others' actions. In the words of Veena Das, societal crisis caused by violence leads to the "withdrawal of trust from normally functioning words" (1998a, 115), which in turn leads to the production of panic-laden rumor and ethnic hatred.

In April 2003, I visited Mr. Ngendakumana[4] and his wife Beatrice in their home in a small town south of Brussels. Mr. Ngendakumana is in his fifties, well dressed, polite, and extremely well spoken. His wife is equally elegant, in a modest fashion that suits her age and status. Seated in big leather sofas in the living room that is heavily decorated with religious motifs and Burundian souvenirs, he serves beer, cake, and coffee and then proceeds to explain the main objectives of his organization for the protection of Tutsi in Burundi. This leads to more general reflections on the nature of the conflict in Burundi and its historical background, as these interviews so often do. While he elegantly draws the general lines, his wife often interferes with a "Monsieur . . ." whereupon she gives a heartbreaking and personal account of what the Hutu did to her relatives, her neighbors, or her friends. "Monsieur, it was awful. They killed my aunt and her six children. I don't understand how they could do it. They were neighbors! Not even an animal—not even a snake—would do such a thing." Her husband quickly—and slightly impatiently—guides the discussion back on track and attempts to conclude in more theoretical terms. However, she returns with photos of school boys who were massacred in their school in 1993. Apparently, the Hutu pupils were told to leave the school, so that they could kill the Tutsi, but the Hutu pupils had refused, and they were all killed. "Why doesn't this happen more often? Why don't people help their neighbors and, for instance, refuse to sort the Hutu from the Tutsi when buses are stopped?" she asks. She was especially upset by the fact that neighbors, people you had been close to, could suddenly turn round and kill you. She explains how some Hutu are very nice and friendly and mentions some of their neighbors and the house girls that they had employed in the house. But even they changed when the killings started, she says. Not that their maid came to kill them, but she was no longer to be trusted because there were rumors about maids suddenly turning against their employers, "employers who had treated them so well all these years," she says. Rather than continue their loyalty, rather than pay back the kindness that their Tutsi employer had given them, they all of a sudden decided to side with their ethnic compatriots and attack the Tutsi.

What is central to Beatrice's narrative, what upsets her the most, is the fact that loyalties can shift so suddenly. These were loyalties that had been built up through a lifetime and rested on mutual, personal relationships, and all of a sudden, the person that she had trusted was no longer to be trusted. The fact that it was intimates who turned against them in the heat of the violence is more disturbing than if it had been total strangers. What is particularly disquieting to her is the fact that she thought that she knew this or that person due to many years of familiarity, but when this person changed identity, she no longer recognized him or her. She realizes that the knowledge that she assumed to have about her close neighbors was false. When the Hutu neighbor betrayed her, he was not changing his identity; he was revealing his true identity—his ethnic identity. His identity as friendly neighbor had been deceptive. Beatrice realizes that she had lived in a world of illusion and deception and could no longer trust her surroundings or her own abilities to judge the identities of others.

To become intimate, one has to lower one's guard and let the other get close. In this situation, one is exposed and vulnerable—the other has access to one's secrets and knows one's weaknesses—therefore, trust is so much the more important among intimates. You can mistrust strangers and keep them at arm's length, but in order to function with kin, neighbors, and other intimate relations, you have to trust that they will not betray you. While Beatrice would never let a total stranger enter her house—let alone take care of her children—she did so with her Hutu maid.[5] This trust was based on intimate knowledge that stemmed from personal experience through many years of interaction. Yet this knowledge is not enough to establish a trusting relationship. However long and close the relationship, one can never know the other entirely; there is always a residue of doubt about his true identity and his true intentions. Therefore, in order to establish an intimate relationship of trust, you must simply have faith in him despite the nagging doubt. To be intimate, you must believe that he is being truthful and honest and that he is not hiding anything from you—in particular his true intentions and identity—and belief, as Søren Kierkegaard claims, is not based on knowledge but on a "leap of faith." According to Kierkegaard, truth and deception are equally widespread ([1847] 1963, 220), which means that we cannot use knowledge to determine whether something is true or false, whether someone is telling us the truth or betraying us. Whether we choose to have faith in others and believe that they are being truthful to us or we choose to hedge our bets and be suspicious in order to avoid being deceived is a choice we make; it is a pure choice beyond knowledge. Whereas Kierkegaard claims that we have to trust and have faith in others, I would argue that we have to find a strange compromise: we act "as if" we believe. We trust our intimates because we must, not because we really have faith in them. So while Beatrice trusted her neighbors and her maid because she (thought she) knew them, she also trusted them because she had chosen to have faith in them.[6] However, in the event of mass violence, their actions revealed that she had made the wrong choice. Not only did this challenge her ability to predict their natures, it also made her lose faith, and this is what disturbs her the most.

Disclosing True Identities

The question arises, for Beatrice, whether the maid ever was what she appeared to be in the first place, whether beneath the surface she always had been the "ethnic other," capable of brutal actions. The sense of betrayal stems, therefore, not only from the sudden shift in loyalty but also from the fact that one might have been betrayed all along. Perhaps the maid never really was a friend in the first place; she had just pretended to be. And if the friendly servant simply was a surface, hiding a true kernel, was the person in question aware of this? Perhaps the Hutu servant did not know that she was carrying this ethnic monster, capable of doing the most inhuman things, inside her. Perhaps the monster simply emerges in certain circumstances after lying dormant for years.[7] The dilemma remains open for Beatrice. She cannot determine once and for all whether these Hutu had always hidden their true identities, pretending to be friends, until the day they decided to come out in the open and show their true identities, or whether the Hutu—at least, the common people like the servants—were themselves taken aback by their own transformation. In the latter case, they must feel betrayed themselves because they really believed that they could be friends with the Tutsi until the day they realized that it was false and that they must kill the Tutsi.

The Tutsi-dominated government held the perception that the Hutu peasants were unaware of their ethnicity until they were embroiled in frenzied violence in 1972. After the 1972 massacres in which up to 150,000 Hutu were killed by the Tutsi-dominated army, following a Hutu uprising in the south of the country, the official government discourse claimed that Burundians were essentially one people in one nation and that ethnic categories were fabricated by the Belgian colonizers in order to divide and rule the Burundian people. The government's "White Paper on the Real Causes and Consequences of the Attempted Genocide Against the Tutsi Ethny [*sic*] in Burundi" (Embassy of the Republic of Burundi in Washington, 1972), written shortly after the massacres in 1972 as a defense of government policies, argues that ethnicity is an invention of colonialism and that any ethnic resurgence in the country must be attributed to neocolonial conspiracies:

If tribalism is to be mentioned think of the one *you dissipated into our society.* You craftily took advantage of *the naivety or the cupidity of certain of our citizens.* In a few years you *destroyed the secular product of our ancestors. You distinguished between the Burundese citizens libelling them as Hutu and Tutsi.* You did not stop there. *You convinced Hutu of the necessity of massacring Tutsi.* (1972, 1; original emphasis)

When explaining what it saw as a Hutu genocide of the Tutsi, the embassy did not put the blame on the Hutu peasants but on outside influence, claiming that the Hutu were not interested in killing their countrymen but had been convinced to do so by neocolonialists and Congolese Mulelist rebels. Whereas the uneducated Hutu were, therefore, believed to be innocent, the educated elite were systematically killed by the army in revenge. This in many ways resembles nationalist tropes around the world where antagonisms within the nation are attributed to outside influence that pollutes the national fabric. And while the uneducated are the most easily manipulated, they are also the most innocent by default. The educated Hutu, on the other hand, are held responsible for their actions and treated as traitors due to their foreign connections. As we shall see below, the nation is not only threatened by infiltration from outside but also by seepage and leakage from the inside out—in the shape of the traitor who transgresses boundaries.

While the government of the time distinguished between innocent Hutu, culprits, and foreign influence, the questions of intent and of knowing remain central for many Burundians—Hutu and Tutsi—when coming to terms with massive violence. Often the answer is ambiguous.

The following example illustrates how Burundians tarry with the question, as it reveals their greatest fear: that the traitor is not a victim of manipulation but actually knows all along his or her intentions. In 1998, I was asking Hutu refugees in Lukole refugee camp in western Tanzania about their personal experiences of ethnic conflict and their childhood memories of ethnic relations. They emphasized again and again that there used not to be any problems between Hutu and Tutsi. A young man explains to me:

Hutu refugee: At that time it was . . . for Hutu children they were not well taught. That's why Hutu have had no problem. But if I try to analyze it now, I see that at that time we had a problem even [though] it was not easy to see. . . . Now I can see we had a problem because . . . , for example, it was not easy to share . . . the same glass with a Tutsi if you are a Hutu child. That's why if I try to analyze nowadays I can see that at that time it was a problem.

Author: Do you think that the Tutsi children themselves they were aware? Their parents told them, "This one is a Hutu. Don't share!"

Hutu refugee: While Hutu were—what can I say—like blind at that time, the Tutsi themselves were well taught about the system about the Tutsi and not to cooperate . . . to cooperate but to have a certain—what can I call it—not to approach them.

When the refugee was a child, he had no problems with the Tutsi children and could hardly tell the difference, yet the Tutsi children knew all along. This is what he refers to by saying "if I try to analyze it now." With hindsight, he can see the problems between Hutu and Tutsi that he did not see then because he was "blind at that time." Before, when the Hutu could not yet see, there was a semblance of harmony, but it was only artificial, he argues, because the Tutsi had other plans all along. This makes the crime of the Tutsi all the worse in his opinion; not only did they want to oppress and exterminate the Hutu, but they also hid their true intentions and pretended to be friendly with the Hutu who blindly believed them. The refugee's narrative is not unique. Most Hutu that I interviewed had narratives built along the same model. First, there had been harmonious relations between Hutu and Tutsi, they explained. Later, this had been disturbed, and ethnic division became apparent. But the harmony had been artificial, and ethnic conflict had always existed under the surface; it was only because they were "blind" that they could not see ethnic differences. The conflict became open either because the Hutu themselves became more mature and opened their eyes or because the Tutsi revealed their true intentions in specific historic moments and "killed the Hutu openly." The Tutsi, they claimed, had known all along, and their apparent friendship had been false. In fact, many Hutu claim that they prefer Tutsi violence because it is more honest than the deceptive, superficial friendship that the Tutsi used to offer before things "became open."

These theories about Tutsi hatching plots behind the scenes draw on a long history of ethnic stereotypes in the Great Lakes region, that claim that Tutsi are cunning, lazy, arrogant, intelligent and secretive. Hutu, on the other hand, are supposed to be happy-go-lucky natives, not very intellectually minded but honest and hard-working. As opposed to the Tutsi, the Hutu do not hide their emotions but get angry and then forget and forgive (Maquet 1961; Malkki 1995; Turner 2001). These stereotypes can be traced back to the early colonialists and missionaries who classified the population into races and created the "Hamitic thesis" (Gahama 1983; Prunier 1995; Mamdani 2001).

While academic scholarship may see ethnicity as a construct, Hutu refugees understand nonethnic national unity as a construct that hides a deeper "reality"—the reality of ethnicity. When they become aware of the reality, there is a strong sense of having been deceived and betrayed by the Tutsi who "knew" all these years while pretending to be friends. In this manner, the real Tutsi is the stereotypical other, while the false one is the one pretending to be your friendly neighbor. His treason consists less in wanting to kill the Hutu and more in pretending to be friends in the first place. However, there is a further twist to the deception of the Tutsi in these Hutu narratives. For while the friendly Tutsi schoolmate might be concealing his true identity and pretending to be a friend, his true identity is difficult to define in itself. What is it exactly that the Tutsi is hiding? Who is it behind the friendly mask? It appears that the act of concealment is the most defining characteristic of the Tutsi; he is deceptive at the core, according to the Hutu refugees.

The concept of deception is central in a forceful article by Arjun Appadurai on the brutality of ethnic violence in the era of globalization (1998). He argues that the body of the ethnic other can be deceptive. Thus, Tutsi do not always have long noses, and Hutu do not always have thick shins: "In a word, real bodies in history betray the cosmologies that they are meant to encode. So the ethnic body, both of the victim and the killer, is itself potentially deceptive" (1998; 232).

In other words, the Tutsi schoolmate who appeared to be just another little boy from the village (perhaps even with a flat nose) was deceiving his Hutu friends by hiding his true identity. The sense of betrayal and uncertainty about the other pushes people to commit horrific acts of what Appadurai terms "vivisectionist violence" against neighbors and old friends. One tries to stabilize the body of the ethnic other through these macabre acts of unmasking the specific body in order to find the true ethnic body. Appadurai is, in other words, explaining how individuals come to terms with the incongruence between individual experiences of the specific members of the other ethnic group and larger ideological constructs about the true nature of the other—hence, his expression elsewhere of "ethnic implosion" (1996). When violence occurs—at the moment of a larger event in society—both Hutu and Tutsi reveal their true, ethnic identities. On the one hand, they are betraying their previous identities as friends and neighbors; on the other hand, they are revealing their true colors—and the deceptiveness of their previous apparent identities. We might take the argument a step further. In Appadurai's view, the individual is deceptive while ethnic categories are stable. According to the categories that Appadurai refers to—drawing on Liisa Malkki's work among Burundian Hutu refugees in the 1980s (1995)—Tutsi are tall and slim and have long noses, while Tutsi in real life may, in fact, be short and stocky with flat noses. Today, however, Hutu have a much more ambiguous knowledge of Tutsi than when Malkki did fieldwork and would not categorically define them according to such "body maps" (Turner 2001, 2005). Rather, they would define Tutsi by their deceptiveness. Seeing as Tutsi look the same, speak the same language, and live in the same places as the Hutu, the only way of defining them is by their ability to lie and deceive. By defining Tutsi as inherently deceptive, any Tutsi who acts like a Hutu or who acts friendly is proving his deceptiveness and hence his existence as an ethnic category. In this sense, ethnic categories become tautological, self-fulfilling, and impossible to disprove. Rather than look for the real Tutsi beneath the skin of the individual, as Appadurai claims, the Hutu are trying to pinpoint the deceptiveness of sociality in general. Vivisectionist violence becomes an impossible task of exposing deceit.

Large-scale ethnic violence damages trust and results in lack of faith in others and in society at large. It introduces deception and treachery in sociality, when one no longer can trust one's intimates and no longer trust their identity, and results in doubt about the very appearance of things. What if things are something else than they appear to be? What if they have a secret other side? Achille Mbembe argues that in Africa "everything almost always conceals something else" (2001, 148). One cannot take anything at face value because inherent in everything that is said is its opposite: the unsaid, the secret. Everything has its double, and this secret, invisible, and unspeakable double is just as important as the visible world in determining the fate of things. Hence, the invisible is not simply the opposite of the visible. "The invisible was in the visible and vice versa," Mbembe asserts (145). The spirit world might be invisible, but it is not distinct as such; it is a part of everything. In other words, we can never trust what we see or hear. Since we can never know what is unseen and unheard, this fear of the invisible, secret side of society is expressed in the fear of betrayal. Betrayal might be avoided through knowledge, but a certain amount of doubt about sociality will always remain; by defining Tutsi as deceptive and treacherous, the doubt about society is projected onto the Tutsi. Tutsi secrets incarnate the unknown side of sociality and allow Hutu to try to come to terms with the dark sides of intimate relations.

Turncoats Betraying Themselves

Defining ethnicity in the Great Lakes has proven very difficult since Hutu and Tutsi share the same language, religion, and culture and live in the same places. However, in precolonial times, Tutsi tended to belong to the ruling elite, while Hutu predominantly were peasants. Although this was only a tendency, and scholars are keen to point out the fluidity of these categories, especially in Burundi, which in pre-colonial times was less hierarchic and centralized than in Rwanda.[8] There were Hutu who had large herds of cattle and Tutsi who had none, and although they were rare, even some chiefs were Hutu—until the Belgian administrative reforms in the 1930s put an end to this (Gahama 1983, Lemarchand 1996). A wealthy and powerful Hutu could even change his ethnicity and officially become a Tutsi through the ritual of *kwihuture*. In this sense, an ethnic category—by definition, an intrinsic categorization—is made to fit a sociopolitical reality. The social fact that some Hutu would fit the sociopolitical characteristics of Tutsiness may be used as proof that they are indeed not racial/ethnic categories (as has been emphasized by scholars and politicians in the region). However, the opposite also happened, as the process of *kwihuture* stabilized the ethnic system, adjusting the categories to reality and validating rules of inherent ethnic qualities. This practice recreates social order but also creates its own excess in the process. For while the ceremony assures that the ethnic system once again fits reality at one level, it also undermines it at another. Despite the ritual, everyone knows that the new Tutsi was actually born a Hutu. However, this knowledge cannot be expressed in public due to the publicly sanctified metamorphosis from Hutu to Tutsi. It remains a public secret (Taussig 1999) that creates a fundamental doubt about the ethnic identity of others.[9] Are they what they appear to be, are they what they officially are said to be, or are they what they initially were? So, although *kwihuture* is celebrated in academia as marking the flexibility of ethnicity and used to counter primordialist explanations, it seems to be disquieting for many Hutu, not only because it spreads doubt about identities but also because these Hutu are, in fact, traitors of their own ethnicity. Although *kwihuture* is no longer practiced, the theme of Hutu becoming like Tutsi is still prevalent among the Hutu.

In my conversations with Burundian Hutu, the theme of Hutu wanting to be like Tutsi emerges again and again. It always focuses on the Hutu elite—whether political or economic—who can afford a lifestyle like the Tutsi and, therefore, forget their own Hutu origins, which are based on being the salt of the earth. Hutu are meant to be the underdogs, and suffering is a major part of their identity (Malkki 1995; Turner 2001). According to such Hutu discourse, once an individual Hutu is given the opportunity to become wealthy or to be allowed into the inner circles of power, he is tempted to forget his humble background and, hence, his Hutuness. With ethnicity corresponding to class to some degree in the Great Lakes region, social mobility gets tangled up in issues of ethnicity, and Hutu who climb the social ladder are vulnerable to accusations of ethnic treachery. This reflects a central dilemma in Hutu ideology that concerns the role of the elite. On the one hand, the Hutu acknowledge the need to become educated and powerful in order to compete with the Tutsi and not always to be deceived by them. On the other hand, the Hutu risk loosing their Hutu identity as the downtrodden, suffering masses in the process. Once they get the knowledge and the power, they gradually get the habits of the Tutsi as well. Power corrupts. So, the balancing act, according to Hutu traitor narratives, consists in accumulating "intelligence" in order to gain access to the "Tutsi secrets" of power (Turner 2005) without loosing one's true Hutu identity.

In an unpublished book called "The Persecution of the Hutus of Burundi," Remy Gahutu, founder of the first Hutu party in exile, explores how the autochthonous Hutu lost the land that was rightfully theirs to the Tutsi invaders. Throughout his analysis of the postcolonial regimes, Gahutu focuses on the use of secrets and lies, covering up the Tutsi's "customary cruelty" (Gahutu, n.d.,) and hiding the true intentions of the regime.[10] However, he also puts the blame on the Hutu themselves. The problem, he claims, is the Hutu who are tempted to become like the Tutsi. They are individuals who choose to abandon their ethnic community for reasons of personal gain. When Hutu, for personal reasons and due to the inferiority complex of the underdog, choose to turn their backs on their ethnicity, the Hutu people can never succeed because they lose their most wealthy and educated individuals. These turncoats are betraying not only the Hutu cause but also their true Hutu identity and ultimately themselves. They will never be happy as long as they deny their authentic identity, he claims. When politicians on both sides join peace talks and decide to negotiate a power-sharing deal with their opponents, they are frequently accused of belonging to this category of traitors, of preferring the short-term benefits (the Mercedes Benz) to the long-term struggle. Rather than struggle to topple Tutsi power and rather than endure the suffering of their Hutu compatriots, they take the easy way out and think of themselves before the group. The issue of individual politicians' defecting and siding with the enemy is a recurring theme and central to Burundians' understanding of the political field. These rumors have always been around but became very evident during the precarious period when Burundi went from full-scale, uncompromising civil war between the Tutsi-dominated government army and various Hutu rebel movements to peace negotiations and power sharing in a transitional regime. It was widely held by the Burundians whom I have interviewed in Burundi and the diaspora that new leaders emerged and new factions of parties were created when individuals wanted a slice of the peace cake. So if the main faction of a rebel group rejected the Arusha Peace Accords, another faction would emerge and agree to them.

To understand this complex process of factionalism, Burundians would most often see the leaders of the new factions as traitors. Being tempted by the big houses, the Mercedes, and the power, they split the party and sign accords with the enemy. They are similar to the turncoats who seek individual fortune by betraying their own group. In a sense, they are perceived to be politically weak and are the subjects of public ridicule. Such traitors are, however, not completely harmless, as it is believed their their weakness—their desire to take the shortcuts without paying the price of fighting—can harm the movement. By bargaining with the Tutsi, they are jeopardizing Hutu unity and, hence, Hutu strength. I argued earlier that an individual can be perceived as treacherous because he or she might look or behave like a friend while secretly harboring loyalties to a hostile ethnic other. In the case of Hutu who sell out in order to gain power and prestige and join the ranks of the Tutsi, a similar logic is at play, although in an inverse manner. They are also pretending to be something else than they really are. But rather than betraying their neighbor or schoolmate from the other ethnic group, they are betraying their own ethnic group—and ultimately themselves. While the former kind of betrayal is a betrayal of intimate trust, based on concrete relationships, the latter is a public and general betrayal of group loyalty. The stories about Hutu turncoats reveal another imagination of sociality: the sociality of common ethnicity that is believed to be more true and profound than the lived sociality of neighbors, classmates, or even spouses. This lived sociality is always deceptive and treacherous.

Tutsi Women, Temptation, and Deception

One of the strongest symbols of Hutu who lack pride in their own ethnicity and try to become like the Tutsi is Hutu men who marry Tutsi women. According to such narratives, the problem with marrying Tutsi women is that these women never lose their loyalty to the Tutsi. So although these elite Hutu believe that they are powerful and have become like the Tutsi, they are seen to be deceiving themselves. While discussing politics with some of the clandestine Hutu refugees in Nairobi in May 2004, I was told how wealthy Hutu like to marry the beautiful and prestigious Tutsi women. The problem is, they said, that these women will have some of their children with a Tutsi—"even their own brother," one of them added, with a mixture of disgust and glee. In this way, the wealthy Hutu who marries a Tutsi ends up paying for the education and upbringing of Tutsi offspring. At some point, the mother tells her Tutsi children who they really are and treats them better than the other mixed-blood siblings. Furthermore, in the case of conflict, like in 1993, these wives side with the Tutsi. They might hide their husband in the house, but when the Tutsi militias arrive, they will loudly proclaim that they do not know his whereabouts, while silently pointing toward his hiding place. The act of loudly proclaiming to be loyal to her husband while silently betraying him and siding with her coethnics vividly illustrates the perception of open and hidden identities. The hidden ones are the most important in critical events.

Such narratives about Hutu men marrying Tutsi women convey the sense that the most intimate relations are perceived also to be the most dangerous. The closer you allow someone to get to you, the more exposed and vulnerable you are. They express deep-seated fears of betrayal within the family and of not knowing the real identity of your kin. As Peter Geschiere has observed, there is a dark side of kinship that is expressed in the frightening realization that there is jealousy and aggression in the family where there should, officially, be love and solidarity (1997, 212). While kinship is based on loyalty and trust, it is also within the family that we are most vulnerable and most exposed to betrayal. Likewise, Veena Das reminds us that we must not only look at "true kinship" but also at "a repudiation of 'false kinship', through which previous intimacies between communities are disavowed" (1998a, 111). The metaphors of true and false kinship "create intense feelings of love and hate, fidelity and betrayal" (ibid.). In other words, kinship brings us together but is always destabilized by the fear that it is false. One cannot live without the intimacy of the family, even though one fears the deadly dangers that it harbors (Geschiere 1997, 212).

While the Hutu men who marry Tutsi women are perceived to be turning their backs on their Hutu identity, they are paradoxically reaffirming their Hutuness because their gullibility, a stereotypical Hutu trait, allows them to be deceived in this manner. They are blinded by power and wealth, but first and foremost by the seductive beauty of the Tutsi women, a superficial beauty that only the most naive Hutu will be deceived by. The apparent beauty of the Tutsi women is a widespread stereotype, but most Hutu men with whom I have spoken reject its truth and claim that they are not more beautiful than Hutu women. Such statements are made to confirm their own maturity and prove that they are not naive enough to be lured by the "Tutsi belles." In informal conversations, however, other images of the Tutsi women emerge, especially the stories about the Hutu elite marrying Tutsi women that draw on—and hence reproduce—perceptions of Tutsi beauty. "Tutsified" Hutu are shown to be the most naive while true Hutu can see through the fraud and deceit of the Tutsi femmes fatales. As in the case of *kwihuture*, the Hutu men apparently (that is to say, at the level of appearance) achieve higher status by marrying Tutsi women, but in the case of violent events, true identities surface, and the Tutsi wives turn against their naïve Hutu husbands; thus, the turncoats end up more vulnerable than the common Hutu who remained true to their identity.

The story of Tutsi women having children through extramarital relations with Tutsi men is significant in several manners. It testifies to the assumed deceitful character of the Tutsi, and it draws on an archetypal narrative about the parasitic nature of the other. Following the logic of witchcraft accusations (Geschiere 1997; Apter 1999; Comaroff and Comaroff 1999; Bastian 2003), body part rumors (Scheper-Hughes 1996; Campion-Vincent 1997; White 1997), and urban legend (Fine 1986), the other is assumed to gain strength by stealing something from "us," usually something very intimate and linked to the body. In Burundi, the Hutu claim that the Tutsi "eat our sweat," signifying that they become wealthy and powerful from Hutu labor. Similarly, stories circulate in Burundi and Rwanda that the *mwami* (king) used Hutu testicles to adorn the royal drum, an instrument that contributed to his sacred power. I was told in the refugee camps in Tanzania that in 1993, when Paul Kagame was still the leader of the Tutsi rebel group, the Rwandan Patriotic Front (RPF), he needed the brain and testicles of a Hutu president in order to make a magic charm that could help him on the battlefield. Consequently, he plotted with Tutsi officers in Burundi to abduct and kill Burundi's president, Melchior Ndadaye, in October 1993. In these cases, the "other" takes reproduction and the ability to think from "us" in order to defeat us. So when the Hutu husband and father brings up and feeds Tutsi offspring, like cuckoos they squeeze the other birds out of the nest, effectively preventing the Hutu elite from reproducing—and hence from threatening Tutsi sovereignty.[11] The nuclear family, ideally the cradle of trust and reproduction, has its dark side, haunted by betrayal.

The behavior of the Tutsi wives testifies, according to these narratives, to the moral decay of the Tutsi and the lengths to which they will go to stay in power. It is a common theme in Burundi and Rwanda that they use their women like prostitutes to seduce Hutu, Belgian soldiers, and even Bill Clinton in order to remain in power.[12] Their desire for power is so strong that they are ready to sacrifice their sisters and daughters, it appears. However, there is also a sense in these narratives that the women are not simply sacrificed and that they actually take perverse enjoyment in these morally deviant political plots. In the interview with young Hutu men in Nairobi, the storyteller finds the fact that they even have sex with their brothers morally repulsive but also fascinating. The other is seen to have unbridled, excessive enjoyment, while "we" know how to moderate ourselves. In Slavoj Žižek's words, "We always impute to the 'other' an excessive enjoyment; s/he wants to steal our enjoyment . . . and/or has access to some secret, perverse enjoyment" (1990, 53–54). Although we dislike the surplus and excess in the way the other organizes enjoyment, a nagging doubt lingers whether the other might actually be enjoying more than we—and that we are wrong and he is right. Whereas this is a general predicament of nationalist ideology, as Žižek contends, I argue that it has specific meaning in relation to traitors. The traitor is excessive by nature because he by definition transgresses the moral, normative boundaries of society and does as he pleases. He follows his own desires and takes pleasure in doing so. According to this discourse, it is not only the Tutsi who take pleasure in seducing Hutu and others with their beautiful women; Hutu men who marry Tutsi—or in other ways strive for personal power and prestige among the Tutsi—have access to enjoyment that is out of bonds for the average Hutu. That is why narratives about traitors are so keen to demonstrate how they will be punished for their actions in the end.

The elite Hutu are at once the only hope for Hutu progress and liberation—being able to discover and dismantle the Tutsi secrets (Turner 2005)—while at the same time being at risk of becoming contaminated by the Tutsi. But even their attempts at personal gain fail because the Tutsi never truly accept them and always side with fellow Tutsi in critical situations. The position of the elite is, in other words, potentially the position of the traitor, it is argued, since Hutu are prevented from ever gaining power and wealth unless they give up their Hutuness.

Conclusion

This chapter has illustrated that ethnicity in Burundi is ambiguous and elusive and seems to be able to change from one moment to another.

While it might not be important to define ethnic categories in times of peace, it becomes an urgent necessity during massive violence. The split-second decision whether someone is Hutu or Tutsi, taken by drunken Hutu militias manning roadblocks or by vigilante Tutsi youth keeping the streets of the capital "clean," can be fatal. There is no in-between in these situations. For these reasons, many Burundians see the ethnic conflict in terms of being closed or open. In their eyes, the conflict is always there, but at times it is latent under the surface, while at other times it surfaces and becomes open. Although the conflict becomes more violent when open, it also becomes more honest because this is when individuals show their true intentions. When the individual changes identity from the friendly neighbor and becomes the ethnic other, he betrays, in a sense, these neighbors who believed that he was a friend they could trust. But, in fact, it is claimed, he was more of a traitor before because he was pretending to be what he was not: a friend. Only when the conflict becomes open does he reveal his true loyalty, according to these narratives. The question and insecurity linger on both sides, however, how much he knew all along. Was he deliberately hiding his true identity, as the Tutsi children were assumed to be, or was he surprised by it himself? These traitors remove all faith in one's intimates and one's personal experiences and produce a fundamental instability and fragility of sociality.

The Hutu elite play a particularly ambiguous role in Burundi: positioned as the potential traitor due to their ability to transgress ethnic borders. Hutu who become wealthy and powerful are easily accused of deceiving their ethnic brothers and, ultimately, themselves because they transgress the boundaries of ethnic belonging. Meanwhile, their alleged treason to their group spurs debates about the boundaries of belonging in more qualitative terms. In recounting the stories about businessmen and politicians who have married Tutsi women, the Hutu are able to debate what it means to be truly Hutu. The elusive nature of ethnicity in Burundi, where individuals can slip from one category to another, calls for constant boundary making and monitoring. The twist to these stories is that, although the turncoats apparently slip into another ethnic skin, in a modern version of the *kwihuture* ritual, they will never escape their true identity. There is a price to be paid for trying to slip from one ethnic category to another. The past will catch up with these traitors because the Tutsi will always remember who they really are. A common theme in the above-mentioned narratives is that the truth is exposed in critical, violent events. This is when the Tutsi wives and their Tutsi children shift loyalty and uncover their true identity by turning against the Hutu husband/father. According to Hutu ideology, the temptations of power, beauty, and wealth corrupt the minds of the gullible Hutu, making the dream of Hutu power a self-defeating illusion. In other words, we see different kinds of narratives about traitors in Burundi's elusive ethnic landscape. On the one hand, we see the traitor who pretends to be nonethnic but who maintains ethnic loyalties deep down and who activates these loyalties in times of crisis. On the other hand, we find the traitor who betrays his ethnic group and tries to become something else. In both cases, however, ethnicity is seen as the most profound of identities, although both examples produce an imagination of an equally slippery identity and an equally deceptive and deceitful sociality.

Chapter 6
In Praise of Traitors: Intimacy, Betrayal, and the Sri Lankan Tamil Community

Sharika Thiranagama

In a 2006 Canadian Sri Lankan Tamil pamphlet called *Thurohi* (Traitor), the author tells his diasporic audience, "many of us fled and came to this country. Why? Our life's duty is to survive. *But what is our historical duty? To be traitors*" (Jeeva 2006, 3; emphasis added).[1] The war between the Sri Lankan state and the separatist Liberation Tigers of Tamil Eelam (LTTE) drew in Sri Lanka's three largest ethnic groups: the majority Sinhalese, the minority Sri Lankan Tamils, and Sri Lankan Muslims; the latter, while war-affected, were not active in the conflict. The primary battlefields and areas of LTTE control were northern and eastern Sri Lanka. In May 2009 the war came to a bloody close in a stand-off with the Sri Lankan Army and the death of LTTE leader Velupillai Prabhakaran and most senior leadership. This end came long after the writing of this chapter and is not its subject. But it is now even more urgent to examine the consequences of the war and LTTE culture of terror on Tamil society and political culture. I examine how in this war treachery came to be seen as *the* ultimate ethical act. I discuss how individuals in a community of potential traitors come to reformulate ideas of intimacy and ways to fashion meaningful social and political roles in the heart of terror.

"The traitor is more dishonorable than the enemy," Prabhakaran announced in his annual Heroes Day speech.[2] The enemy so named is the "Sinhalese" Sri Lankan government. That the Tamil traitor is considered more abhorrent than the enemy reveals that the LTTE was fighting a war on two fronts, one against an external enemy, the other against an internal foe, in an effort to define a people and a place, a task that brooks no opposition and necessitates frequent cleansing. The traitor had become the central figure by which the LTTE poses questions of community, loyalty, and Tamilness.

Tamils had come to fear being marked as traitors. Treasonous acts were ever-expanding, from open political action to being seen talking or transacting with the Sri Lankan Army to refusing to pay LTTE taxes. The categorization of treason remained stable only to those to whom one was considered treasonous: the LTTE. Thousands had been arrested and fined, and many killed. The reason given for almost all extrajudicial killings in the LTTE-controlled north and east was the needful cleansing of traitors. This heightened following the split of the LTTE into two factions, both claiming that those who support the others are traitors, further exacerbating the surveillance and violence enacted against Tamils. This situation has received little attention in academic work (including my own), which has concentrated on the interethnic and countrywide tensions of the civil war. The actions of the LTTE toward its own population, for whom it promised liberation and a Tamil homeland (Tamil Eelam) have remained "our secret," one shared among Tamils, a story about the relationship between not the self and the other but the self and "ourselves".

This chapter draws from research undertaken with those who were labeled traitors, my own fieldwork among Tamils in Sri Lanka, and a new dissident consciousness epitomized in pamphlets, plays, and dissident poetry that assert that to be a traitor is the only way to occupy a position that can speak about "our secret," the LTTE. I attempt to set some of the groundwork for a good consideration of treason within the specific political context of Sri Lanka, as well as a more general framework for understanding why it is possible to make some lives forfeit merely by labeling them traitor. I argue that the potency, possibility, and abhorrence of treason are produced by our senses of intimacy with others and our fears that intimacy may be brittle and fragile.

The first section gives a detailed introduction to the LTTE and its rise to power. I then move, in the second section, to discuss the structural positioning of "the traitor" and the connection between senses of intimacy and the moral abhorrence of treason. I pose this within a Sri Lankan context, where I disentangle the LTTE's "fear of traitors" from civilian "fear of betrayal"—being betrayed by each other to the LTTE as traitors. Both play with two different senses of the intimate. The first notion takes from Herzfeld's (1997) suggestion that a sense of "cultural intimacy" exists among those who share codes, practices, language, and a sense of "rueful self-recognition." The second is the sense of closeness we feel for intimates, those we live, socialize, and work with. I suggest, first, that the LTTE was able to exert power over Tamils because it operated from within the community and within a sense of the intimate.

However, I then examine how intimacy becomes constantly reformulated as people search for ways of being social with each other. Finally, I conclude by pointing to the ways in which those who have been labeled traitors come to acknowledge and make treason the grounds by which they find a way of speaking about Tamil politics, refusing, reversing, and, finally, as with Jeeva above, harnessing the power of treason as needful diagnostic.

A Culture of Political Cleansing

The LTTE was focused in both real and symbolic senses on its leader Vellupillai Prabhakaran. This has become even more evident in their current collapse following his death. The military wings included a conventional land and artillery army, a navy (the Sea Tigers), intelligence wings, and special suicide squads (the Black Tigers).[3] Its primary features were consistent: a pyramidal structure, the use of suicide bombings and cyanide capsules, an extensive intelligence network, and a prioritization of eliminating traitors within the Tamil community, and, thus, its reliance on fear and intimidation to control Tamil politics. Fear of its intelligence network, divided into military and internal intelligence, was widespread. Internal intelligence was involved in surveillance, incarceration, and elimination of both LTTE cadres and the general population. Intelligence cadres both infiltrate and mobilize others to inform on their neighbors, kin, and fellow cadres. The LTTE is also marked by its excessive fetishization of its own agency—marking distinctions through constant use of flags, uniforms, its own law code and judiciary, a continuous stream of propaganda, relentless pursuit of a party line, and not least its ritualization of the Tamil calendrical year through public events and celebrations devoted to its "martyrs."

Cadres were both voluntarily and forcibly recruited. From the 1990s, forced recruitment rose, with the LTTE particularly focused on recruiting children. Its extensive recruitment and use of child soldiers, the infamous "baby brigades" as it names them, have been heavily criticized.[4] The 2002 ceasefire did not halt such recruitment; families in eastern Sri Lanka were told that each family should contribute one child to the LTTE. This large-scale conscription, whether voluntary or forced, means that most families have a connection to or a family member in the LTTE. Uniformed cadres are clearly separated from the civilian population, renamed, and their loyalties reoriented toward the movement.

However, the LTTE also possesses a more civilian face. The LTTE is brother, sister, son, cousin, and the uniformed young men and women patrolling the area or demanding taxes from each Tamil in his or her house. Clearly distinguishing the LTTE is complex, given its intimate ties within Tamil families. Moreover, the LTTE also strove to militarize civilian space in other ways. It maintained a loose network of long-term and short-term loyalties and informers who offer information for gain or as a result of coercion. Civilians caught in the struggle for survival existed in a state of constant complicity. These two features meant that the intimacy of the LTTE presence among the civilian population has led to a situation where networks of trust were increasingly shrinking, while fear of other Tamils increases. Other Tamils may be informers ready to denounce, or they may be LTTE cadres in civilian gear. Later sections of this chapter deal with the effects of LTTE power within civilian life. Here, I offer a brief history of the rise of the LTTE and the ways in which the pursuit of treason became embedded in Tamil nationalism

The Rise of the LTTE

Sri Lanka's postcolonial history of state and minority relations has been extensively documented, so I will be brief here. Continued anti-Tamil state discrimination and the inability of the Tamil parliamentary parties, such as the Tamil United Liberation Front (TULF), to resolve discrimination led to the creation of many small Tamil militant groups in the 1970s. Militants called for the creation of a separate Tamil homeland comprising the Tamil majority areas of the north and east. Popular support for militancy increased as a series of anti-Tamil riots in 1977 and 1983—following earlier anti-Tamil riots in 1956, 1958, and 1971—pushed Tamil minorities to an impasse. After the 1983 riots, recruitment to the militant groups swelled into the thousands, and the Indians took a more central role in arming and training militant groups (Krishna 1999). The secretive, highly disciplined, and militarily effective LTTE emerged as the self declared "sole representative of the Tamil people" in 1986, when it proscribed or absorbed other militant groups (such as the Tamil Eelam Liberation Organization, TELO, and the Eelam People's Revolutionary Liberation Front, EPRLF) and families associated with them in a year of intense fratricidal conflict. They labeled militants from the other groups and their families, not freedom fighters, but "traitors to the Tamil nation." The subsequent alliance of these other militant groups with Indian rule in the north (1987–90) and attendant misrule also soured the reputation of these groups among the civilian population. The continuing excessive violence of the Sri Lanka Army ensured that the LTTE is for many Tamils the lesser "evil"—less a politics of popular support and more a politics of popular desperation and brinkmanship.

The Indian Peace Keeping Force (IPKF) entered Sri Lanka in 1987 to broker and maintain a settlement; however, relations between the IPKF and the LTTE broke down into a bloody war. In 1990, the IPKF withdrew, and soon after, peace talks between the Sri Lankan government and the LTTE collapsed into Eelam War II. The LTTE began to set up aspects of a parallel state in the northern and eastern areas under their control, including a judiciary, police force, and taxation system.[5] In 1995, after the Sri Lankan army takeover of northern Jaffna, the LTTE moved its capital to the Vanni region in north-central Sri Lanka and remains in informal control of much of the north and east. In 2009, the Sri Lankan army renewed its military campaign against the LTTE, pushing it into an ever shrinking northeastern coastal strip. The LTTE forced around 300,000 civilians to march with them as human shields. This precipitated an immense humanitarian crisis, with the Sri Lankan army continuously shelling a small area where civilians were crammed in temporary shelters and bunkers, and the LTTE forcibly conscripting civilians and shooting any who tried to escape. In May 2009, in the final battle, LTTE leader Prabhakaran was killed under still mysterious circumstances and the senior leadership of the LTTE decimated by the Sri Lankan Army. While the war is over, the Sri Lankan government has indefinitely interned in camps the 300,000 or so Tamil civilians from the war zones for ''security clearance,'' leaving the future for reconciliation, and the ending of this agony for those already traumatized Tamils, uncertain.

Tamil Militancy and Violence

The centrality of the traitor to LTTE demonstrations of its sovereignty has to be put in the context of a larger strand of Tamil nationalism that legitimated political killings. For Tamil nationalism, the creation of Tamil Eelam necessitated both internal and external processes: the Sinhalese state had to be opposed as an enemy of Tamils, and Sri Lankan Tamils had to be fashioned into new political subjects, fit residents of a potential Tamil Eelam/homeland. Legitimizations of political killings became normalized in militant movements and accepted within Tamil nationalist discourse, evident in the traitor killings from 1975 onward and internal purges within all militant movements.

The first public killing of a traitor was the July 1975 assassination of Alfred Duraippah, the mayor of Jaffna. One of the three assassins was a young Prabhakaran, the LTTE leader. Duraippah was a highly popular politician, and he attracted great resentment from the Tamil nationalist parliamentary parties (the Federal Party). Further, Duraippah had allied himself with the Sri Lankan national party, the Sri Lanka Freedom Party (SLFP). His assassination was celebrated jubilantly by Tamil politicians, militants, and militant sympathizers, although reputedly thousands of ordinary Jaffna Tamils attended his funeral. Many of the ex-militants from all parties that I interviewed told me quite unequivocally that, at the time of the murder, they had supported and celebrated the killing. Kugamoorthy, a former TELO cadre, now in his forties and resident in London, told me,

> My feeling at that time was that it was a good thing. He was a traitor and needed to be eliminated. . . . the TULF [formerly the Federal Party] . . . bear a responsibility for such a culture of violence. They didn't shoot but they talked . . . on their platform about how one day Duraippah would die and he was a Tamil traitor. . . . We rejoiced. . . . We thought, however young we were then, that one should shoot the enemy. . . . We didn't understand where this would bring us.

While Prabhakaran claimed responsibility for the killing, it was undoubtedly an act that found favor across the Tamil nationalist spectrum. Duraippah's killing was the first in the beginning of high profile murders of individuals accused of collaborating with the government and extending by the mid-1980s also to the (LTTE-led) execution of criminals.[6] Killings were routinized and internalized within the movements. It soon became clear that all the Tamil militant movements were internally purging their cadres and eliminating dissent. By 1985, the People's Liberation Organization of Tamil Eelam (PLOTE) and TELO began to implode with brutal internal killings and factional fights. Civilians had begun to talk about "the boys" killing "boys" (Swamy 2003; Hoole et al. 1990). Any sign of dissent was immediately stamped down and named as treason.

Thus, to some extent, the cleansing of traitors—*Thurohi olippu*—as a political practice could be described as nascent within all the militant structures and embedded within a larger Tamil nationalist discourse. When I interviewed ex-militants from the other Tamil militant movements, many used their present designation by the LTTE as traitors to reflect back on this past, treason providing a lens by which the violence of the past as well as their own activism and desire to fight for Tamil rights could be understood. Nonetheless, identifying treason was undoubtedly shaped by the LTTE into its own signature to indicate that no collaboration or ambiguity would be tolerated in the Tamil national consciousness that had to be formed to create the new Tamil Eelam. The LTTE was also particularly intolerant of internal dissent given its prioritization of military discipline and obedience. Vijitharan, who had been a member of the LTTE from the ages fifteen to eighteen, told me in 1983,

> Before you did something you couldn't ask why. . . . If I was told to kill you, I would kill you. After that I can come and ask why I was meant to shoot you. . . . The answer was, "Do what Prabhakaran tells you and remain quiet." . . . We

were soldiers and we had to do what we were told. . . . In the LTTE, if you are told to kill someone, you kill them. That is their structure and strength.

When he was undergoing training in India, Vijitharan began to notice cadres going missing from the training camps:

One night in our camp, they came and took someone from our batch away, . . . named him a traitor and shot him. . . . At that time, I began to hear stories about Pottu Amman [the LTTE intelligence chief], that he had a green boat on which he used to take people away, cut them up, and throw them into the sea, people who wanted to go back.[7]

Further, the LTTE attack on other Tamil militant groups transformed political killings and the attribution of treason to new levels. When the LTTE became the sole Tamil power, it identified itself as the only route to an ultimate good, Tamil Eelam. Thereby it was able to define treason, first, as that which was against the LTTE and, second, that opposing the LTTE was the same as treason against one's own self-determination and national homeland. All forms of political action such as human rights activism not allied with the LTTE were described as treasonous. This fixing is crucial as Tamil dissidents also see treason as opposition to the LTTE.

Demonstrations of the "rightful" elimination of traitors provided the means by which everyday policing was legitimated and political sovereignty claimed.[8] Governance of Tamil areas converted everyday coercion and incarceration into acts against "traitors." After 1990, the LTTE consolidated its penitentiary structures. Thevan, a former government clerk and an EPRLF supporter, was arrested and tortured in one of the LTTE's largest traitor prisons. Given his qualifications, he was made by the LTTE guards to record the names and "treasonous deeds" of those imprisoned. He reckoned the count of those in the prison was at around 3,000 and the human rights group University Teachers for Human Rights–Jaffna (UTHR-J) estimates the total imprisoned to be around 4,000 in 1992.[9] Among those imprisoned were those who had failed to pay taxes; criticized the LTTE, or were businessmen, civilian activists, relatives of other traitors, militants from other movements, and LTTE cadres.[10] These numbers give some idea of the immensity and ordinariness of the practice of detaining traitors, either permanently or temporarily, as the supracrime under which various other crimes were subsumed. Treason evidently had a structural ability to convert and justify murder into necessary cleansing and rightful policing of boundaries. Traitor killing could somehow become accommodated as a necessary good. Why?

Making Lives Forfeit: The Dark Side of Intimacy

This chapter explores two related questions. First, why was the LTTE so concerned with the problem of treason? Second, why could extrajudicial killings of "traitors" be considered legitimate? The first question points to the tangled nature of sovereignty in Sri Lanka and the ways in which LTTE authority over Tamils was based on and asserted itself around ethnic intimacy between ruled and ruler. More generally, I suggest that any state-in-the-making is integrally concerned with the problems of traitors. The second question concerns the perceived abhorrent nature of treason: betrayal of the intimate by the intimate.

Baumann (1991) argues that modern states are characterized by a constant ordering and classifying, based on distinctions between "us friends" and "those enemies" who are not "us." The attempt to order, Bauman argues, has the task of preventing ambivalence but inevitably produces its own ambivalence, the suspicion of both that which it cannot name and make adequate to a name, all that is arbitrary, random and undecidable, which defies easy classification and separation. He positions the "intrusive" figure of the Simmellian stranger, who comes from somewhere "over there" into "here." The stranger is *neither* friend nor enemy and may even be *both*. Thus, by threatening the seeming neatness of the friend/enemy distinction, the stranger strikes at the very basis of social life and the possibility of sociation. Strangers are, Baumann argues (following Derrida), "undecidables," being

neither/nor . . . they militate against the either/or. . . . [T]heir underdetermination is their potency: because they are nothing, they may be all . . . .[O]ppositions enable knowledge and action; undecidables paralyse them. . . . [U]ndecidables brutally expose the artifice, the fragility, the sham of the most vital of separations. . . . [T]hey bring the outside into the inside, and poison the comfort of order with suspicion of chaos. (1991, 56)

Reversing Baumann, the traitor, I suggest, is an "undecidable," analogous though not identical to the stranger. If strangers disturb the distinctions between friends and enemies, traitors go even further: they disturb the fabric of intimacy between friends. They reveal that, in fact, those we were intimate with can also be "neither/nor" and betray us and, further, that this suspicion can be ever-present in social life.

In other words, traitors are distinct from enemies and strangers by virtue of being potentially ourselves, a betrayal from within. When I asked Tamils if Sinhalese or Muslims could be considered traitors, the answer was unequivocal—only Tamils could be traitors; Sinhalese and Muslims were instead *ethiri* (enemies). Ethnic lines drew the boundaries of treason; Muslims, though Tamil-speaking and sharing the north and east with Tamils, were nonetheless, by being a different ethnicity, also clearly differentiated.[11] The greatest betrayal comes from *within* the line that one has constructed between the "inside" and the "outside," the self and the other. However, the figure of the traitor is also simultaneously inside and outside the community.[12] The community itself is bounded through the definition of who can be considered a traitor and be continually expelled outside in order to "cleanse" society. This community is then unbound continually since, in necessitating expulsion, the traitor must thus be acknowledged to be inside all along, an inadmissible acknowledgment of disunity.

An important parallel to the prosecution and labeling of treason can be understood through studies of witchcraft accusations. Most show us that, characteristically, those who are accused are known to accusers and that witches are considered to emanate from "within" communities rather than outside (e.g., Briggs 2002). Geschiere (1997) in his study of witchcraft in Cameroon locates witchcraft at the heart of sociality, as the "dark side of kinship" (1997, 212). In Cameroon, the first search for the source of witchcraft is to look within the family and the house. This *djambe le njaw,* "witchcraft from inside the house," is considered the most terrifying because, for the Maka, those with whom one is intimate, by their knowledge, can inflict the most harm—"witches have a hold over their intimates" (45). The belief that witches devour their kin and offer them up is a further example of the link that witchcraft fundamentally originates from and tears at the heart of intimacy (40).

Geschiere argues that these discourses are rooted in the double-edged nature of kinship and intimacy. The family, which is ideally premised around trust, solidarity, and amity, is most often equally filled with jealously, inequality, conflict, and aggression. One's natural allies, necessary to survival, may covertly work against one:

[in Africa] the family remains the cornerstone of social life, and one cannot live without its intimacy. . . . [Y]et it is precisely this intimacy that harbors deadly dangers since it is the breeding ground of witchcraft. . . . [T]he continuing force of this discourse is that it expresses the permanent struggle of living in this dark threat from inside. (1997, 212)

Discourses on witchcraft come from the awareness that kinship and intimacy are powerful because they are double-edged. The greatest trust is placed in intimates because the greatest betrayals come from those with whom one is intimate, not from strangers. This question about trust, risk, and intimacy is existential because, as the Maka say, one has to find a way to "live with one's sorcerer" (Geschiere 1997, 42). Geschiere's work on the doubledness of kinship and intimacy illuminates, analogically if not directly, the peculiarity of the concept of treason and the fear of treachery. Treason too is seen as a betrayal of the intimate. Here, intimacy refers to, first, that of home and kin and, second, "cultural inti-macy," the idealized notion of one's ethnic group—that is, Tamil-ness—as a set of shared codes, language, practices, sentiments, and belonging (Herzfeld 1997).

Thus, I argue that the fear of and the power wielded by the traitor derives from something inherent to the way in which we understand sociality, the necessity and hidden fears of being intimate with others.[13] Specific political campaigns against traitors gain their moral legitimacy through their resonance with this twinning of trust and suspicion within social life. The killing of traitors is considered acceptable, and the lives of traitors can be considered forfeit in Sri Lanka and elsewhere because treason is seen to emanate from the intimate, cultural, and immediate. The betrayal *of* and *from* the intimate is considered logically and morally more reprehensible and fearful than the betrayal by outsiders. Treason is the ultimate transgression. There is an important distinction, however, between the intimacy of home and kin and that of ethnicity. They are often moral claims of different sorts, however much political groups attempt to make them align. Treason often opens up inherent conflicts between betrayal of one's family and that of one's ethnic group, as I dis-cuss in later sections. Moreover, the notion of ethnic intimacy has to be historicized here as a consequence of deepening supralocal ethnic iden-tification. While Tamils and Muslims, for example, share neighborhoods and the same language, one kind of intimacy, ethnic intimacy is com-pletely disavowed by both.

Interviewing those labeled as traitors by the LTTE made this clear: the stain of treason was related closely to the idea that treason was betraying one's own self as a Tamil. Enemies betray other people; traitors betray those who are like them. As Kugamoorthy explained to me,

Nobody would like to be called a traitor. . . . treachery is about betraying trust, betraying a cause, or betraying your people, your relations, your kin, your ethnic group. . . . You can have a feeling of being a Tamil. To not have that feeling can be seen as a betrayal. They [the LTTE] say "be a Tamil like this." . . . This is the essence of the LTTE victory. It has given this feeling to people . . . that they have to be "Tamil," they have to act "Tamil" and those that do not have this feeling in that way are traitors. When you forget this feeling of being Tamil, then this is the same as being a traitor.

George and Muttu, two ex-EPRLF brothers I interviewed in Toronto, were equally clear on the abhorrence of treason. The LTTE could excuse traitor killings, they explained, because "betraying your own peo-ple" was so terrible. Treason silenced questions about legitimacy. Saying that someone was a traitor, Muttu said, meant that no one questioned punishment. Thus, even among those I interviewed whose own lives had become forfeit, it was clear that treason and the traitor occupied a special place within moral categories. It was a category that put those who were labeled as such beyond the pale.

However, this does not fully explain why LTTE political practice was premised upon a search for traitors. A fear of traitors, those who may oppose the LTTE and thus disturb the seeming unity of the Tamil nation, was a genuine anxiety for the LTTE and the basis for its extensive surveillance network. LTTE power rested fundamentally on being acknowledged by Tamils as their legitimate rulers. It always feared that, without constant coercion and seduction, its Tamil population could potentially repudiate its claim to represent them and turn instead to the nonethnic enemy state to satisfy their aspirations. The LTTE did not have unchallenged territorial sovereignty. Northern and eastern Sri Lanka was a patchwork of crisscrossing and fragmented sovereignties, gray zones where the Sri Lankan state and the LTTE coexisted. Furthermore, these areas are not solely Tamil—Muslims and Sinhalese make up nearly two-thirds of the claimed eastern province. The LTTE controlled territories, but it was still a state-in-the-making. Tamil Eelam was identical with the war for Tamil Eelam. The LTTE was more afraid of ordinary Tamils—the source of their power and weakness—than of any Sinhalese soldier carrying a gun. A nationalism that *has not* become a nation-state—where certain territory could define friends and enemies—generates and eliminates not strangers (in fact, they welcome supporters who see the legitimacy of the cause) but traitors. This nationalism that has to create a territory and a people at the same time is, I suggest, continually disturbed by the fear of disunity. The power of unity must be built on demonstrating that treachery cannot be tolerated by showing its existence and elimination. Yet by doing this, the unity becomes more evidently fragile and less self-evident, and constant vigilance is needed. A never-ending search for traitors becomes, equally, an anxious base for unity.

Thus, any analysis of treason must see it as both a historical and politically specific phenomena and also explore the moral valence of treason or rather betrayal as a fear built into (however various and different) notions of intimacy. In the next section, I move to draw out how Sri Lankan Tamils in Sri Lanka attempted to live intimate lives in the shadow of treason.

Living in the Shadow of Treason

Even if treachery had become marked by the LTTE as that which was opposed to them, betrayal, however, is more democratic; the fear of betrayal paralyzed Sri Lankan Tamil society. Other Tamils, people tell you, may turn out to be LTTE; therefore, it is best to be constantly on one's guard. Furthermore, there are things that everyone knows and no one knows; dangerous knowledge if uttered makes one culpable to witnessing it. I was repeatedly told by Tamils, "there is no trust (*nambikkai*) among Tamils anymore"—the stock representation of civilian life in the north and east. The Tamil community had become solidified in opposition to the Sri Lankan state, which viewed all Tamils as potential terrorists. However, internal to this ethnic border was the dismemberment of networks of work and trust that had existed between families and within villages, as a result of pervasive LTTE presence. This can be described as "internal terror," both due to the operation of terror within the Tamil community and the internalization of the fear of terror by individuals.

Moreover, if the LTTE governed Tamils as if they were a community of potential traitors, then the traitor is for Tamils not "other" but a constantly potential self that has to be guarded against. In such a situation, how does one continue to be intimate with others in the shadow of treason? What are the ways in which, as trust shrinks, new forms or prostheses of intimacy come to be developed. This section tracks how those I interviewed attempted to ask this very question: what can the intimate possibly be in "this age of the traitor"? (Jeeva 2006).

Internalizing Terror

Fieldwork among Tamils, in Sri Lanka and Canada, was marked by fear and suspicion. I too became infected with fear for those I interviewed. In Toronto, walking fast with Vimaleswaran through labyrinthine walkways in a housing estate, trying to outpace two Tamil men who had stared at us too intently, I was breathing heavily and quickly, fear for him drilling through my head. I knew that this was probably coincidence, that nothing would happen to him, that they were going home or, like us, visiting some other Tamils. Still, I could not stop being afraid. Vimaleswaran walked more calmly and told me a parable. Taking security precautions, he said, was different from being afraid to live and speak openly. Carrying a torchlight and stick against a snake outside the house is not the same as being too scared to leave the house at night because there is a snake outside. With a quizzical look, he said "maybe they are afraid of us; maybe they think we are the LTTE and following them." I had to laugh. The men turned, and we walked on ahead and never saw them again. He had taught me another thing about the kind of terror that pervaded the Sri Lankan Tamil community. Those who I and others looked at wondering if they were really LTTE were looking at us and wondering if we were LTTE. This is what the phrase "there is no trust between Tamils anymore" means in the context it was uttered. Conversations between Tamils were governed by all kinds of procedures and questions subtly to ascertain political positions and whether the other person would turn out to be an LTTE informer.

These fears were equally high *within* the LTTE. Ranjan, formerly a high-ranking cadre for ten years, described a silent collective awareness of repression and authoritarianism in the ranks, fear of other cadres, and the pyramidal structures of personal gain within the LTTE that rewarded loyalty only to Prabhakaran, not to each other:

What I think, you will also think. But neither of us can talk about what we think. . . . What you are feeling, I will understand and you will understand what I feel. But we can't talk about it. If we talk then there is trouble. . . . Then you will write a letter saying that how I came to you and what I said. The next day they will take me and shoot me. That's what happens. That's why nobody talks. . . . If you inform on someone else then you get a promotion.

They were sending us to fight. But we could never talk back or argue with them. If we said anything about the leader or anything, then they would say we were traitors.

For civilians, fears were heightened by the possibility of personal disputes and conflicts around land, family, and internal religious affairs assuming new proportions if one side went to the LTTE. When accusations of treachery are also used to settle private disputes, everyday life with others is governed with uncertainty, constantly marked by the fear of, and the ready availability of, such accusations.

Not to be seen as a traitor was of paramount importance. Kugamoorthy and I were discussing popular attendance at the LTTE's national commemoration of Heroes Day:

Ordinary people go either by force or they feel guilty that they have not died and they worship and celebrate these people out of that guilt. Finally, they go because they want to show that they are not traitors. To do that alone a thousand people will go. This is not about political meanings and understanding of the struggle, this is to show that one is not a traitor to other people and the LTTE. . . . You can create yourself as a not-traitor by going.

Being a traitor was, then, not an "other" but a constantly possible self that one could slip into if one was not careful. Guarding against betrayal was anticipation not of the treason of others but the treachery of oneself.

This was the guessing game that civilians and the LTTE coproduced, acute as the categories of treasonous acts grew ever wider and wider alongside the frustrations of life under LTTE control. The ever-looming possibility of punishment encouraged civilians and cadres to internalize the probable consequences of transgression and to censor themselves. Furthermore, loyalties were deliberately reoriented away from each other and toward the LTTE; Tamils were constantly enjoined to betray each other, creating high levels of anxiety and suspicion.

The main casualties of LTTE terror were feelings of closeness and intimacy among Sri Lankan Tamils. In fact, only other Tamils and those who knew your movements and everyday life could betray you to the LTTE. This uncertainty about others is also produced, I argue, by the ways in which the LTTE inserted itself into social life and can be seen as an "intimate" power. The LTTE reproduced and embedded itself in everyday forms of sociality, serving to destabilize any sense of implicit trust within those networks. Living with treason, then, was different from "living with one's sorcerer." Living with witchcraft, Geschiere (1997) suggests, is a normalized part of kinship; living with treason, however, serves to bring about new forms and imaginations of sociality.

The Power of Intimacy

Sritharan had left his small militant group, and, living in Jaffna, he had begun helping dissidents and collecting information on human rights abuses. At this time, an undercover, high-ranking LTTE cadre had moved in with Sritharan's relative next door. They became very good friends, often eating and spending time together, unaware of each other's political affiliation and involvement. In fact, the LTTE were at the time searching for Sritharan but they only knew his assumed militant nom de guerre, and in Jaffna he was living under his real name. Sritharan recalled that his relative had tried subtly to warn him several times, stopping Sritharan from criticizing the LTTE too much. When Sritharan's cover was blown, he had been forced to leave Jaffna and live underground. It was only at this point that both Sritharan and his friend found out about each other. Sritharan's former friend led the search for him in Jaffna, and because they were so close, he knew all Sritharan's friends, his family, and all the possible places he could have gone. When I ask Sritharan whether he saw this as a *thuroham* (betrayal), he smiled and told me that this was not treason; "this is just how they are," he said. Instead, Sritharan pointed out how it is those with whom one shares social relations—who "know" you—who can really wield power over you. This is central to how people attempt to navigate sociality with others.

Sritharan's story illustrates both how LTTE presence was woven into the fabric of everyday life and how this affected ordinary networks of trust. The LTTE was drawn from and often indistinguishable from the civilian population. Extensive recruitment in schools and its policy of demanding that families contribute children to its organization meant that the LTTE was also one's family and social circle. Its maintenance of informal networks of informers and loyalties meant that knowing who was LTTE and who was civilian was very difficult. This is why civilians were so uncertain whom they could trust. Second, the LTTE were interested in the kinds of preemptive knowing that civilians (and anthropologists) employed to live or observe everyday life, poisoning that sociality further. Alagan pointed this out to me when I interviewed him in Canada. Alagan had joined the Communist party when he was still at school and had left school in the 1960s to become an activist in the "Peking branch." In his sixties and still politically active against the LTTE, he had been arrested and tortured by them and now lived on the run underground, writing articles in Tamil under anonymous names. When I interviewed Alagan and we talked about his arrest and torture, he disconcertingly told me that the questions that the LTTE asked him were the same as the ones I had been asking him: "They interviewed me like you are interviewing me, about my childhood, about every little detail, about how I got into politics, every relative and their movements, homes." Uncomfortable suddenly about my own questions, I examined my own enterprise and LTTE interrogations anew. What were we both after? I was trying to find out Alagan's political affiliations, how he ended up a dissident, his convictions, and the effects of his experiences, his family, his ideas about sociality, and what it meant to be Tamil for him. The LTTE's intelligence worked along the same lines. Alagan related to me how the LTTE cadres who tortured him boasted to him of how they were building up an archive of traitors and their families, compiling information on every aspect of their social relations. They would be watched, continually under suspicion. Alagan's wife and children had become, after his detention, a traitor's family, living underground and on the run. His wife's relatives were also once arrested by the LTTE. They were now marked as possible targets of accusation, unless they remained quiescent.

That the LTTE was building up archives of Tamil sociality was emphasized to me by Vimaleswaran, a journalist and human rights activist. He told me that his ambiguous origin was one of the reasons that he had successfully avoided arrest by the LTTE. Vimaleswaran's mother was from the north; but his father was a Malaiyaha Tamil from the hill country, and he initially grew up in a Sinhalese area. He has, in his own reckoning, successfully avoided capture because he did not really have an *ur* (natal village); thus the LTTE have found it hard to trace him. Not being from Jaffna, Vimaleswaran cannot be pinned down, and his family, neighbors and friends recorded and information collected on whom he might contact or visit. Further, his visits to his mother's natal home are too infrequent to give away information. The LTTE's intelligence, Vimaleswaran told me, works on the principle that everyone has a natal village. A cadre in each village will keep a diary or have a set of informers on the movements and networks of those in the village. This is how their intelligence network was built. The LTTE intelligence network was embedded in, builds up an archive of, and poisons everyday sociality among Tamils. For Tamils, as with the Maka (Geschiere 1997), both the greatest trust and the greatest danger come from those intimates who "know" you. In war time, these forms of sociality acquire a potency and power that enjoin civilians to regard ordinary information as secrets to be kept.

Most important, the LTTE reconfigured being Tamil around the ethnic cultural intimacy produced by shared knowledge of itself (LTTE) and the possibility of its rule over the individual—wherever that person is—simply because he or she is Tamil. This secret was what Michael Taussig calls a "public secret" as "that which is generally known, but cannot be articulated" (1999, 5). In Colombia, Taussig argues, disappearances, murders, and violence by different actors were public secrets, where "we all 'knew' this, and they 'knew' we 'knew' but there was no way it could be easily articulated," the obvious becoming animated by "the spectral radiance of the unsaid" (6). In such a way, the LTTE was constantly animated by being unsaid and yet present. The LTTE's power lay in being a public secret.[14] The possibility of internal terror was coproduced by the LTTE and civilians. The latter censored themselves, with or without enforcement, in the face of the seeming omniscience, secrecy, and unpredictability of LTTE power. We all knew that the LTTE was killing Tamils and recruiting children, and Tamils would talk to each other knowing that there was a possibility that any Tamil you could meet could be an LTTE cadre or informer. Everyone tried to double guess each other around the secret—LTTE terror. Yet, in public, this could never be articulated because articulating what one knew was dangerous. Knowing was essential—otherwise, LTTE terror could not effectively intimidate or silence—but speaking about it was dangerous.

Being Tamil meant that the LTTE was "our secret." Everyone assumed that being Tamil put you in possession of that secret alongside them. It was taken for granted that all conversations were multilayered, allusive, double-voiced. This was the secret of being Tamil. Even if Tamils could not trust other Tamils, they nonetheless also believed that only other Tamils could understand the predicament that all found themselves in because only other Tamils were subject to LTTE power. When I interviewed people, I was told that they could talk to me because I could "understand." What this meant was that, as a Tamil, I too knew about the LTTE and would be careful, and, thus, I was risking myself as much as they were in talking to me. Even in Muslim refugee camps, which were not riven through with internal terror but where Tamils who arrived could still be the LTTE and thus feared, I was introduced by my guide Farook as: "name, Sharika; *ur* (home) Nallur, Jaffna; she herself has *known* the LTTE so you can talk openly and trust her." Only other Tamils were presumed to know the rules of the game and could read between the lines. "Outsiders," Sinhalese, and foreign journalists who reported that Tamils seemed to support the LTTE publicly were regarded with disdain: they "weren't in the know," "they didn't know the rules of the game," and they saw clarity in ambiguity.[15] Thus, the possibility of being a traitor has in a very real way come to mark what it means to be Sri Lankan Tamil. Postcolonial Sri Lankan Tamil identity, which initially became defined around a common group discriminated against by the state, is now equally defined as a group that the LTTE has the possibility to rule.[16] Knowing the LTTE drew the inside of the community; Tamils who could always be potential traitors were more like each other than the Sinhalese who could speak out but were not targeted as traitors. Treachery and secrecy came to define who knew and, thus, a macabre ethnic difference even more.

Secrecy and Speech

The operation of terror works on the sociality of your own ethnic group, your own language and codes, your neighbors and sometimes even your kin. Such poison then affects relations that we have with people we feel close to, not with those who are distant. It is our sense of intimacy that is most affected and transformed in a time of internal terror. However, our analysis cannot stop at the description of how technologies of terror work because it is clear that, despite being marked, shaped, and reconstituted by the impact of fear and terror, lives, intimacies, secrets, memories, and conversations continue apace. How then did people attempt to repopulate this world of intimacy? I suggest that the possibility of speech and secrecy came to shape the possibility of intimacy and sociality.

One Tamil language magazine *Amuddu*, run briefly from Colombo, found that its prose competition on the topic "You are being watched" brought a continuous stream of letters and submissions from northern Jaffna. Most submissions were anonymous entries, uninterested in winning the prize. The then editor of *Amuddu* felt that this was simply out of the sheer pleasure of letting speech flow (personal communication). In interviews with Tamil civilians, the most common representation of the effects of LTTE power on ordinary life centered on LTTE control over public speech, a condition that all were subject to, whether dissidents or not. Without exception, all would stress that "one couldn't speak freely." Rajan, a twenty-one-year-old civilian, was one of many who described LTTE rule through control over speech:

Now can I say to somebody high up in the LTTE, what you have done is wrong, this is all wrong? Can I say that? No. Tomorrow I will not be there. So I cannot talk about my opinions or my beliefs freely. I have not got free speech or freedom to write. I can't criticise them in a paper. So then what?

As I heard more and more of these "shortcuts," I came to realize that the possibility of speaking freely was, for Tamils, not about an abstract right of freedom of speech. These descriptions and complaints about guarding one's tongue were indicative of people's articulation of the *very possibility of sociality.* Speaking freely was about being social, about being connected to others. It was this that people were inquiring about and attempting to formulate through their relationships with others.

The politics of speaking and silence became central to my then doctoral research (Thiranagama 2006). I noted, as Lisa Wedeen (1999) points out, that public conformity does not necessarily preclude speech but that this speech (and politics) moves elsewhere into the "interior":

prohibiting public announcements does not prevent people from talking privately amongst those they trust. The realms of the forbidden, the taboo, and the clandestine expands as the official political realm contracts. Commonplace events become titillating bits of information or gossip to be guarded, cherished and revealed among friends. (Wedeen 1999, 45)

Then, I had posited that, in the face of public conformity, a notion of "inner life" and the "private" had expanded in significance, suggesting a world of knowing silence in public and the expansion and the valorization of the private homes, rooms, and small networks of trust. However, placing the question of treason center stage requires moving away from the interior to the double-edged notion of the intimate. If betrayal is so pervasive, emanating from a fear of those we live with and share our lives with; if violence and punishment create ethnic boundaries; and if the selective sharing of information and the creation of secrets are both crucial for individual survival, then notions of public and private/the interior suggest inappropriately spatially and socially stable spheres. In fact, the LTTE and traitors threatened each other because they were both public and private. Heterogeneous networks of trust created notions of private and public, rather than the other way around, and in a way that was not necessarily coterminous with spatial understandings of private and public.

The possibility of trust was a constant theme in conversations, and free speech was the measurement of this trust. Interviewees talked all the time about how one was safe and with whom one could be safe. Often, many would say that they were most safe with their kin. For twenty-year-old Alexander, trying to survive in Jaffna without joining the LTTE, "home" is the safest place. Alexander tells me that he can only talk freely inside his home because "they are my *sondakaran* (kin/relatives); we can talk freely among ourselves." When I asked him whether he can trust his friends and whether it is possible to argue with a pro-LTTE friend, he immediately said "you have to be careful because if they are in or involved in the movement, they will tell local command." "Home," he tells me, is trustworthy because "it is your relations . . . in public you never know who is a member of their intelligence . . . you never know who will report you." This was the most common response I received from civilians.

This might seem the standard anthropological answer, that it was on structures of kinship that people fell back in relation to obligation, refuge, and mutual protection. In fact, rather than reflecting structures of kinship, these statements muddied considerably traditional notions of kin to make new ways of imagining relatedness around one could be intimate around, whom one could trust. This trust was through whom one could *speak to*, and this was not necessarily one's family.

While the home and family are valorized as intimate and safe, it is families and homes that have been, through mass displacement, child recruitment, and internal terror, most under attack, these changes being the means by which Tamils measure the impact of civil war. For example, twenty-one-year-old Rajan and his parents, forcibly displaced twice from their home, also lived in fear that his teenage brother would either run away to the LTTE or be requisitioned; the effect of LTTE rule was, thus, the threat of dismembering home and family constantly from within. Second, one could not always speak to family members openly, either for fear of endangering them by knowledge or because of uncertainty about their political loyalties. Many of those arrested and tortured by the LTTE were taken in because they are brothers, sisters, cousins, and parents of people formerly in other militant movements. Many had to distance themselves from their families in order to preserve their family's safety in Sri Lanka.

Sakthi, a member of the former militant group EPRLF, responded to my questions with an equally common statement from ex-militants about the bonds of shared experience, understanding, and speech as the basis for trust:

Uravu [kindred] is for us only those who we have worked with in the struggle. . . . Because of your background, we trust you a little to speak with you, but we can't talk with everyone. Even with our school friends we can't talk, not even small talk. Even if we go home, we are frightened, we can't even ask or answer the basic questions, how are you, where are you living, what work are you doing? . . . We only talk to those who have trust with us and who know all our histories. . . . People who are kin to us . . . they are not in this kind of world. They won't understand our troubles.[17]

Thus, selective circulation of secrets and speech served to render a sense of intimacy and sociality possible, ones that have to be continually reinvented.

If terror works on alienating one's sense of the intimate, then the ways in which people attempted to repopulate their senses of the intimate, I suggest, was through the possibility of speech. It is not that one can speak to those one is intimate with; instead, I propose here that one is intimate with those you can speak to. Through asking about how to speak and whom to speak to, new homes, new friends, and new neighbors come to populate the intimate, one way of living life in the shadow of treason. The other way, which I come to now, is to turn from the fear of marking oneself as traitor to making it crucial to one's own sense of political purpose: to speak *in praise of traitors*.

In Praise of Traitors

In September 2006, I attended a Tamil "literary conference" in London, an annual meeting of Sri Lankan Tamil dissidents from around Europe. Although only around forty to fifty people attended, I was told that, in other years in Paris and Berlin, there was nearly double the attendance.[18] The conference has been held for over a decade now, mainly between Berlin, Paris, and London, the three active centers of the European dissident scene. Attendees were predominantly left-wing; many were former members of militant groups from a generation that joined in the 1970s and 1980s. It is not a formal affair; it is equally seen as a way for families, isolated from mainstream Tamil society due to their dissidence, to stay in touch with each other. I arrived in time to hear a session given by Senthan, who distributed Jeeva's pamphlet, which I quoted at the beginning of this chapter. Senthan's talk paid tribute to the memory of Kethesh Loganathan, who had been assassinated the previous month in Sri Lanka for being a traitor. Kethesh an ex-EPRLF member and NGO activist, had most recently moved to the Sri Lankan government's Peace Secretariat in an effort to influence policy, a move that had been heavily criticized all around. It was most probably for this, given the political credibility and flair he could have given the government, that he was killed by the LTTE. He was also one of the many EPRLF members killed throughout 2002–2006. Senthan asked the audience to reflect on Tamil nationalism and its history of violence. To general applause, he argued that we should be proud of being traitors, reading out Jeeva's pamphlet:

It is to my pride that I am called a traitor. The word has filled with political power. We will continuously chant it. First Alfred Duraippah, Sunderam, Oberoi Thevan, Mano Master, Anandarajah begin the long list of traitors, then

Vimaleswaran, Rajani, Selvi, Yogeswaran, Neelan, Rajan Sathiyamoorthy, Pathmanabha, Robert . . . endlessly this list stretches on, let us be proud that it continues with Ketheswaran.

Senthan's and Jeeva's pride in being traitors and the audience applause are what makes treason in Sri Lanka unique. Traitor killing has become so ubiquitous and the category of treason so stretched that it turned from an extraordinary phenomenon to a possible way of life. Being a traitor is a constantly potential self for civilians. It forms the ground around which people fashion their behavior, their notions of intimacy, inside and outside. Thus, the traitor as this constantly potential self was also fertile ground for the fashioning of a new political role. It is to this new political role that I move in concluding this chapter.

To return to earlier parallels, studies of witchcraft are often dominated by research into "cultures of accusation." Here, I have tried to lay some of the grounds by which accusations of treachery come to be made meaningful. However, this is the point of departure. A study of a culture of accusations would, in the last instance, remap Tamil sociality through LTTE categories. Moreover, studies of witchcraft rarely produce witches, but here there really are traitors. Sri Lankan Tamil society continues to produce ever more traitors; moreover, these traitors acknowledge that, in some crucial way, they are indeed traitors. It is this I set out to document—what traitors themselves actually thought about becoming traitors. Did figuring themselves as traitors mean that one could find a new way of occupying a dismembered political world?

In the case of many who were ex-militants, though not in the case of those who had noncombatant backgrounds, the history of violence, purging, and militancy was one they shared. When EPRLF members were being killed some human rights agencies such as Amnesty International would not cover it in their reports because, as they pointed out, these organizations highlighted only the deaths of civilians. EPRLF, EPDP, and PLOTE members were being counted as paramilitaries, not innocent victims.[19] In the case of the ex-militants I interviewed, there was no "innocent" political role they could assume given their past histories. Yet were they then to acknowledge that their lives could be made forfeit? What did it mean to live with treason in your life? Acknowledging this treason takes different forms.[20] Here, I identify the three most common responses: refusal, reversal, and sublation.

For Alagan, whom we met earlier, from a Maoist background, the word "traitor" was preserved in its horror. Being a traitor's family had meant that his wife, his children, and her family also lived in fear. For many of those who become traitors, the difficulty does not lie in acknowledging oneself as a traitor. It is the responsibility one has to take in relation to one's relatives, friends, and neighbors. For him, traitor was a role that had been applied to him but one he could not accept. As he told me, trembling with anger, "I have worked all my life for the people's struggle, for oppressed-caste villages and Tamil rights, and then they come and call me a traitor!" He told me that the reason he had become a political activist was that he loved to be with people: he liked to organize, to keep contacts, to meet people and talk everyday. Now he has only ten people he feels he can trust and talk to freely. The LTTE, he says with sadness, have taken away his two loves, "to be with people and to write."

Kugamoorthy is an example of reversal. For him, while "everyone is frightened of being called a traitor, . . . it is a question of human nature" he states, "I don't mind being called a traitor because I understand the politics":

This is the heart of our politics, "Tamil," "betrayal," and "traitor." We are stuck in a kind of politics which is about eliminating traitors—that is all. Whatever comes out of this is not about politics.

For Kugamoorthy, while treason is so associated with the LTTE that it becomes something meaningless, the power of betrayal and treachery cannot be dismissed. Thus, while he first told me, "Myself, I don't think that such a thing exists. The LTTE may use betrayal and traitor for their politics, but I think there is no such thing," he immediately followed this statement by saying:

In my opinion, it is the LTTE who are the greatest traitors . . . the LTTE who has betrayed its own cause and its people. It has no concern for those people's lives. The LTTE can say other people are traitors but. . . . when we can look at it through a different history . . . then we can see that we have accepted the greatest betrayal of all. This will never change. There is only a final end in the LTTE.

I heard this sentiment often from many accused as traitors: an acknowledgment of treason was about a message that had missed its mark. The LTTE was seen as committing the ultimate betrayal: working along the structure of the intimate, it had betrayed its own people.

The third acknowledgment of treason is (Hegelian) sublation, where a form is preserved and simultaneously transcended. A new social form is made that retains the figure of the traitor as a powerful and corrosive force for social order. Treachery is not refused, reversed to the accuser, but maintained as the core of a new social form.[21] This third form, as with writers like Jeeva and many of those I interviewed such as Vimaleswaran, was to acknowledge treason by inhabiting it fully. Jeeva's conclusion to his pamphlet summarizes well, if more eloquently than most, this position:

Those who were once ashamed and cowed when the whites called them black, are now declaring themselves with pride to be black. Those who were oppressed and discriminated against by upper-castes as untouchable now stand upright and announce proudly that they are Dalits. . . . Many of us fled and came to this country. Why? Our life's duty is to survive. But what is our historical duty? To be traitors! Let the spirit of Kethesh and other deceased traitors give strength to us so we can also convert ourselves into traitors like those thousands of traitors killed, then and now. Long live traitors! Yes we are all traitors now. (2006, 3)

If naming someone a traitor means that questions about his or her execution are silenced, as a consequence of the moral aversion to the figure of the traitor who betrays her own kind, then this moral aversion imbues the figure of the traitor with a tremendous power. The figure of the traitor, which for the LTTE was the most feared figure, becomes in the hands of those labeled as such, a means by which to oppose power, not with innocence but with power—as Jeeva says, "The word has filled with political power" (ibid). Vimaleswaran asked me if "in this situation, can we be anything but traitors?" If the LTTE defined treason as an act opposed to the LTTE, then further, I found in my interviews, for Tamils who commit such acts of treachery, sociality can be stabilized around shared fates, other traitors whom one can trust. This latter threatens the LTTE the most because it questions the very basis on which the LTTE can maintain the moral valency of treason and thus maintain its own rule.

Thus, in Sri Lanka, increasingly, dissidents argue that treachery is the only ethical position. Beginning and ending with this moment, I suggest that this provides a fertile basis for examining the traitor as a significant figure both in the specific way in which the LTTE in Sri Lanka sought to insert itself as quasi-state and, more generally, in violent and uncertain processes of state making. This analysis of the LTTE is perhaps even more pertinent in the current climate and can be equally applied to the Sri Lankan government which is now busy labeling and harassing "Sinhalese traitors." In Sri Lanka, all perspectives—those of the LTTE and others—posit being potential traitors as the line by which inside, outside, community, trust, sociality, and being Tamil has come to be negotiated. Through the figure of the traitor, we can understand the ways in which violent ethnic nationalism is as equally concerned with policing itself as it is concerned with erecting boundaries between friends and enemies. From the case of Sri Lankan traitors, we can understand that the acknowledgment of treason as an ethical act questions the very basis of ethnic intimacy.

Chapter 7
Treason and Contested Moralities in a Coloured Township, Cape Town

Steffen Jensen

In a newspaper interview from 2006, influential South African columnist, writer, and anti-apartheid activist Fred Khumalo suggested that to reduce crime all South Africans should become *impimpis*. The *impimpi* was the despised traitor of the struggle against apartheid, those who informed against his or her comrades to the security forces or collaborated with the regime. Through his or her actions, the *impipi* had forfeited all rights of life and could be killed. *Impipi* killings became emblematic of the struggle against apartheid during the late 1980s. The logic behind Khumalo's statement was that only by leaving behind mistaken loyalties toward those members of the community who commit crime could crime be stopped. In a paradoxical move, the struggle against apartheid was once again played out in contemporary South African politics, as the ultimate villain of yesteryear, at least discursively, became the hero of post-apartheid South Africa; to end the reign of criminals, community members had to come forward, inform, collaborate, and thereby assist the new state in fulfilling the dream of a free, democratic, and prospering South Africa.

Khumalo's plea to collaborate with the state and the police is not new; under the guise of community policing, it is arguably one of the constitutive elements in post-apartheid policing. Community policing was introduced as a central element in police transformation with the Police Act of 1996 and developed with moderate success through the following decade. The often blatant failure of instituting and organizing community collaboration in policing forms the backdrop to the remark on the need to become *impipis*. And in many ways, Khumalo has struck upon an uncomfortable truth. As I have argued elsewhere (Jensen 2005), to be at war with crime is, in many parts of South Africa, tantamount to being at war with one's own family, neighbors, and friends. Hence, to collaborate with the police constitutes remarkably unpopular actions in some quarters; it is tantamount to treason.

Treason is one of the crimes that carry the highest legal sanctions and moral outrage. It is thought to be a relatively simple task to define what amounts to treason, although it can be difficult to establish legally who the traitor is because some treacherous acts are hidden. In his article on the Russian-Polish relations in the nineteenth century, Patrice Dabrowski outlines what he calls the ABC of treason, "Apostasy," "Betrayal," and "Collaboration" (Dabrowski 2003). This means that treason amounts to denouncing one's identity, betraying it, and collaborating with the enemy. In other words, treason means acting against one's natural polity on behalf of those who wish to destroy it. In this line of thinking, treason is the opposite of the polity. However, as argued in the introduction to this volume, nations, polities, moral communities, and so on are always constructed and performed—and by implication, so is treason. In fact, treason does not stand in radical opposition to loyalties, solidarities, and communities. It is the constitutive outside of these entities; rather than destroying them, betrayal constitutes the outer boundaries of the moral community, that which is included through its formative exclusion. Hence, when a traitor-to-be is accused of denouncing his or her community, the accuser lends materiality to what was supposedly always there—the community. Furthermore, as the editors also point out, there is a temporal dimension to treason; sometimes people remain the same while historical and political developments render their loyalties illegitimate, indeed treacherous. Both the substantive and the temporal dimensions emerge in what follows.

Most accounts of treason clearly concern the betrayal of one's country. It is, as Dabrowski asserts in the Russian-Polish case, the flipside of nationalism. However, in this chapter I argue that, although the emblematic form of treason is national betrayal, the figure of the traitor or the grammar of treason can be expanded to encompass other forms. Hence, I explore how the figure of the traitor can be used to shed light on the contested forms of gendered morality that exist in coloured urban areas in Cape Town. There is, to my mind, an added bonus in exploring the claustrophobic world of the underbelly of Cape Town through the lens of the traitor: not only does it help us understand this world, but the exercise also contributes to our understanding of treason as rather more mundane. I argue that, especially in situations of flux and instability, betrayal or feelings of betrayal are always possibilities. In a sense, the intimate and claustrophobic township world that I describe below is constituted in part through a string of small betrayals that people must engage in to survive, and that they experience and talk about to make sense of marginalization and misfortune.[1] In this way, betrayal (both as acts and as experiences) is central in constituting different sets of moral selves.

Along these lines, I argue that different, competing groups of women employ figures akin to the traitor, as they attempt to promote or defend their version of what the moral community in the township should be. Here, I need to make a brief detour to consider the concept of community in a South African context. For decades, the concept has played a key role both during apartheid and in the post-apartheid period. The apartheid regime ruled through specific versions of ethnic or tribal communities, and at the same time, "community" became central to understanding concepts of people's power in the struggle against apartheid. Likewise, in the post-apartheid period, the concept occupies a central role in "addressing the injustices of the past" as part of community development, community policing, and so on. In this way, community has always been an overdetermined concept, pregnant with political salience. This, however, also suggests that the concept is of little analytical value. Rather, it must be analyzed both as a battlefield and as a political discourse. In my use of the concept throughout this chapter, I stress the inherently contested character of community by talking about particular competing versions of moral communities—moral communities that are, invariably and inevitably, betrayed.

In the intimate and claustrophobic world of the coloured township, at least two competing versions of the moral community exist. They revolve around the relationship to the police and the broader state, as well as to the gangs and other violent male groups. This analysis suggests that the moral community, made up of the particular township that I call Valencia Park, presumed to have a singular identitary reality, is utterly fraught and riddled with ambiguities and power struggles. To know exactly, under these circumstances, who is betraying the moral community is almost impossible, as the township community cannot be stabilized as the presumed moral reality that would allow us unequivocally to distribute the titles hero and villain. Nonetheless, it is exactly through the categories of the treacherous that the loyalties, solidarities, and communities become tangibly real—at least for a while—because in the intimate world of the township, most absolute claims to morality or its opposite, the treacherous acts that endanger the community, suffer defeat or must be renegotiated, sometimes for tactical reasons, to enable people—neighbors and indeed families—to go on living next to each other, while having intimate knowledge of one's own and others' treacherous acts. This is, as also argued in the introduction to this volume, predicated on the ultimately unstable subjectivities and polities of the modern, postcolonial world.

To complicate the scenario further, coloureds, not least the ones in the townships, have historically been ambiguous, racially and politically, as their allegiances to either of the dominant groups (whites and Africans respectively) have been questioned. On the one hand, coloureds occupied a position—although marginal—within white South Africa, and they received more state attention (for better or for worse) and had better options than Africans (Goldin 1989). On the other hand, coloreds were incorporated into the struggle through the generic terms "black" and "oppressed" (Norval 1996). However, neither side was absolutely certain of where coloured loyalties lay. This ambiguity has persisted in post-1994 South Africa (Eldridge and Seekings 1996). In this way, coloureds, through their structural position in South African society, arguably were and are always already in danger of being accused of betrayal. Hence, I argue that the small and quotidian betrayals of township compatriots merge with a larger narrative of coloureds' historical betrayal.

My argument proceeds in three sections. First, I explore the ways in which the apartheid regime structured the ways in which women could become moral individuals, indeed quasi-citizens, which in no small measure, related to the status of coloured men as always already potentially criminal and hence radical noncitizens. Second, I explore the situated struggles between two groups of women: one group that I call the respectable mothers and one that I call the activists. Finally, I bring the two analyses together in a conclusion on the status of betrayal, which evolves around notions of contested moralities and complicity.

Structuring Women's Morality and Treason

Without the consent or the knowledge of women in the townships, the apartheid state in its governmental form made a deal with them.[2] The deal was this: if women acted as the intermediaries for the state in its attempt to safeguard children against the ravages of township life, notably the dangers represented by irresponsible fathers and *skollies*, the archtypical coloured criminal, the state would provide for the women as mothers of children and potential homemakers. Clearly, the deal was not part of a conscious plot to destroy families in the townships. The alliance was based on an understanding of why coloured families were so dysfunctional, an understanding deriving from stereotypes of the coloured man as inherently criminal, irresponsible, and morally weak. It developed incrementally over forty years of intervention. This had consequences beyond courses in cooking and sewing, which were popular with state agencies from the 1970s, and imprisonment rates for coloured men. It also structured resource allocations within the coloured nuclear family in relation to the labor market. Apartheid's Coloured Labour Preference Policy in and around Cape Town and the subsequent influx-control mechanisms shielded coloured employment from African competition. Furthermore, the regime promoted textiles and leather industries in the Western Cape, which de facto privileged female entrance into the labor market. As a consequence, thousands of coloured women ended up working in the industrial zones of Cape Town. Coloured men still occupied the better-paid jobs. However, a significant number of men found themselves in temporary and casual employment in the building and construction sector or out of work entirely.[3] This led to a feminization of the lower parts of the formal labor market. A second way in which gender relations were structured during the apartheid era was through the social grant system that bankrolled many coloured township families for decades (supporting the claim that coloureds were privileged and in the pocket of the regime, later used to substantiate claims regarding their questionable allegiances). These grants were primarily paid to women as mothers, rather than to households. In this way, many men became marginal in the economic life of households, a burden rather than a provider.

This system underwent significant changes after 1994. Influx controls were lifted allowing Africans legal rights to the city. Global economic forces hollowed out the job opportunities that had previously been extended to coloured women, and unemployment among women rose markedly. The welfare system was revamped to the economic detriment of coloured women, who had received the bulk of state welfare before. The system was primarily revamped for fiscal reasons. However, local representatives of the state also explained the reduction of welfare with an incipient "culture of dependency" among coloured women, which led them to think that "they are entitled to money," as a senior welfare official put it. Few coloured women directly blamed the government for the cuts. Rhoda, whom we shall meet later, suggested that the real problem lay with those coloured women who cheated the system, squandering millions and rendering real suffering coloureds (like herself) vulnerable to governmental wrath. Like so many township women, however, Rhoda was faced with a paradox. Official, dominant discourse suggested that the welfare grant was only for those who really needed it. As such, moral conduct was premised on not cheating, which Rhoda also invoked. However, in everyday life moral conduct related to the ability to provide for families, presenting Rhoda with hard choices.

In conditions of poverty, welfare became part of complex livelihood strategies. Elaine Salo (2004) illustrates that, in these situations, being able to negotiate complicated welfare systems, cope with the frequently humiliating treatment coloured women received at the hands of welfare officials, and transmitting knowledge of the grant system to the less well-informed or younger women became central in the mothers' moral claims. Rhoda excelled in this, and she was one of those whom younger women went to in order to learn about the system and how to beat it. Although she received the grant, she had several jobs and was able to mediate contact between younger women and the labor market. As such, she incarnated the paradox township women faced, caught as she was between the official notions of morality and demands put on her to provide for her family.

To deal with the double problem of dependency and fiscal restraints, the new state was changing its contract with the women: there was now more emphasis on partnerships and "equal" relations between state and mothers who were charged with bringing up children. The new insistence on partnerships was meant to produce responsible mothers—unlike the previous approach that had produced only dependency among mothers, thereby falling short of its goal of generating some level of gendered citizenship for women in the townships.

The dismantling of the welfare schemes for coloured women was not designed to produce responsible mothers, but few state officials protested against it, one housing manager arguing "Now these people must go to work." As the deracialization of the welfare schemes was only one part of what Salo terms "the unravelling of the economic scaffolding of local personhood" (2003)—the other being the decrease in industrial employment—it is difficult to see where employment could come from. However, dismantling the welfare state was cast as central for the strategy to empower women to take control of their own lives and develop a sense of responsibility toward their children. The elaborate welfare grants and the protected employment opportunities produced particular circumstances for local personhood and identity, and when they changed, the parameters for the production of personhood—even citizenship—changed quite dramatically (Salo 2004). To compensate, the state extended to women the more intangible and vague offer of partnership for women to participate in the upliftment of the township through community work. Different groups of women were able to benefit very differently. Some lost out. For others, the new partnerships became central in the generation of resources. This produced new tensions as women had to negotiate between everyday livelihood exigencies and dominant ideas of community work as living *for* the community, not *off* the community. Out of these transformations, two groups of women emerged: the mothers and the activists. It is to their power struggles around stabilizing particular versions of the moral community that I now turn.

Contested and Betrayed Moralities

Coloured men, especially from the townships, were associated with violence through the racial stereotypes that posited them as capable of engaging in destructive and damaging violence, thereby effectively situating them as people with no rights or chances of citizenship (Jensen 2006).[4] Although few township women engaged in acts of violence, they were associated with the violence through the men in their lives. Women dealt very differently with the threat of marking by proxy, however; what permeated discourses and practices surrounding violence was that a woman's respectability could be permanently compromised if she was associated too closely with violence. Some women were in a better position to defer violence, while other women faced difficult dilemmas because their men or sons were involved in a variety of gang-related practices, including substance abuse and violence. The question then became how to handle the association with violence in such a way as to emerge as respectable while maintaining a good relationship with, for instance, family members who otherwise threatened to compromise one's moral standing.

Not all women tried to explain away their male relatives' violence. A significant number of women in Valencia Park would go to great length to exonerate and even defend their sons and husbands. Rhoda was an example of this kind of mother. She was accorded great respect in one of the gang territories. On several occasions, she testified as a character witness in court proceedings against boys in her area. She scolded the police when they came to arrest the boys, and she intervened to protect them when outside gangs came to the area where she stayed. She said,

> I would like someone to explain to me what a gangster is, because I don't see neither of these boys shooting and killing each other. I don't regard them as gangsters, because these boys, if they fight, if they make a noise or whatever they do, you can still talk to them and tell them that they must stop making a noise or you can stop the fight they are having. Now a gangster is someone that, if they fight, you can't stop them fighting or you can't even talk to them or skel [scold] them and say "julle het al weer geraas gemaak, hoekom het julle geskiet?" [You have made noise again. Why did you shoot?]

Rhoda did recognize that the boys could be troublesome, but she denied that this might qualify as gangsterism. The boys listened to her and accepted her judgments. They were respectful of her and other mothers. Therefore they were not gangsters. This understanding of the boys evidently animated the women's relationship with the police, which historically was markedly hostile.[5] Fifty-year-old Faudilla described the police in these terms:

Oh!! They [are] corrupt. When you phone the police now, they come tomorrow. The people must first die here. They don't even come to the right place. First they drive ten times around the block, then they will come to you. To me it looks like they are afraid to come here. When they hear about the shooting, they always come when the shooting is over, but while they are shooting, they don't come.

Together with the image of cops taking bribes, Faudilla also evoked images of drunken police officers, another recurrent theme when the mothers discussed the police. Added to this were frequent skirmishes with the police when raids in search of drugs and suspects were being carried out or when the sons or husbands of the women were arrested. This totality points to a highly antagonistic relationship with the police. Faudilla said,

The police came here one day and they searched here for drugs and so forth and they took this one guy. He was shouting, so I went down. Right now I'm shouting at the police to leave him alone. Right so I got him out of their hands. Then one of the police said I'm interfering with their work! The more they want to grab him the more I fight them. "Let him go!" and I tore him free. Then this cop stands there with a gun to my head and tells me that I am interfering with his work!

Faudilla stressed her own agency and capability of coping with the police, but in many cases, the encounters with the police were violent as well as humiliating. The police would arrest the wrong people and transgress codes of decency; they were insensitive, violent, and drunk, and appeared afraid of the townships. "Corrupt" stood for the collective category encompassing all these different negative immoral traits attributed to the generic police officer. There were also strong connotations of defending the area from intruders, even when the boys had been arrested for pushing drugs.

Apart from the emotional ties Faudilla and Rhoda had to their sons and husbands, there were structural reasons for the loyalty to their men and hatred of the police. Elaine Salo (2006) argues convincingly that the township she worked in, Manenberg, was divided up into different subcommunities that correlated with gang territories. Inside each of the territories, adult mothers were dominant. They derived their dominance from a combination of the position they occupied as the privileged beneficiaries of welfare grants, their access to the labor market, and historical notions of respectability, tied up with motherhood. As such, they defined and policed what it meant to be respectable inside the territory. Men occupied a double position within this version of the moral community. First, they needed to be strong and able to defend their turf. On the streets of the townships, this was to be an *ouen.* For people from other parts of the township, *ouens* were often considered to be gangsters, but in relation to the mothers, being an *ouen* from here was not necessarily to be a gangster. The second role they occupied, which Salo brings out, was that of good sons or *goeie seuns*. Hence, the moral habitus of young men, or *ouens*, depended less on their destructive practices as gangsters than on their kinship with respectable women. According to Salo, respectable mothers "render the gang ideology, practices, and aesthetics socially invisible" (Salo 2004, 211), subsumed under the narrative of the good son. In return for the respectability conferred upon young men, the livelihoods they accessed, and the protection they got vis à vis the state, the young men, through the rites of the gang, policed gang members inside the moral community. If a young man stole from within the community or attracted outside attention, it was the gang's prerogative to punish the one who had compromised the moral community. Good sons were defined in relation to their kin but also as a function of their respect for the mothers. Salo discusses in detail the practices in relation to fatherhood, the time when good sons asserted their autonomy vis à vis the mothers. Although premarital sex per definition ran counter to respectability, the ensuing pregnancy could be turned into a source of morality, if the good son went and told the mother of the daughter, thereby paying tribute to and respecting her house. In this way, the strategic alliance between mothers and young men was perpetuated after the young men assumed autonomy.

Salo's analysis explains the paradoxical support that women gave to men who seemed to compromise all claims to respectability. When Anthony, a leader of local gang, died, one important concern was who would now protect the area from outside gang attacks and who would control the *laaities* (young ones) inside the territory. Anthony was the incarnation of Salo's young man in alliance with mothers. He was always respectful and often asked for the advice of mother figures such as Rhoda. He would parade around the area carrying his infant baby, showing his commitment to fatherhood. And if some of the young boys acted badly, he would punish them for their insolence. In this regard, his reputation for violence around Valencia Park and his drug-dealing activities were subsumed under the greater narratives of the good son, the responsible father, his respect for the mothers of the area, and his defense of the territory.

If we relate this to the issue of treason, it is clear that betrayal of the moral community does not consist in supporting the good sons and responsible fathers; it consists in bringing in the police, which Faudilla and Rhoda, along with the boys, would fight. However, in the post-apartheid moment, bringing in and supporting the police in the fight against gangs and crime was exactly what the government suggested. Not only would it be the right thing to do, it almost became a moral prerequisite, not only for the police but also for many residents within Valencia Park. Against this perception, Rhoda and Faudilla argued that their boys were not gangsters and that the police should go looking for those responsible for the killings that went on elsewhere, more precisely across the road in the adjacent gang territory. This gang brought violence into Rhoda and Faudilla's section of the township. For instance, in relation to the killing of Anthony, the women were adamant in their defense of Anthony's excellent qualities, while demanding that the police go to the adjacent gang territory to look for the guilty party, a recently released gangster named Donkey.

The construction of a moral community based in the alliance between respectable mothers and good sons was, however, far from uncontested among women in the township. A rape case provided an example of the struggles between different versions of the moral community. Five boys from an apartment block in Rhoda's section had raped a girl who lived in the same block. The circumstances around the rape were uncertain. At first, the girl refused to report the incident, but eventually she went to the police. The police forgot, as they often do, to take her to the district surgeon for examination, making the case virtually impossible to prosecute. Tensions ran high in the block, as different women sided either with the girl or with the boys. Those arguing against the girl said that she had wanted it, that she had always been sleeping around, and that she was drunk, and only when people found out—because the boys bragged about it—did she report it. However, others argued against the boys and held that their attack on the girl had been so brutal that nothing excused their actions.

In the block, there were several well-respected women, but none of them had been able to influence the boys not to rape the girl; moreover, they became entangled in the rape case, as three out of four sided with the boys.[6] A woman from another block reflected on one of these women:

Cheryl sort of went to those guys, spoke to them, but she never went to the girl, the victim. And I mean, Cheryl being a woman, I would have first gone to the victim, speak to her and I would have been more on her side.

She and other women criticized Cheryl for taking sides, asserting, "You've got to be neutral." One woman went to see the girl afterward and sent her off to yet another woman who subsequently advised her to go to the Independent Complaints' Directorate to complain about the police's lack of professionalism in handling the rape case.

At stake in the rape case were two different renditions of the moral community of women. One side was the alliance between mothers and good sons. In this version of the moral community, the girl who was raped had forfeited the protection extended to her as a good daughter. She had been drinking and was often found in the company of boys. Hence, the verdict of the mothers of the boys was severe. They sought local resolution to the conflict and did not support the girl in her endeavors to seek outside mediation through the police—an act that would have betrayed the community, that is, the respectable mothers. If she had behaved according to the (mothers') standards for young, respectable girls, she would never have been attacked in the first place.

The respectable mothers' version of the moral community was contested by another group of women whom I call the activists. They were the ones who convinced the girl that she should seek outside assistance from the state. Their version of the moral community was not based on the understanding that the boys necessarily were good sons before they were trouble. Furthermore, the moral community was less localized in particular gang territories and drew its strength from the new political dispensation and the state's attempts to create partnerships with local communities on the Cape Flats. They sat on a number of different political and crime-fighting forums: the Safer Schools project, the Advice Office, the community policing forum and the local branch of the African National Congress (ANC). As their version of the moral community was different, so was that which constituted betrayal. The tables were turned half circle. Whereas Rhoda and Faudilla saw the police as the threat, these women saw betrayal in not bringing in the police. For them, a section of the police were allies in the community's struggle to rid itself of the scourge of crime and gang-related violence. These women's relationship to the police was quite different from the outright hostility, characterizing Faudilla and Rhoda's approach to the police. They expressed understanding of the difficulties the police faced. However, their support was never unqualified, and they publicly criticized the police. These women had considerable knowledge of the work of different police units and institutional priorities. They also differentiated between police officers and sought to work with those they knew and trusted. One said,

Generally the police are corrupt, but that should not prevent us from working with them. We need them as they need us. What I do is that I find particular police officers that I can work with, and I support this police officer because the ones we can trust have a hard time.

In these women's understanding, betrayal of the community was not necessarily about cooperation with the police. Rather, betrayal of the community rested in the willful collaboration with and protection of the gangs. The clash between these two different renditions of moral communities—mothers and activists—was fought primarily in the realm of community work.

Treason and Moral Politics

Like "community," community work carried out by community workers was a politically salient concept and a category of undisputed good: a community worker was charged or had charged herself with the task of realizing the potentials of the community, which often lay dormant due to injustice and oppression. As such, community work was intimately connected to the struggle against apartheid. These remarks suggest that community work, like community itself, is of doubtful analytical value. Instead, we need to focus on the struggles around community work and how the community, as a moral entity, is portrayed. These struggles often featured women as central actors. In its ideological constitution, community work was not solely the domain of women. It was perceived to be nongendered, neutral, and self-sacrificing. Only the interests of the community should be at the heart of community politics. However, in everyday political life, community work was thoroughly gendered, in terms of both numbers and ideological underpinnings. Women constituted the overwhelming majority of community workers. Women performed most church work. Women de facto ran most of the organizations and associations in the township. In all the community meetings I attended, women were either in the majority or the only ones there. The ideological underpinning of community work was also gendered, as it resembled an enactment of female virtues: helpful, caring, considerate, unselfish, and respectable. By engaging in acts of community work, women enacted the very ideology of the good woman. The rationales behind each of these women's actions differed, as did the practices and modes of service. Some women defined their moral community inside particular gang areas; some focused on church work; and others focused on party politics and relations to the state. But the drive behind at least some of these women's commitment to do community work were apparently similar: community work allowed them to emerge as respectable in situations of marginalization and violence, often perpetuated by those closest to them.

In Salo's analysis, the version of the moral community as enacted in an alliance between respectable mothers and good sons was dominant. It would seem, however, that this was changing, partly due to socioeconomic transformations on the labor market and in relation to welfare systems. As the deracialization of the public sector and the labor market proceeded, the grant system and coloured women's privileged access to the labor market were eroded. The new poorly paid white-collar employment opportunities in the post-apartheid urban economy were extended primarily to relatively well-educated young women, which again challenged the dominance of older women. These processes potentially endangered the dominance of the territorialized version of the moral community. Although no economic rewards were being offered or expected for community work, some women saw the state's pledge of partnership as an opportunity to access recognition and resources. Hence the state, and thereby the police, increased in importance in comparison to the apartheid period because police and state in post-apartheid South Africa became avenues of accessing resources and recognition through partnerships.

Rhoda, one of the main protagonists of the territorialized version of morality and its links with the good son*s*, also engaged in community politics as a livelihood strategy. Other community workers condoned this on an everyday level. One noted, with reference to Rhoda, "We know we all have to eat and feed our children." However, as conflicts escalated between the different forms of morality, the attempt to generate livelihoods out of community work came back to haunt Rhoda. This related to the ideological construction of community work.

Community work was about representing poor, often illiterate, people of the townships. Historically, the state played an ambivalent role in the world of community work. On the one hand, it was contrasted with the community as an alienating, oppressive entity, from which the community workers needed to protect the people of Valencia Park. On the other hand, the community workers needed the state to obtain resources with which to help the community. Community workers derived their legitimacy through being recognized as representatives of the people through their ability to mediate on their behalf. Clearly the relationship to the state, in no small measure, was determined by the version of moral community that individual women propagated. However, although the state was perceived in hostile terms, enemies were also sometimes sought within the community—enemies such as some of the community workers who pretended to be working for the community but in reality were pursuing other agendas. The narratives could take at least two forms: first, that the "so-called" community workers were "not representative" and, second, that they did not really care about the people but used them for other ends. The true community worker, in this view, worked only *for* the people, with no other motive than wanting to help the illiterate and poor people of the township and did not live *off* the people. To fulfill the requirements of this ideologized community worker was, of course, as impossible as the fulfillment of community itself. Nonetheless, there were narratives relating to the idea of ulterior motives that worked to discredit a community worker.

Community work was organized in informal alliances that were inherently unstable. Often an alliance was defined on the basis of its members' perceived success or failure in mediating contact with the state, and allies fought internally over resource allocation and state recognition. The logic of community work, ideologically framed as unselfish and unpaid work, was that there were never enough resources to satisfy all. Community work revolved around a few core individuals who accessed most of the allocated resources and remunerated work, rendering them vulnerable to accusations of corruption and self-enrichment. As such, community work was structured by systemic relations between individuals and to the state. However, community workers also subscribed to different renditions of what constituted the moral community. Let me illustrate this ethnographically.

Tension had been building between Rhoda and her former allies. A climax was reached when the police raided Rhoda's house. She accused former friends of telling the police that she was hiding weapons and drugs. The next week one of them was quoted in a local newspaper, telling the press that they had been collaborating with the police on the gang war haunting the township. This gave Rhoda the leverage to attack her former friends, as the agents behind her humiliation. Her fury related to the humiliation itself and the way in which her respectability had been compromised, and she shouted to me, "This is a respectable house." The precursor to her humiliation also related to the boys in her area. Rhoda and another community worker, Tasneem, had been pitched against each other during the aftermath of a shooting incident. Tasneem's son had almost been caught in the crossfire when somebody shot in his general direction, and a boy of seventeen had been arrested and charged with attempted murder. Rhoda defended the boy, saying that he did not shoot and that she knew who had. She also accused Tasneem of wanting to turn the boy into a gangster (in Rhoda's point of view, the consequence of a stay in prison) and said that she, Tasneem, knew nothing about what went on in her section as she was a resident of the adjacent area. The members of the faction defended themselves by saying that they knew nothing about how the police came to choose Rhoda's house—not entirely truthful, as one woman admitted to me—but, as she was the only one complaining, there was probably some truth in the charges against her. This was especially because, as Jainap, one of the core members of the faction, put it, "She always covers up for the boys in the [area]."

What Jainap invoked was the problematic alliance between Rhoda as a mother and the good sons of the area. She thereby challenged the legitimacy of the very alliance at the center of Rhoda's moral claims. Jainap, originally from the same apartment blocks as well, had a much less idealized idea of her own brothers and the boys around her. She noted that most of them were too useless to belong to gangs. After a member of her household killed another man in a row and joined a local gang, she did not excuse him: "If he is a gangster and killer, he must go to jail. I don't want to protect him no more." For Jainap, taking a stand against the boys who cause havoc was an essential part of her moral claims—in sharp contrast to Rhoda's moral community. Hence, the alliance between respectable mothers and good sons was reconfigured to one of women of doubtful morality "covering up for the gangsters":

If she [Rhoda] is keeping illegal guns in her house, yes, then I don't want to associate with her. I respect her as a person, as somebody I grew up in front of, but as a person being involved with her in the community field, as a community worker, then, no, I don't want to associate with her.

As hostilities between the two groups of women gained momentum, I was drawn into the conflict. Before, I could engage with different members of the faction, which at that time still included Rhoda. When the conflict erupted, a member of the group that opposed Rhoda, Lisbeth, asked rhetorically why I [the fieldworker] spent time with what she called "filth." She explained that "filth" included, inter alia, welfare fraud, lack of responsibility toward children, and always "defending the boys." These traits of immorality were all employed to describe Rhoda. Rhoda on her part asserted her morality and insisted that the young man was a good boy and neighbor and that he always listened to her. Rhoda furthermore evoked the strength of her alliance in terms that fed into community politics, when she noted that, in fact, Tasneem had no right to speak on behalf of the people in the apartment blocks because she (Tasneem) did not live there. She furthered her own claims of representability by delegitimizing the claims Tasneem might make and by evoking her privileged access to her neighbors for whom Tasneem had the audacity to speak.

Thus, any informal alliance was an amorphous and precarious body, negotiated during intense power struggles to define its inner and outer boundaries. However, the struggles also bore witness to the existence of different gender relations. Rhoda evoked a moral community that was based around the alliance between mothers and good sons. Tasneem and Jainap, on the other hand, evoked a wider moral community than the township, one that aimed to establish post-apartheid political identities that transcended localized renditions of the moral community. Inherent in these two renditions of moral communities were very different notions of what it meant to be respectable. In most cases, these variations mattered little, and they resurfaced as politically effective only in times of conflict. In such times, community workers used accusations of moral shortcomings to delegitimize their rival community representatives. In extreme cases, the delegitimization involved bringing in the police, but most often it took the form of slanderous gossip, or in Afrikaans, *skinner stories*. The shortcomings did not necessarily lead to the demise of somebody's reputation. Skinner stories were more exactly strategic reservoirs employed in times of crises. Skinner stories functioned as a constant threat of delegitimization that was readily available and could be evoked and revoked when expedient. When people were back in favor again—since none of the moral shortcomings prevented a community worker from doing her job—the threat of evoking the skinner story was held over until the next time, such as the allegation that Rhoda was hiding weapons and drugs. Proof was necessary only when people *did not* want to marginalize somebody, not if a person was to be discredited. In other words, Rhoda's relationship with the boys in the area would not necessarily provoke accusations of betraying the community—in fact, at times it legitimized her, as her former allies acknowledged. Her relationship only became treacherous as other problems emerged. Apart from vindicating the suggestion of the editors of this volume that betrayal has a temporal dimension to it, this is also suggestive of the fractured and multifaceted nature of community politics and its constitutive outside, the treacherous acts of working against the community. Even the most virulent denunciation of particular treacherous acts is only temporary in intimate community and family politics.

Betrayal, Community, and Complicity

As we have seen, women in Valencia Park were faced with multiple paradoxes in their attempts to be perceived as respectable individuals. Structural and changing relations with the state, with the labor market, and with violence committed by those closest to them animated the ways in which, in everyday life, they attempted to reconcile dominant versions of morality with their experiences of violence, poverty, and marginalization. For almost a century, dominant (state) renditions of female moral comportment were tied up with the role of the mother. In the post-apartheid moment little changed in this respect. However, the circumstances under which women could emerge as respectable mothers have changed substantially in the past decade. With the phasing out of the maintenance grant and less privileged access to industrial labor, women have been forced to seek new ways of emerging as moral individuals. One of the ways in which the realignment of motherhood has occurred is through the time-honored sphere of community work. There were different ways of conducting community work, understood as the service that members of a particular locality provided to other residents of the area. Some, like Rhoda, saw the community in highly localized ways; she was a respectable mother of good sons rather than of gangsters. Others, like Jainap and Tasneem, saw the community as part of a wider district, drawing on an activist notion of the struggle against apartheid. Although the territories from which they drew their legitimacy differed in scale, the female community workers all participated in the performative production of gendered moral communities in which the moral disavowal of other forms of morality was a centrally constitutive element.

Moral communities were not gendered solely because a majority of women performed them. Men figured differently in each moral community, In Rhoda's rendition, the moral community was premised on an alliance between mothers and sons, who were good sons if they listened and respected the women of the area—almost regardless of their activities outside the boundaries of the moral community. Jainap and Tasneem distinguished between men along the lines of the threat they posed to the moral community in terms of the law. These different models of moral femininity existed side by side, although hardly in a nonconflictual manner; in fact, each derived strength partly from excluding the other. For instance, Lisbeth's suggestion that Rhoda was "filth" was a clash between different moral communities, as Lisbeth attacked the core of Rhoda's morality. And Rhoda's suggestion that Tasneem had no right to speak because she came from elsewhere was a comment on claims to morality. The performance of different moral communities through exclusion had been going on for a long time. However, as the state approached the townships differently—inviting partnerships rather than extending welfare services—the different renditions' relative strength shifted. Clearly, adherence to the penal codes constituted a prerequisite for partnership. Although Rhoda insisted that the boys were not gangsters and Faudilla was prepared to fight with the police, they had to face the dominant (state) view that their sons were trouble rather than good sons. However, Tasneem and Jainap also had their trouble with their association to violence. Apart from being linked to the police, at one stage they had also been active in a Muslim-dominated vigilante group that, during 1998 and 1999, turned extremely violent, executing drug dealers and setting bombs off at police stations (Dixon and Johns 2001). Again, this fact was common knowledge and only a problem in some instances.

During the course of this chapter, I have made substantive reference to how the township is shot through by power struggles as to the definition of what constitutes a moral community and who can make moral claims. In places like the coloured township, these inherently gendered moral claims are always precarious, as they rely on problematic relations to the state and to structures of male violence. This foregrounds the issue of complicity, also raised by the editors of this volume. In the chapter, I have explored the ways in which different groups of women have different levels of complicity with state, especially police, structures and with structures of violence. However, there is a historical structuration of the struggles between the different versions of community in Valencia Park and how complicity has played itself out. This relates to the coloured group as a whole.

During apartheid, coloureds occupied a particular position within the South African racial hierarchy. I have hinted at this special position above in discussing the alliance between the state and women in the townships. The apartheid regime worked hard to realize the dream of separate development, that is, specific forms of governance for different racial groups. As part of the separate development for coloureds, they were extended services not extended to Africans in the form of housing, welfare, education, access to the labor market, etc. Africans, on the other hand, received the brunt of apartheid police repression, were subject to influx control mechanisms, were paid lower salaries, and had very little education. Hence, coloureds were in general thought to have had an easier time during apartheid and were in many ways seen as complicit with the regime. During the struggle, many coloureds took active part in the resistance. However, it was a tenet in most informal discussions with both Africans and coloureds that the coloureds were not really trusted as fully committed to the struggle. As democracy dawned on South Africa, this image of the untrustworthy and complicit coloureds was confirmed, as coloureds in Cape Town voted massively for the National Party, the old apartheid party. These political allegiances have continued; coloureds are instrumental in preserving the only non-ANC political entity in the country, the City of Cape Town. Hence, it is fair to say that the ANC and Africans in general have never really trusted the coloureds and their loyalty to the new South Africa: coloureds are the *impimpis* of the new South Africa.

This form of complicity also plays itself out in the moral contestations taking place between Rhoda and Faudilla on the one side and Tasneem and Jainap on the other. Part of the implicit accusation that Tasneem and Jainap, firm supporters of the ANC, level at Rhoda and Faudilla is their political disloyalty and the fact that, in shunning the police and the institutions of the new order, they are in fact colluding with the old order. Rhoda's wavering political alliances (she has shifted between the ANC and the Democratic Alliance) are used to substantiate this claim. Faudilla and Rhoda, on the other hand, protest against the intrusion of the malign state that historically has targeted coloureds, while suggesting that the new state is also against coloureds. Hence, there are different levels of complicity and betrayal. Most often, these forms of complicity go unspoken or are only hinted at, but they relate to the complex position of coloureds within the moral community of the new South Africa.

All these diverse processes of solidarity, loyalties, and betrayal locally, past and present, I suggest, are played out in the struggles around competing moral claims in the township. What entities are the different women loyal to? The new South Africa? The community? Forces destroying the community? These uncertainties are played out in the half-light of public secrets or the skinner stories: without openly stating it or admitting to it, everybody knows about the complicit relations between Rhoda and the apartheid state that she vows to oppose; everybody knows about different women's relationship to structures of male violence—the gangs, the vigilante groups; everybody knows that some women have an unhealthy relationship with the police that cannot be aired but that is used against other women to discredit them or to work for the community—the latter not being strong enough a reason to "betray" people to the police. Everybody knows, but these most often remain unsaid, unspoken, only hinted at. In the claustrophobic, racially compromised, and morally contested space of the townships, few secrets remain such for long. In such spaces, the traitor, as a mundane figure and a mark, will be a constant element in ongoing struggles for recognition of moral claims.

Chapter 8
In a Treacherous State: The Fear of Collaboration Among West Bank Palestinians

Tobias Kelly

Khalil was one of the largest building contractors in the West Bank Palestinian village of Bayt Hajjar. I had just spent the day with him, visiting one of his projects, where he was providing laborers to help build a new suburb in the rapidly expanding settlement of Halamish. For many Palestinians, the presence of Israeli settlements is the major obstacle to a just and lasting peace. The fact that it is often Palestinians who work and build the settlements is, therefore, highly controversial. Although I knew from other people that Khalil worked in the settlements, I had expected him to be reluctant to talk to me about it. However, within hours of first being introduced by a mutual friend, he started to talk about his work in Halamish. When Khalil had asked me if I wanted to join him as he inspected his projects, I jumped at the chance, intrigued if slightly apprehensive. Khalil and I spent the day together in Halamish, as he negotiated new contracts, spoke to his workers, and inspected the site. In the evening, we drove back to the village of Bayt Hajjar, where we were both staying, along a road nominally reserved for Israeli settlers. We both sat uncomfortably low in our seats as we drove quickly through the dark. There had been several sniper attacks by Palestinians on Israeli vehicles in recent weeks, and for any armed Palestinian sitting among the olive trees, it would be impossible to tell if the driver of the car was an Israeli settler or not. As we neared the village, we drove past a large 4 × 4 vehicle parked under a bridge. Almost immediately, Khalil began to get visibly agitated. When I asked him what the matter was, he explained that the driver of the 4 by 4 was another labor contractor from the village, but that he was also a well known *muta'awin* (collaborator) with the Israeli secret police and was probably waiting under the bridge to meet his handler. Khalil told me that the contractor and all collaborators like him were a *sarataan* (cancer). Throughout my stay in the West Bank, talk of collaborators was endemic. Rumors and accusation would be met with counteraccusation, and suspicions spread quickly. While waiting for buses, drinking coffee in cafes, or chatting in front of shops, people would talk about little else. The possibility of collaboration seemed to be everywhere. Even Khalil, who earned his living carrying out an activity that many Palestinians considered tantamount to working for the Israeli occupation, would get visibly upset and worried about the prospect of collaborators living in Bayt Hajjar.

This chapter explores why suspicion about collaboration was so ubiquitous among West Bank Palestinians. Based on fieldwork carried out in 2000–2002, during the first two years of the second intifada, it examines the dilemmas of reproducing Palestinian citizens in a half (mis)formed state. In the face of an Israeli occupation that threatened to end aspirations for an effective Palestinian state, the claims of Palestinian nationalism have often been given a tangible presence through everyday relationships. From the 1970s onward, Palestinians in the West Bank attempted to lay the basis for their own state from the ground up. Not only were numerous committees, trade unions, women's groups, and voluntary organizations established, but the desire for Palestinian statehood was also seen as being embedded in commonplace activities. The style of wedding celebration or a person's choice of employment, for example, reflected a particular set of nationalist aspirations (Jean-Klein 2001). In this process, personal desires and family responsibilities merged with the project of Palestinian statehood. However, in a tragic embrace, the everyday actions and intimate relationships upon which the Palestinian state would be built have also been implicated in the very regime that they wish to deny. Given the political, economic, and social entrenchment of Israeli occupation, complicity with the Israeli state runs through the most seemingly mundane activity. The dominance of the Israeli occupation has been a constant and unavoidable fact of life. In his analysis of the logic of emancipation, Ernesto Laclau (1996) argues that groups struggling for independence necessarily contain elements of the forces they seek to overcome. For Laclau, the penetration of the oppressor into the everyday life of the oppressed necessitates the need for emancipation and also makes complete separation impossible. As such, national liberation movements are forced to build their new nations on foundations produced by the very regimes they are opposed to. For Palestinians, going to work, earning a living, or even building a house can mean relying on people acting in the name of the Israeli state. Behind every Palestinian *muwatin* (citizen/national), there is, therefore, also a subject, subordinate to the whims of the Israeli military occupation.

Rumor and suspicion about collaboration and complicity spread, not because people do not know what their friends, neighbors, relatives, and colleagues are doing but because they are all too aware of what is possible or even necessary. Social and political analysis all too often assumes that it is difference that causes conflict and fear. However, antagonism can also be rooted in a frightening mutual recognition. It is not just the unknown that produces apprehension but the all too knowable. Far from intimacy and knowledge creating a sense of warm familiarity, they can also lead to their own type of fear. People can simply know too much about each other and what they are capable of, precisely because they face the same dilemmas and pressures. The embedding of politics within intimate relations, therefore, invites constant reflection on the potentially dark side of intimacy, on the forms of betrayal and disappointment that can mark relationships with those closest to you (compare Geschiere 1997). As such, this chapter examines how, throughout the Israeli occupation, two intifadas, and the Oslo Peace Process, Palestinians have been forced constantly to renegotiate the boundaries of complicity and betrayal in their everyday lives. The everyday potential for collaboration creates powerful feelings of vulnerability and suspicion, inviting constant reflection on the moral, economic, and political possibility of the Palestinian *watan* (nation).

Living with the Israeli Occupation

Since the Israeli occupation of the West Bank, the Palestinian residents of the region have been in a quandary over how to deal with the overwhelming presence of the Israeli state in their lives. In Bayt Hajjar, Israeli government officials came to the village within weeks of the 1967 occupation, looking for people to work in the construction and farming industries inside Israel. At first, the villagers were uncertain as to whether to accept the work. Not only might it be very dangerous, but they also did not want to be accused of being *muta'awineen* (collaborators). Senior Palestinian politicians were telling laborers not to go to work in Israel, and there were even a few attacks on the buses used to transport the laborers to Israeli warehouses, factories, and kibbutzes. However, many of the residents of the village felt that they had very little choice, as they had no other way of supporting their families. The West Bank economy was stagnant, and they could not make any money from their dry fields. Following the 1967 occupation, the West Bank went through a process that one commentator has called "de-development" (Roy 1995). The Israeli government placed heavy import duties on West Bank agricultural produce and restricted the use of irrigation. At the same time, Israeli agricultural goods were able to flow into the West

Bank. The Israeli military had closed down all West Bank banks after 1967, so there were few opportunities for investment. The result was an unprofitable agricultural sector, few jobs in the West Bank, and the dependency of West Bank labor on the Israeli economy. Such economic integration was designed to produce political acquiescence. In this context, within a few years of the occupation, virtually all the men in Bayt Hajjar were working in Israel.

At the same time as the economic integration into the Israeli economy, there was also an effective territorial expansion of the Israeli state into the West Bank. During the 1970s and 1980s, Bayt Hajjar was surrounded on two sides by Israeli settlements, built on land expropriated from nearby villages. Many of the village residents, Khalil among them, went to work in the new settlements. In particular, one of the settlements was built on the remains of the Palestinian village of Bayt Nuba that had been destroyed by the Israeli military in 1967. Some of the displaced people from Bayt Nuba now lived in Bayt Hajjar and went to work in the turkey sheds that had been built by the new Israeli settlement directly over their former homes. By the early 1970s, driving into Israel from Bayt Hajjar was just a simple matter of taking the rough roads past the new settlement of Mevo Horon. The few villagers who had cars could drive them directly into Israel, while others would catch the Israeli-run bus, which used to drive into the center of the village to pick up workers. In this period, trips to the beaches, restaurants, and nightclubs of Tel Aviv became a regular feature of life.

At a political level, there were several attempts by the Israeli military to exercise control over the West Bank. The position of the *mukhtar* (village head man) has its roots in the late Ottoman Empire and has historically been used to mediate between the members of particular *hamula* (clan) and the state. In the 1970s, the Israeli military tried to use the *mukhtar* to administer the Palestinian population of the West Bank. In Bayt Hajjar, a man called Hakam Karim was the *mukhtar* of the largest of the Bayt Hajjar's four *humayil* (clans). Hakam was often called upon by the Israeli military to undertake routine administrative tasks or to take the Israeli army to the homes of suspected nationalist activists. Furthermore, all permits from the Israeli military, whether for travel, building, or agriculture, had to be applied for through the *mukhtar*. This began to cause friction in the village, as it was claimed that, rather than make life easier for the residents, Hakam was merely facilitating the Israeli occupation. The role of *mukhtar*, which had previously been based on the fact that land was held at the *hamula* (clan level), had already also been undermined by the privatization of property in the late British Mandate. The growth of wage labor in Israel had also undermined Hakam's relative affluence. The largest house in the village was now owned by a contractor who took men to work in Israel. While the rest of the village had become wage laborers in Israel or were trying to get to the university, none of Hakam's sons or grandchildren had received his secondary school leaving certificate, and all were made to work on the fields practically as soon as they could walk. In this context, instead of being respected, Hakam was widely seen as a figure of fun for being attached to an outdated way of life.

In a further attempt to consolidate their political control of the West Bank, in the early 1980s, the Israeli government tried to set up Village Leagues. Members were allowed to carry arms and enforce their own sense of law and order in the villages. The leagues were supposedly run along clan lines but were directly controlled by the Israeli military. Those Palestinians who joined up were armed and offered Israeli protection. The *mukhtar* Hakam initially saw this as an opportunity to strengthen his declining influence. However, in the neighboring village of Bayt Ur al-Tahta, several members of the Village Leagues were killed by fellow villagers for collaborating with the Israeli military. Hakam quickly avoided having any obvious role in the institution. Although the Village Leagues continued for a few years in Bayt Hajjar, it was on an individual and largely clandestine basis.

In December 1987, after years of gradually rising tensions, civil disturbances began to spread from the Gaza Strip to the West Bank. In Bayt Hajjar, as elsewhere in the West Bank, the village *shabaab* (youth) led a number of demonstrations against the constant Israeli patrols. The village's schools were soon closed down by the Israeli military, as they were accused of inciting violence. In response, several of the teachers decided to run informal lessons that took place in the mosque or in people's homes. Agricultural committees were also set up in some of the villages to the north of Bayt Hajjar. These committees were associated with the main political factions of the Palestinian Liberation Organization (PLO) and aimed at encouraging the *fallaheen* (peasants) to return to their land. Groups of *shabaab* began to set up roadblocks on the outskirts of the village, blocking the road with burning tires in order to try and stop people from going to work in Israel. However, it soon became clear that a complete boycott of work in the Israeli economy was not feasible in Bayt Hajjar. The village's land was not productive enough to support large families and the new consumption patterns that had developed since the Israeli occupation. At the same time, there were few opportunities for employment in the West Bank. Some of the men were at this time working in a toilet paper factory in Ramallah, but they were earning only NIS 20 ($5) a day compared to the NIS 120 ($30) that could be earned by building houses in Israel. The Palestinian nationalist movement, therefore, soon stopped calling for a permanent boycott of work in Israel but would intermittently call a one-day national strike. Many of the workers in Bayt Hajjar would try to ignore these as much as possible, by either leaving earlier and earlier to get to work or by staying overnight in Israel if they knew there was going to be a strike the next day. Very few people would criticize them publicly, as most of the rest of the village was behaving in exactly the same way. Despite the daily clashes with the Israeli military in Bayt Hajjar, many of the workers continued to go to work in Israel or in the newly expanded settlements in the West Bank.

The first intifada, therefore, took place in the context of the residents of Bayt Hajjar's economic and administrative dependency on the Israeli occupation and, as such, can be understood as an attempt to break with the dependency on the Israeli military. According to the Palestinian sociologist Salim Tamari, the committees and organizations that developed during the late 1980s sought to "out-administer" the occupation, by literally "shaking it off" through the creation of a viable set of Palestinian political, social, and economic institutions from below (Tamari 1990; see also Hilterman 1991). However, at the same time, many of these attempts to create an independent Palestinian space existed in tension with the fact that the villagers of Bayt Hajjar not only depended on the Israeli economy for work but also relied on the Israeli occupation for the provision of basic services. The Israel military's policy of trying to bring political acquiescence through access to the Israeli economy was arguably so successful that, by the time I arrived in Bayt Hajjar in the late 1990s, some people were openly saying that if there was ever a final peace agreement between Israel and the PLO, they wanted to be annexed to Israel. They would quickly add that they loved Palestine, but they had to feed their children, and access to the Israeli economy gave them the best opportunity of doing so. Attempts to reproduce Palestinian families seemingly conflicted with the desire to reproduce an independent and sovereign Palestinian nation.

The Oslo Peace Process

In 1993 the government of Israeli and the PLO signed the Oslo Accords. For the Israeli state, the violence of the first intifada had demonstrated that it could not maintain control over the Palestinian population of the West Bank and Gaza Strip while simultaneously claiming to be a liberal democracy. The Oslo Accords helped ease these tensions by passing partial responsibility for the Palestinian population of the West Bank and Gaza Strip to the newly formed Palestinian National Authority (PNA). Above all, the PNA would be responsible for controlling Palestinian militants. For the PLO, led by Yasser Arafat in distant Tunis, the Oslo

Accords came at a crucial juncture, as the PLO had been weakened by its support for Saddam Hussein in the first Gulf War, and offered an opportunity to "return" to the West Bank and Gaza Strip.

Although the Peace Process represented an important symbolic change in its mutual recognition of the Israeli state and the PLO, it did not fundamentally alter the structures through which the West Bank and Gaza Strip were ruled. Although the PNA took over responsibility for the daily lives of many Palestinians, the system of Israeli military regulations remained in place. While the PNA was given responsibility for policing and civil matters, such as school and hospitals, the Israeli state retained ultimate security control of the area and responsibility for all Israeli citizens. Furthermore, Israel remained the only state in the region, and the economic and political resources of the PNA were far smaller than those available to the Israeli state. Fundamental issues, such as the borders of any Palestinian state or the fate of Palestinian refugees, were never addressed, but left to final status negotiations that have never been finalized.

For the residents of Bayt Hajjar, the creation of the PNA saw the creation of a new municipality in place of the *mukhtar,* and the schools reopened under the control of the PNA Ministry of Education. The newly appointed mayor of the village, Iyyad Abdallah, was a veteran activist in Yasser Arafat's Fatah movement and part of a new generation of political leaders who had risen to prominence, as the *mukhtar,* Hakam, had decreased in influence. In the early 1980s, Iyyad Abdallah had been arrested by the Israeli police after being accused of planting a bomb in Israeli-controlled Canada Park. After spending several years in an Israeli prison, Iyyad was released shortly before the creation of the PNA in the mid-1990s. As with many Fatah activists, alongside his role as mayor, Iyyad was also given a job in the PNA. He worked at the newly created District Coordination Office (DCO) that was set up to liaise between the PNA and the Israeli state in routine administrative matters. Although Iyyad had left school without any qualifications, after spending so many years in Israeli jails he was fluent in Hebrew. With the Oslo Peace Process, his language skills were much needed in order to coordinate between the PNA and the Israeli state. Iyyad's family began to prosper with his new job, and he was able to build a new home on the outskirts of the village and buy a new Japanese car.

Many of the other former nationalist activists in Bayt Hajjar went to work for the newly created PNA security forces. My landlord's uncle returned to the West Bank, after living in exile with the PLO for over twenty years, to take a position as chief mechanic with the Palestinian civil police. Others went to work for the *mukhabarat* (secret police) or the Preventative Security. This continuity between former political activists and officers in the PNA security forces was reflected up to the highest level. The one-time head of the Preventative Security in the Gaza Strip, Muhammad Dahlan, had helped found the Fatah youth movement, known as the *shabiba*, in the West Bank in the early 1980s before being deported to Jordan in 1988. Under the Oslo Accords, the PNA security forces fast became the largest part of the PNA. Importantly, this expansion was tacitly condoned by the Israeli military, as the PNA played a major role in cracking down on opposition to the continued Israeli occupation and rounded up thousands of activists from the Popular Front for the Liberation of Palestine (PFLP) and Hamas. For the Israeli military, the new PNA security forces provided vital intelligence and coercive capacity in its struggle with more militant elements of the Palestinian national movement.

Although the PNA was now nominally responsible for the provision of water, planning permission, schooling, and rubbish collection within the newly drawn municipal boundaries of Bayt Hajjar, the residents of the village remained dependent on the Israeli state in many other ways. The land directly outside the village was under direct Israeli control, and in order to travel anywhere, people had to pass through Israeli checkpoints. Electricity and water were still hooked up to the main grids that were in Israeli hands. The power in the village was often cut off for days on end when the electricity substation up the hill malfunctioned and Israeli officials did not get around to mending it. The amount of water flowing into the village was limited by the Israeli military, which meant that there was not enough water to irrigate any crops. The physical size of the village was also limited since, although the PNA controlled planning within the municipal boundaries, outside the boundaries permission was at the discretion of the Israeli military, permission that was almost never granted.

Following the signing of the Oslo Accords, many of the workers in Bayt Hajjar continued to go to work in the Israeli economy. There were few jobs to be had in the stagnant Palestinian economy apart from in the PNA security forces, and the wages paid by the PNA were generally very low. However, throughout the 1990s, the Israeli military had restricted the availability of permits to enter Israel. Many people had their applications for a permit turned down on "security" grounds. My neighbor's brother, Hani, had been refused a permit and then had been summoned to the Israeli military base at Beit El, just to the north of Ramallah. Once there, he was told that he would be granted a permit only if he agreed to work with the Israeli secret police. It was impossible to tell how many people in Bayt Hajjar accepted these offers. It was widely assumed that several labor contractors from the village were collaborating with the Israeli military, due to the ease with which they received permits for their workers. The contractor that Khalil and I saw waiting under the bridge was particularly prominent in these rumors, as was Khalil.

Given the restrictions on permits to enter the pre-1967 borders of Israel, many people from Bayt Hajjar went to work in the fast expanding settlements that surrounded the village. As the settlements were in the West Bank, Palestinians usually did not require a permit to enter them. Palestinian workers in the settlements have been highly controversial. There were several attempts by the PNA in the 1990s to prevent Palestinians from working in Israel, and PNA police officers were sent to physically stop workers from entering Israeli settlements (Kelly 2006). However, these campaigns usually failed due to lack of other available jobs for West Bank Palestinians. When I asked people in Bayt Hajjar how they felt about working in the settlements, they would usually just shrug their shoulders and say that it was only work and they had to find a way to earn a living. Similarly, when I asked how people felt about Khalil for actually building the ever-expanding settlements, people would say that he was "a good man" because he provided much-needed jobs.

The increase in checkpoints and the difficulties in gaining permits meant that many of the residents of Bayt Hajjar tried to gain alternative forms of identification that could be used to earn a living. In particular, a large number of people held Israeli identity cards. Holding an Israeli identity card had important advantages in that it granted access to the benefits of the Israeli welfare state, such as schooling and health insurance, which were considered to be considerably better than those available in the West Bank. I knew of one man, living in Bayt Hajjar but holding an Israeli identity card, who every morning would drive his children across the unmarked border into Israel so they could attend a school in Israel, which was far better resourced than the PNA-run school in Bayt Hajjar. The richest people in the village were overwhelmingly people such as Khalil, who held foreign citizenship or Israeli identity cards and could pass relatively easily through checkpoints. Most of these people were contractors who specialized in providing Palestinian labor for Israeli employers. Still others had set themselves up as merchants.

In the 1970s, gaining an Israeli identity card was widely seen as treacherous. However, by the time of my fieldwork, there were, I estimated, more than 200 men, in a village of around 7,000 people, who had Israeli identity documents. The most common way of gaining an Israeli identity card was through marriage to an Israeli citizen. Khalil had himself married a Palestinian citizen of Israel and now kept a house in Bayt Hajjar as well as a small flat in the nearby Israeli town of Ramle.[1] A far more notorious way of obtaining an Israeli identity card was by directly collaborating with the Israeli military. It was widely suspected that several of the larger labor contractors in the village, who used to take laborers to the factories of Tel Aviv or Jerusalem, had managed to obtain Israeli identity cards through such means. There were also often repeated rumors in Bayt Hajjar that Jibril Rajoub, the former head of the one of the largest of the new PNA security forces, had received an Israeli identity card and had a large house in the Israeli town of Herzilya due to his services to the Israeli secret services.

Under the Oslo Accords, access to the warehouses and factories of Tel Aviv and Jerusalem became more and more difficult for the residents of Bayt Hajjar, as permits became scarcer and checkpoints increased. In the midst of this partial separation, new ways had to be found to earn a living that often involved new forms of complicity with the Israeli state, such as working in Israeli settlements or holding Israeli identity cards. At the same time, the creation of the PNA saw the category of the collaborator become increasingly problematic. Following the Oslo Accords, many of the activities that would previously have been deemed to be collaboration were now being carried out by people who had seemingly impeccable national credentials. Iyyad, the village mayor, who had once set off bombs near Israeli targets, now sat at a desk just a stone's throw from an Israeli military officer. The rhetoric of "peace" with Israel that was built into the Oslo Accords made talk of collaborators politically problematic. As such, far from being self-evident and given once and for all, notions of collaboration were produced by the shifting moral, economic, and political evaluations created by the wider political climate.

The Second Intifada

In late September 2000, violent clashes broke out between stone-throwing Palestinians and Israeli soldiers. These soon turned into gun battles between armed Palestinians and Israeli troops. Many of the residents of Bayt Hajjar, as with other Palestinians, were deeply disillusioned with the Oslo Peace Process. Since the 1990s, as work in Israel had become more and more difficult, unemployment had grown. The village was also increasingly surrounded by expanding Israeli settlements. Finally, PNA officials, Iyyad Abdallah among them, were widely seen as corrupt and self-interested. When the second intifada broke out, many people in the village were not surprised, as they said that the Oslo Peace Process had not been going anywhere. Although Bayt Hajjar was far away from the main centers of violence, many of the roads around the village were sealed by Israeli military checkpoints and work inside Israel became increasingly difficult, leading to mass unemployment.

Those people who had taken jobs with the PNA found themselves in an increasingly awkward position. The District Coordination Office, where Iyyad Abdallah, the mayor of Bayt Hajjar, worked, had become the scene of violent clashes between the Israelis military and armed Palestinians. The second intifada left Iyyad in a difficult situation. To work in an office expressly created to coordinate with the Israeli state was increasingly problematic. Iyyad, therefore, stopped going to work and would often be seen driving around the village, seemingly with nothing to do. Iyyad was not alone, and many former activists who had taken up administrative positions with the PNA in the wake of the Oslo Accords found that history had overtaken them. They had received their jobs due to their credentials in the nationalist movement, but in the context of the second intifada, these same jobs came dangerously close to looking like collaboration. Some people who worked for the PNA were directly accused of collaboration. In April 2002, Jibril Rajoub, at that time head of the most powerful PNA security force, handed several Hamas prisoners over to the Israeli military, after his compound was surrounded by Israeli tanks. Poster and leaflets printed in the following days directly accused him of working for the Israeli military. Similarly, Mousa Arafat, the nephew of Yasser Arafat and the former head of military intelligence, was widely known by the Hebrew version of his name, Moshe, because of his ties to the Israeli security forces. He was later assassinated in 2004 by unknown assailants in the Gaza Strip.

At the same time as the intifada continued, the PNA became less and less able to provide even basic services to the people of Bayt Hajjar. The Israeli military accused sections of the Palestinian security forces of being involved in attacks on Israeli soldiers and civilians. The result was that it frequently bombed Palestinian police stations and prisons and arrested members of the PNA security forces. Fearing that they would be arrested if stopped on the road between Bayt Hajjar and Ramallah, the people in the village who worked for the security forces stayed in Ramallah. The PNA police presence, always patchy, became nonexistent in Bayt Hajjar. Furthermore, due to an ongoing financial crisis, the PNA intermittently stopped paying the wages of its employees, and teachers, municipality workers, and nurses had to go for months without any money. As the second intifada progressed, many Palestinians increasingly questioned the ability of the PNA and its security forces to look after their basic interests, both personal and national. One common joke, playing on the identical Arabic spelling, claimed that there was no *sulta* (authority), only *salata* (salad).

The Meanings of Collaboration

In order to understand the meanings and implications of collaboration, it is important to understand its place in the history of the Palestinian national movement. The label has been applied across a wide spectrum of behavior over the past hundred years (see, for example, Cohen 2007). Perhaps the oldest subcategory is the *samsar* (land dealer). The *samsar* is a person accused of selling land to Jews or the Israeli state. In the first half of the twentieth century, the Zionist movement had gained a foothold in what was then British Mandate Palestine through buying land from Palestinian land owners. Since this period, Palestinians who have continued to sell land to Jews have been seen as *khawana* (traitors) to the Palestinian national movement. Other collaborators have included the *wasit* (middleman) who liaised between the Israel military and individual military and the *jawasis* (spies) who worked directly for the Israeli security services. Although the figure of the collaborator has long been present in Palestinian national history, it was during the first intifada of the late 1980s that it gained particular prominence. Indeed, one commentator has claimed that, in the later years of the first intifada, the Palestinian national movement in the West Bank was effectively turned into a network of young men largely concerned with rooting out collaborators (Jean-Klein 2008). As part of the attempt to disengage from the institutions of Israeli rule, the Palestinian national movement ordered all employees of the Israeli administration to resign. Collaborators were now being defined by the Palestinian political leadership as those who worked openly for the Israeli administration, as well as those who carried out activities for the Israeli security services. This category included officers in the pre-Oslo police force, members of the Israeli-controlled municipalities, and those who worked in the Village Leagues.

Perhaps the most feared type of collaborators were was the *jawasis* (spies) who work for the Israeli secret service. Often basic services, such as permits for work in Israel or permission to build a new house, were only granted in return for providing information on fellow villagers to the Israeli secret service. Before the Oslo Accords, all permits were issued directly by the Israeli administration, so any request for permission was also potentially an opportunity to pass on information. At other times, criminal charges were dropped or shortened in return for collaboration. Many *jawasis* are also recruited in prison and asked to spy on fellow inmates. Although the large numbers of Palestinians being held in Israeli jails have represented a considerable mobilizing and educational force in the development of Palestinian nationalism, it also represented an opportunity for the recruitment of collaborators to the Israeli security forces. The tactics of the Israeli security services of recruiting spies in return for services or lenient treatment from the criminal justice system mean that anybody who received planning permission or a permit to enter Israel, as well as those who received relatively light sentences, is seen by many Palestinians as being potentially suspicious.

The figure of the collaborator also has strong moral overtones. In the late 1980s, as the internal campaign during the first intifada against collaborators was reaching its peak, an internal Fatah document defined collaborators as "people who have lost all shame, honor and conscience."[2] Drug dealers and prostitutes have been seen as collaborators, partly on the grounds that they lower the moral fiber of Palestinians and partly because their activities made them vulnerable to exploitation by the Israeli security services. During the first intifada, a book known as *ad-dahiyyah taataraf* (the victim confesses) appeared across the West Bank. The book describes the life of a man called Mazen Fahwenani from Jenin in the north of the West Bank. It sets out in detail how Fahwenani recruited dozens of Palestinian men and women to work for the Israeli secret service. In particular, Fahwenani reportedly specialized in setting "honey traps" in order to take pictures of people in sexually compromising positions, then using these pictures to blackmail them. Irrespective of whether the book described real events, it was widely circulated and read, providing the dominant popular image of the period of collaborators as morally dubious. In Bayt Hajjar, Khalil's brother, who was widely suspected of passing on small bits of information to the Israeli secret police, was also suspected of being a minor drug dealer, selling small amounts of cannabis to the village youth. Stories abounded about the time, in the early 1990s, when he had been arrested by the Israeli police for trying to grow marijuana in one of his family's fields on the hills above Bayt Hajjar. He had been released after a few days, further increasing the suspicion that he had done a deal with the Israeli security forces. Whether the claims of drug dealing or collaboration came first is largely irrelevant, as, for many people in Bayt Hajjar, they were closely related. Accusation of financial *fasad* (corruption) among PNA officials were also often linked to accusations of collaboration. Since Iyyad had been made mayor, not only had he employed many of his own relatives in the only jobs available in the municipality—collecting rubbish—he had also been able to move into a much larger home and buy a car. In popular conceptions, the moral corruption of financial self-interest is often linked to the moral corruption of collaboration with the Israeli military.

It is important to recognize that there was not always an absolute condemnation of people accused of acting as Israeli spies. There were numerous stories of people being forced to collaborate by the Israeli military, which invoked as much pity as anger. Sometimes this involved blackmail for inappropriate moral behavior, but, more often than not, it involved someone who was desperate for work and had therefore passed on limited pieces of information to the Israeli military in return for a permit to work in Israel or the shortening of a lengthy jail sentence.

Such people were felt to be *masakeen* (unfortunate, deserving of pity), as they had been caught in a near-impossible bind. Collaboration was seen as a tragic outcome of the wider recognition that personal desire, family obligations, and national aspirations could often not be fitted into a seamless whole. This tragedy was felt to be a product of the wider Palestinian situation, where the Israeli military controlled virtually every aspect of life. As such, there was a widespread recognition that even the most morally and politically principled person could become a collaborator.

The ambiguous nature of the category of the collaborator means that it is often possible for people, widely thought of as being collaborators, to carry on living relatively freely in the West Bank. This was particularly so in the period after the first intifada and in the first years of the PNA. In Bayt Hajjar, I was constantly being told that several people who lived nearby were collaborators. One example was a man who, a few years before the creation of the PNA, was rumored to have stabbed his brother in the center of the village over a disputed piece of land. He had never been prosecuted, it was claimed, because he acted as an informant for the Israeli military. I was told by my landlord late in my stay that many of the people in the village assumed that I was working for the Israeli security services, as I kept asking questions that they could not see the point of. The only reason that the issue had not been taken further was that they could not believe someone working for the Israeli security forces would speak Arabic so badly and behave in a way that was so obviously suspicious.

The ambiguity in its meanings and implications means that charges of collaboration are often subject to counteraccusations and used to settle personal rivalries. Khalil's claim that the labor contractor we passed under the bridge was a collaborator has to be seen in the context of his rivalry for contracts and the recruitment of laborers within the village. Khalil was similarly implicitly accused by other contractors of collaboration due to his work in the settlements. One contractor told me he thought it was *mukhjil* (shameful) that Khalil carried out such work, not knowing that I knew he himself supplied laborers to another settlement. Often accusations were indirect and insinuated. Direct accusations were most often made either through graffiti scrawled on the village streets or through posters put up overnight. Clearly, some people were more susceptible to accusation than others. The work that Khalil performed in the settlements made him particularly vulnerable, but a sense of a lack of moral righteousness also made people more prone to accusation. Khalil's brother was forever tainted by the accusation of growing marijuana. However, the opaqueness of these accusations meant that they were never entirely trusted. People were well aware that accusations of collaboration were often personally motivated, but they, nevertheless, left traces of suspicion. The Israeli military reportedly played on this ambiguity, issuing false communiqués from the Palestinian national movement, condemning figures who had never done so for collaborating, thereby creating considerable uncertainty as to whom to believe. Friend and enemy, the trustworthy and the untrustworthy became increasingly difficult to tell apart.

Throughout the first years of the second intifada, talk of collaboration and collaborators was everywhere, filling innumerable conversations as people waited for buses, sat outside cafes, or met in the street. Accusations and counteraccusations were spread in a cycle of rumor and gossip. However, accusations were not just motivated by a cynical desire to slander and spread gossip but by a profound sense that the potential for collaboration seemed endemic. Bauman (1991) has famously argued that the unknown stranger produces particular forms of anxiety and suspicion. However, collaborators were feared and suspected not because they were beyond the moral pale and unknown but because they were all too understandable and all too recognizable. It was not difference that caused anxiety but similarity. Closeness does not only produce a benign sense of intimacy but also a feeling of malignant possibility. Collaborators are not a distant "other" but a distorted and all too familiar self.[3] Precisely because people were aware of the ways in which complicity was inherent in many of their everyday actions, the collaborator stood like a mirror in which they could see their own potential, frightening reflection. The fear of collaboration does not come from not knowing what is behind appearance but by being all too aware of what might be there. This does not mean that all people saw themselves as potential Israeli spies, rather that they recognized that some form of complicity with the Israeli occupation was implicit in many of their everyday actions. People knew the pressures that might force them to cooperate with the Israeli state.

Palestinians have been faced with the competing ethical demands of supporting their families and tacit cooperation with the Israeli occupation. While aspirations for Palestinian statehood have often been rooted in mundane hopes and desires, all too often these hopes have been unattainable without the indirect support of the Israeli state. Given the economic, social, and political dominance of the occupation, personal ambitions, familial responsibilities, and collective goals often come into conflict. In this situation, there is no simple solution, no pure ethical moment, as not all duties can be reconciled. People are forced constantly to negotiate the shifting boundaries of permissible and impermissible complicity. As such, collaboration is not a one-off event but the product of many "small-scale treacheries" forced on people as they try and provide for their families.[4] It is important to stress here that many, if not most, West Bank Palestinians have found ways to oppose the Israeli occupation. For some, this has meant joining armed militant groups; for others, this has seen them refusing to work in Israeli settlements and to participate in many activities in between. Most have also made the ethical decision not to work as Israeli spies. However, these choices have often come at great personal cost, either in terms of loss of life, long periods in jail, or loss of income. The key point is that, for many of the residents of Bayt Hajjar, there has been no straight forward resolution to the tension between complicity with the Israeli state, however subtle, and the need to provide for families or fulfill personal ambitions. In such a situation, it is crucial to move beyond the logic of binary oppositions of Israeli versus Palestinian in order to understand how aspirations, hopes, and fears can become mutually, if antagonistically, entangled within one another. Political conflicts should not be seen simply as the marking of difference but as also the product of tension between competing ethical and social projects that blur the boundary between consent and coercion, loyalty and betrayal.

Assassinations

In early November 2000, the Israeli military began to assassinate Palestinian activists, often by using helicopters hovering in the skies above Palestinian towns and villages. In the months and years that followed, dozens of activists were killed in similar ways in the middle of Palestinian areas. It seemed that the reach of the Israeli military was everywhere, spreading considerable fear, both among activists and ordinary Palestinians. The Israeli policy of assassinating prominent nationalist activists using helicopter gunships, bombs, and snipers was also widely seen as relying on local Palestinian collaborators on the ground. In Bayt Hajjar, throughout the intifada, Israeli troops would make constant raids, usually in the middle of the night. During these raids, they would often be led by a masked Palestinian who would show them the way. Sometimes these people would be physically coerced to act effectively as human shields. Other times, they appeared to have a longer-term relationship with the Israeli troops. It was widely assumed in the village that these people lived in Bayt Hajjar.

Throughout the second intifada, the PNA seemed to be on the brink of collapse. In the spring of 2002, the Israeli military was a ubiquitous presence in the center of Palestinian towns. Yasser Arafat was holed up in the half-destroyed remains of his Ramallah compound, without electricity or running water, unable to leave. Palestinian security officers were also being arrested in their thousands, and those that remained were too afraid to wear their uniforms or carry their weapons. Many civil servants just stopped going to work, as the Israeli military raided the offices of the PNA and carried away boxes of documents and computer hard drives. As activist after activist was assassinated or arrested, Palestinian *jawasis* (spies) were widely seen as responsible for the ease by which the Israeli military reached into the heart of Palestinian communities. The fear of spies was matched by constant talk of *mustarabeen* (undercover Israeli hit squads—literally "fake Arabs") who would infiltrate Palestinian towns, passing as locals, before killing or kidnapping their targets. Much to my panic, I was once accused by a small child while queuing for bus of being a *mustarab*, only for the child to be told not to be stupid, as the whole point of the *mustarabeen* was that they were difficult to tell from a Palestinian.

A year into the intifada, Palestinians began actively to punish people accused of direct collaboration with the Israeli security services. In March 2002, near to where the buses between Bayt Hajjar and Ramallah dropped off their passengers, a Palestinian from the refugee camp of Amari, stripped to the waist and his hands tied behind his back, was marched into the main traffic circle in the town by masked gunmen and shot dead. He was then hung by the feet from the large scaffold that stood in the center of the circle and left to swing upside down as the cars drove past. The gunmen, faces covered with head scarves, announced that the man was a collaborator with Israeli intelligence and had taken part in the assassination of three members of the Al-Aqsa Martyrs Brigade. The brigades were a partly clandestine militia, made up of local Fatah activists, and would increasingly play a leading role in the second intifada, launching attacks on Israeli soldiers and civilians.[5] The brigades were a far from unified movement, but rather a loose amalgam of local cells all using the same name. In many towns and villages, there were several rival groups answering to the name of the brigades. Those accused of collaboration by the brigades were often subjected to summary trials and forced to confess their crimes before being executed. Fearing that it was increasingly looking redundant at best, or as acquiescing to the Israeli occupation at worst, and unable directly to confront the Israeli military, the PNA also started to arrest suspected collaborators. By September 2001, the PNA was said to be holding 450 suspects in the West Bank. However, the masked members of the al-Aqsa Martyrs Brigade carried out most of the punishments of suspected collaborators. By the spring of 2002, the brigades were executing scores of Palestinians for allegedly collaborating with the Israeli state, reaching a peak in March and April 2002, when nearly sixty people were killed.[6]

Against this background of suspicion, anxiety, and confusion, nothing is more definitive than bloodshed. As the Palestinian national movement became more and more fragmented, the PNA teetering on the brink of collapse, and numerous armed groups seeking to impose their own particular visions of justice, the taking of life gave an undeniable tangibility to the pretension to speak in the name of the Palestinian people. In the face of political fragmentation, there is a hard reality to the claim to power seen in the taking of life. Arjun Appadurai (1998) has argued that, in contexts of uncertainty over loyalty, violence often acts as a marker of certainty. While the ubiquitous possibility of collaboration caused disquiet, unease, and ethical confusion, the killing of those accused of collaboration cut through these ambiguities with a gruesome absoluteness. However, at the same time, rather than mark the reassuring presence of the Palestinian state-building project, the execution of suspected collaborators only served to increase the anxieties of the residents of Bayt Hajjar. Their killings only functioned to highlight the fact that there was no functioning state or legal system that could hold collaborators to account in a transparent and just manner. On several occasions, people were assassinated only later to be exonerated publicly by the brigades or the PNA security forces. Sometimes, this appeared to be a case of mistaken identity, but often it seemed to be a case of people using accusations of collaboration to settle scores in the context of particular local rivalries. My landlord constantly lamented the killing of collaborators. While he said that collaborators were a *sarataan* (cancer) that deserved to be killed, he thought that public executions showed a lack of *hadarat* (civilization). He complained about the inability of the PNA to bring suspects to justice in any way that vaguely resembled the *siyadat al-qanun* (rule of law). The masked men of the brigades, faces covered with headscarves and communicating through graffiti and posters put up in the dead of the night, were almost as spectral as the collaborator. Instead of creating a form of dead certainty, the killing of suspected collaborators only added to the fear and confusion.

Conclusion

The fear of treachery haunts Palestinian nationalism. All political movements that claim to act in the name of the "people" are faced with the problem that the people have no tangible presence. Citizens are never self-evident, and their unity cannot be taken for granted but must be constantly marked through the political rituals, institutions, and performances of statecraft (Balibar 2003). The will of the "people of Israel" is made tangible, for example, through the planting of flags, the celebration of Independence Day, the holding of elections, and the actions of the Israeli military. The dominant and concrete presence of the Israeli state gives the claims of Israeli popular sovereignty a very real, if contested, presence of its own. For West Bank Palestinians, in contrast, the existence of a half (mis)formed state, in the shape of the PNA, has meant that the responsibility for reproducing Palestinian citizens has lain in a host of everyday activities. Tasks as seemingly mundane as going to work, earning a living, or trying to build a home have, therefore, been given a particular political and ethical charge. Yet the very activities through which attempts are made to reproduce the Palestinian people are also entangled with the overwhelming presence of the Israeli state. For West Bank Palestinians, behind even the most mundane activity stands the economic, administrative, and military power of the Israeli state. To paraphrase Bauman (1991), collaborators stand for both the cunning of enemies and the treacherousness of friends. Collaborators represent both the dominating presence of the Israeli state and the weaknesses of the Palestinian national movement.

The fear and hatred created by the figure of the collaborator are products of what might be called "epistemic murk" (Taussig 1984), the difficulty of telling truth from illusion, friend from enemy, protector from persecutor. Indeed, with the creation of the PNA, embedded as it is within the security and administrative structures of the Israeli state, the Palestinian national movement was itself in danger of becoming a collaborator. For many people, it became impossible to tell who was speaking in the name of the Palestinian people and who was serving the interests of the Israeli occupation. As such, the seeming ubiquity of collaboration causes a constant reflection on the moral, political, and economic possibilities of a Palestinian state. The collaborator has a double in the shape of the undercover Israeli *mustarabeen*. However, collaborators provoke a far stronger fear. While it is possible to unmask *mustarabeen* as Israelis, a collaborator comes from within the very heart of the Palestinian community. The sense of vulnerability they create is not just simply that people might not be who they seem to be, but rather an anxiety that, in the face of the pervasive presence of the Israeli state, the Palestinian state-building project is too fragile. Collaborators, therefore, produce a collective sense of vulnerability, a longing for a state that might protect its people in the face of the overwhelming presence of the Israeli state and the potential for Palestinian corruption (compare Wedeen 2003). It is not just loyalty that is in question but also the very possibility of a national project within which Palestinians had invested their hopes and desires. The fear of the collaborator, then, is not simply that, when you "'tear off the mask'" (Fitzpatrick 2005) there will be an Israeli underneath but something far more frightening: that just possibly, there will be nothing.

Chapter 9
The Glass Agency: Iranian War Veterans as Heroes or Traitors?

Kamran Rastegar

The profile of the traitor is a fluid one, reflecting changing circumstances and anxieties around the social value of certain kinds of ideological commitment. Wartime is the condition where the traitor's features are most sharply defined, even if the criteria for what constitutes traitorous action are contested in the period of active conflict. However, the period following the cessation of a war may often be marked by deep ambivalence, where the unavoidable traumas of war bring to the fore questions about the ideological commitments that had been mobilized in support of the war. In any postwar environment, the reversion of society to a peacetime footing exacts a price on those who had been closest to the heart of the ideological exigencies of the war. Unless they are able to transform themselves, the heroes of the war risk drinking a bitter tea representing the decreasing social value of their ideological commitments—not always in terms of what was considered to be their sacrifice, but rather in terms of social accommodation of the ideals and degree of zeal they once exemplified. As the political grounds shift, it is possible for this kind of commitment to change quality from being seen as heroic to becoming seen, at first, as possibly undesirable or excessive and, in certain conditions, even being recoded as traitorous.

This discussion will examine how the ideological commitment demanded by the post-revolutionary Iranian regime in the Iran-Iraq war has been read within postwar Iranian cinema, through the case study of one film that centrally engages the problem of the shifting nature of the hero-traitor dialectic in this period. Ebrahim Hatamikia's action-drama *Ajans-e Shisheh-i* (*The Glass Agency*, 1997) is one of a series of films from the postwar period dealing directly with the lingering traumas of the war and, in particular, asking questions about the values surrounding the categories of both hero and traitor. Here, Iranian cinema will be treated as part of the "ideological state apparatus" of the Islamic Republic, acting with all the diversity and ambiguity with which Louis Althusser initially invested this category (Althusser 1971, 146). As such, Iranian popular cinema may be seen to present insights into the intermediary role cultural discourse plays in debates around concepts such as martyrs for the nation, as well as traitors to the nation.

In Iran, the eight-year war with Iraq (1980–88), resulted in the emergence of an official cultural paradigm for the Islamic Republic both through the repressive domestic ideological climate that the war produced and in the intense pressure for personal sacrifices on the part of individual Iranians during the course of the war. In some senses, its representation through the ideological state apparatuses of the Islamic Republic was, and remains, the purest distillation of the official ideological paradigm of postrevolutionary Iran.[1] The war is still commonly cited in official discourse as the exemplary ground for the sacrifices that the revolutionary society was meant to be built upon—the veterans of this war would then act as ciphers for the commitment to this sacrifice, and their "sacred defense" (as the war was called) of Iran would determine the baseline from which the revolution's aims would be measured.

In Iran, narratives of the war themselves tend to center on themes of sacrifice and the deep personal commitment of fighting men to the defense of the nation and the revolution. While these themes are common to many postwar contexts, in Iran the archetype of the hero is more problematic than in some other contexts. Iran's armed forces comprised not only the traditional armed forces, which had been decimated by postrevolutionary purges of officers loyal to the shah's regime, but also included the *pasdaran-e enqelabi* (revolutionary guard), a military institution founded to counterbalance the traditional armed forces, as well as the Basij, an irregular militia of highly ideologically committed but poorly trained, lightly armed volunteers. These groups to some extent can be mapped against ethnic and class divisions within Iranian society, with the Basij drawing membership from the poorest urban and rural communities.[2] The efficacy of the Basij as dedicated foot soldiers to conservative elements in postrevolutionary society has been displayed on a continuing basis since the end of the war, with more spectacular examples being their mobilization to intimidate and deploy violence against student demonstrators in 1999 and 2001. The sudden appearance of groups of motor bike-riding men, generally dressed in civilian clothing at demonstrations or acts of public protest has been one of the most effective mechanisms for the pacification of public dissent at the disposal of conservative factions in the Iranian government.[3]

However, these ideological accumulations around war narratives are often quite fragile. The codification of an official cultural paradigm of heroism through the experience of the war has resulted in an ambivalent representation of both the traitor and hero in Iranian postrevolutionary cultural production within the official cultural discourse of the Islamic Republic. Yet the war and its terms of reference have not as yet been dispelled as cultural reference points; the war still constitutes the apex of postrevolutionary ideological commitment, at least by the most hard-line (what Ervand Abrahamian calls "Khomeinist") elements in Iranian government and society.[4] It is by looking at this ideological core that one may begin to map a movement of representational politics in postrevolutionary Iran; for; despite the "sacredness" of the war, its history and aftermath serve as fertile grounds for critical debates over ideological matters in postrevolutionary Iran.

Ebrahim Hatamikia first emerged as a popular filmmaker in Iran during the early 1990s, as a leading light of Iran's "Sacred Defense" film "genre"—a term identifying films relating directly to the Iran-Iraq war.[5] To date, his filmography includes some ten or so feature-length films; the narrative of nearly every one of these films has concerned the war itself or the postwar lives of men who fought in it. Hatamikia's work may best be termed as essentially commercial in terms of its production context and formally highly conscious of the typologies of popular genres such as the social melodrama and the action-thriller—which tend to predominate in Iran's domestic film industry—even if most commentators see his films as more artfully working within these formal and production contexts. His films have been very popular inside Iran: several of his films have been among the biggest box-office successes in their years of release. Yet his work is distinguished from the mainstream of commercial filmmaking not only by its relative technical sophistication but also, and just as importantly, by its ambivalent characterization of social questions infrequently addressed in popular culture in Iran. His work has not escaped controversy—one film, *The Dead Wave* (2001), was banned from screening when it was completed—but as he is not identified with Iran's cosmopolitan auteur filmmaking economy (which has won praise and adulation in international film festivals since the 1990s), he has been able to remain nominally more acceptable to hard-line elements, even when they have despaired of the content of his work. To a great extent, this is also because Hatamikia is a former Basij member himself, and his own experience as a front-line war documentarian working with the military has given him credibility that the intellectually sophisticated Iranian art-house filmmakers lack. Yet, within the sanctioned framework of sacred-defense cinema, Hatamikia has been able to use his own legitimacy, as well as the legitimacy of the topic of the war, to raise questions concerning the culturalist projects of the Islamic Republic. In a social sense, his films are seen by Iranian viewers to be vehicles for examining the regime's ideology in a complex manner, at times approaching or even crossing the government's so-called red lines—issues that are not outlined but that most public discourse in Iran tends to avoid. His films continue to be debated at great length in the Iranian press, with nuanced ideological subtexts read into them by critics and common viewers alike.

Hatamikia has found continual inspiration in the shifting social memory of the war and the ongoing postwar traumas that have affected Iranian society since the end of the war. One of his most popular films, *The Glass Agency* (1997), directly addresses questions of how those who fought in the war have interacted with and been reintegrated into a peacetime society. The *Glass Agency* follows the story of a Tehran taxi driver, Kazem, who happens upon his old war comrade Abbas on a traffic-clogged street in the capital. Abbas and his wife Nargess have traveled to the city from their rural farm to find medical treatment for him. A wartime wound has afflicted him since his time in the trenches; however, recently he has become incapacitated and is unable to work his farm, hence his decision to come to the capital to seek help from a medical specialist. Kazem then takes Abbas to see another fellow former fighter, who is now a prominent doctor in Tehran. The diagnosis is unsettling— Abbas needs immediate surgery, of a kind too delicate to carry out in an Iranian hospital. The doctor recommends immediate departure for London, where a colleague will agree to carry out the surgery for free. All that remains is for Abbas to purchase an airline ticket for the next flight to London.

Kazem takes responsibility for Abbas, insisting he and Nargess stay at his home with his family while travel arrangements are made. He and Abbas spend a frustrating day seeking funds from government agencies to help pay for his airline ticket; despite his status as a war veteran, even a foundation whose mission it is to assist veterans refuses immediate action, and they are told a committee will look at his application for funding at some undisclosed period in the future. To make matters worse, it is the eve of the Persian New Year, and many offices are closing. Now desperate, Kazem decides to sell his taxi to pay for the ticket and insists that he accompany Abbas to London to look after him. The problems they encounter are representative of a common theme in many postwar films in both Iran and elsewhere, which present a critique of the limitations that exist in the services governments provide for those who previously sacrificed themselves for the nation. Even the fact that Abbas needs to seek treatment in London is coded as a point of humiliation for the proud former fighters, who are at the mercy of both unsympathetic government officials and foreign doctors.

These initial scenes display a set of tropes generally familiar to the postwar film genre—touching upon the comradeship of the former fighters despite the passing of years, the withering regard of official institutions toward their predicament, and the apathy of swathes of society for their dedication and sacrifices. Here these general themes are given an Iranian particularity through references to the ideological context of the war; but interestingly, in the first sequences of the film, these references are very subtle. Neither Kazem nor Abbas directly invokes this commitment, yet references surround them, reinforcing the fact that their wartime duty was not only to the nation but also to a universalist ideological struggle defined by postrevolutionary political discourse.

After these initial scenes, the action then moves to what will be the main setting for the film, an up-market travel agency. Inside the agency Kazem, accompanied by Abbas, waits impatiently to purchase their tickets to London. He has arranged with a potential buyer of his car to meet at the agency where he will take the money directly to buy two tickets he has reserved on the next morning's sold-out flight to London. The agents are impatient—there are several people on a waiting list who would gladly purchase the tickets right away, and Kazem's buyer is late. The head of the agency threatens to sell the tickets, and Kazem appeals to his nationalist sentiments by informing him of the purpose of the travel. Unmoved by Abbas's plight, the agency owner harangues Kazem for holding up his business with matters that are not the owner's responsibility.

In a stylized sequence, Kazem loses his temper and smashes a window in the manager's office upon which an employee of the agency runs to get a policeman. Kazem's violent outburst is represented not in film language conventional to the action genre but through a new film language. The action is relayed in slow motion, in brief edits, set against a choralesque soundtrack, exiting the realism of the narrative. The Iranian audience would find resonances in this scene with the metaphysical eruptions that are a convention within sacred-defense films. Surreal elements—achieved through techniques such as slow-motion, unconventional editing, and haunting or rhythmic soundtrack choices—are used within these films to signal the entrance of a character or characters into a state of higher or alternate consciousness, associated with wartime and the experience of entering front-line combat. The policeman rushes into the agency but is overpowered by Kazem, who rips the policeman's gun from his hands.

In this economic sequence, Kazem transforms from being a neglected, working-class war veteran to an ideologically recommitted fighter willing to use violence to achieve his goals. While his explosion is cathartic, and the film directs audience identification very much

Figure 9.1. Scene from *The Glass Agency* (dir. Ebrahim Hatamikia): Kazem smashes a window in the travel agency.

toward him, the mise-en-scène and soundtrack also establish that what is happening is a tragedy rather than a triumph. By choosing to transition Kazem's character from a browbeaten cabbie to a gun-wielding hostage taker through this delicate and evocative sequence, the actions that follow this set of events are tinged with a tragic and ambivalent tenor.

Now armed, Kazem locks the front door of the agency, trapping the employees and a number of customers inside as hostages. He demands that Abbas and he be put on the London flight. Shortly afterward, police and soldiers surround the agency. The first hostage negotiator to arrive is Ahmad, who by chance is a former Basij comrade of Abbas and Kazem. Distressed, he promises to try to help them resolve the issue, using language and gestures that testify to his empathy with their plight. But shortly, another negotiator, Salahshur, arrives on the scene, apparently from the intelligence services. Rather than display camaraderie and empathy as Ahmad has, his style is one of sarcasm and arrogance, willfully projecting disinterest toward the circumstances surrounding the men's desperate act. The arrangement of the two negotiators sets up a tension within the story between two differing modes of reading the crisis of the traumatized veterans. This tension is further developed in the responses of the fifteen or so hostages who similarly treat their captors either with a measure of empathy or with hostility and anger at the references to the sacrifices of these men during the war and after.

In one scene, one of the hostages attempts to bribe Abbas to let him and his wife leave the agency. He offers to "pay my portion" to be released and pleads that his wife needs medicine that she does not have with her. When Abbas hesitates, the woman becomes angry and shouts, "What more do you want from us, you're given jobs, given places in the universities, and now you hold us here?" She refers to legal and social programs that ensure that war veterans are given preferential treatment in employment and in gaining admission to highly competitive universities. Her response sets in motion the recoding of the legacy of the war veterans as something other than heroic. The woman's accusations strike bitterly at the heart of postwar anxieties over the priority given to the men who fought in the war where the distribution of meager social services are concerned. Rather than being rightful claimants to a superior position in the dispersal of social assistance, the veterans are here intimated to be the opposite, parasites draining the life from postwar Iranian society. Furthermore, by staging this hostage drama, the woman intimates that they have become something much worse—crossing over from being unproductive members of society into being actual traitors. She directs her criticism not at a personal level, but rather as a challenge of the ideological justification for their actions. Abbas, unable to reply to her charges, ushers her quickly out the door.

The film progresses on a narrative sustained by the tension between these two poles, developed within the relationship between Kazem (and to a lesser extent, Abbas, who is too ill to become very involved) and Salahshur. After a series of events, Salahshur returns to negotiate with Kazem again. He addresses him in the center of the travel agency surrounded by an audience of hostages.

Salahshur. Well . . . ok, I've done my research. Imagine, at one time being a sergeant, then to have to become a taxi driver, with a half-built house, a boy nearly in university . . . it must be difficult. Of course, there aren't very many people like this . . . but there are some.

Kazem: Do you think we cost anyone more than the cost of a single one of those high-rise buildings being built everywhere? Isn't it better we be out in the open? Or would you rather we were sent to a museum or put in a zoo, where you could really do some research on us?!

Salahshur. (looking at the hostages for support) Did I insult him?

Kazem: Did you fight at the front?

Salahshur. Where I've been was no less than having been at the front.

Kazem: (Runs over to him and shouts various military instructions at him, as if to test his knowledge of them.)

Salahshur. (Pauses as if to see if Kazem is finished) Now can I ask you a question? No doubt in elementary school you were shown a map of Iran—it's shaped a bit like a cat—(draws a map in the air, then begins to point to the imaginary countries around it): Armenia, Azerbaijan, Turkistan, Afghanistan, Pakistan . . . the little bitty Gulf Arab countries . . . Kuwait, Saudi Arabia, Iraq, Turkey. Do you know what all these countries think about that cat? If you did, I'm sure you'd never let a sergeant embarrass us like you're doing right now. (Slides a rolling chair toward Kazem). . . . Your decade's over, commander! If you weren't holding that gun in your hands, who would even listen to you? It's the only thing that

Figure 9.2. Scene from T*he Glass Agency*: Salahshur confronts Kazem.

gives you power. You spoke for a whole decade, said what you wanted to, and the rest of us shut up and listened. Whatever you did, we were quiet—you took what you wanted, we stayed quiet, you gave what you wanted, we stayed quiet. But now allow us to speak for once! Do you want, ladies and gentlemen, for another one of these neighbors to attack us?
A hostage. Never!
Salahshur. Would you like it if—God forbid—there was another war?
A hostage. Never . . . (others murmur in agreement)
Salahshur. Our decade is the decade of stability! Security! When is this country going to be blessed with security? When is that son of yours going to be able to start to make plans for his own future?! It's not my decade . . . it's your son's. . . .
Kazem: (Screams) Get out![6]

This confrontation plays out the central ideological tension within the film, the tension between the legacy of the veterans, the ideals they were supposed to be fighting for, and the proper way to memorialize the history of the war. Here, Salahshur, instead of displaying humility and empathy, mocks Kazem as one whose time is over and who is now irrelevant to the new national context. Kazem makes reference to legitimizing elements by asking Salahshur if he served at the front and whether he understands certain military commands. By refusing to go along with these means of measuring political and ideological legitimacy, Salahshur again emphasizes the irrelevance of Kazem's way of thinking. Going even farther, in Salahshur's logic, Kazem is acting as a traitor in jeopardizing the present aims of the nation: security and stability. While his previous sacrifices and ideological commitment were idealized

Figure 9.3. Scene from *The Glass Agency*: Kazem carries Abbas to the car that is to take them to the airport.

within the wartime national narrative, Kazem's insistence on a social rec-ognition of these sacrifices—written into his sense of justification in hav-ing taking the hostages—now transforms his ideological commitment into a traitorous act.

Eventually an agreement is reached by the negotiators to take Kazem and Abbas to the airport early the next morning, to be given seats on the London flight. After many diversions, they leave the agency the next morning and enter the car that is to take them to the airport, only to find that Salahshur has laid a trap for them (see Figure 9.3). The driver in the car does not have the keys; they cannot escape. Just as Salahshur steps up to the car to apprehend them, a helicopter descends and lands in the street. Ahmad emerges from inside it, bearing a letter from a "high authority" giving him the right to take them to the airplane instead. Salahshur is furious but realizes he has lost the struggle; and after an argument between the negotiators, Ahmad transports them to the airport (see Figure 9.4).

The final scene of the film takes place on the airplane, with Kazem and Abbas sitting in the first-class area, accompanied by Ahmad who is escorting them to the U.K. They seem happy and at ease and joke with each other as the flight gets under way. However, just as a flight atten-dant tells them that that the airplane is to leave Iranian airspace, Kazem

Figure 9.4. Scene from *The Glass Agency*: Ahmad stops Salahshur.

turns to Abbas, finding that he has quietly died (see Figure 9.5). Thus, the film ends on a distinctly ambivalent note. While in a narrative sense, the veterans prevailed in their struggle against Salahshur, vindicating themselves in the face of his accusations of their traitorous actions (especially with the dispensation given them to be allowed to leave—presumably from the Supreme Leader), Abbas's death transforms the victory into a tragedy. It may even be that the hostage-taking itself was the cause of his death, given that he had been strongly cautioned by the doctor to avoid stressful situations and to "always laugh." In either case, this late cause for Kazem, the Basiji—his latter-day front—ends with the death of his old comrade, and the failure of his final mission.

It is important to note that *The Glass Agency* was released in 1997, just as the "reformist" movement led by Muhammad Khatami was gaining political ascendancy in the Iranian domestic scene. This political moment was one where a number of previously taboo subjects were slowly opened to public debate. The film posits a tension over the ideological legacy of the Iran-Iraq war and, in particular, the social value to be accorded to the continuation of a commitment to the most extreme aspects of the war's legacy, represented by the Basij, within a changing Iranian political context. The ambivalence of the ending sets out questions for the future of this legacy, even as the film itself steps back from

Figure 9.5. Scene from *The Glass Agency*: Kazem dies.

affording legitimacy to those characters within the film who accuse Kazem and Abbas of acting as traitors. Yet, within the confines of official discourse over the war—a topic much more sensitive than myriad other areas where criticism of and dissent from official positions has been tolerated—the fact that this film does give voice to this view is significant. While the characters who represent this opinion are not, in the end, those the film asks the audience to identify with, they are also not shown to be outside the limits of reasonable discourse about the war.

The Glass Agency is not the only film to take on the subject of the war critically. But it marks a moment in the development of public discourse around the war when the legacy of the war is no longer beyond question. By going as far as it does to incorporate criticism of, if not the war, the acceptability of a continued pursuit of the war's ideological aims within a postwar society, it marks a milestone in how the war is valued. While at its core the film treats the ideologically inflected characters of Kazem, Abbas, and their supporters with great sympathy—even, in a sense, mourning the dissipation of social cohesion over the centrality of the purported aims of the war (which were always identified with revolutionary aspirations such as social justice and the elimination of poverty)—Salahshur, with his discourse of realpolitik and pragmatism, represents a retreat from these goals to those of a postwar setting: national security and economic stability. While the film also represents Salahshur's anger and the frustrations of the hostages in very sympathetic terms, it posits the clash of these positions—considering the hostage takers as heroes or traitors—as fundamentally tragic. The death of Abbas in the final sequence of the film is predicated on the symbolic evacuation of that which he represents from the national scene.

This analysis, through its reading of *The Glass Agency*, only begins to elaborate on the fabric of the conflict between the continuation of the wartime ideological commitments and an attempt to move the national ideological framework beyond the context of the war. One reason for the widespread popularity of the film was the fact that it was a public means of engaging in a debate about this issue, which had already been at the center of private discourse among Iranians for some time. The opening presented by the film was to acknowledge that, in many ways, the commitments of the war were now not only perhaps irrelevant to postwar social, economic, and cultural problems but that, in some cases, acting on these commitments may now appear to be traitorous. Yet through presenting the story through the eyes of Kazem and Abbas, and thus inviting audience identification with them, the recoding of Basij war veterans as traitors is not the goal of the film. Instead, by allowing an open engagement with a logic that would find their actions to be those of traitors, the film uses the uncertainty of the category of the traitor as a way to reflect upon the political past and future of Iran.

Chapter 10

The Man in the White Raincoat: Betrayal and the Historian's Task

István Rév

In the late morning of 30 October 1956, revolutionaries attacked the headquarters of the Budapest Party committee, next to the City Opera in the eighth district of the city. Most probably, it was not a well-planned, premeditated siege; the attack was triggered by unsubstantiated and never-confirmed rumors about the existence of underground prisons and torture chambers with hundreds of prisoners, women and children among them. The Ministry of Defense sent six tanks to assist the communist defenders, but the head of the unit and the driver of the leading tank were both unfamiliar with that part of the city. The tanks, which had come to Budapest from a location sixty kilometers away, mistakenly started shelling the party headquarters, from whose windows the defenders were shooting at the attacking crowd. In the process, they completely ruined the City Opera, while the insurgents in their turn stormed and occupied the party headquarters, brutally killing the parliamentarians who had been sent out under a white flag to negotiate a ceasefire. "We fucked up," said Major Gallo, the head of the unit, summarizing the results of the unlucky expedition at his post-revolutionary trial in 1957 (Eörsi 2006, 80). Altogether 26 communists were killed in what turned out to be the bloodiest anti-Communist atrocity during the thirteen days of the 1956 revolution. There is speculation, even today, that the Soviets eventually decided to come back to defeat the revolution by military might as a consequence of the bloodbath on October 30. Several Western photographers and photojournalists were on the square at the time of the siege. George Sadovy sent a photo report to *Life*, which was reproduced all over the world. A number of film crews documented the events, and after the defeat of the revolution, the photographs and the footage of the fighting were used by the Communist courts that tried the so-called counterrevolutionaries involved in the storming of the building.

Some of the footage shows a man in a white raincoat in front of the fallen building after the fighting, carrying a machine gun on his shoulder. He is hard to identify, as his features are barely visible; and in a curious way, men in photographs from 1950s Hungary look surprisingly similar, even when the pictures were taken from relatively close up. Communism was a society of visible uniformity: there was only a very limited choice of clothing, the state-owned hairdressing salons offered the same haircut, and it would have been dangerous in any case to try to be markedly different from the majority. Nevertheless, there is only one person wearing a white raincoat among the armed revolutionaries in the photographs.

The Informer and the Historian

On 26 January 2006, *Élet és Irodalom* (Life and Literature), one of the most influential Hungarian cultural weeklies, published a long article titled "The Identification of an Informer" (Gervai 2006). It was a few days before the opening of the annual Hungarian Film Festival with István Szabó's new film *Rokonok* (Relatives). "The Identification of an Informer" is a piece of accidental investigative journalism. The author, a film critic, while working on a monograph on the history of Hungarian film in the past decades, stumbled upon a file in the Historical Archive of the Secret Services, which contains the 48 reports written between 1957 and 1963 by an informer under the pseudonym Endre Kékesi. At the end of his lengthy investigative report, he reveals that the person under the alias was a member of the famous class of 1956 at the Budapest Film Academy and none other than the only Hungarian film director to receive an Academy Award for the best foreign-language film—*Mephisto*, in 1982: István Szabó, who also received the award for best screenplay at the 1981 Cannes Film Festival.

The reports of the informer are in general quite uninteresting; there is no downright damaging information about any of the seventy-two people about whom Szabó reported during his six years as an informer. However, we can never be sure about the consequences of seemingly innocent sentences sent to the secret police, who arranged and rearranged information received from different sources and used it in ways that would have been unimaginable to the naïve informer, who tried not to harm those whom he betrayed.

The next day, István Szabó gave an interview to the Hungarian daily with the largest circulation, the former official newspaper of the Communist Party:

I am grateful to fate, and in retrospect, I can be very proud of what happened. My work for the state security was the bravest and most daring act of my whole life. With the help of my work for the security services, we managed to prevent one of our classmates being caught after the 1956 revolution and saved him from the gallows. . . . We succeeded, and he became a world famous film director. . . . I made a life-long commitment to my friends not to talk about this affair. But fifty years have passed since then, the regime has changed, and something for which one would have been hanged has turned into a glorious heroic act. . . . I am talking about Pál Gábor, [director of *Vera Angi*, 1979, a deservedly famous film about the Stalinist period in Hungary] who was my classmate in 1956. On the day of the siege of the party headquarters, I visited another classmate of ours. Then, unannounced, Pál Gábor arrived with a gun on his shoulder and said that he had come from Köztársaság Square, where they had stormed and occupied the building. . . . Then the Soviets came in, and by that time Pali was very frightened. We promised each other that we would never talk about his participation in the storming of the building, and we would save him in every conceivable way. . . . I was arrested with two of my classmates in February 1957. The reason is unknown to me to this day. We were held at the police station for three days, and we had to tell them everything about our classmates and also about ourselves. One of the two is still alive, and I do not have the right to reveal his name. The other was Ferenc Kardos [another film director], who is no longer alive. On the third day, they forced me to sign a paper to the effect that I would report about life at the Film Academy. . . . When I came out, I went to Gyöngyössy [another classmate, who would also become a film director] and told him everything. He was much older than most of us, very experienced, having already spent three years in prison in the early 1950s, and he persuaded me to accept that role, which would enable us to misinform the authorities and save our friend from the square. . . . This did not seem to be too great a sacrifice for a friend. I really wanted to protect my classmates. This was my only ambition. I do not know how it was possible that, although he was visible in that newsreel among the gunmen in front of the party headquarters, he was not recognized and arrested. . . . In 1958 while working as an assistant at the documentary film studio, I chanced to open the door of an editing room, and to my horror, I glanced at footages from a documentary made on the square. I immediately recognized Pál Gábor in a white raincoat with a gun in his hand. It was a horrible moment. In the evening, I ran up to Gyöngyössy, and told him what I had seen. He asked me who else had seen the footage. I answered that there were only two people in the editing room, and nobody else had seen the pictures. It was he who told Pali what I had seen. (Szabó 2006; translation is mine)

From Szabó's words, it is fair to assume that what he felt in the face of the revelation was most probably shame; that is why it was so important for him to present his deed as a heroic act. The deeply buried secret had suddenly surfaced. Having been exposed, he felt it necessary to emphasize that he was proud of his act, which he did not consider as surrender but rather as a sacrifice laid under mortally dangerous conditions on the altar of friendship. Pride is the opposite of shame, if shame is, as Bernard Williams, the moral philosopher, formulated its primary meaning: "being seen, inappropriately, by the wrong people, in the wrong condition" (1993, 78). Szabó insisted that his was an act of bravery, which is furthest from what one can be ashamed of, for "shame is the emotion of self-protection," as Gabrielle Taylor remarked (1985, 81). He obviously did not feel any guilt. Szabó repeated several times in the interview that his enemies wanted to destroy him, that the news of the revelation was sent to the international media in order to undermine his position as an internationally acclaimed artist, that the aim was to break his artistic career. He was afraid of the loss of his standing in the eyes of others. Whereas shame can be considered as more self-centered, self-directed, guilt is directed to the other, the victim of the shameful act; guilt is closely connected to the acceptance of responsibility. Guilt and responsibility for one's despicable actions are related to the idea of reparation, compensation, and healing. All such notions were apparently absent in Szabó's reaction.

Two days later, the best-informed historian of the 1956 armed struggle contradicted Szabó's claims. The historian stated with confidence that the man in the white raincoat was not Pál Gábor but László Marsányi, a twenty-one-year-old artisan, the head of a small insurgent group, who lived in the eighth district of Budapest and emigrated to the West after the revolution, at which point he disappeared from the sight of the authorities, the police, and scholars. Eight members of his group were identified, arrested, and tried; seven of them were sentenced to death and executed. The historian felt it important to note that all those who had been so visible in the pictures taken at the site of the siege of the building—and had not emigrated in the meantime—were arrested and tried and, in most cases, sentenced to death. The authorities did not let anybody escape who could be identified in the photographs.[1]

The next day, the media found László Marsányi in Australia; he had not visited Hungary since he left at the end of 1956. He confirmed that he had been among the fighters on the square, but the quality of the photograph he received made it impossible for him to state with confidence that he recognized himself. The surviving members of the 1956 Film Academy class called an international press conference in defense of their friend István Szabó. All five filmmakers, whom Szabó had reported on, claimed that they recognized beyond doubt their former classmate, Pál Gábor, in the pictures. They are outstanding, although somewhat elderly visual artists with—one would think—above-average visual skills and excellent eyes, which should enable them to identify images. A few days later, one of them published an essay, in the same journal that had revealed Szabó's past, in which he confessed that he had been one of the two men arrested together with Szabó and also recruited by the secret police as an informer (Kézdi-Kovács 2006).

August 2006 saw the publication of an interview with György Hoffmann, a former photojournalist of MTI, the Hungarian National News Agency. Hoffmann had taken pictures in the square and sold them to well-known Western photographers, who could pay him more than he would have received had he sold them under his own name:

Laci Marsányi was my classmate at school, we sat together on the same bench for three years, and I am sure that it is not him in the photograph. I met Marsányi several times during the revolution, and he did not wear such a long coat; he wore a rather short coat instead. I remember this very well; there are things that remain inscribed in one's memory forever.[2]

A copy of the documentary on the siege of the party headquarters with the man in the white raincoat is in the collection of the OSA Archivum, where I work. I know the film in which the man in front of the besieged building appears for less than two seconds. When Szabó accidentally caught a glimpse of the footage through the open door of the editing room, it would have impossible for him to recognize his classmate. Even when the film is slowed down or stopped and the frame is enlarged (none of which was possible for Szabó at that moment back in 1958) it is still impossible to identify the figure with any certainty. It is, therefore, highly unlikely that Szabó was able to recognize Pál Gábor in the footage. Gábor's widow has declined to tell in public what she knows.

A long and heated media battle started, centering on the case of the famous film director but with more far-reaching moral implications in a country where, after more than one-and-a-half decades, there is still no proper legal method of dealing with former informers and with the documents of the former secret services in general. Historians who work on morally loaded events of the recent past, in particular on issues related to the life and work of former informers, have often been publicly accused of inappropriate treatment of contentious and sensitive events.

Uncovering Betrayal

In Hungary, unlike Germany, there was no Gauck Commission, no general vetting of former Stasi agents; in contrast to Czechoslovakia, no lustration; as opposed to Poland, no systematic (although always unsuccessful and invidious) attempts to identify the informers of the past regime. As an almost natural consequence of the peaceful, negotiated nature of the political transition of 1989 in Hungary, based on mutual self-restraint and compromise, not only could the members of the former *nomenklatura* retain their positions in public life, but—except for a small and well-defined group of elected officials (members of Parliament and the government, editors-in-chief of the public media)—

nobody was required to undergo an examination of his or her former connections with one particular branch of the secret service, the branch responsible for fighting the so-called internal enemy. This restraint meant that former members of the intelligence and counter-intelligence agencies, even if elected to high public office, were not obliged to reveal their past. In 2002, immediately after the general election, an opposition newspaper revealed that the newly elected prime minister—a former deputy prime minister of the pre-1989 regime—had been a top-secret counter-intelligence officer from the late 1970s.

Until recently, files on former informers were available only to well-defined groups of individuals: people who had been informed on or researchers who had received permission from the special archival commission set up by the government. In the past few years, files of other branches of the former secret services, including selected, pre-1989 documents from the archives of the intelligence and counterintelligence services, have become available to researchers with permission from the same archival commission. Nevertheless, even today the successor services have far-reaching discretionary rights in deciding which documents to transfer to the Historical Archive of the Former Secret Services; and in the absence of proper inventories, indexes, and catalogs, the researcher is completely dependent on the intentions and the good or bad will of the institutions and the archivist. Nobody has an overview of the extent or the exact nature of the files. Researchers are working in the dark, and the availability of documents is a matter of sheer luck and the helpfulness of civil servants, who do not know whom they are supposed to be helping: the institutions, the victims, the researchers, the public, or the data protection ombudsman, whose overriding priority is to protect the privacy and informational self-determination of those individuals about whom information is available in the depths of the archive.

According to the law, information concerning public figures should become public, but the status of public figure is dependent on the consent of the individual; if the famous film director, who later became the powerful and highly influential head of a state-owned film studio under Communism, does not consider himself a public figure, information about his former secret life is not public information. The consequence of this situation is that politically sensitive information about selected individuals is leaked in the service of the ever-changing political needs of the day. My agent only served the public good, while your agent was a morally corrupt traitor. In the past one-and-and-a-half decades, the revelations have customarily been followed by expressions of sympathy and solidarity, as if the identification of important publicly known figures as former informers could mitigate the collaborationist past of the wider public. In this situation, the historian has a distinctive role and a special responsibility. It cannot be denied that the informer is the collaborator of the historian. The informer's reports are invaluable sources for the historian, who would not be able to understand the crucial issues of the buried and forgotten past without the rediscovered secret reports of this dubious character. The secret police archives are gold mines for the historian, who, nevertheless, cannot be unambiguously grateful for the help provided by the informer.

Responsibility in István Szabó's Films

Szabó, in the interviews he gave after the revelation, repeatedly claimed that, although he had remained silent about his past for sixteen years even after the collapse of Communism, he was under oath (allegedly to his friends) not to speak and that in any case, he had treated the problem of his past in his own films. As he claimed, his film Bizalom (*Confidence*, 1979), nominated for an Oscar, could already serve as a key to his thinking about the central moral issues that confront the individual under dictatorship. "In *Confidence*," Szabó confided in the pages of *Film Quarterly*, "the Gestapo of suspicion and distrust haunts the protagonists" (quoted in Hughes 1982, 13). *Confidence* is a peculiar love story, created under the spell of Ingmar Bergman's 1968 *Shame*. It is set during the short-lived but tragic rule of the fascist Arrow Cross at the end of World War II in Hungary. The protagonist, an underground resistance fighter, falls in love with the wife of another partisan. The man is unable to have any real confidence in the woman, who loves him and whom he should trust not only as a lover but also as a coconspirator. He is unable to trust her because he cannot forget that it was his previous lover, in Germany in 1933, who had given him up to the Nazis. The film depicts a perverted world, where nobody can be trusted, where anybody might be reported on, betrayed, let down, and disappear without a trace.

Szabó's next film *Mephisto* was based on Klaus Mann's novel of the same title. The protagonist of the novel is Hendrik Höfgen, whose real life model was Gustaf Gründgens, the famous German actor and stage director. Gustaf (later Gustav) Gründgens had played a role in Klaus Mann's first play, *Anja und Esther*, together with Klaus Mann's sister, Erika Mann, and Pamela Wedekind, the eldest daughter of the dramatist Frank Wedekind. The play, which portrayed a lesbian relationship, was staged at the Hamburger Kammerspiele, where Gründgens played more than seventy roles between 1923 and 1928. There are reasons to suppose that Klaus Mann became intimately attracted to Gründgens, who in 1926 married Erica Mann, although she was in love with Pamela Wedekind. Erika Mann and Gründgens divorced in 1929. During the time of the

Weimar Republic, Gründgens, Bertolt Brecht's favorite actor, flirted with the communists and he even planned—as Szabó showed in his *Mephisto*—to direct some sketches under the title Revolutionary Theater. Max Reinhardt, one of the founders of modern theater, invited him to Berlin; and in the 1932–33 season Gründgens played Mephisto in Goethe's *Faust* for the first time under Reinhardt's direction. In 1931, Gründgens played the role of Schraenker, the crime boss, in Fritz Lang's first talking movie, *M. Eine Stadt sucht einen Mörder*, which was seen by some, including Siegfried Kracauer and Klaus Mann, as a premonition of the Nazis' rise to power (Mann 1941). Although the film was banned by the Nazis, a part of it, the speech made before the court by the serial killer Hans Becker, played by the Hungarian-born Jewish actor Peter Lorre, was later taken out of context by Joseph Goebbels and inserted into the most famous Nazi anti-Semitic propaganda film, *Der ewige Jude* (The Eternal Jew, 1940) as an ersatz confession of Jewish guilt.

After Hitler came to power, Gründgens found a patron in Hermann Goering, who was married to an actress. Goebbels, the Nazi propaganda minister, himself a failed novelist, intensely disliked the homosexual Gründgens, but in 1934 he appointed him director of the Prussian Staatstheater in Berlin. Like Wilhelm Furtwängler, Gründgens was also appointed a member of the Prussian State Council. He became one of the most recognizable faces of Nazi cultural policy and propaganda, acting and directing both on stage and on the screen. Influenced by the Nazi "total-war" efforts, he volunteered for the front in 1943. He was stationed at an airbase near Amsterdam and then recalled to continue his politically engaged *kultur efforts* at the Staatstheater. After the war, he was incarcerated in a Soviet prisoner-of-war camp; but following his anti-Nazi investigation trial, he was rehabilitated and continued his theatrical career, first in East, later in West Berlin, Düsseldorf, and Hamburg. In 1954, the Federal Republic decorated him with the German Service Cross, the highest civilian award, for his services to postwar German culture. In 1957, Gründgens directed Goethe's *Faust* in the Deutsches Schauspielhaus in Hamburg. He played Mephistopheles once more, and the performance was turned into a film, directed by Peter Gorski, Gründgens's postwar companion and adopted son. He died of an overdose of sleeping pills in Manila, where he stopped on his round-the-world travels after retiring from the stage in Hamburg. He left a short note behind, asking not to be woken, as he wanted to have a long sleep.

On 22 December 1999, on the hundredth anniversary of Gründgens's birth, an exhibition opened in the Berlin Staatsbibliothek, "Gustav Gründgens—A German Career." As part of the anniversary celebrations, his life was turned into a television documentary, and his films were shown in German cinemas. At the entrance to the exhibition hung

a poster with a quotation from Gründgens, from the time following the
war: "I want to be regarded as someone who preserved and nourished
the flame in a dark period and someone who can relate how it was, how
it is now, and how one can possibly rebuild" At the time of the centenary, the *Frankfurter Allgemeine Zeitung* wrote that Gründgens was "a par-
ticipant who did not collaborate."

Szabó's *Mephisto*—in George Steiner's words—presented the unholy
fusion between Kultur and barbarism (Hughes 1982, 14). However,
Klaus Maria Brandauer, the Austrian actor who played Hendrik Höfgen
(Gründgens's personification) in Szabó's *Mephisto*, told Lawrence Van
Gelder, the film critic of the *New York Times*,

I saw him only in his films, but I read his books. For me, he was the most important figure of the German language theater in the whole century. He was not
only an actor but a director and the president of a big theatre. His life was theater. Only theater. The stage was for him the world in which he was able to live.
. . . He saved Polish people, Jewish people from his theater during the war, and
after the war the Communist actor Ernst Busch from East Berlin said to the military government: Mr. Gründgens was a very honorable man during the war. And
for that reason Gründgens became *free*. (Van Gelder 21 March 1982).

Brandauer gave a stunning performance in *Mephisto*. Klaus Mann portrayed the Gründgens of the novel as follows:

Hendrik Höfgen—typecast as an elegant blackguard, murderer in evening dress,
scheming courtier—see nothing, hear nothing. He has nothing to do with the
city of Berlin. Nothing but stages, film studio, dressing rooms, a few night-clubs,
a few fashionable drawing rooms are real to him. Does he not feel the change
in the seasons? . . . The actor Höfgen lives from one first night to the next, from
one film to another, his calendar composed of performance days and rehearsal
days. He scarcely notices that the snow melts, that the trees and bushes are in
bud or in full leaf, that there are flowers and earth and streams. Encapsulated
by his ambition as in a prison cell, insatiable and tireless, always in a state of
extreme hysterical tension, Hendrik embraces a destiny that seems to him excep-
tional but is in fact nothing but a vulgar arabesque at the edge of an enterprise
doomed to collapse. (Mann 1995, 146)

The audience of the film, however, sees not only an uncontrollably
vain character but also a great actor. Brandauer knows, exactly as Gründgens did, that Mephisto is his real chance for fame. He told Van Gelder,
"For an actor, the principal role in *Mephisto* is a dream—the portrait of
an artist in moral decay, the opportunity to sweep through a panorama
of roles, to sing, to dance, to rage, to rut, to swagger before underlings
and cower in the presence of overwhelming power, to depict public confidence and private agony" (Van Gelder 21 March 1982). Brandauer
takes to it like a fish to water; this is his supreme moment, the height of
his artistic career. And he does not only excel in portraying a character

who deems no price too high to pay for success, who is willing to serve the darkest powers for a chance to act out his exhibitionism, but he also succeeds in persuading the audience of the film that he is playing a great actor. "To act the part of Höfgen was like therapy for me, because Mr. Höfgen is an actor and I am, too; so he is a brother to me. We all have vanities. We want to have the love of the audience. We want to have success, and sometimes we make great compromises with the public to win success." (Van Gelder 21 March 1982). There is something chilling and deeply unnerving in this fine performance: Brandauer manages to substantiate Gründgens's claim to have been the man "who preserved and nourished the flame in a dark period."

After the revelation that he had been an informer, Szabó insisted that, although he had remained silent about the details of his career, in his films he had returned time and time again to this most personal issue of his life and had courageously faced the moral lessons of his secret: "We want to do nothing more than tell the story of what has happened to us," as he stated in an interview he gave in 1982, after the American opening of *Mephisto*. However, in the same interview, he claimed that

we are often unable to carry out the more difficult tasks set for us by history. But it's not always people who are to blame for that. The human tasks set by history in this century may be unique in their difficulty. As has also been stated, history is a kind of director deciding the roles we play in our individual lives. . . . The dice are thrown by history. (Hughes 1982, 14–18)

Art, Politics, Morality

We should remember that Szabó finished working on *Mephisto* in 1981. In 1976, Leni Riefenstahl's spectacular and disquieting photo album on the males of a Sudanese tribe, *The Last of the Nuba*, was published. Susan Sontag's famous and scandalous review, "Fascinating Fascism," triggered by the publication of Riefenstahl's book, appeared in the *New York Review of Books* in the same year. (It was republished in her celebrated book of essays *Under the Sign of Saturn* in 1980). The cover of *The Last of the Nuba* asserted that Riefenstahl sprang to international fame "during Germany's blighted and momentous 1930s." Many Nazi works of art were exhibited in public for the time after World War II at the 1974 Frankfurt am Main exhibition Art in the Third Reich. In 1977, the Haus der Kunst in Munich organized the Die Dreissiger Jahre: Schauplatz Deutschland exhibition that traveled to Essen and then to Zurich. Ursus Books published a massive catalog of the works on show. The Utopia and Apocalypse: A View of Art in Germany 1910–1939 exhibition opened in London in 1978. In 1981, the Realism exhibition was organized in Paris. The Thirties: Art and Culture in Italy show opened in Milan in 1982.

When Szabó turned to the art and culture of the Third Reich, he was not a solitary artist, working in a cultural vacuum, who had suddenly discovered the sunken world of the 1930s and 1940s. Susan Sontag remarked that it was not that Riefenstahl's Nazi past has suddenly become acceptable, but that, simply, with the turn of the cultural wheel, it no longer mattered in the way it did before.

In several interviews he gave after the collapse of Communism, Szabó reiterated that that he had turned to Nazi Germany as the setting of some of his films because it would have been politically impossible to portray another totalitarian regime, that is, Hungary or the Soviet Union. The Third Reich, according to him, served as a laboratory to test general moral problems, a substitute for Communism, as he knew it from personal experience. But he turned to Germany even after the fall of the Communist regime when he was no longer forced to replace his personal experiences with stories set in pre- or postwar Germany. In 2001, he finished *Taking Sides*, a film whose protagonist was Wilhelm Furtwängler, another emblematic figure of German culture. It seems that apart from the alleged historical analogies, there was something else that pulled Szabó toward Germany. As the unsettling case of the film *Mephisto* has already indicated, the deeper reasons may be found somewhere else.

Three years after his son published *Mephisto* and eight years before he would finish *Doktor Faustus*, Thomas Mann wrote a strange piece on Hitler for *Esquire* magazine, in which he claimed that "the moral sphere . . . is really not altogether the artist's concern" (cited in Lepenies 2006, 46). In his Tanner Lecture delivered at Harvard, Wolf Lepenies, the cultural sociologist and German public intellectual, argues that, in Germany from as early as the nineteenth century, but especially after the devastating defeat in World War I, culture became accepted as a compensation for politics; when this happened, the absence of morality in the public sphere was also accepted (Lepenies 1999). Lepenies claims that "The aesthetic appeal first of fascism and later of National Socialism was not a superficial phenomenon. It must be one of the core elements in any attempt to explain the attractiveness of Nazi ideology for a large segment of the German bourgeoisie and many German artists and intellectuals" (Lepenies 1999, 174–75). Lepenies here follows Fritz Stern, one of the leading historians of the modern German ideology, who wrote that German public life could be understood by reference to the preeminence of culture that prevailed in Germany from the beginning of the nineteenth century. According to Lepenies,

1933 was not a break, it was the fulfillment of German history. As Gottfried Benn [the German writer, who was blacklisted after the war] put it, the new state had to be commended not least because it promised to give culture its due: the separation between politics and culture was about the end. In the state of the Nazis, the cultural nation would be reborn. (1999, 177)

There was something unsettling in German culture that Walter Benjamin called the aestheticization of politics, the perverted "aesthetic appeal first of fascism and later of National Socialism [that] was not a superficial phenomenon" (Lepenies 2006, 47) and that was an inherent part of Nazi self-identity. One should look beyond Szabó's words when he claims that he escaped (in his films) from the Communist censors to the stage set of the Third Reich.

The Germany Szabó discovered for his moralizing films was fascinated by its own culture, the special standing and treatment of the artist, who decided to stay at home, serve his country, and keep culture alive, even in the darkest of all times. The productive artist, according to this deep-rooted conviction of Germany in Szabó's films, has a responsibility; his acts cannot be judged on the basis of simple political or moral standards. His case is complex and complicated, and this should be taken into account when portraying and judging his life and achievements.

Another Szabó film is pertinent. *Taking Sides*, based on the South-African Ronald Harwood's play (he too came from the world of a repressive regime) of the same title, presents Dr. Wilhelm Furtwängler's so-called de-Nazification investigation in a ruined Berlin, after the fall of the Nazi regime. It was once remarked that conductors in our time fall readily into two categories: Wilhelm Furtwängler and all the others. Among those who recognized this truth early on was Adolf Hitler, possessor of perhaps the best musical ear of any twentieth-century statesman—except for Ignaz Paderewski [the famed concert pianist, composer, and prime minister of Poland in 1919]. Despite many importunities and provocations in later years, Hitler never wavered in this judgment. A photograph of the Führer reaching upward to the podium to shake the conductor's hand after a 1935 concert of the Berlin Philharmonic is remarkable testimony—such expressions of respect by Hitler were rare (Grey 1994, 1).

Furtwängler (1886–1954) one of the most acclaimed conductors in the history of Western classical music and Arturo Toscanini's great rival, was head of the Berlin Philharmonic Orchestra. He came from a very prominent, strict, serious, German upper-middle-class family. His father, Adolf Furtwängler, a classical archaeologist, was one of the founders of Greek studies in Germany, director of the Museum of Antiquities in Berlin. Wilhelm Furtwängler's private tutors included the famous archaeologist Ludwig Curtius, whom the Nazis forced into exile, and the Beethoven expert Walter Riezler. Wilhelm Furtwängler succeeded

Arthur Nikisch as the conductor of the Leipzig Gewandhaus Orchestra and the Berlin Philharmonic; he was the musical director of the Vienna Philharmonic, and the head of the Bayreuth Festival. At the end of 1933 Goebbels set up the Reichsmusikkammer, the National Chamber of Music, headed by Richard Strauss, and Furtwängler was installed as its vice-president, while Goering appointed him to the Prussian State Council. Although he resigned from both bodies as a consequence of his disagreement about the interpretation Paul Hindemith's opera *Mathis der Maler*, he remained in Germany as one of the most important cultural figures who did not choose or were not forced to emigrate. Having been cleared by the civilian authorities in his de-Nazification trial, he returned to the Berlin Philharmonic to conduct his first post-war concert in May 1947. At end of the concert, the ovation lasted an hour and 15 minutes, and there were 47 curtain calls.

Even in the field of culture, classical music occupied a special position in Germany, particularly under totalitarian and autocratic regimes, as Benjamin Korstvedt reminds us:

Artistic bolshevism was carried to extremes. Against all this there was but one remedy: a return to the pure sources. What art was purer than that born of the deep religiosity of Bach, Beethoven and Bruckner! Especially Bruckner's God-consecrated art . . . [*Besonders Bruckners gottgeweihte Kunst*]—stated the official Bruckner biography, published in 1936, two years before the *Anschluss*. (quoted in Korstvedt 1996, 136)

In *Taking Sides*, a major in the U.S. army—played by Harvey Keitel—an insurance assessor in civilian life, is instructed to investigate the links between Furtwängler and the Nazis. The major is shown documentary films of the horrors of the Bergen-Belsen concentration camp, and he is told to do whatever it takes to get proof of Furtwängler's collaboration with the Nazis. The American officer interviews members of Furtwängler's orchestra, but they point out that the conductor refused to shake hands with Hitler, which was why he carried his baton in his right hand, and that he helped Jewish musicians to escape from Germany. However, the American insurance broker reminds himself that Furtwängler conducted even on the eve of the Nazi Rally and Hitler's birthday and that it was his performance of Bruckner's Seventh Symphony that was broadcast over the radio when Hitler committed suicide. There is a Soviet colonel in the film, a curator from the Leningrad Museum of Art, an expert on German art and culture, who tries to persuade the American to drop the investigation because he has been instructed to take Furtwängler with him to occupy a leading musical position in the Soviet Union. The Soviet colonel confides to his American colleague that unless he manages to take Furtwängler to the Soviet Union, as a war trophy, his life is in mortal danger.

In the course of the interrogation, the major repeatedly humiliates Furtwängler, whom he describes as Hitler's bandleader. The insurance broker turned investigator discovers that a second violinist in the Berlin Philharmonic had been a member of the Nazi party and an informer for the Nazis. The violinist, personified by Ulrich Tukur, who played with great empathy a cynical high-ranking Stasi officer in the Oscar winning 2006 German film, *The Lives of Others* (*Das Leben der Anderen*), explains that he had been a member of the Austrian Communist Party, and when the Nazis found this out, he had no choice but to agree to become an informer; that is how he could become a second violinist in the orchestra, which had been purged of Jewish musicians. The American threatens the former informer and offers him a way out, if he tells everything damaging he knows about the conductor. The frightened musician first calls Furtwängler "a man of genius" but later confides that the conductor had not only arranged to send an art critic he disapproved of to the Russian front but had also sent Hitler a telegram wishing him a happy birthday.

Furtwängler tries to explain to the determined and uncultured American that it was important for him to stay in Germany because music has the ability to promote liberty, humanity, and justice and that he had no idea of what was happening in Germany. He asserts that he did not leave Germany "because I am not Jewish, and because I tried to help from the inside." The American remains unconvinced and confronts Furtwängler with anti-Semitic statements he made during the Nazi rule. The major recounts that when Hitler shot himself, the radio played one of Furtwängler's recordings. "When the devil died, they wanted his bandleader to conduct the funeral march." In the end Furtwängler is charged with serving the Nazi regime and uttering anti-Semitic statements. Eventually, he is acquitted of all the charges. As the synopsis of the film states, "The film ends with footage of the Berlin Philharmonic Orchestra performing for top Nazi party officials and Furtwängler shaking the hand of the Führer. As he takes a bow, he rubs his hand on a handkerchief in an apparent attempt to rub away all contact with Hitler." The apparently nonrepresentational and thus polysemous facade of music makes the musician a perfect example for István Szabó. ("Music is music," as Edward Said recalled his childhood discovery in his memoirs). As a result of the perceived surface neutrality of music, it seems as if the isolated composer or conductor had been engaged only in the pursuit of his artistic vocation, independent of the political, social, ideological, and cultural environment of his existence.

Taking Sides, produced before the revelation of his past, as Szabó has put it in an interview, was prompted by the need to rebuff numerous attempts in post-Communist Eastern and Central Europe to bring to book famous artists and intellectuals who worked during Communism, in order, he said, to invite people not to judge the situation in black and white terms and to understand better the complexity of art and politics in a totalitarian regime.

According to musicologists and cultural historians, the real strength of musical life in Weimar Germany was not in composition but in performance or, more precisely, in performers. "The strength of German music in the 1920's lay in conductors. To mention only the most famous names—Furtwängler, Karl Muck, Bruno Walter, Fritz Busch, Erich Kleiber, Otto Klemperer and [Hungarian-born] George Szell [besides] Kanppertsbusch, Fritz Zweig, Hans Rosbaud, Artur Rother" (Lippman 1993, 45). After Hitler came to power, the Jewish musicians, including Klemperer, Walter, and Szell, left together with the non-Jewish Kleiber and Busch. Wilhelm Furtwängler, Szabó's protagonist, however, decided to stay.

As the centenary of Furtwängler's birth was approaching, his widow Elisabeth Furtwängler invited the music historian Fred Prieberg to write a book about him. The book, *Kraftprobe*, was published in 1986, triggering a renewed debate about the life and character of the conductor. Prieberg argued that "only as an accomplice of Hitler's barbarism was [he] able to save Jews . . . he lived for years in a complex world that placed almost unbearable strain on his nerves. . . . He was a double agent, living every moment under threat of discovery" (1991, 101). As Chris Walton remarked in 2004: "Prieberg had the strong view that Furtwängler's critics in the anti-fascist camp were led by their blind hatred, their criticism being a result of their having been themselves ideologically infected by the Nazis" (2004, 9).

At the end of his book *The Devil's Music Master*, Sam Shirakawa provides a long list of names of the Jews Furtwängler saved or tried to save during the Nazi regime. However, a closer look at Furtwängler's writings and statements makes Prieberg's claim—even from the perspective of the revisionist literature of the past two decades and despite the Furtwängler renaissance—quite problematic. Furtwängler, who dreaded atonality, was a staunch supporter of "organic" music, so dear to Nazi ideologues and music theoreticians because of the close association of the organic with the notions of social Darwinism. In an undated memorandum, Furtwängler says,

The cultural policy of the National Socialists consists primarily in the battle to defeat the demoralizing influence of Jews and others in cultural life. This struggle makes it necessary that public cultural institutions and institutions for artists themselves be reorganized by the party according to political criteria. . . . The task was in essence not so difficult, since futurism and Bolshevism in our cultural life had already been more or less defeated before the National Socialists took power and had been dismissed by all seriously-minded Germans; there remained only to make the Jews and the main exponents of futurism and Bolshevism disappear. (quoted in Walton 2004, 13)

Albert Speer, in his memoirs *Inside the Third Reich*, tells a story about the final concert he organized for the Berlin Philharmonic during the last days of the war. Speer, according to his recollections, had promised Furtwängler that he would warn him when the end was near, by ordering Bruckner's Romantic Symphony to be performed as a signal that he should pack and go into hiding. The concert was held on 12 April 1945 (Furtwängler was already in Switzerland by that time) at the Bluthner Hall, near Potsdamer Platz in Berlin.

In his own defense, Szabó stated that in his works he had confronted those moral issues hidden in his past that had tormented him. He claimed that he had done what an artist could do: he had transformed specific issues into products of high aesthetic quality and thereby formulated the particular in a general way with a universal moral message for the well-being and enlightenment of the wider public. By fictionalizing his personal concerns, his own biography, he had turned necessity into artistic virtue. Private ethical issues are, however, not my concern here; I would rather address the options available to a historian in a morally charged case, particularly, in the case of events of recent history.

Historical Moralizing

As opposed to the options available to the artist, the work of the historian contains an element of hopeless, although, not necessarily naïve, specificity. In a particular and limited sense, there is not much difference between the natural sciences and the historical profession: both require experiments that can be repeated and then checked, verified, confirmed, or falsified using the same data. The facts the historian uncovers in support of his or her claims should be accessible from different angles. For a historian, one of the most important data is the set of proper names, names of individuals connected to certain events, since "Sentences containing proper names can be used to make identity statements which convey factual and not merely linguistic information" (Searle 1969, 165). Historians go back to archives, sources, and documents to find, to check, and to verify names in order to ascertain the assertions of fellow historians and to analyze the names in a new or different context. "The thread of Ariadne that leads the researcher through the archival labyrinth is the same thread that distinguishes one individual from another in all societies known to us: the name" (Ginzburg and Poni 1991, 5). The historian cannot subsume the documents related to István Szabó's actions in the figure, the life, and the actions of Wilhelm Furtwängler by overlooking the specificities of the character and the context. Although a work of history can serve as an allegory, it can have that function only if—as Marc Bloch defined history—it is about a man in time, an identifiable man in well-defined times.

The historians who uncovered documents about one-time informers of the Communist regime have often been accused of illegitimate moralizing. According to their critics, they are not entitled to moral judgment, to a "moral zoology," as employed by Hippolyte Taine when he examined the protagonists of the French Revolution, with the attitude of a "'supreme and imperturbable judge" (Ginzburg 1999, 14). This criticism, in fact contains two assertions: (1) the historian does not, cannot, know all the relevant facts; and (2) the historian has no right to moralize, to judge. The two assumptions are naturally connected: the historian is not entitled to moral judgment since he is not in possession of all the relevant facts; some things always remain hidden from sight. Accurate philosophers would tend to define this stand as epistemological particularism. These are both reasonable postulates. The historian never knows all the relevant facts: important details cannot ever be recovered, some were never recorded in the first place, some are utterly misrepresented in the surviving documents, etc. All these factors make historical reconstruction extremely risky and difficult but not, perhaps, hopeless or impossible.

There is an implicit and specific moral particularism at work here. The basic assumption is that, in general, the historian is never in a position to discover all the important and relevant facts, and this is particularly so when he or she is working with the utterly unreliable documents of the former secret police. A fact that can make a (moral) difference in one case can make a completely different difference in another case. Facts—pertaining to possible moral outcomes—can have variable relevance (and the historian does not even know whether a particular fact, or the lack of it, is relevant). The same fact, depending on the complexities of the particular situation, can count either in favor of or against the behavior of the historical actor. In order to arrive at any moral conclusion, it would be essential to comprehend all the relevant nonmoral features of the historical event under scrutiny. The historian cannot say that what mattered in a particular case should also matter in another. This emphasis on the specificities of particular—and never fully knowable—historical facts serves as a general blank acquittal from possible historical responsibility: the (unknown, undisclosed, unattainable, perished, destroyed) particular facts would shed a different light on the historical act, the (moral) consequences of which would be essentially different if all the facts could have properly been taken into consideration.

Although we usually do not know all the relevant facts—even in our ordinary everyday life, as Ignazio Silone put it, "Behind every secret there is another secret"—we are still able to form reasonable, usable opinions about incidents in the lives of others, despite the fact that those others are different from us, have a different gender, a different past, come with a different tradition, were raised in a different environment, have different reflexes, react in a different way. Historians, in each epoch, in a slightly or grossly different way, are trained to reconstruct incidents of the past on the basis of critical interpretation of only partially available sources and their connections. It is not only by aiming at absolute knowledge, based on all the facts, that the historian can achieve objectivity, which, nevertheless, does not equal certainty. In principle, the serious historian can have access to enough documentary sources to base his or her claims on secure foundations.

Historical interpretation—despite all the hopes and efforts to the contrary—cannot be formalized in a mechanical way. The historian might fail, even if he or she tries to be faithful to the two virtues of truth, sincerity and accuracy, which become essential virtues and guarantees of serious scholarly work, especially in the absence of easily formalizable rules of historical reconstruction. (Accuracy is the virtue of carefully investigating and deliberating over the evidence for and against a belief before asserting it. And sincerity is the virtue of genuinely expressing to others what one in fact believes—in the case of history—on the basis of facts (see Williams 2001). It is difficult to accept that the skeptics are in a better position to deliver the truth about historical reconstruction than are historians in delivering truthful accounts about incidents of the past.

The historian, unlike the detective, the police officer, the investigative journalist, the prosecutor, or the judge, is not supposed to reconstruct—beyond reasonable doubt—the incidents of the past. This would be a mistaken expectation. Honest, sincere academic history writing should be the testimony of truthful efforts of reconstruction, rather than pretending to be a faithful and complete rendering of the incidents of the past. A historical work is at least as much the portrait of the protagonist of the story narrated as it is the portrait of the author of the text as a historian trying to make sense of and negotiate with the sources. The historical truth is that it is never possible to arrive at absolute reconstruction even if it is supported by reasonable and acceptable evidence; uncertainty (in historical reconstructions) is an unavoidable part of the assertion of knowledge of the past.

Historians can offer only afterthoughts, and as in the case of any afterthought, the historian's effort carries an unavoidable element of uncertainty and not only in the sense that historical argumentation can resort to conjectures and inferences: even the outcome of a historical investigation might—in fact, should—remain, to a smaller or larger degree, devoid of absolute certainty. In consequence of this unavoidable element of historical reconstruction, the historian cannot usurp the role of the judge and would do better to stay away from general moral judgment too. Still, accurately researched and sincerely stated uncertainties might provide protection from the dangers of unreflexive conviction of historical certainty, the mother of narrow-minded preconceptions and intolerance.

Surprisingly, those who are skeptical about the possibility of making the recent past intelligible do not hesitate when making strong assertions about heroic figures of the distant national past. Skeptics have no difficulty in portraying and attributing motivations to Saint Stephen (967–1038), the first Hungarian king, although the only surviving document of a more or less personal nature that could be connected to his person is his "Admonition" addressed to his son, and even in this case, the exact authorship of this document, a *Libellus de institutione morum* that follows Carolingian models, is highly questionable. Skeptics are more doubtful when the object of historical investigation is a figure of the recent past or a living person. The closer the historical actor in time, the more particular, more complex, and less penetrable his or her motivations supposedly become; the task set for the historian is more demanding the closer we get to our present, the more information we have or might have. The large quantity of (potentially) available and oftentimes contradictory information, should—according to the skeptics—constrain or silence the historian. Still, most of us, including the skeptics, living under the rule of law, accept the fact that judges, who deliver verdicts of life and death, are entitled to administer justice, although, as we know, not even the judge can ever be in possession of all the relevant facts and motives that would make the actions of the defendants completely transparent.[3] The courts, while carefully weighing the deeds and motivations of contemporaries, can naturally make mistakes; justice is not exempt from occasional miscarriage, but if the possibility of ever arriving at an intelligible reconstruction of past events were denied to the courts, as is so often done in the case of historical reconstruction, none of us would have the chance to live under the rule of law.

Still, the assertions of the skeptics are not without merit. By definition, the historian is always late; he or she never arrives in time. The historian arrives on the scene when the action is already irreversibly over, after all have taken their bets, and the immediate consequences of the act are already in existence. As the historian comes after the fact, he is in no position to intervene in a direct way, to change the course of events, to tell the protagonists what they should or ought to do. As David Hume formulated it in his *Treatise on Human Nature:* one cannot infer an "ought" from an "is." On the basis of the available documentary evidence, the historian is entitled to narrate that which most probably happened. What ought to have happened—although it concerns the historian—is beyond his or her reach. The available (and always partial) sources attest only to what could have taken place. As the pragmatist philosopher Hilary Putnam formulates it, "The purpose of the historian cannot be to perform a speech-act of condemning long-dead [or even still living] persons; rather his aim is to make the historical event intelligible, and to do this he employs a description which is itself made available by a moral point of view" (2005, 74).

In societies that have recently experienced political transition, especially in the former communist countries, there is a special breed of doubters. Long decades of mostly ideologically driven, centrally commissioned, and censored historical narratives in the service of continuously changing political needs have gravely undermined the credibility of historical work. The loss of belief in the possibility of authentic historical reconstruction affects primarily the work of historians working on modern and recent historical events, but even medieval studies—as countless attempts after 1989 of constructing a new Middle Ages in all the East and Central European countries testify—have not been spared blunt and wholesale revisionism. The opening (followed, in some countries by the renewed closure) of the archives after the fall of the Berlin Wall created the perception that "facts" that might prove the opposite of any openly stated historical assertion are just there, hidden in the depths of the so far well guarded archives, awaiting discovery, rescue, and reworking. Anything, even a retroactive historical miracle, might be possible, based on newly discovered relevant facts; the past should not forget the people of the new world who are waiting for an appropriate prehistory.

Probably, the most significant reason behind the epistemic doubts, however, is the newly experienced instability of the self. In the face of the unexpected changes that contradicted almost all existential expectations, everybody's life is now seen in a new light. Except for the few truly courageous members of the democratic opposition, almost everybody had to make his or her smaller or graver compromises during the long decades of a rule that mocked and undermined the respect and self-respect of human dignity. To acknowledge the past is not an easy thing for most of us. In this context, one is tempted to accept Ian Hacking's overly paradoxical formulation: "It is almost as if retroactive redescription changes the past" (1995, 243). The rejection of any alleged attempt at moralizing should be understood from this perspective. Hiding behind the veil of historical particularism, the specificities of the (partly unknown and unknowable) historical circumstances that purportedly prevent any generalizable moral conclusion is a by-product of the post-transition predicament.

In the overly politicized atmosphere of the former communist world, moral judgments about historical events have always been suspected either of being politically motivated or of having a hidden political agenda. Historical arguments in East and Central Europe were used in the twentieth century, and even earlier, in deciding highly contested political issues. Insistence on the privileged nature of historical particularities has served to keep the space for politically charged arguments and counterarguments, accusations and counteraccusations, wide open. The issue of the former agent is an instructive case in point. Large segments of the political left, especially the supporters of the successor parties—who, in the face of revelations, usually feel, at least indirectly, implicated—customarily play down the political, social, and moral significance of the detected act, especially if the person involved has remained—at least nominally—broadly faithful to his or her former political allegiance. In such cases, the case for the defense centers on the biographical particularities of the person (István Szabó was just nineteen years old when he was recruited); the relative and isolated nature of his deeds, notably in the light of his subsequent service to the country; the objectively patriotic nature of the act (as in the case of Péter Medgyessy, the prime minister and former counterintelligence officer, who allegedly neutralized the Soviets at the time of Hungary's entry into the International Monetary Fund); the popularity of the person (as in the case of the popular radio broadcaster who commentated live when Hungary famously defeated England by 6 to 3 at Wembley Stadium in 1953). When the accusations affect individuals who are directly or indirectly connected to the political right, as with the revelations about prominent figures of the ecclesiastical hierarchy, the arguments coming from the right either point at those groups that might have had a vested interest in the revelation (Jewish groups that supposedly conspired in the fall of Stanislaw Wielgus, appointed archbishop of Poland), or as opposed to the concrete deeds of the informer, they emphasize the role of the Communist officers who recruited the person in order to compromise him or his institution. The skeptics, when judging the reconstructions of politically sensitive cases, usually give up the requirement of the constraint of consistency and do not apply the same (moral) principles—even if they explicitly adhered to them—to similar cases, if consistency, in the light of the unearthed documents, would require them to form a critical opinion about political or ideological bedfellows. The charged atmosphere turns ethical utterances into purportedly political propaganda. Nevertheless, as human beings with ethical sensitivity and as researchers who use documents in which description is intermixed with value judgment, historians cannot avoid taking an ethical stance.

Thick Description

In order to preserve the credibility of serious historical scholarship—especially in the milieu of extremely sensitive and self-destructively doubting post-transition societies—it is advisable for the historian to be particularly cautious with direct moral judgments—and also with claims about the certainty of reconstruction. In the midst of a "memory epidemic," it is important to maintain and emphasize the distinction between historians and activists of historical memory. Historical memory operates in the present; it maintains that the past is not past but an aspect of the present that can and should be redressed. Historical memory craves for justice: either legal or moral or both. Historical memory is an inherently moralizing attitude to the events of the past.

It is useful in this context to turn around the classic question whether one can derive values from facts and ask the following: is it possible to use sources without confusing descriptive facts with evaluative judgments? The question is particularly pertinent for the historian writing for a skeptical audience. Evaluation and description are mixed and often interdependent in the sources, which are usually overlooked by cautious positivists. According to pragmatist philosophers, the distinction between facts and values is at the very least hopelessly fuzzy (Putnam 1981, 128), and one cannot easily be "disentangled" from the other. "The terms one uses even in description in history and in sociology and the other social sciences are invariably ethically colored," argues Hilary Putnam (2003, 63). Although the radical positivist claim of a strict and clear fact/value dichotomy might be far-fetched, it would be difficult for the historian to overlook the fact/value distinction, especially since courts customarily distinguish two types of statements—facts and value judgments (opinions)—when deciding defamation cases against historians. After the advent of positivism, historians became more careful in sticking to facts and in trying to suppress their unavoidable personal sympathies. What a typical French judge holds desirable about a historian is, in fact, a not uncommon view: "In the judge's view, the image of the 'good' historian [is]: meticulous, scrupulous, always moderate in opinion and tone, apparently neutral, without avowed passion, or irritating nerve. He resembles the good judge like a brother does" (Bredin 1984, 111).

The historian is concerned. For historians who have a genuine interest in the topic of their research, the object of their inquiry is not only a matter of fact but also a matter of concern; and ethics can be conceived as a system of interrelated concerns (Putnam 2005, 22). Historians too are moral beings, but as historians, they do not possess the professional tools that would allow them to moralize. Historians are in the business of presenting the concrete, the named, the particular, and not in that of explaining what makes an act just or unjust in a general sense. That task is left to others; privileged among them is the reader of the historical narrative.

Historians are not well equipped to play the role of the moral philosopher by using prescriptive, so-called "thin" concepts like "good," "bad," or "ought," so "dear to moral philosophers, which supposedly reward the reflective search after truth and explain what it is about action . . . that accounts for its rightness or wrongness in universal terms" (Hollis 1995, 176). The historian, fortunately, has not been left completely without tools to reconstruct past incidents in an ethically sensitive way, while at the same time preserving scholarly credibility. The solution, however, is not to oppose insistence on the particular with historical generalization.

As opposed to thin concepts like "good," "bad," or "ought," our languages recognize so-called "thick" concepts that operate close to the ground. Thick concepts, like "treachery, promise, brutality, courage"— the examples Bernard Williams (1985) uses in his deeply skeptical *Ethics and the Limits of Philosophy*—are more specific notions than those that could be defined as thin ethical concepts. Thick concepts—according to some philosophers—express an uneasy union of fact and value:

> The way these notions are applied is determined by what the world is like (for instance, by how someone has behaved), and yet, at the same time, their application usually involves a certain valuation of the situation, of persons or actions. . . . A term of this kind involves a descriptive complex to which a prescription has been attached, expressive of the values of the individual or of the society. (Williams 1985, 129–30)

Thick concepts can be firmly attached to the description of events, making use of the factual basis of the sources, without resorting to mostly prescriptive concepts that cannot be factually verified by the documents. However, by using such concepts, the historian is capable of establishing his or her ethical position, without gravely undermining the factual foundations of the historian's effort.

Thick concepts have been mentioned in the philosophical literature from the middle of the 1950s (in the works of Iris Murdoch, Philippa Foot, and John McDowell), but the distinction between thin and thick concepts came into circulation after the publication of Williams's *Ethics and the Limits of Philosophy* in 1985. One would presume that Williams's formulation of the juxtaposition of thin and thick concepts comes from the work of his Oxford colleague Gilbert Ryle (1900–1976). But we know from Williams himself that his so-called ethnographic stance on the notion of thin and thick was influenced by Clifford Geertz, and the marks of this anthropological genealogy have been retained by Williams (1986). Geertz admitted that he had borrowed the notion of thick description from none other than the philosopher Gilbert Ryle. "What defines [anthropology]," writes Geertz, "is the kind of intellectual effort it is: an elaborate venture in, to borrow a notion from Gilbert Ryle, 'thick description'" (1973, 6). The philosopher was influenced by the anthropologist, who, in turn, had borrowed the concept from a philosopher. This mixed parenthood contributes to the usefulness of the distinction between thick and thin for the historical profession. The connection between thick description, as practiced by anthropologists and historians, and thick moral concepts is not only philological and historiographical, but theoretical as well; and this is what offers the chance for historians to make exceptionally good use of them.

A parallel reading of Williams's and Geertz's texts—which, to my knowledge, no scholar has attempted so far—seems particularly useful for a historian. Geertz's idea of culture is compatible with Williams's notion of thick ethical concepts: both are, to a degree, descriptive and prescriptive: "what we call our data are really our own constructions of other people's constructions of what they and their compatriots are up to," claims Geertz (1973, 9), emphasizing that the empirical facts are themselves mediated through the way in which the actors involved in the historical incidents perceived and—unavoidably—evaluated their experiences. Williams argues:

How we "go on" from one application of a concept to another is a function of the kind of interest in what the concept represents, and we should not assume that we could see how people "go on" if we did not share the evaluative perspective in which this kind of concept has its point. An insightful observer can indeed come to understand and anticipate the use of the concept without actually sharing the values of the people who use it. . . . But in imaginatively anticipating the use of the concept, the observer also has to grasp imaginatively its evaluative point. He cannot stand quite outside the evaluative interests of the community he is observing, and pick up the concept simply as a device for dividing up in a rather strange way certain neutral features of the world. (Williams 1985, 141–42)

There are philosophers who argue that the nature of thick concepts, their saturation with descriptive elements, renders them nontransportable from one context to another, thus undermining moral universalism and encouraging particularism (O'Neill 1996). For historians, this is not an insurmountable weakness of thick concepts, as they try to refrain from judging the historical events under reconstruction on universal moral grounds. Historians aim, rather, to grasp the specificities of the situation. "Thick description cannot be cashed out in culture-or context-neutral terms, but rather implicates a rich set of values and commitments, which inform, guide, and motivate action" (Garfield 2000, 180), and this is exactly what makes them attractive and suitable tools for those historians whose ambition is to grasp the peculiarities of a particular situation.

Even for those historians who follow the words of Lev. 19:16, "Thou shalt not go up and down as a talebearer among thy people: neither shalt thou stand against the blood of thy neighbour", in an uncompromising way and are convinced that being an informer is a moral wrong, the historical context makes a (moral) difference. The historical question is not whether it is a general moral wrong to harm your neighbor or inform about your friend; the question the historian asks is rather what happened in this or that concrete situation, how and why and to what avail. It is obvious that the valence of so-called nonmoral facts is historically sensitive; depending on the context of the past event and on the interest, the position, and the historical embeddedness of the scholar, the meaning and significance of nonmoral facts differ.

It seems that Williams's ethnographic stance made him receptive to the concerns and approach of the anthropologist, whose primary task is to describe and make intelligible what has taken place, what has presumably been experienced by the actors themselves:

The sympathetic observer can follow the practice of the people he is observing; he can report, anticipate, and even take part in discussions of the use they make of their concept. But, as with some other concepts of theirs, relating to religion, for instance, or to witchcraft, he may not be ultimately identified with the use of the concept: it may not really be his. (1985, 142)

More than a decade after the publication of *Ethics and the Limits of Philosophy,* Williams wrote, "If we concentrate on thick concepts, we do indeed have something like the notion of a helpful informant" (1996, 27). Thickness, thus, is not just a style of narrating and focusing on the relevant details, not just concentrating on intentions, expectations, circumstances, and purposes that supposedly provide actions with their meaning—as Ryle asserted in his original papers—but also the choice of appropriate thick concepts in appropriate contexts (1971, 465–96).[4] Those concepts are suggestive: they keep the direction of the observation and description near the site of the action, closer to the ground, while behaving almost as if a local informer aided the work of the outside observer, who tries to make sense of the way in which the natives (of different localities or times or minds) are trying to give meaning to the actions of their world.

Contrary to Williams's implicit assumption, whether an utterance could or should be treated as a thick concept is not automatic or just linguistically determined; thick concepts are made and determined by their site, their location in the course of the reconstruction of the event. A descriptive term, depending on the context and the intention of the user, might behave as a thick concept, while a thick concept might be turned into a moral concept if it used in a specific site.

At this point, it becomes really difficult to distinguish the words of the philosopher from the text of the anthropologist. The point for now is only that ethnography is thick description:

What the ethnographer is in fact faced with . . . is a multiplicity of complex conceptual structures, many of them superimposed upon or knotted into one another, which are at once strange, irregular, and inexplicit, and which he must contrive somehow first to grasp and then to render. . . . Doing ethnography is like trying to read (in the sense of "construct a reading of") a manuscript—foreign, faded, full of ellipses, incoherencies, suspicious emendations, and tendentious commentaries, but written not in conventionalized graphs of sound but in transient examples of shaped behaviour. (Geertz 1973, 9–10)

The advice given by Geertz—"for [anthropological] theory [it is necessary] to stay rather closer to the ground than tends to be the case in sciences more able to give themselves over to imaginative abstraction" (1973, 24)—finds an echo in the supposition of the philosopher, namely, that "the middle distance is critical . . . where people do their best with what they are given" (Hollis 1995, 176–77). An important looping effect is at work here: it is not only with the help of thick concepts that the historian is capable of credible, meaningful, and sincere description; but by aiming at sharply focused and intense historical reconstruction, it might become possible to find the right conceptual tools. As Ian Hacking asserts, "Only by immersion in real-life complexities can one hope to get a clarification of language that fits lived experience" (2003, 124). Immersion means getting close to and focused on the—sometimes controversial—details of the lived experience of the past.

It is the narrative reconstruction of the concrete incident of the past that suggests the moral (in the sense of the message conveyed or the lesson to be learned from a story) since the historical narrative cannot be just the actual application of general, codifiable moral norms even if the historian follows moral principles. The historian is not necessarily a moral particularist: she or he may well embrace moral principles, but it is the emerging nonmoral facts of the whole story under reconstruction that stipulate the moral evaluation of the acts of the protagonists. The moral evaluation does not come as a revelation but as the probable outcome of painstaking scrutiny of the nonmoral features of the whole event, context, or situation; it would be a mistake to mix up this epistemological assertion with the unsound metaphysical claim "that the overall balance of reason is what makes the right actions right and wrong actions wrong" (Berker 2007, 115).

Writing about Geertz—without mentioning Bernard Williams and the issue of thick moral concept—Stephen Greenblatt argues: "As Geertz's famous essay deploys the term, however, thickness begins to slide almost imperceptibly from the description to the thing described. . . . Thickness no longer seems extrinsic to the object" (1977, 17). It was not due only to Geertz's observational and analytic abilities that he was able to show that the complexities of the objects of his research were "actually inscribed in the textual fragments" he used. The fecund hybrid nature of those thick concepts he employed "helped to create as well as to disclose the effect of compression," and it also stipulates a strong ethical commitment (Greenblatt 1977, 18). Thick moral concepts might help in keeping clear of the moral high ground, close to the scene of action, where reflection on historical events does not threaten to rob thick concepts of their power to guide. An important looping effect is at work here: it is not only with the help of the thick concepts that the historian is capable of credible, meaningful and sincere description, but by aiming at sharply focused and intense historical reconstruction, it may also become possible to find the right conceptual tools.

Afterword: Questions of Judgment

Stephan Feuchtwang

In their Introduction, Tobias Kelly and Sharika Thiranagama draw two themes from the chapters of this book. One is the intimacy of accusations of treachery. The other is what is performed by accusations of treachery, the re-creation of the boundaries of an object of greater loyalty: a people and its sovereignty.

Most of the chapters that follow dwell on the construction of figures of treason and betrayal and their realization in the persecution of actual populations. They focus on the intimacy of these greater loyalties and betrayals. But beside them, equally as figures in media and mind, and realized in actual conduct, are representations of what is immediately intimate, the local, the familial, the neighborly, and the friend. They are the originals that are projected and enlarged by analogy to country, state, and people. They are landmarks and features, loved trees or houses, often in more than one place, often across borders, graves or other locations of the recently dead, or of neighbors, or of friends. We each entertain several such figures to which we count ourselves as answerable and to which we are attached. Together and separately they become homelands by analogy and by extension. In reverse, patriotism or partisan passion in a civil war recruit into sacrifice of life, into fighting together, a selective and vivid commitment to fellow-soldiers as friends-in-extremity, another intimacy derived from the larger figure of loyalty and its leaders; both the iconic and charismatic figure of a leader and the immediacy of comrades may be invoked at the same time. This amounts to an earnest and deadly as well as an enlarging and ennobling play between the local, the familial, and their analogues, a play between two intimacies. The analogues become the intimacy of comradeship (female, male, and both) tearing into the intimate relations of locality, neighborhood, friendship, and family, breaking families or cleansing them into communities of people and their betrayers.

After the tearing apart, after the cleansing that is never complete and never can be, in the fragile time of peace that must follow, the figures of home, not their analogues, are vital for diplomacy across the rifts of the larger loyalties that had been mobilized. Along with and despite the new intimacies of war, they are vital for the reconstitution of everyday sociality. I want in this Afterword to turn to these figures of peace. They are figures of containment of hostility and tension, ideals of hospitality, of manners, of being polite to those with whom we share facilities and services, joined by figures of local home and of family and its internal conflicts, rivalries, and secrets, containers despite the tensions and hostilities the figures of others may arouse and despite the inherent hostilities generated by repeated encounters. I want to suggest how noble they are beside the more practiced nobility of the greater causes. I think all the chapters of this book point in this direction, which is after all the subject to which most ethnography draws our empathy. To put it baldly, I want to try out the thought that the necessary duplicity of these local and intimate relations is good.

It is right as an anthropologist and as a human being to sympathize with those caught between warring sides. But I don't want simply to say "hooray for traitors." That is too easy. It would deny the other moral feeling, which I share, the honourable feeling by which we condemn traitors. Perhaps this feeling should be confined to specified targets such as arms dealers selling to both sides. But it is not easy to say what honour should include and exclude. Should it exclude people who can afford not to collaborate with an oppressive occupying power but do? Or should it exclude those who wastefully and knowingly for their own glory put at risk the lives of others laying down their lives for a cherished and threatened country? Should it exclude those who sabotage for selfish gain a cherished ideal for which many are willing to make sacrifices? These are questions about patriots who can be traitors to the cause they profess. The high moral ground of patriotism is often exploited by vindictive gangs or worse, much worse than rogues.

But is duplicity wrong in other cases? Both moral grounds, that of higher loyalty and that of everyday civility, may be combined with self-interested exploitation. How do we combine the high moral ground with the low moral ground, and where do we draw lines dividing warm sympathy and admiration from cooler description? I am aware of and am indeed reflecting upon the way ethnographic description and the writing of history use adjectives of judgment that are implicitly moral. My concern will be how we write as well as what we write about traitors. But first I want briefly to claim the full historical and geographical scope of this inquiry.

The Predicament of Traitors

In their introduction, Kelly and Thiranagama focus on the most sympathetic traitor predicaments, people caught between conflicting loyalties
that change over time, and people turned into scapegoat targets for
accusations of disloyalty. They try to indicate the prevalence of this predicament, saying it is most acute and concrete in postcolonial states. I
would suggest it is much more general. It is not just a feature of postcolonial states, even when we add post-Soviet states. Everywhere we are subject to the changing figures of what is mobilized as pure and noble and
deserving of our greatest priorities of life and loyalty. Everywhere we are
subject to or participate ourselves in new appeals to spiritual union, to
stand up for ideology or principle, or to defend race or ethnicity as a
definition of homeland.

The traitor predicament is no less concrete in the longer-lived nations
subjected by their governments to recomposition of their populations
by repatriation and by immigration during and since the Second World
War, which turned into local civil wars in many countries of Europe as
well as the rest of the world. Racist or ethnicist or religio-ethnic or ideological purification are and have been at the heart of political history.
The condition of civil war in the world was produced and exacerbated
by the Cold hot Wars. Civil war and "crisis states," not interstate war but
proxy wars within states and their enclaves, is the condition of the present era. So the two intimacies and the potential of violence of the
greater upon the smaller is everywhere.

So much for geography and immediate history, but we should also
specify the time more conceptually and I will now suggest why, before
turning to questions of sympathetic description.

Exaggeration of Differences, Universal and Specific

Home and the strange are linked by shared place—the same town, country, and institution. This sharing with people who are more or less similar but different is the ground for rumor and accusation of treachery.
The chasm into which we can find ourselves looking when faced with a
double who is strange, an other who could be but isn't "me," is part of
the human condition—we know our self through others who are never
self-same. Homi Bhabha has built upon this basis, principally upon
Freud's notion of the Uncanny (the *Unheimlich*), a theory of projected
hatred of what the self finds unacceptable according to its idealizations
of who "I" am, namely, projection and expulsion of what is unacceptable according to figures of family, friends, and home into larger communities of identification.

These are not just fantasies. They are based on selected but real differences, and those differences are not always slight. Projected hatred exaggerates differences, but does not create those differences out of nothing. The differences can be as great and as visible as a completely different way of life, such as that of the Roma from the settled villager, or the observer of another religion, or as little and as barely distinguishable as the converted Christian and assimilated German Jew in Christian Germany. But persecution brings both into a populist regime of visibility and sovereignty that marks and separates these sharers in our home space, separating them out from our home space into border regions or ghettoes of exclusion. They are nevertheless close because they share the homeland locally, are met on common grounds and in shared facilities, and can be attractive, each to the other.

In "The Other Question," Bhabha (1994) describes stereotyped images in colonial discourse as a doubling, dividing the self to serve the fantastic desire to be pure in origin and projecting everything else into the colonial other. Doubling entails disavowal. In fact there are two disavowals. One is the refusal to see in the other a replica of the (mixed) self. The second is the refusal to see the other as the same but different. The repetition of the projection is compelled by disavowal, by the unrelenting pressure of refusal that seeks security in the assertion of the stereotype as the real. Once the stereotype has been used, offering realization of the desire for purity, it produces it own dynamic of compulsive repetition and demonization. Disavowal of the human in the demonic subhuman involves a compulsive refusal of similarity. And it is not confined to the colonial or to the postcolonial situation.

Suspicion of the stranger, even within the rules of hospitality, is surely a universal human condition. For instance, to be alone in a Zafimaniry village in Madagascar is to be non-kin and therefore to be under suspicion of being a witch. A stranger, including the anthropologist, is greeted by some construction of intimate kinship with his or her hosts and is urged to share their food: "come and eat, my child" or "my mother" or "my young sibling" (Bloch 1999, 141). Yet, hidden within this commensality, within its intimacy, there is also sibling rivalry. Eating together holds a danger of intimacy that could be poisonous. "The Zafimaniry are as obsessed by the theme of poisoning as they are by the theme of domestic openness" (144). Equivalent suspicions can be found in every intimate relation. Hospitality is everywhere compromised by senses of exclusive belonging. But this universal suspicion is now politicized by the analogical projection of self into a greater community, of people, religion, country, and state: politicized paranoia. Instead of witchcraft accusation, the force of rumor generates fear of neighbors and accusations of treason leading to purification purges (see, for instance, Das 1998). Witchcraft accusation or the discovery and elimination of sorcerers continues to flourish in these politicized conditions, but it signals a violent way of withdrawing from the results of more widespread and politicized violence (Allen and Turton 1996, 12–13).

I shall stress turning back to the homely and the civil. But I do not mean to imply a return to what went historically before, to a time before that of populist patriotism in which we live. I mean simply backing away from the analogues and projections of the homely, from the imagined community that is created by accusations of treason at the expense of the analogized figures of home. As the chapter by Richard Whitecross points out, what preceded were historically other analogical pairs with home and family and friendships, pairing them with, for instance, religious brotherhoods, apprenticeships, mercenary troops, feudal bonds, courts, or loyalty to a monarch. It is a great mistake to describe familial, ancestral, homely, and civil intimacies and their figures as primordial loyalties. To do so is to reify them as the true basis for the larger scale formations of nations and ethnicities in so-called modernity. They are no more primordial than are the greater loyalties because they are remade in the course of the creation of these larger analogues and their political economies.

Turning Back from the Figure of the Traitor

Simon Turner's chapter starts out from and dwells upon the figure of the traitor. Starting from the figure, the question becomes "when" and "with what bodies" the traitor is realized, personified—and attacked. Starting from the figure of the traitor, it is therefore possible to say, as he does, "The betrayal lies in pretending that ethnicity does not matter while in fact it does."

This is without doubt a good portrayal of how the accuser feels. In the everyday intimacies of friendship and neighborhood there is a conflict between the knowledge of ethnicity and the practice of sociality, and it can be turned into a conflict of loyalties. The conflict as I would describe it is one between the everyday, figures of home and civility, and the more generalized and abstract one of "people." But I am proposing something opposite this first proposition, moving back from the point of view of the figure of the greater loyalty and toward a second proposition in Turner's chapter. There is no question in my mind that the first proposition, the one quoted above, and its morality are secondary in both senses; it is derived and it is morally inferior. I am putting manners, courtesy and decency before patriotism and above being a traitor to my ethnicity. But once the figure of the traitor has been realized and honoring "my" people has been acted out, the sociality that was betrayed cannot easily be resumed.

Since the violence has been so intimate, is repair of now even more tense intimacy possible? It may always break down again into violence. Civil war creates new figures of loyalty, themselves betrayed by the blurring of friend/enemy lines, by the new tense intimacies of ambiguity. The tools of peace and restored sociality are not as satisfying as patriotism or friendship based on fighting comradeship, nor as fearful and unsharable as the comradeship of having committed atrocities together. As Turner writes in a vitally important second proposition, "we have to find a strange compromise; people act as if they believe—they trust their intimates because they must, not because they really have faith in them."

Turner dwells on the potential for further violence, one that makes the ethnic stereotype of the deceptive Tutsi true, realizing the demon figure on real people by mutilation and death, making visible what is concealed. Instead I want to dwell on leaving the invisible invisible, containing it again by the necessary deceptions and leaps of faith by which sociality is repaired, even across the figurations of ethnic identity after ethnic cleansing. In the Burundi case this entails making compromises between the myths of autochthony (we are the people of this earth) and the myths of the invading stranger state or the international conspiracy. It means holding resentment in, recognizing dependency and dominance only enough to reduce it, not acting to replace it with its pure mirror of "us" in power.

I want us to consider compromising great loyalties. I am trying to suggest that we see figures of intimacy as the necessary tempers, the bases for peace-making diplomacy, restoring us after the violent fluctuations and assaults induced by the larger analogical, political, religious, and communal or ethnic calls on loyalty. I say that the intimate figures are a necessary foil to the democratic and populist appeals of their analogues, indeed, that they are the democratic superior, sovereign to those appeals, even when those larger appeals are themselves intimate, infiltrating or rather suffusing the figures of more immediate intimacy and after they have split apart what were neighbours, friends, family, and home. I am suggesting a political and moral philosophy that tests these analogical appeals to intimacy upon the sovereign grounds of truly local and intimate figures of reciprocity, obligation, and manners.

Reincorporating Traitors

Instead of seeing how the traitor is made explicit, I would refer instead to the laughter and theater that after the Ugandan civil war had died down Teso people performed fearfully to reintegrate violent gangs, former youth who had killed their own fellow villagers. The war between a rebel army and the state army broke down into militia groups attacking their own people and looting the wealth of their own areas (de Berry 1998, 6). The bitter memories of this violence among the violated is described by Teso as "too much thinking," an ingestion of bitter words, which can not only be heard in an inner dialogue but also tasted and otherwise felt in the stomach, causing ulcers, depression, and emaciation. The cure is to substitute sweet words, ironic jokes, for the bitter, for instance, by giving nicknames to both violators and violated. The humiliated and impoverished victims call the cheapest footwear they are reduced to wear "what-to-dos" instead of the shaming "car-tyre sandals"; one young man who in "thinking too much" had attempted suicide by swallowing chloroquin was nicknamed "chloroquin" and could laugh about it. Violators joined in plays for a church group enacting the recent past as entertainment as well as education.

The nearest equivalent in this book is *The Glass Agency*, the Iranian film about the afterlife of the heroes who sacrificed their bodies and willingly saw their comrades-in-arms sacrifice their lives for the Islamic Republic against infidel Iraq. Kamran Rastegar dwells, as I do, on the return to ambivalence and peace, in which the self-sacrificer is an embarrassment. He comes from a time of the silencing of the ambivalent, when everyone else had to keep quiet except the callers and responders to heroic self-sacrifice, who have now to become invisible and silent, ghosts of that time. The film brings the ghost back to visibility. It offers its audience a space in which to bring the two times together, in a compromising present. Jo de Berry's example of Teso theater undertakes a far greater compromise with local killers and their leaders. They are not heroes. They have become violent traitors. The self-sacrificing hero of the Islamic Republic in the film is not a hero turned gangster; he is a hero among compromisers who could themselves be thought of as traitors. But turning back to the compromises of local sociality means finding ways of living in one case with violent heroes, and in the other with heroes-become-traitors. It is in both cases a more homely heroism.

Nayanika Mookherji presents another scenario of a turn to peace after a war, this time a war of independence for Bangladesh. The traitors during that war have been incorporated in positions of power, just as Nazis and their collaborators were in Germany in order that there could be a viable administration of the new government (the alternative, dismissing all of them, would have been to prolong foreign occupation in Germany, and Iraq 2002–10 is an example of the consequence of doing that, a civil war under occupation). Like Turner, Mookherji dwells on the politics of exposing, making visible these traitors in government. It is part

of a politics of compromise with a time when rape, mutilation, and killing were weapons of civil war, against the secularist independence of
Bangladesh. "Bangladesh's 'genocidal' birth" she writes "represents to
the left-liberals the unresolved, unreconciled history of the nation, the
wound of the nation still raw, gaping and unhealed in the present. This
thus necessitates the need for an 'epic culture' of heroes and villains,
the need for identifying the Islamicist collaborator all over Bangladesh.
... Through the block or obstacle of the Islamicist collaborator the fantasy of the full Bangladeshi identity is sustained as this identity is yet to
be." Her description draws our sympathies to these secular left-liberals.
In the other direction, she draws sympathy to those targeted by purifiers,
Biharis caught between the sides in the war of independence. From her
description it is more difficult to have sympathy with powerful opportun-
ist ex-collaborators in government. Is this the moral line to draw, in
which we join in condemnation? Should we focus on the current politics
and acts of these former collaborators, to describe what they do or do
not do for descriptive judgement? Or should we constantly recall their
past in a time of war, which is to support in Bangladesh a politics of
purge such as that which Julia Strauss in her chapter describes with negative connotation on both sides of the Chinese civil war as they persisted
on either side of the Taiwan Straits?

From my own reading and research on China and Taiwan, I think that
for the sake of symmetry Julia Strauss underestimates the popular base
of the Communist forces that created the People's Republic of China
(PRC). They led what was to a great extent a popular war against a venal
Nationalist government whose occupation of Taiwan, immediately alienating its welcome there, was typical of what it had become on the Mainland. But she rightly notes the similarities of both sides' purges by police
action. In the People's Republic, the cultivation of a populace by mass
mobilization campaigns was self-alienated by the ludicrous bureaucratization of meeting quotas of found and exposed traitors, campaigns that,
as she writes, "invited 'the masses' to participate in the state's terror."
Recalling a past of treacherous compromise and hypocrisy in Bangladeshi politicians is of course not a call for such a purge, but it does constantly resurrect a past that has been surpassed, compromised, perhaps
in ways that could be deemed necessary.

In Taiwan, the rump of the Republic of China kept itself alien from
the population by military action and secret trials against dissidents. I
would add that there was also an equivalent of the PRC's mass campaigns in Taiwan, in the form of the New Life Movement (an invocation
of Confucian virtue and National loyalty) that the Nationalists had
started in government in the mainland and continued in Taiwan in state
schools.

Unlike Bangladesh, Rwanda, and Sri Lanka, these Chinese purifica-
tions were not campaigns of targeting ethnically defined populations.
They were rival claims to define and represent the "people" defined in
terms of two historical ideologies: one of a people's revolution, the other
of a people's historical essence and its modern destiny. That did not prevent there being ex-Communists among the purgers in the Republic of
China on Taiwan and ex-Nationalists in the PRC. And in both there were
many similar targets, ex-collaborators with the Japanese occupation and
colonial regime respectively, not to mention ex-warlords and bandit
chiefs in both. They were rich material for accusation and purge and
very difficult to sort into sheer opportunists and more ideologically committed "collaborators." We can sympathize with the traitors' predicament of intentions or commitments between or other than those of the
sides that came to dominate and demand loyalty. How about sympathy
with a far more easily condemnable collaboration with an enemy occupation force?

For instance, thousands of local government officials and thousands
more leaders of associations that moved between charitable work and
the running of houses of prostitution continued to work under the occupying Japanese regime in the Mainland, condemnable as traitors by both
Nationalists and Communists. Timothy Brook (2005) argues that they
were puppets, in the sense that they had no choice but to obey or to
continue their former activities and in some cases to thrive by currying
favor with Japanese rulers. Prominent among them were those who had,
like so many other educated Chinese, been to Japanese universities.
More clear-cut would be to condemn the Chinese troops of the puppet
regime for the atrocities they committed, or for the exactions of high
taxes in areas of starvation and prevention of movement out of them
during the famine of 1942 (Thaxton 1997, 210, 262). But that is condemnation for atrocity, not treason, for what they did, just as it is possible to condemn troops and leaders of the patriotic Nationalists for
plundering villages (200).

With these examples we can now include the collaborators in Bangladesh's government. Collaborators are fixers. Fixers, those who are
skilled in making arrangements, in interpretation and mediation, or in
finding supplies, entrepreneurs within command economies, or in occupied territories running rackets (such as the deals done by Yossarian, the
hero of Joseph Heller's hilarious and terrifying novel *Catch 22* about the
U.S. armed forces in Italy during the Second World War), can all be
accused of criminal fraternization, collaboration, counterrevolution, or
treason. When found to be in breech of a law, their actions are criminal.
I am suggesting something similar in our judgmental descriptions. We
must describe and weigh acts of duplicity, judging whether they on bal-

ance save lives, make survival more possible, or destroy lives, and whether what they did outweighs what they are doing now and its usefulness. Their skills and experience can be vital for postwar settlement, and it is by what they do that they should be described and judged, not as a labelled figure.

Tobias Kelly's chapter describes how specific acts of collaboration are singled out: selling Palestinian land to the occupying force and its settlers; spying for the occupying force. These are labels for condemned acts of political crime, but they are, as he points out for spies, often an enforced choice under extreme pressure and threat. So the suspicion of acting as a spy was accompanied by pity in the judgment of other Palestinians. Going further, gangs of Fatah patriots committing assassinations of suspected spies were as condemnable as the secret occupation-force Israeli assassinations of Palestinian patriotic activists. Such violence demarcates but is as dubious as that of collaboration. Law, legal process in the judgment of acts, on the contrary, is on the side of peace and civilization. The judgment of Kelly's landlord offers a model on drawing the line: "While he said that collaborators were a *sarataan* (cancer) that deserved to be killed, he thought that public executions showed a lack of *hadarat* (civilization). He complained about the inability of the PNA to bring the suspected to justice in any way that vaguely resembled the *siyadat al-qanun* (rule of law)." The judgment of acts is better than the judgement of people, and legal process is better than summary justice in the judgement of acts, condemnation and sentence. But of course, law can support summary justice, can make statutory and total the suspicion of a traitor in a friend/enemy distinction that makes potential traitors of any of the subjects of law, as Antigone became in Sophocles' play about the law of warrior king Creon. Law can be bad. But judgmental decisions reached after due investigation of actions and governed not only by laws but also by equity, the necessary compromises of applying law and legal principle with current reality, is certainly on the side of civilization.

Nations of Collaborators

When a government becomes so alienated from its popular base in a state of emergency that every situation is one of being threatened from within as well as without, the whole population is definable as a people betraying itself—a nation of collaborators. Lars Buur's chapter describes Frelimo's government in Mozambique approaching this state of affairs: "the Frelimo government created the dissent against itself by acting against livelihood strategies as though they were dissent strategies. In the context of newly independent Mozambique, surrounded as it was by enemies and steeped in military discourses, such 'dissent,' constructed as treason, justified an extreme set of responses to protect the 'freedoms' of the revolution." In fact only some of the population were singled out for deportation to forced labor camps as collaborators with the enemy. But as Buur points out, when the political crisis accompanies an economic crisis in which many if not all those outside a government-linked elite are able to survive only by disapproved means, the enemy within is literally everywhere. Since many relied on speculation and hoarding, they were potentially exemplars of the widely disseminated cartoon figure of the traitor. Most significantly from the point of view I am suggesting, Buur notes that whether or not one became a captive to the category "traitor" was something that depended on the civility and ethical discretion of the police, who had become the clearest instantiation of the sovereign power of the People. The agents of state coercion themselves became honorably duplicitous, at least to the people benefiting from their discretion.

I have elsewhere described this as a situation of aggravated indifference, a government of the People alienating itself from its people (Feuchtwang 2006). We might say that this is the extremity of political crime. From the point of view of the people with all their own, homely figures of livelihood strategy and civility as criteria, such an alienated government is as much a hero traitor as the boy gangs in Uganda are. But nothing is so straightforward. The analogous figures of popular sovereignty are imbued with the promises and aspirations invested in a state leadership, even if its current officials and (most of) its leaders are a bitter disappointment or only look after their own. Suspicion of government officials and leaders has its counterpoint in expectations of good government, engendered by figures of the ideal—such as that of Samora Machel in the case of Frelimo—long presented by the same regime. The state is indispensable for development beyond the bare livelihood strategies to which the regime or a combination of external pressures and civil war has reduced its population. So, a combination of criteria of judgment is inevitable, on the one hand the homely and civil, and on the other the political ideal. Between them they constitute the sovereignty of the actual people in all their ambivalence and with all the motives hidden behind those figures.

Steffen Jensen's chapter might be a description of a version of what I mean, exacerbated by sharp political rivalry and violence. It describes how dependence on the state is an issue of distance. Either there is complete distrust of the police and government welfare schemes in favor of locally organized good gangs, or there is reserved support for police and government and condemnation of the same gangs. Both positions start from what is good for their locality. Denunciation in gossip for betraying family or community to the police or government is a border-setting performance of family, community, and state. Denunciation in gossip for shielding criminally bad boys is another such border-setting performance, an adjustment to legal enforcement and state grants. Each presents different priorities in an assertion of respectability in a situation of dire hardship. But these differences, which could become polarized into political violence, are tempered for survival and for living with neighbors; gossip and denunciation are rhetorical tactics that sustain different and rival versions of moral community but usually without the lasting intimate effects of openly violent rivalry between opposed ideas of the nation and their accusations of treason.

Conclusion

I am suggesting something more than "intimacy," something that is captured neither by the various ways of saying that friend and enemy distinctions are not decidable, nor by the insight that we are all our own traitors, strangers to ourselves. In the first place there is the difference between larger analogues and projections and the more immediately experienced and transmitted figures of homely intimacy that are the source of the analogues. In the second place, real differences, not necessarily small, and real actions are identified and exaggerated to make suspected betrayal visible.

The loyalties and civilities of the local and the homely are intimate. So are their analogical projects of identification with a larger community and a state. The intimacy of and the figure of the home, a remembered house, a tree, to which I have referred is inspired by Sharika Thiranagama's (2007) poignant account of Jaffna Muslims as well as Jaffna Tamils betrayed and dislocated by the militant leadership of "their" liberation in Sri Lanka. The distinction between two intimacies has its point of departure in something she writes in her chapter in this book (197): "intimacy refers to, first, that of home and kin and, second, "cultural intimacy," the idealized notion of one's ethnic group—that is, Tamilness—as a set of shared codes, language, practices, sentiments, and belonging" (Herzfeld 1997). But I want to stress the difference: Herzfeld's cultural intimacy is an ironic intimacy between rulers and ruled, a reservation of the privilege to ridicule the larger identity.

I have tried to draw, in this conclusion to a book about the figures and persecutions of traitors and collaborators, the worthiness of this irony, this rhetorical disguise, this compromise. The traitor predicaments described in this book are the most violent instances of the two intimacies at odds. But I would say they are always distinguishable and in tension, not because homely loyalties may be transnational. So too are many identifications with a greater community, such as to centers of religious and political authority across the border of Bhutan, described by Richard Whitecross in his chapter. These larger loyalties, supposedly reinforcing each other can also become the subject of accusations of the "anti-national," for instance, the crossed loyalties of the sacred and the secular, where the secular monarch or titular head of a nation is legitimated by a transcendent figure and his successors and embodiments. The distinction I am stressing is another one of supposedly reinforcing loyalties, between the two intimacies of home and of larger community. They are different because they are different kinds of experience and representation. And I give priority to the first because from it comes the possibilities of peaceful diplomacy and compromise: good duplicity.

I would go beyond the reading of Sophocles' *Antigone* to which the introduction refers. The drama is constructed around a contradiction between the law enacted by human rulers, in this case a friend-enemy definition of loyalty, and the law of life and death, which Sophocles presents as a law or fate in the hands of the gods, of the Furies, and of the dead, and as the proper conduct of rites, of family, identified by his character Creon as the world of women. The king (Creon) is forced by the law of gods and the family to compromise the friend/enemy law of the state and is destroyed in the process. The king's hubris has caused him to err, in my reading, by causing him to confuse two acts, that of betrayal of the state by Polyneices, who fought for another state against what had been his own, and that of family duty to a brother (Polyneices) by a sister Antigone, which crosses the line of friend/enemy but is not treason and causes no-one's death. Creon could not see the wisdom and lack of contradiction between honoring both loyalties, to state and to family. Beyond that, he could not see that the latter is healing and noble, particularly because it combines love with respect for law, including that of the state. Antigone's higher honor is in a situation of bad law, one that forces the two acts into a contradiction, in which case she gives priority to love and respect. I go further in extending the law of family to respect and civility to those with whom we share facilities but who may be strange and appear threatening.

In other words, I am saying that there is nobility in ambivalence and duplicity. It is noble to desist from projection, to recognize mixture and difference and to hold in the unsettling challenges to figures of ourselves and our cherished ideals. The honor of duplicity is to honor the challenge to principle, question principle, defend it, change it, and not act abstractly on it, removing the challenge or wishing it to be removed. Good duplicity is also to tolerate, by good manners, one's hatred or any other emotion in what Kelly and Thiranagama call "the dark side of familial and community life" instead of turning it into "a legitimate instrument of violent sovereignty." In sum, I want to draw attention to the ideals and the figures that are our internalized representations of civilization and that bind us to honor civility.

Notes

Introduction: Specters of Treason

We are indebted to Thomas Blom Hansen and the two anonymous reviewers for University of Pennsylvania Press for their insightful comments that helped us clarify our arguments considerably.

1. We thank one of the anonymous reviewers particularly for helping clarify our argument here.

Chapter 1. Xiconhoca: Mozambique's Ubiquitous Post-Independence Traitor

I would like to thank all participants at the Traitors workshop at the University of Edinburgh and the Popular Governance or Criminalization seminar at the University of Oxford who shared their generous comments. I am also grateful to Kate Meagher, Dennis Rodgers, Morten Nielsen, Obede Baloi, Alison Stent, Tobias Kelly, and Sharika Thiranagama for commenting so helpfully on the chapter in draft form. The usual disclaimers apply.

1. All names are pseudonyms except for those of historical figures.

2. Operation Production refers to the 1983 post-independence government operation aimed at "solving" the problem of urban unemployment (informality, delinquency, etc.) by forcibly removing from the main urban centers all those described as "unproductive." Thousands of people were arrested, uprooted from their homes, and flown to Niassa and other centers of real or imagined food production where they would help produce food for the country. The action accounts for some of the worst violations of human rights in the country, but there are no published figures for the operation. Many of the victims of Operation Production eventually escaped and made their own way back home. Others died in the attempt or joined or were press-ganged by the Renamo rebels.

3. The then governor of the Province of Niassa, David Simango, had announced as early as February 2003 that the government planned to evacuate to their "original" home areas about one thousand people who were deported from other parts of the country to Niassa during 1983 (Mozambique News Agency, *AIM Reports* 248, 19 February 2003).

4. I have elsewhere analyzed the continuation of the political ethos of monism and suggested that, despite the switch to a liberal democracy, the ideological and symbolic terrain is still haunted by the politics of difference between "friends" and "enemies" emanating from the internal war between Renamo and Frelimo (see Buur 2007a, b; Kyed and Buur 2006).

5. The category of the traitor or internal enemy exceeded the Renamo resistance in many ways.

6. Moreover, the new nation-states in southern Africa confronted the highly charged ideological dialectical opposition of East-West proxy confrontation besides de facto remnants of colonialism and, for southern Africa, the all-embracing shadow of apartheid.

7. Frelimo document quoted in Hall and Young (1997, 60).

8. The figure of Xiconhoca has usually been mentioned in passing in the academic literature in terms of the fight against corruption and immorality (Harrison 1999), the redrawing of the relationship between peasants and state institutions (Harrison 1998), the struggle over excessive bureaucratization (Henriksen 1978), struggles between formal and informal economies (Chingono 1996), or as a popular communicative device (Hall and Young 1997). I will not contest any of these interpretations because they all point toward particular moral, ethical, and ideological fault lines in the Mozambican attempt to produce a new society.

9. It is interesting that all of Xiconhoca's disparate characteristics get linked to each other by and through the body; once an ordinary and innocent informal trader is linked to a racketeer and speculator, he automatically becomes a rumormonger and an alcoholic as well.

10. Interestingly, Chingono (1996, 41) mentions that when Renamo made their first attack on a co-operative shop in Sofala in 1977, they gave the shopkeeper a poster to pass on to Samora Machel depicting him "as a monkey sitting on a throne." It was, therefore, not solely Frelimo who relied on this medium (for the use of cartoons in political struggles in general, see Mbembé 2001).

11. See Kyed and Buur (2006) and Buur and Kyed (2006) for analysis of the recognition of traditional authorities in Mozambique. For an analysis of state recognition of traditional authorities in sub-Saharan Africa, see Buur and Kyed (2007).

12. The party adhered to the Stalinist dictum "National in Form and Socialist in Content" (see Roepstroff 1996, 70–74 for a discussion of the narration of the Soviet understanding of the relationship between nationalism and socialism in general).

13. The Frelimo narrative about backwardness and the influence of the traditional, all underpinned by the figure of the New Man, has obviously very strong resonances with developments in other countries where communist parties ruled, such as in the early years of the Soviet Union. Due to space constraints, I cannot explore these links here.

14. As Alexander recounts, most of the depictions of "immaturity" echo the general language of Frelimo during the war with Renamo, where Renamo was described as brutal, uncivilized, poorly educated, and rural, while Frelimo was depicted as civilized, literate, and urban (1997, 8). Since the war, this language has continued to circulate in the national media debate, especially around elections.

15. See the special one year after independence edition of *Noticias* for Samora Machel's explanation of how this could be achieved (No. 1 Especial, 1976, 20–21, 59–61)

16. For a reference to Samora's emphasis on the moral regeneration of the population, see ibid., 101.

17. From the outset of independence, discussion of everyday economic governance in the Frelimo-controlled media featured articles on ruthless operators

who speculated on the prices of staple products, framed by elaborate explanations of structural weaknesses such as problems with the state marketing board Agricom, lack of materials for the industry, national transport infrastructure, the lack of transport, and so forth (see, for example, *Noticias*, 19 September 1976, 2; *Noticias* No. 1 Especial, 1976, 50).

18. One of the few writers who acknowledged this struggle from the outset is Henriksen, stating "fear of economic breakdown may have temporarily displaced earlier fears of neo-colonialism," even though he saw it as a passing phenomenon (1978, 461).

19. See ibid., 17–20. The newspaper *Tempo* announced the creation of two hundred people's shops in 1977 "in the struggle against speculation by private companies" (15 May 1977; see also Henriksen 1978, 460), but this was a priority right from the beginning of the new regime (see *Noticias*, No. 1 Especial, 1976, 24, 113).

20. Just as the word *enemy* was drawn from military language, the only language Frelimo knew. See *Noticias*, 1 July 1976, 3; 11 August 1976, 3; 13 August 1976, 2; 18 August 1976.

Chapter 2. Denunciatory Practices and the Constitutive Role of Collaboration in the Bangladesh War

My thanks go to the editors Sharika Thiranagama and Toby Kelly for organizing the Traitors workshop, for putting together this edited collection, and for their comments and suggestions. I am also grateful to Saydia Kamal for her photograph and granting me the permission to reproduce it in this chapter. The illustrations of the posters have been drawn from the Web site of International Institute of Social History, Amsterdam, which is the safe keeper of collections. All reasonable effort has been made to trace the illustrators of these posters.

1. The loss of the intellectuals is considered a significant loss in Bangladesh and is commemorated each year on 14 December on the Martyred Intellectual Day (see Mookherjee 2007).

2. For further discussion on these numbers, see Mookherjee (forthcoming 2011).

3. In 1946, just before the independence and partition of India in 1947, the Nizam of Hyderabad, who was unwilling to accept the annexation of his kingdom to India, formed a volunteer corps of Razakars for resisting the entry of the Indian army into his kingdom. This is referred to as the Razakar Movement. In 1971, a Razakar force was also formed by the Pakistan government after this model with an enrollment of 96 loyalist activists. This force was subsequently formed in different parts of East Pakistan and constituted nearly 50,000 collaborators.

4. While Bengali nationalism seeks a pan-Bengal (including Bengalis in India) bonding beyond religion, Bangladeshi nationalism primarily refers to those residing within the territorial boundaries of Bangladesh with a reference to their Muslim identity.

5. Most people, including those in the Awami League, criticize Mujib for this amnesty. Some Awami Leaguers defend Mujib by reiterating that Razakars who had conducted grave and specific crimes were not released.

6. After the war, 42 cases were filed against the collaborators by the family members of the slain intellectuals till March 1973. However, over the years, no progress was made. On 24 September 1997, Farida Banu, sister of slain intellec-

tual Ghyasuddin Ahmed, filed a case; subsequently, some police investigations were carried out. However, as the old files and police records became untraceable, there was little progress.

7. For Azum's role, see Guhathakurta (1996, 6).

8. Jahanara Imam, author of *The Days of 1971* (1993), a woman from an upper-middle-class family and mother and wife of martyred liberation fighter led Gono Adalat. She has become iconic among the cultural elite and the middle class as a mother figure who succeeded in mobilizing public opinion against the fundamentalists and in favor of proliberation forces. She died of cancer in 1994.

9. In the 1990s there were many cases of violence against women, ranging from safe custody rapes and deaths by police, acid-throwing cases, rapes by ordinary citizens, fatwas, and attacks against female NGO workers.

10. In Rwanda, too, Tutsis were referred to as "imposters" or a "race of foreigners" (Taylor 1999, 90).

11. This comment was made by Mujib in 1972 in the context of criticizing the rampant corruption involved in the distribution of Red Cross blankets after the war and highlighting his helplessness in rooting out those involved.

12. Enayetpur is a village in western Bangladesh. Predominantly inhabited by Muslim residents, it has a population of nine hundred, with five households owning land and the large majority of villagers being landless daily wage laborers.

13. C. Taylor (2002, 168) has also used the tropes of flows and blockages to refer to various instances of violence in the case of the Rwandan genocide. Barriers were these liminal sites where "blocked beings" could be reconfigured through torture so that they become "categorical abomination" and in turn cast out of the nation.

Chapter 3. Intimacy, Loyalty, and State Formation: The Specter of the "Anti-National"

This chapter draws on fieldwork undertaken in 1999–2001 for Whitecross (2002). Fieldwork was made possible by an Economic and Social Research Council (ESRC) PhD Research Studentship. Additional fieldwork was undertaken in 2003 and 2004 with support from the Carnegie Trust for the Universities of Scotland (2002), an ESRC Postdoctoral Fellowship (2003), Society for South Asian Studies (UK) (2003), Frederick Williamson Memorial Trust, Cambridge (2003), and a University of Edinburgh Research Award (2004). I wish to thank the editors for inviting me to participate in the Traitors Workshop, Edinburgh. Hugo Gorringe, Laura Jeffrey, and the participants in the workshop provided invaluable comments and insights. All errors are, of course, my own.

1. Drukpa refers to the Druk Kagyu sect of Himalayan Buddhism to which the founding zhabdrung, Ngawang Namgyal belonged. The term Drukpa is used to refer both to his system of government and more recently to Bhutanese nationals, especially those from the north, and is used in counterpoint to the term *Lhotshampa* (see Hutt 2003).

2. *Dzong* refers to fortress/monasteries built at strategic sites across Bhutan. They were centers of government and centers of religious activity, especially for rituals for the protection and welfare of the country and the Druk Kagyu school. Due to their dual function, there is no simple translation appropriate; therefore, the term *dzong* has been retained.

3. Dzongkha is a dialect of western Bhutan that became the official language

of government in the seventeenth century. In the 1960s it became the official language of Bhutan.

4. Aris (1998, 122) notes that this text was submitted to the National Assembly but was never approved for publication.

5. The most recent incarnation of the zhabdrung died in Manali, Himachal Pradesh, in 2003.

6. There are three main ethnic groups in Bhutan: Ngalong, Sharchop and Lhotshampa. In addition, there are approximately another sixteen linguistic groups. With the exception of the Lhotshampa, all these groups share common religious and social practices, and their languages are part of the Tibeto-Burman groups of languages. The Lhotshampa, on the other hand, are primarily Hindu and speak Nepali.

7. See Hutt (2003) for details of the conflict between the Lhotshampa and Bhutanese authorities in the late 1980s and its peak in 1990–91.

8. To what extent they were seen as being Bhutanese is difficult to comment on. They did settle and interacted with the royal government, including paying taxes. The term Lhotshampa suggests that they were accepted as settlers in the southern areas that had not previously been cultivated by the northern Bhutanese.

9. I do not examine this in great detail. See Hutt 2003 and Strawn 1994.

10. Whitecross (2009) examines in more detail the citizenship legislation and the effects on the Lhotshampa.

11. From 1846 to 1951, although the Shah dynasty remained on the Nepalese throne, effective political control was held by the Rana family, who became hereditary prime ministers. The Rana regime was eventually brought down by an alliance between the monarchy and modernizing intellectuals and support from the newly independent India. Direct royal rule was imposed by King Mahendra in 1961 and lasted until 1979. See Whelpton (2005).

12. The archival reports of the National Assembly indicate an emerging emphasis on dress and national identity as early as 1964. During the debates in 1964, Bhutanese national dress was discussed and made a requirement for all Bhutanese women, army personnel, and guides entering public buildings.

13. There is very little information available on who created or why the concept of Tsa Wa Sum was developed. However, as I discuss below, the shift in its meaning from "government" to "people" arguably reflects a conscious attempt by the Bhutanese state to create, even in the absence of democratic elections or participation in governance, a common identity shared by all Bhutanese.

14. English translation of the Third Draft Constitution (issued 7 August 2007). The Dzongkha specifically uses the term Tsa Wa Sum.

15. I do not discuss the role of village volunteers. However, it is worth noting that the role has recently been formalized in the reintroduction of militias based on the seventeenth-century *pazap* system of military service. This was particularly noticeable in 2003–4 at the height of the campaign by the Bhutanese to remove ULFA/Bodo guerrillas from their camps in southern Bhutan. ULFA is the acronym for the United Liberation Front of Assam. The Bodo are a tribal people in the North-East Frontier region of India seeking to create an independent state. A number of political parties support an armed struggle against India, including the National Democratic Front for Bodoland and the Bodo Liberation Tigers.

16. Until 2004, *Kuensel* was the only weekly newspaper in Bhutan. This newspaper was owned by the government until 1992.

17. See note 7 above.

18. I do not focus here on the implications of this refusal to acknowledge the possibility of northern Bhutanese being "anti-nationals" due to the complexity of the issue.

19. Draft translation of autobiography of T. N. Rizal provided by Michael Hutt (SOAS) 30 November 2006.

20. Prior to his abduction/extradition, Rizal had set up the People's Forum for Human Rights in Kathmandu.

21. In 1994, a joint verification process was established by the governments of Bhutan and Nepal. Under the terms of this agreement, two teams of Bhutanese and Nepalese officials would examine each of the refugees' claims to Bhutanese citizenship. Those who were deemed to be refugees would be permitted to return and resettle in Bhutan. Following the verification process at one camp, 70.55 percent were categorized as having voluntarily emigrated from Bhutan and only 2.4 percent as "genuine refugees." None of those recognized as "genuine refugees" have returned to Bhutan. In December 2003, the joint verification process was disrupted when frustrated refugees in the Jhapa camp attacked the Bhutanese officials. Since then, the process has been in abeyance. In 2007, the governments of Norway, Canada, and the United States agreed to accept approximately half of the refugees.

22. *Kuensel,* "Ngolops Should Be Punished," 8 July 2000, 1.

23. *Kuensel,* "111 Sentenced for Collaborating with Militants," 4 September 2004, 1.

24. Ibid., 20.

25. Phuntsho makes a mistake here—Rizal did not establish the Bhutan People's Party; see note 14 above.

26. Concerns over increasingly violence by supporters of Gorkhaland have reemerged in 2008.

Chapter 4. Traitors, Terror, and Regime Consolidation on the Two Sides of the Taiwan Straits: "Revolutionaries" and "Reactionaries" from 1949 to 1956

Research for this chapter was generously supported by a Fulbright Research Fellowship for Taiwan (2005–6), the British Academy, and a Chiang Ching-kuo Foundation research grant (2006–8).

1. Virtually the entirety of the CCP and GMD leadership had rubbed shoulders and served together during the period of the First United Front in the mid-1920s, and undoubtedly there was some degree of contact between individuals on both sides in later periods after the purges of 1927. Many families had individuals who aligned with different sides; for examples, see Cheek (1997).

2. The 800,000 figure was released at the Eighth Party Congress in September, 1956 (Domes 1973, 2). The figure of 2,000,000 was mentioned in a work report of 1952, also cited by Domes, who "conservatively" estimates the total numbers executed to be upwards of 3,000,000.

3. Shanghai Municipal Archives (hereafter SMA), B1/2/1339, "Fan'geming zuifan chuxing fenlei tongjibiao," (Statistical form on classification and punishment of counterrevolutionaries), 1951. In Shanghai, the vast majority were apprehended and dispatched in the spring and early summer of 1951, with very few executions thereafter; upsurges of the campaign went on significantly thereafter in remote inland areas.

4. The chief documentary collection for the early 1950s era is *Taiwan diqu jieyan shiqi 50 niandai zhengzhi anjian huibian* (Compilation of political cases from

the martial-law era Taiwan in the 1950s), vols. 1–5 (Nantou: Taiwan Document Commission, 1998), hereafter cited as NZASH. Most of these documents have been assembled from the Taiwan Provincial Security Command (Taiwan sheng bao' an silingbu). There were five different island-wide organizations entrusted with running the White Terror in the early 1950s: in addition to the Taiwan provincial police bureau, the Constitutional Military Headquarters (Xianfabin silingbu), the Ministry of Interior Investigation Bureau (Neizheng bu diaocha ju), and the Ministry of Defense Internal Security Bureau (Guofang bu baomi ju). Responsibilities between these different organizations overlapped, lines of reporting were unclear, and the standard by which individuals were either counted or left out of the final statistics was at best vague.

5. NZASH suggests both higher and lower numbers, 1: 127. The collection of these numbers was nonstandard and inconsistent between different particular organizations. 1952 was the one year that full figures were given for each of the organizations involved in the suppression in Taiwan, and if we extrapolate proportionally on the basis of the figures from 1952, the total numbers for 1950, 1953, and 1954 would have to be increased by 116 percent, for a total of 11,672.

6. The total population of the greater Shanghai area was 5,400,000 in 1950; that of Taiwan, roughly 7,500,000.

7. NZASH, 1: 129, 2: 80, 88, 122.

8. NZASH, vol. 2, "Jilong shi gongzuo weiyuanhui Zhong ji jiedong deng ren anjian" (Jilong municipal working committee case on Zhong Jiedong et al.), 8–11; "Gaoxiong shi gongzuo weiyuanhui dengren an" (case on Gaoxiong municipal work committee et al.), 23–24.

9. NZASH, vol. 2, "Taibei shi gongzuo weiyuanhui Guo Xiuzong deng ren an" (case on Taibei municipal work committee: Guo Xiuzong et al.), 69–73.

10. NZASH, vol. 2 "Zhongyang shehuibu xiaxie jinjian die Su yilin deng ren an" (case on Central Ministry of Social Affairs: Su Yilin et al.), 328–29.

11. Some of the following details on the Campaign to Suppress Counterrevolutionaries draw on Strauss (2002).

12. SMA C21/2/179. 'Shanghai shiwei guanyu fandong tewu dangtuandengji gongzuo zhishi" (Shanghai Municipal Committee directive on classification of counterrevolutionary parties and corps), 10 December 1950.

13. QDA (Qingpu District Archives). 1/1/38, "Bei douzheng zhi duixiang qingkuang tongjibiao" (Statistics on targets struggled against), February–March 1951.

14. SMA C21/1/98, Zhang Ben, "Wuyue siri shicheng nianqing ganbu jinian wusi qingnian jieji zhongguo xinminzhu zhuyi qingniantuan chengli erzhou nian daihui shang de baogao" (Report on the second anniversary of the Youth Cadres' Commemoration of May Fourth and China's New Democracy Youth Corps Municipal Invitation), 4 May 1951.

15. Martial law (*jieyan fa*) was first promulgated (on a limited basis) in November 1934 at the time that the Guomindang military was "pacifying" the Jiangxi Soviet base area. It was revised on 19 May 1948, again on 14 January 1949 (immediately after Chiang Kai-shek himself arrived in Taiwan), and passed by the Legislative Yuan over a year later on 14 March 1950. A range of martial executive orders (*Taiwansheng jieyan ling*) particular to Taiwan was passed in the aftermath of the crackdown on the university demonstrations of 6 April 1949, and two sets of special regulations for "rectifying" sedition (*zhengzhi panluan tiaoli*) and cleaning out bandit spies (*zhenluan shiqi qianqing feidie tiaoli*), were promulgated on 21 June 1949 and 13 June 1950. See *Zhanhou Taiwan Minzhu*

yundong shiliao huibian [Compilation of postwar Taiwan materials on democratic movements], vol. 1 (Taipei: Guoshiguan, 2000), 16–22, 25–34, for complete texts.

16. NZASH, "Sujian feifa fenlei tongjibiao" (Statistics and classification on cleaning out traitorous bandits) (1952), 59.

17. NZASH, "Taiwan sheng bao'an silingbu junfachu, 41 niandu shenjie anjian gao shenfen tongjibiao" (Taiwan Provincial Security Command, martial law section: 1952 statistical review of high status cases), 85. These figures, of course, do not include those concurrently being purged from the Guomindang as part of its rectification, nor those purged from the military. Those two campaigns, concurrently run by the organizations in question, would put the figures much higher.

18. SMA A22/2/50, "Shifu jiguan ganbu buchong tianbiaozhong de xuanchuan jiaoyu gongzuo zongjie" (Summary work report on municipal organization cadre supplementary forms on propaganda and education), 31 July 1951.

19. SMA C21/2/179, "Shanghai shiwei guanyu fandong tewu dangtuan dengji gongzuo zhishi" (Shanghai Municipal Committee directive on the registration work of counterrevolutionary special affairs party and corps), 10 December 1951.

20. SMA C1/1/28, "Shanghai gongren canjia zhenya Fan'geming yundong zongjie baogao" (Summary report on Shanghai workers' participation in the Campaign to Suppress Counterrevolutionaries), July or August 1951.

21. NZASH (1), "Taiwan jingbeizongbu gongzuo baogao jielu 38 nian" (Taiwan Garrison Command work report quarterly record 1949), 5–7.

22. NZASH (1), "Taiwan jingbei zongbu gongzuo baogao 41 nian" (Taiwan Garrison Command work report 1952), 51–52.

23. NZASH (1), "Taiwan Bao''an siling bu qingkuang shenji jihua" (Taiwan Security Headquarters situational collected reports); "Taiwan Jingbei zongbu gongzuo baogao 39 nian" (Taiwan Garrison Command work report 1950), 17.

24. NZASH (1), "Taiwan jingbei zongbu gongzuo baogao" (Taiwan Garrison Command work report 1952), 50.

25. The following section is drawn from Strauss (2002).

26. SMA C1/1/128, "Shanghai gongren canjia zhenfan yundong zongjie baogao" (summary report), and SMA C21/1/98, Zhang Ben.

27. This discussion is based on SMA B123/2/1036, "Di'yi shangye ju zhuanmen xiaozu guanyu liangge duoyue laide suqing ancang fangeming douzheng de chubu zongjie" (No. 1 Commercial Bureau special small groups preliminary report on struggle against hidden counterrevolutionaries in the last two months), 30 September 1955.

Chapter 5. Betraying Trust and the Elusive Nature of Ethnicity in Burundi

1. For a debate on these positions, see Mamdani (2001).

2. I am aware that far from all Hutu ascribe to these at times paranoid perceptions. However, their logic is enlightening for an understanding of the ambiguous position of ethnicity in a part of the world where ethnic imaginaries can have fatal consequences.

3. This chapter is based on fieldwork from Burundi and among Burundians in exile over a number of years (1997–2004). Many of the same patterns occur in Rwanda, however, despite the very different postcolonial political history.

4. Pseudonym.

5. After the killings, Beatrice no longer trusts her Hutu maid, while she might trust a Tutsi she has never met before. She feels that she no longer knows her maid, while she knows a Tutsi. This is knowledge based not on intimate relations but on ethnic stereotypes.

6. Žižek develops this paradox by claiming that we act *as if* we believe in ideologies in order to prop up the ideologies because we know that, if we did not, they would fall apart, and we do not want them to do that. We need to believe in them because we want them to be true (Žižek 1992).

7. Evans-Pritchard ([1937] 1976) found similar dilemmas in Azande society concerning those possessed by witchcraft: the moral dilemma for the community was always whether the carrier was aware of the power inside him or not. Was he using it purposefully, or did it just take over his body? This has profound importance for the kind of steps to be taken against a witch.

8. See especially his lengthy comparison of the two in Lemarchand (1970).

9. The paradox of changing ethnicity remains at the level of knowing/not knowing and of acting "as if."

10. On the issue of secrets and lies, see also Turner (2005). On the perceptions of the international community and conspiracy theories, see Turner (2002, 2004).

11. Das finds a similar logic at play between Hindu and Sikhs. Sikhs are compared to a snake who would turn around and bite the hand that feeds it milk. If you feed the Sikh children, they will grow up to be snakes, not men (1998a, 121).

12. See Jean-Pierre Chrétien's analysis of the Rwandan media in connection with the 1994 genocide (Chrétien 1995) and Turner (2004) respectively.

Chapter 6. In Praise of Traitors: Intimacy, Betrayal, and the Sri Lankan Tamil Community

Thanks are due to participants in the Traitors workshop Edinburgh and the LSE Anthropology departmental seminar where this material was first presented. The Pembroke Center, Brown University, funded a postdoctoral fellowship that made the research possible and provided a warm, supportive, and intellectually nourishing home. Tobias Kelly and Peter Geschiere gave highly instructive comments on versions of this chapter, which undoubtedly made it better. R. Murugan kindly gave his time and helped me for no reason at all. Most of all, I wish to thank Manoranjan and those I interviewed for their help, courage, and commitment.

1. Pamphlet translated from Tamil with the kind help of R. Murugan.

2. Heroes Day is the national LTTE celebration day; it commemorates the "martyrs" who have died in combat for the LTTE.

3. Willingness to commit suicide if captured is a more generalized phenomenon; all cadres carry a cyanide capsule around their necks.

4. Children are recruited into the baby brigades and then later sorted into adult male and female brigades (40 percent of children recruited are girls). Human Rights Watch reports that, in 1990, between 40 and 60 percent of LTTE combatants killed on the battleground were children under the age of eighteen (see Human Rights Watch 2004)

5. This state can be considered both parallel and parasitic: paralleling the coercive and military structures of state, but continuing to be parasitic on the Sri Lankan state's national funding of teachers, hospitals, social welfare programs and the provision of rations.

6. Early assassinations range from Anandarajah, the principal of a Jaffna school killed for organizing a football match between Jaffna schools and the Sri Lankan Army, to the execution of six criminals in 1984 (Sabalingam www.sangam.org, http://www.sangam.org/articles/view2/?uid = 527 31.

7. See UTHR (J), report 9, chap. 3.2.

8. This was further emphasized in eastern Sri Lanka by the 2002 split of the LTTE into northern and eastern factions, both claiming that civilians working with the other are traitors.

9. See UTHR (J) Report 9 (1992 and Report 10 (1993). Reports describe prison camps and give detailed description of the torture at the largest prison camp, Thunnukai, through the testimony of escapees in Report 9, chap. 3, and in Report 10, chap. 4. In 9 (3.2.3) and 10 (4.2–7) a sample of those detained at Thunnakai and other camps in 1992 is described.

10. The majority of incarcerated civilians in Thunnakai, Thevan told me, were from lower-caste backgrounds, whose families found it more difficult to use influence or to raise money to effect their release.

11. I deal with the relationship between Tamils and Muslims and the history of the ethnicization of Muslim identity elsewhere (Thiranagama 2006).

12. See Agamben's discussion of *Homo Sacer*, especially his discussion of the bandit, which provided some of the sense for how I view the traitor. Especially significant is his description of the ban that makes some lives outside the law.

13. This is analogous to the ways in which Freud analyzes the fears, tensions, and ambiguities of the bourgeois family.

14. Taussig's description of the fetishization of the public secret is particularly apt for how the LTTE represents its own power. He argues that the power of the public secret is the power that secrecy lends to certain objects, forces, and knowledge; the public secret encircles a void that remains inviolate: "it is the skin of the secret that vibrates with sacred light, intimation of the *public secret* within" (1999, 58).

15. Moreover, criticism of the LTTE often came from Sinhala politicians and journalists and was certainly not out of concern for Tamils. Thus, it was even more "our secret."

16. Ram Mannikalingam suggests that being Tamil in Sri Lanka is about not being able to assume indifference to the LTTE (personal communication). While a Sinhalese can assume indifference to the LTTE, a Tamil has to assume a position, whether of support, studied neutrality, opposition, etc.

17. These circles are also vulnerable. One faction of the EPRLF under Suresh Premachandran joined the LTTE recently despite the murder of many former comrades by the LTTE. Current EPRLF members, now called EPRLF (v) are in greater danger because those who knew them intimately are now working in conjunction with LTTE intelligence.

18. Estimating the size of the Sri Lankan Tamil dissident community is complex. An active group of Sri Lankan Tamils across Europe and Canada who are involved in writing and criticizing openly would be around 200. However, a person may be regarded as a dissident for any reason ranging from refusing to pay LTTE taxes to not encouraging LTTE conversation in the house. Although ex-members of the LTTE and other militant groups might number into the thousands, those who were willing to talk about this problem in their homes or to others could be a few hundred. I would suggest that dissidence consists of a series of everyday refusals to internalize LTTE rhetoric, which muddies the notion of a dissident community.

19. In 2007, the EPDP became involved in an alliance with the Sri Lankan state in murdering and abducting Tamil civilians. The EPRLF remains neutral.

20. By "acknowledgment," I mean that, the role of a traitor to the LTTE is accepted even if the sense is refused.

21. I do not mean by this that the other two forms I identify are lesser or earlier forms.

Chapter 7. Treason and Contested Moralities in a Coloured Township, Cape Town

1. As Fitzpatrick and Gellately (1997, 15) argue, denunciations and accusations of betrayal are often made by ordinary people against neighbors, families, and acquaintances for quite personal reasons, which do not necessarily correspond to the overall, often national conflicts.

2. Most analyses of the apartheid state explores the state's undeniable potential for violent oppression (e.g., Beinart 2001; Brogden and Shearing 1993), forced removals (Western 1996), and political exclusion build on racial categories that the state legalized in the different pieces of apartheid legislation (Lewis 1987). Complementary to the view of the state as repressive, I argue that, at least for coloureds, the state engaged in a wide-ranging biopolitical endeavor. This endeavor evolved around negative stereotypes of coloured men as always already criminal. Over the twentieth century, this biopolitical regime evolved, consisting among others in extremely high rates of male incarceration and female welfare provisions. For elaboration, see Jensen 2001. For similar approaches to analyzing coloured history, see Badroodien (1999) and Salo (2003).

3. The Theron Commission of Inquiry asserted in 1976 that some 29 percent of coloured men were unemployable due to physical weakness, lack of education, alcohol abuse, or other problems related to coloured men (Republic of South Africa 1976).

4. The stereotypes tainted all coloured men to greater or lesser extent. Men in the townships faced the most difficulties in emerging as moral people, while the responsible, middle-class—often religious—coloured man has had a social position in Cape Town's social economy for decades. For distribution of stereotypes to different groups, see Adhikari 2005 and Western 1996.

5. Since at least the 1980s, rioting against the police constituted a virtuous act for people opposed to the regime. In the same period, in Cape Town as well as in Johannesburg (Glaser 2000), gang violence was seen as integral to the struggle.

6. To make matters worse, after the case was abandoned, the boys continuously bragged about it around the area. In the end, the brother of the girl attacked one of the boys, who then went to the police to lay a charge of assault.

Chapter 8. In a Treacherous State: The Fear of Collaboration Among West Bank Palestinians

I am indebted to the participants at the Traitors workshop, in particular, Sharika Thiranagama and Heonik Kwon for their insightful comments. At a later stage, Lori Allen provided invaluable help in clarifying my arguments.

1. In 2003, the Israeli Knesset passed a law that explicitly prevented West Bank Palestinians from gaining Israeli identity cards through marriage to Israeli citizens.

2. Untitled, no date. On file with author.

3. Sharika Thiranagama, personal communication.

4. I am indebted to Richard Whitecross for this formulation.

5. Fatah has historically been the largest and most powerful Palestinian nationalist faction in the West Bank and has controlled the PNA since its creation in the early 1990s.

6. Toward the end of the first intifada, which lasted from late 1987 to 1992, more Palestinians were being killed by other Palestinians than by the Israeli military. In the first year of the *intifada* 20 suspected collaborators were killed, rising to 100 the year after that. Between January 1988 and April 1994 the number of suspected collaborators killed by other Palestinians rose to an estimated 800 (see PHRMG 2001). For figures on the second intifada, see the reports of BTselem, http://www.btselem.org/English/Statistics/Casualties_Data.asp?Category = 25 &region = TER.

Chapter 9. *The Glass Agency*: Iranian War Veterans as Heroes or Traitors?

1. For more on the domestic impact of the Iran-Iraq war, see Dilip Hiro (1991, 40–70).

2. For more on the history of the Basij, see Kamrava (2000, 84–86).

3. For a description of the Basij role in the crackdown, see Khajehpour (2002).

4. Abrahamian defines Khomeinism as a movement that "like Latin American populism, claimed to be a return to 'native roots' and a means for eradicating 'cosmopolitan ideas' . . . [it] used organizations and plebiscitary politics to mobilize the masses but at the same time distrusted any form of political pluralism" (1993, 38).

5. For more on sacred defense cinema, see Varzi (2006, 76–105).

6. Dialogue transcribed from commercial video copy of *Ajans-e Shishe-i* (*The Glass Agency*, 1997), and translated by author.

Chapter 10. The Man in the White Raincoat: Betrayal and the Historian's Task

An earlier version of this chapter appeared as "The Man in the White Raincoat," in *Past for the Eyes: East European Representations of Communism in Cinema and Museums After 1989*, ed. Oksana Sarkisova and Peter Apor (Budapest: Central European University Press, 2007).

1. "Ki a ballonkabátos férfi?" (Who Is the Man in the Raincoat?) *Népszabadság*, 30 January 2006, www.nol.hu/cikk/392467/ (accessed 28 March 2007).

2. Interview with György Hoffmann, 21 August 2006, http://1956.mti.hu/Pages/Hoffmann.aspx (accessed March 27, 2007).

3. Reasons render actions eligible and actions motivated by them intelligible (see Raz 1999). "A reason is roughly the presence of an evaluative feature and of the facts which connect it to the action in the right way" (Raz 2006, 109).

4. See also Bernard Williams (2002).

Bibliography

Abrahamian, Ervand. 1993. *Khomeinism: Essays on the Islamic Republic.* Berkeley: University of California Press.

Adhikari, Mohamed. 2005. *Not White Enough, Not Black Enough: Racial Identity in the South African Coloured Community.* Cape Town: Double Storey.

Agamben, Giorgio. 1998. *Homo Sacer: Sovereign Power and Bare Life.* Stanford, Calif.: Stanford University Press.

———. 2000. *Means Without End: Notes on Politics.* Trans. Vincenzo Binettie and Cesare Casarino. Theory Out of Bounds Series 20. Minneapolis: University of Minnesota Press.

Ahmed, Rafiduddin. 1988. Conflict and Contradictions in Bengali Islam: Problems of Change and Adjustment. In *Shariat and Ambiguity in South Asian Islam,* ed. Katherine P. Ewing, 114–42. Berkeley: University of California Press.

Alazad, Alauddin. 1984. Ghatok 195 ("Collaborators 195"). In *Muktijuddher Kobita,* comp. Abul Hasnat. Dhaka: Shondhani Prokashoni.

Alexander, Jocelyn. 1997. The Local State in Post-War Mozambique: Political Practices and Ideas About Authority. *Africa* 67 (1): 1–26.

Ali, Tariq. 1983. *Can Pakistan Survive? The Death of a State.* London: Penguin.

Allen, Tim and David Turton. 1996. Introduction. In *In Search of Cool Ground: War Flight and Homecoming in Northeast Africa,* ed. Tim Allen and David Turton, 1–22. London: UNRISD with James Currey.

Althusser, Louis. 1971. *Lenin and Philosophy and Other Essays.* New York: Monthly Review Press.

Amnesty International. 1983. *Reports of the Use of the Death Penalty in the People's Republic of Mozambique.* July. New York: Amnesty International.

———. 1984. *Reports of the Use of Flogging in the People's Republic of Mozambique.* February. New York: Amnesty International.

———. 1985. *Reports of the Use of Torture in the People's Republic of Mozambique.* April. New York: Amnesty International.

Appadurai, Arjun. 1996. *Modernity at Large: Cultural Dimensions of Globalization.* Minneapolis: University of Minnesota Press.

———. 1998. Dead Certainty: Ethnic Violence in the Era of Globalisation. *Public Culture* 10 (2): 225–47.

———. 2006. *Fear of Small Numbers: An Essay on the Geography of Anger.* Durham, N.C: Duke University Press.

Apter, Andrew. 1999. IBB = 419: Nigerian Democracy and the Politics of Illusion. In *Civil Society and Political Imagination in Africa,* ed. Jean Comaroff and John Comaroff, 267–308. Chicago: University of Chicago Press.

Arendt, Hannah. 1958. *The Origins of Totalitarianism.* London: Secker and Warburg.

———. 1999. *The Human Condition.* Trans. Margaret Canovan. Chicago: University of Chicago Press.

Aretxaga, Begona. 1997. *Shattering Silence: Women, Nationalism, and Political Subjectivity in Northern Ireland.* Princeton, N.J.: Princeton University Press.

Aris, Michael. 1987. The Boneless Tongue: Alternative Voices from Bhutan in the Context of Lamaist Societies. *Past and Present* 115: 131–64.

———. 1998. *The Raven Crown: the Origins of Buddhist Monarchy in Bhutan.* London: Serindia Press.

Artur, D. R. and Bernard Weimer. 1998. Decentralisation and Democratisation in Post-War Mozambique: What Role of Traditional African Authority in Local Government Reform? Paper presented at 14th Congress of the International Union of Anthropological and Ethnological Sciences, Williamsburg, Virginia.

Asad, Talal. 1993. *Genealogies of Religion: Discipline and Reasons of Power in Christianity and Islam.* Baltimore: Johns Hopkins University Press.

Badroodien, Azeem. 1999. Race, Crime, Welfare and State: Social Institutions in South Africa from the 1940s. *Social Dynamics* 25 (2): 49–73.

Balibar, Étienne. 1998. Violence, Ideality and Cruelty. *New Formations* 35: 718.

———. 2003. *We, the People of Europe? Reflections on Transnational Citizenship.* Trans. James Swenson. Princeton, N.J.: Princeton University Press

Barry, Sebastian. 2005. *A Long Long Way.* London: Faber.

Bastian, Misty. 2003. "Diabolic Realities": Narratives of Conspiracy, Transparency, and "Ritual Murder" in the Nigerian Popular Print and Electronic Media. In *Transparency and Conspiracy: Ethnographies of Suspicion in the New World Order*, ed. Harry West and Todd Sanders, 65–92. Durham, N.C.: Duke University Press.

Bauman, Zygmunt. 1991. *Modernity and Ambivalence.* Cambridge: Polity.

Beinart, William. 2001. *Twentieth Century South Africa.* Oxford: Oxford University Press.

Berker, Selim. 2007. Particular Reasons. *Ethics* 118 (1): 109–39.

Berry, Joanna de. 1998. "Look Back in Laughter": Humour and the Memory of War in East Uganda. Paper presented to the research seminar of the Department of Anthropology, London School of Economics, 30 October.

———. 2000. Life After Loss: An Anthropological Study of Post-War Recovery, Teso, East Uganda, with Special Reference to Young People. Ph.D. dissertation, London School of Economics, University of London.

Bhabha, Homi. 1994. The Other Question: Stereotype, Discrimination, and the Discourse of Colonialism. In *The Location of Culture*, 66–84. New York: Routledge.

Billig, Michael. 1995. *Banal Nationalism.* London: Sage.

Bloch, Maurice. 1999. Commensality and Poisoning. Special Issue, *Food: Nature and Culture. Social Research* 66 (1): 133–51.

Bornstein, Avram S. 2002. *Crossing the Green Line Between the West Bank and Israel.* Philadelphia: University of Pennsylvania Press.

Bose, Sarmila. 2005. Anatomy of Violence: Analysis of Civil War in East Pakistan in 1971. *Economic and Political Weekly*, 8 October, 4463–71.

Botstein, Leon. 1993. The Future of a Tradition. *Musical Quarterly* 77 (2):155–60.

Bradburn, Howard. 1995 *Dispatches: War Crimes File.* London: Twenty Twenty Television.

Bredin, Jean-Denis, 1984. Le Droit, le juge, et l'historien. *Le Débat* 32: 93–111.

Briggs, Robin. 1996. Author's Response. *Reviews in History* 4. http://www.history.ac.uk/reviews/paper/witch.html.

———. 2002. *Witches and Neighbours: The Social and Cultural Context of European Witchcraft*. Oxford: Blackwell.

Brogden, Mike and Clifford Shearing. 1993. *Policing for a New South Africa*. London: Routledge.

Brook, Timothy. 2005. *Collaboration: Japanese Agents and Local Elites in Wartime China*. Cambridge, Mass.: Harvard University Press.

Burton, Richard. 2001. *Blood in the City: Violence and Revelation in Paris, 1789–1945*. Ithaca, N.Y.: Cornell University Press.

Butalia, Urvashi. 2000. *The Other Side of Silence: Voices from the Partition of India*. Durham, N.C.: Duke University Press

Buur, Lars 2007a. From Traitors to Symbols of Peace: The Shifting Meaning of Informal Traders in Mozambique. Paper presented at Popular Governance or Criminalization? The Informal Economy and Institutional Change, African Studies Seminars, St. Antony's College, Oxford, 30 May.

———. 2007b. People's Party and People's Representation? Becoming a Member of the Mozambican Nation-State Project. Paper presented at Crisis State Research Center, LSE, 21 November.

Buur, Lars and Helene M. Kyed. 2006. Contested Sources of Authority: Re-Claiming State Sovereignty by Formalising Traditional Authority in Mozambique. *Development and Change* 37 (4): 847–69.

———. 2007. *State Recognition and Democratization in Sub-Saharan Africa: A New Dawn for Chiefs?* New York: Palgrave.

Campion-Vincent, Veronique. 1997. Organ Theft Narratives. *Western Folklore* 56 (1): 1–37.

Cheek, Timothy. 1997. *Propaganda and Culture in Mao's China: Deng Tuo and the Intelligentsia*. Oxford: Clarendon.

Chingono, Mark F. 1996. *The State, Violence and Development: The Political Economy of War in Mozambique, 1975–1992*. Aldershot: Avebury.

Chowdhuryy, Kawser. 1992. *Gono Adalat*. Video. Dhaka. Film.

Chrétien, Jean-Paul, Reporters sans Frontières (Association), et al. 1995. *Rwanda, les Médias du génocide*. Paris: Karthala.

Coelho, Jõao Paulo Constantino. 1993. Protected Villages and Communal Villages in the Mozambican Province of Tete 1968–1982: A History of Resettlement Policies, Development and War. Manuscript, Department of Social and Economic Studies, University of Bradford.

———. 2004. The State and Its Public: Notes on State Ritualisation in the Transition from Socialism to Neo-Liberalism in Mozambique. Paper presented at Ritualisation of the State: Neo-Popular State Rituals in Mozambique and South Africa Conference, June, WISER, Johannesburg, in collaboration with the Nordic Africa Institute, Uppsala.

Cohen. Hillel. 2007. *Army of Shadows: Palestinian Collaboration with Zionism, 1917–1948*. Berkeley: University of California Press.

Comaroff, Jean and John Comaroff. 1999. Occult Economies and the Violence of Abstraction: Notes from the South African Postcolony. *American Ethnologist* 26 (2): 297–301.

———. 2003. Transparent Fictions: or, The Conspiracies of a Liberal Imagination: An Afterword. In *Transparency and Conspiracy: Ethnographies of Suspicion in the New World Order*, ed. Harry West and Todd Sanders, 287–301. Durham, N.C.: Duke University Press.

Cutler, S. H. 1982. *The Law of Treason and Treason Trials in Later Medieval France*. Cambridge: Cambridge University Press.

Dabrowski, Patrice. 2003. Russian-Polish Relations Revisited, or The ABC's of "Treason" Under Tsarist Rule. *Kritika: Explorations in Russian and Eurasian History* 4 (1): 177–99.

Das, Veena. 1995. *Critical Events: An Anthropological Perspective on Contemporary India.* Delhi: Oxford University Press.

———. 1998a. Official Narratives, Rumour, and the Social Production of Hate. *Social Identities* 4 (1): 109–30.

———. 1998b. Language and the Body: Transactions in the Construction of Pain. In *Social Suffering,* ed. Arthur Kleinman, Veena Das, and Margaret Lock, 67–92. Berkeley: University of California Press.

Deak, Istvan. 2000a. Introduction. In *The Politics of Retribution in Europe: World War II and Its Aftermath,* ed. Istvan Deak, Jan Gross, and Tony Judt, 3–14. Princeton, N.J.: Princeton University Press.

———. 2000b. A Fatal Compromise? The Debate over Collaboration and Resistance in Hungary. In *The Politics of Retribution in Europe: World War II and its Aftermath,* ed. Istvan Deak, Jan Gross and Tony Judt, 39–73. Princeton, N.J.: Princeton University Press.

Dinerman, Alice. 2006. *Revolution, Counter-Revolution and Revisionism in Postcolonial Africa: The Case of Mozambique, 1975–1994.* London: Routledge.

Dixon, William and Lisa Johns. 2001. *Gangs, Pagad and the State: Vigilantism and Revenge Violence in the Western Cape.* Violence and Transition Series 2. Johannesburg: Centre for the Study of Violence and Reconciliation.

Domes, Jürgen. 1973. *The Internal Politics of China.* New York: Praeger.

Double Ten Directive (Shuangshi Zhishi), 1950/1994. Reprinted in *Jianguo yilai zhongyao wenxian xuanbian* (A Selection of Important Documents since the Founding of the People's Republic of China), Volume 1. Beijing: Zhongyang Wenxian Chubanshe.

DTIPF. 1979. *Xiconhoca o inimigo.* Maputo: Departamento do Trabalho Ideológico do Partido Frelimo.

Eagleton, Terry. 2002. *Sweet Violence: The Idea of the Tragic.* Oxford: Blackwell.

Eldridge, Matt and Jeremy Seekings. 1996. Mandela's Lost Province: The African National Congress and the Western Cape Electorate in the 1994 South African Elections. *Journal of Southern African Studies* 22 (3): 517–40.

Ellis, Stephen and Gerrie ter Haar. 2004. *Worlds of Power: Religious Thought and Political Practice in Africa.* London: Hurst.

Embassy of the Republic of Burundi. 1972. The White Paper on the Real Causes and Consequences of the Attempted Genocide Against the Tutsi Ethny in Burundi. http://www.archive.org/details/TheWhitePaperOnTheRealCauses AndCon sequencesOfTheAttemptedGenocide.

Eörsi, László. 2006. *Köztársaság tér 1956* (Republic Square 1956). Ed. András B. Vágvölgyi. Budapest: 1956 Institute.

Evans-Pritchard, E. E. [1937] 1976. *Witchcraft, Oracles and Magic Among the Azande.* Oxford: Oxford University Press.

Feldman, Allen. 1995. Ethnographic States of Emergency. In *Fieldwork Under Fire: Contemporary Studies of Violence and Survival,* ed. Carolyn Nordstrom and Antonius C. G. M. Robben, 224–53. Berkeley: University of California Press.

Feuchtwang, Stephan. 2006. Images of Sub-Humanity and Their Realization. In Special Issue on State Violence, ed. Tobias Kelly and Alpa Shah. *Critique of Anthropology* 26 (3): 259–78.

Fine, Gary. 1986. Redemption Rumors: Mercantile Legends and Corporate Beneficence. *Journal of American Folklore* 99 (392): 208–22.

Fitzpatrick, Sheila. 2005. *Tear Off the Masks: Identity and Imposture in Twentieth-Century Russia*. Princeton, N.J.: Princeton University Press.

Fitzpatrick, Sheila and Robert Gellately. 1996. Introduction to the Practices of Denunciation in Modern European History. *Journal of Modern History* 68 (4): 747–67.

————. 1997. Introduction to the Practices of Denunciation in Modern European History. In *Accusatory Practices: Denunciation in Modern European History, 1789–1989*, ed. Sheila Fitzpatrick and Robert Gellately, 1–21. Chicago: University of Chicago Press.

Forster, EM. 1972. *Two Cheers for Democracy*. London: Hodder Arnold.

Gahama, Joseph. 1983. *Le Burundi sous Administration Belge*. Paris: Karthala.

Gahutu, Remy. n.d. Persecution of the Hutus of Burundi. Manuscript on file with author.

Garfield, Jay L. 2000. *Moral Particularism*. Oxford: Clarendon.

Geertz, Clifford. 1973. *The Interpretation of Cultures*. New York: Basic Books.

Gervai, András. 2006. Egy ügynök azonosítása [Identifying an Agent]. *Élet és Irodalom* January 26.

Geschiere, Peter. 1997. *The Modernity of Witchcraft: Politics and the Occult in Postcolonial Africa*. Trans. Janet Roitman. Charlottesville: University of Virginia Press.

Ghosh, Papiya. 1998. Partition's Biharis. In *Islam, Communities and the Nation: Muslim Identities in South Asia and Beyond*, ed. Mushirul Hasan, 229–65. Delhi: Manohar.

Gilsenan, Michael. 1977. Against Patron-Client Relationships. In *Patron and Clients in Mediterranean Societies*, ed. Ernest Gellner and John Waterbury, 167–83. London: Duckworth.

Ginzburg, Carlo. 1992. *The Cheese and the Worms: The Cosmos of a Sixteenth-Century Miller*. Trans. John Tedeschi and Anne Tedeschi. Baltimore: Johns Hopkins University Press.

————. 1999. *The Judge and the Historian*. London: Verso

Ginzburg, Carlo and Carlo Poni. [1979] 1991. The Name and the Game: Unequal Exchange and the Historiographic Marketplace. In *Microhistory and the Lost Peoples of Europe*, ed. Edward Muir and Guido Ruggiero, 1–10. Baltimore: Johns Hopkins University Press.

Glaser, Clive. 2000. *Bo-Thotsi: The Youth Gangs of Soweto, 1935–1976*. Oxford: James Currey.

Goldin, Ian. 1989. *Making Race: The Politics and Economics of Coloured Identity in South Africa*. London: Addison-Wesley.

Gorringe, Hugo. 2006. Banal Violence? The Everyday Underpinnings of Collective Violence. *Identities: Global Studies in Culture and Power* 13 (2): 237–60.

Greenblatt, Stephen. 1977. The Touch of the Real. Special issue, The Fate of "Culture": Geertz and Beyond. *Representations* 59 (29):14–29.

Grey, Andrew. 1994. Life of a Much-Maligned Conductor Examined in New Biography. Review of *The Devil's Music Master: The Controversial Life and Career of Wilhelm Furtwängler*, by Sam H. Shirakawa, Institute for Historical Research. http://www.ihr.org/jhr/v14/v14n1p41_Shirakawa.html.

Gross, Jan. 2000. Themes for a Social History of War Experience and Collaboration. In *The Politics of Retribution in Europe: World War II and Its Aftermath*, ed. Istvan Deak, Jan Gross, and Tony Judt, 15–36. Princeton, N.J.: Princeton University Press.

Guhathakurta, Meghna. 1996. *Dhorshon Ekti Juddhaporadh* (Rape Is a War Crime) *Bulletin of Ain-O-Shalish Kendra* (February): 6–8.

Hacking, Ian. 1995. *Rewriting the Soul: Multiple Personality and the Sciences of Memory.* Princeton, N.J.: Princeton University Press.

———. 2003. Indeterminacy in the Past: On the Recent Discussion of Chapter 17 of Rewriting the Soul. *History of the Human Sciences* 16 (2): 117–24.

Hall, Margaret and Tom Young. 1997. *Confronting Leviathan: Mozambique Since Independence.* London: Hurst.

Hanlon, Joseph. 1984. *Mozambique: The Revolution Under Fire.* London: Zed Books.

———. 1991. *Mozambique: Who Calls the Shots?* London: James Currey.

———. 2007. Are Peasants Lazy or Not Supported? News Reports & Clippings Mozambique, April. 115 (20) (April). dev-mozambique-list@open.ac.uk.

Harrison, Graham. 1998. Marketing Legitimacy in Rural Mozambique: The Case of *Mecúfi* District, Northern Mozambique. *Journal of Modern African Studies* 36 (4): 569–91.

———. 1999. Corruption as "Boundary Politics": The State, Democratisation and Mozambique's Unstable Liberalisation. *Third World Quarterly* 20 (3): 537–50.

Hatami-kia, Ebrahim. 1997. *Ajans-e Shishe-i* (The Glass Agency). VCD. Farabi Cinema Foundation, Iran.

Heaney, Seamus, 1998a. Crediting Poetry: The Nobel Lecture 1995. In *Opened Ground: Poems 1966–1996.* London: Faber and Faber.

———. 1998b. Punishment. In *Opened Ground: Poems 1966–1996.* London: Faber and Faber.

Henriksen, Thomas H. 1978. Marxism and Mozambique. *African Affairs* 77 (309): 441–62.

Herzfeld, Michael. 1997. *Cultural Intimacy: Social Poetics in the Nation-State.* New York: Routledge.

Hilterman, Joost R. 1991. *Behind the Intifada: Labor and Women's Movements in the Occupied Territories.* Princeton, N.J.: Princeton University Press.

Hiro, Dilip. 1991. *The Longest War: The Iran-Iraq Military Conflict.* London: Routledge.

Hollis, Martin. 1995. The Shape of a Life. In *World, Mind, and Ethics: Essays on the Ethical Philosophy of Bernard Williams*, ed. J. E. J. Altham and Ross Harison, 170–84. Cambridge: Cambridge University Press.

Homa, Omid. 1994. *Islam and the Post-Revolutionary State in Iran.* New York: St. Martin's.

Hoole Rajan, Kopalasingam. Sritharan, Daya Somasunderam, and Rajani Thiranagama. 1990. *The Broken Palmyra.* Claremont: Sri Lanka Studies Institute.

Hughes, John W. 1982. Mephisto: István Szabó and the Gestapo of Suspicion. *Film Quarterly* 35 (4): 13–18.

Human Rights Organization of Bhutan. 1993. *Annual Report.* Lalitpur: Lumbini Press.

Human Rights Watch. 2004. *Living in Fear: Child Soldiers and the Tamil Tigers in Sri Lanka.* http://hrw.org/reports/2004/srilanka1104/.

Huq, Syed Shamsul. [1976] 1991. Payer Aoaj Paoa Jai (Footsteps can be heard). In *Kabbo Natto Songroho.* Dhaka: Bidyaprokash.

Hutt, Michael. 2003. *Unbecoming Citizens: Culture, Nationhood, and the Flight of Refugees from Bhutan.* Oxford: Oxford University Press.

Imam, Jahanara. 1993. *Ekatorer Dinguli* (The Days of 1971). Dhaka: Shondhani Prokashoni.

Isaacman, Allen. 1982. The Mozambique Cotton Cooperative: The Creation of a Grassroots Alternative to Forced Commodity Production. *African Studies Review* 25 (2/3): 5–25.

Jamieson, Lynn. 1998. *Intimacy: Personal Relationships in Modern Societies.* Cambridge: Polity.

Jean-Klein, Iris. 2001. Nationalism and Resistance: The Two Faces of Everyday Action in Palestine During the Intifada. *Cultural Anthropology* 16 (1): 83–126.

———. 2008. Judging by Aesthetics and "Due Care" in the Management of Collaborators During the First Intifada. In *The Practice of War: Production, Reproduction and Communication of Armed Violence*, ed. Aparna Rao, Michael Bollig, and Monika Bock, 175–214. Oxford: Berghahn.

Jeeva. 2006. "Thurohi." Thursday 22 September 2006. Paris.

Jensen, Steffen. 2001. Claiming Community-Negotiating Crime: State Formation, Neighborhood and Gangs in a Capetonian Township. Ph.D. dissertation, Institute for Development Studies, Roskilde University.

———. 2005. From Development to Security: Political Subjectivity and the South African Transition. *Development and Change* 36 (3): 551–70.

———. 2006. Capetonian Backstreets: Territorializing Young Men. *Ethnography* 7 (3): 275–305.

Jian, Jian. 1993. *Baise Kongbu* (The White Terror). Taibei: Yangzhi Wenhua Shiwu Gufen Youxian Gongsi.

Joshi, Vandana. 2003. *Gender and Power in the Third Reich: Female Denouncers and the Gestapo, 1933–1945.* Houndmills: Palgrave Macmillan

Kalyvas, Stathis. 2006. *The Logic of Violence in Civil War.* Cambridge: Cambridge University Press.

Kamrava, Mehran. 2000. Military Professionalization and Civil-Military Relations in the Middle East. *Political Science Quarterly* 115 (1): 67–92.

Kelly, Tobias. 2006. *Law, Violence and Sovereignty Among West Bank Palestinians.* Cambridge: Cambridge University Press.

Kézdi-Kovács, Zsolt. 2006. Jelentek. *Élet és Irodalom*, February 3.

Khajehpour, Bijan. 2002. Protest and Regime Resilience in Iran. *Middle East Report* November 12). http://www.merip.org/mero/mero121102.html.

Khan, Mushtaq. 2000. Class, Clientalism, and Communal Politics in Contemporary Bangladesh. In *The Making of History: Essays Presented to Irfan Habib*, ed. K. N. Panikkar, Terence Byres, and Utsa Patnaik, 572–606. New Delhi: Tulika.

Kierkegaard, Søren. [1847] 1963. *Kjerlighedens Gjerninger.* København, Gyldendal.

Klein, Melanie, 1967. Love, Guilt and Reparation. In *Love, Hate and Reparation*, ed. Melanie Klein and Joan Riviere, 57–91. London: Hogarth Press.

Korstvedt, Benjamin M. 1996. Anton Bruckner in the Third Reich and After: An Essay on Ideology and Bruckner Reception. *Musical Quarterly* 80 (1): 132–60.

Krishna, Sankaran 1999. *Postcolonial Insecurities: India, Sri Lanka and the Question of Nationhood.* Delhi: Oxford University Press.

Kuensel Online Newspaper (Bhutan). http://www.kuenselonline.com/modules .php?name = News&file = print&sid = 4457

Kyed, Helene M. and Lars Buur. 2006. New Sites of Citizenship: Recognition of Traditional Authority and Group-Based Citizenship in Mozambique. *Journal of Southern African Studies* 32 (3): 563–81.

Laclau, Ernesto. 1996. *Emancipation(s).* London: Verso.

———. 2005. *On Populist Reason.* London: Verso.

Lefort, Claude. 1988. *Democracy and Political Theory.* Trans. David Macey. Oxford: Polity.

Lemarchand, René. 1970. *Rwanda and Burundi.* London: Pall Mall Press.

———. 1996. *Burundi: Ethnic Conflict and Genocide.* Washington, D.C.: Woodrow Wilson Center Press.

Lemon, Rebecca. 2006. *Treason by Words: Literature, Law, and Rebellion in Shakespeare's England.* Ithaca, N.Y.: Cornell University Press.

Lepenies, Wolf. 1999. The End of "German Culture." Tanner Lectures on Human Values, Delivered at Harvard University, Cambridge, Mass., 3–5 November.

———. 2006. *The Seduction of Culture in German History.* Princeton, N.J.: Princeton University Press.

Levi, Primo. 1986. *The Drowned and the Saved.* London: Penguin.

Lévi-Strauss, Claude. 1950. Introduction à l'oeuvre de Marcel Mauss. In *Marcel Mauss, sociologie et anthropologie,* ed. Claude Lévi-Strauss, ix–lii. Paris: Quadrige/PUF.

Lewis, Gavin. 1987. *Between the Wire and the Wall: A History of South African "Coloured" Politics.* Cape Town: David Philips.

Lindisfarne, Nancy. 2002. Starting from Below: Fieldwork, Gender, and Imperialism Now. *Critique of Anthropology* 22 (4): 403–23.

Lippman, Samuel. 1993. Furtwängler and the Nazis. *Commentary* 45 (March).

Lubkemann, Stephen. 2005. Migratory Coping in Wartime Mozambique: An Anthropology of Violence and Displacement in "Fragmented Wars." *Journal of Peace Research* 42 (4): 493–508.

Lucas, Colin. 1997. The Theory and Practice of Denunciation in the French Revolution. In *Accusatory Practices: Denunciation in Modern European History, 1789–1989,* ed. Sheila Fitzpatrick and Robert Gellately, 22–39. Chicago: University of Chicago Press.

Macamo, Elísio. 2003. How Development Aid Changes Societies: Disciplining Mozambique Through Structural Adjustment. http://www.codesria.org/Links/conferences/general_assembly11/pa pers/macamo.p df.

Machel, Samora. [1980] 1985. We Are Declaring War on the Enemy Within. In *Samora Machel: An African Revolutionary: Selected Speeches and Writings,* ed. Barry Munslow. London: Zed Books.

———. 1981. *Sowing the Seeds of Revolution.* Harare: Zimbabwe Publishing House.

Malkki, Liisa.1995. *Purity and Exile: Violence, Memory, and National Cosmology Among Hutu Refugees in Tanzania.* Chicago: University of Chicago Press.

Mamdani, Mahmood. 2001. *When Victims Become Killers: Colonialism, Nativism, and the Genocide in Rwanda.* Princeton, N.J.: Princeton University Press.

Mann, Klaus. 1941. What's Wrong with Anti-Nazi Films? *Decision:* 27–35.

———. 1995. *Mephisto.* Harmondswoth: Penguin.

Maquet, Jaques. 1961. *The Premise of Inequality in Ruanda: A Study of Political Relations in a Central African Kingdom.* London: International African Institute.

Mbembé, Achille. 2001. *On the Postcolony.* Berkeley: University of California Press.

Menon, Ritu and Kamla Bhasin. 1998. *Borders and Boundaries: Women in India's Partition.* New Delhi: Kali for Women.

Monk, Paul. 2002. Green Island Elegy: Human Rights in the Chinese World. http://austhink.org/monk/Island_Elegy.doc.

Mookherjee, Nayanika. 2006. "Remembering to Forget": Public Secrecy and Memory of Sexual Violence in Bangladesh. *Journal of the Royal Anthropological Institute* 12 (2): 433–50.

———. 2007. The "Dead and Their Double Duties": Mourning, Melancholia and the Martyred Intellectual Memorials in Bangladesh. *Space and Culture* 10 (2): 271–91.

———. 2008. Gendered Embodiments: Mapping the Body-Politic of the Raped Woman and the Nation in Bangladesh. *Feminist Review* 88 (1): 36–53.

———. 2011 forthcoming. *The Spectral Wound: Sexual Violence, Public Memories and the Bangladesh War of 1971.* Durham, N.C.: Duke University Press.

Mouffe, Chantal. 2005. *The Return of the Political.* London: Verso.

Narayan Swamy, M. R. 2003 [1994]. *Tigers of Lanka: from Boys to Guerrillas.* Colombo: Vijitha Yapa Publications.

Nasrin, Taslima. 1993. *Shame (Lojja).* Dhaka: Pearl Publications.

National Assembly of Bhutan. 1990. *Report of the Sixty-Ninth Session of the National Assembly. Annexure Two.* Thimphu: Royal Government of Bhutan.

———. 1991. *The Proceedings and Resolutions adopted during the 68th session of the National Assembly.* Thimphu: National Assembly Secretariat.

Navaro-Yashin, Yael. 2002. *Faces of the State: Secularism and Public Life in Turkey.* Princeton, N.J.: Princeton University Press.

Nordstrom, Carolyn and Antonius C. G. M. Robben, eds. 1995. *Fieldwork Under Fire: Contemporary Studies of Violence and Survival.* Berkeley: University of California Press.

Norval, Aletta. 1996. *Deconstructing Apartheid Discourse.* London: Verso.

Nussbaum, Martha. 2001. *The Fragility of Goodness: Luck and Ethics in Greek Tragedy and Philosophy.* Cambridge: Cambridge University Press.

O'Laughlin, Bridget. 2000. Class and the Customary: The Ambiguous Legacy of the Indigenato in Mozambique. *African Affairs* 99: 5–42.

Olsen, Kasper Nefer. 1993. *Offer ogObjekt: En Introduktion til Michel Serres' Statuer.* København: Det kgl. danske Kunstakademi.

O'Neill, Onora. 1996. *Towards Justice and Virtue: A Reconstructive Account of Practical Reasoning.* Cambridge: Cambridge University Press.

Ottaway, D. and Ottaway, M. 1981. *Afrocommunism.* New York: Africana.

PHRMG. 2001. *Human Rights and Legal Position of Palestinian "Collaborators".* Jerusalem: Palestinian Human Rights Monitoring Group.

Phuntsho, Karma. 2004. Echoes of Ancient Ethos: Reflections on Some Popular Bhutanese Social Themes. In *The Spider and the Piglet: Proceedings of the First International Seminar on Bhutan Studies*, 564–79. Thimphu: Centre for Bhutanese Studies.

———. 2006. "Bhutanese reform, Nepalese criticism," Open Democracy. http://www.opendemocracy.net/democracy-protest/bhutan_nepal_3 996.jsp.

Prieberg, Fred. 1991. *The Trial of Strength.* Trans. Christopher Dolan. London: Quartet Books.

Prunier, Gerard. 1995. *The Rwanda Crisis, 1959–1994: History of a Genocide.* London: Hurst.

Putnam, Hilary. 1981. *Reason, Truth and History.* Cambridge: Cambridge University Press.

———. 1984. The Craving for Objectivity. *New Literary History* 15 (2): 229–39.

———. 2003 *The Collapse of the Fact/Value Dichotomy and other Essays.* Cambridge, Mass.: Harvard University Press.

———. 2005. *Ethics Without Ontology.* Cambridge, Mass.: Harvard University Press.

Raz, Joseph. 1999. *Engaging Reason.* Oxford, Oxford University Press.

———. 2006. The Trouble with Particularism. *Mind* 115 (457): 99–120.

Republic of South Africa. 1976. *Commission of Inquiry into Matters Relating to the Coloured Group.* Theron Commission. Pretoria: Government Printer

Rizal, T. K. n.d. *Nirvasan.* Unpublished document, draft translation provided by Professor Michael Hutt.

Roepstorff, Andreas. 1996. Form og Identitet eller *That National Thing:* Et studie I historie, narration og national identitet I Litauen. Manuscript, Moesgaard: Aarhus Universitet.

Roper, Lyndal. 1998. Witchcraft and Fantasy. *History Workshop Journal* 45: 265–71.

Rousso, Henry. 2002. *The Haunting Past: History, Memory, and Justice in Contemporary France.* Philadelphia: University of Pennsylvania Press.

Roy, Asim. 1983. *The Islamic Syncretic Tradition in Bengal.* Princeton, N.J.: University Press.

———. 1996. *Islam in South Asia: A Regional Perspective.* New Delhi: South Asian Publishers.

Roy, Sara. 1995. *The Gaza Strip: The Political Economy of De-Development.* Washington, DC: Institute for Palestine Studies.

Royal Government of Bhutan. 1992. *National Security Act.* Thimphu: Government of Bhutan

———. 2007. *Constitution of Bhutan.* Thimphu: Government of Bhutan.

———. n.d. *Thrimszhung Chenmo* (Supreme Laws). Thimphu: Government of Bhutan.

Ryle, Gilbert. 1971. *Collected Papers.* Vol. 2. *Collected Essays, 1929–1968.* London: Hutchinson.

Saber, M. A. 1989. *Pathor Somoy* (Difficult Times). Dhaka: Pallab.

———. 1991. *Sotero Bochor Pore* (Seventeen Years Later). Dhaka: Ananya.

Salek, Siddik. 1977. *Witness to Surrender.* New Delhi: Oxford University Press.

Salo, Elaine. 2003. Negotiating Gender and Personhood in the New South Africa: Adolescent Women and Gangsters in Manenberg Township on the Cape Flats. *European Journal of Cultural Studies* 6 (3): 345–65.

———. 2004. Respectable Mothers, Tough Men and Good Daughters: Producing Persons in Manenberg Township, South Africa. Ph.D. Dissertation, Emory University

Sanders, Todd and Harry West. 2003. Power Revealed and Concealed in the New World Order. In *Transparency and Conspiracy: Ethnographies of Suspicion in the New World Order,* ed. Harry West and Todd Sanders, 1–37. Durham, N.C.: Duke University Press.

Saul, John S. 1985. *A Difficult Road: The Transition to Socialism in Mozambique.* New York: Monthly Review Press.

Schafer, Jessica. 2001. Guerrillas and Violence in the War in Mozambique: De-Socialization or Re-Socialization. *African Affairs* 100: 215–37.

Scheper-Hughes, Nancy. 1996. Theft of Life: The Globalization of Organ Stealing Rumours. *Anthropology Today* 12 (3): 3–11.

Schmitt, Carl. 1996. *The Concept of the Political.* Chicago: University of Chicago Press.

Scott, James. 1985. *Weapons of the Weak.* New Haven, Conn.: Yale University Press.

Searle, John R. 1969. *Speech Acts: An Essay in the Philosophy of Language.* Cambridge: Cambridge University Press.

Shklar, Judith. 1984. *Ordinary Vices.* Cambridge, Mass.: Belknap Press of Harvard University Press.

Siegel, James. 1998. *A New Criminal Type in Jakarta: Counter-Revolution Today.* Durham, N.C.: Duke University Press.

Silverman, Kaja. 1992. *Male Subjectivity at the Margins.* New York: Routledge.

Simmel, Georg. 1972. *Georg Simmel on Individuality and Social Forms.* Ed. Donald N. Levine. Chicago: University of Chicago Press.

Strauss, Julia C. 2002. Paternalist Terror: The Campaign to Suppress Counterrevolutionaries and Regime Consolidation in the People's Republic of China, 1950–1953. *Comparative Studies in Society and History* 44 (1): 80–105.

Strawn, Christopher. 1994. The Dissidents. In *Bhutan: Perspectives on Conflict and Dissent,* ed. Michael Aris and Michael Hutt, 97–128. Gartmore: Kiscadale.

Szabó, István. 2006. Szembesítés (Taking Sides). *Népszabadság,* 27 January. http://www.nol.hu/cikk/392171.

Tamari, Salim. 1990. Limited Rebellion and Civil Society: The Uprisings Dilemma. *Middle East Report* 164 (5): 4–8.

Taussig, Michael. 1984. Culture of Terror, Space of Death: Roger Casement's Putumanyo Report and the Explanation of Torture. *Comparative Studies in Society and History* 26 (3): 467–97.

———. 1999. *Defacement: Public Secrecy and the Labor of the Negative.* Stanford, Calif.: Stanford University Press.

Taylor, Christopher. 1999. *Sacrifice as Terror: The Rwandan Genocide of 1994.* Oxford: Berg.

———. 2002. The Cultural Face of Terror in the Rwandan Genocide of 1994. In *Annihilating Difference: The Anthropology of Genocide,* ed. Alexander L. Hinton, 137–78. Berkeley: California University Press.

Taylor, Gabrielle. 1985. *Pride, Shame and Guilt.* Oxford: Oxford University Press.

Teltscher, Kate. 2006. *The High Road to China: George Bogle, the Panchen Lama and the First British Expedition to Tibet.* London: Bloomsbury.

Thaxton, Ralph A., Jr. 1997. *Salt of the Earth: The Political Origins of Peasant Protest and Communist Revolution in China.* Berkeley: University of California Press.

Thiranagama, Sharika. 2006. Stories of Home: Generation, Memory, and Displacement Among Jaffna Tamils and Jaffna Muslims. Ph.D. Dissertation, University of Edinburgh.

———. 2007. Moving On? Generating Homes in the Future for Displaced Muslims in Sri Lanka. In *Ghosts of Memory: Essays on Remembrance and Relatedness,* ed. Janet Carsten, 126–49. Oxford: Blackwell.

Trinh, T. Min-Ha. 1989. *Woman, Native, Other: Writing, Postcoloniality, and Feminism.* Indianapolis: Indiana University Press.

Turnaturi. Gabriella. 2007. *Betrayals: The Unpredictability of Human Relations.* Chicago: University of Chicago Press.

Turner, Samuel. 1800. *An Account of an Embassy to the Court of the Teshoo Lama in Tibet.* London: G & W Nicol.

Turner, Simon. 2001. *The Barriers of Innocence: Humanitarian Intervention and Political Imagination in a Refugee camp for Burundians in Tanzania.* International Development Studies. Roskilde: Roskilde University.

———. 2002. Dans l'oeil du cyclone: les réfugiés, l'aide et la communauté internationale en Tanzanie. *Politique africaine* 85: 29–45.

———. 2004. Under the Gaze of the "Big Nations: Refugees, Rumours and the International Community in Tanzania. *African Affairs* 103 (411): 227–47.

———. 2005. "The Tutsi Are Afraid We Will Discover Their Secrets": On Secrecy and Sovereign Power in Burundi. *Social Identities* 11 (1): 37–55.

Ura, Karma. 1996. *The Ballad of Pema Tshewang Tashi: A Wind-Borne Feather.* Bangkok: White Lotus.

UTHR- J, 1992. *Report 9: The Trapped People Among Peacemakers and Warmongers.* http://www.uthr.org/reports.htm.

————. 1993. *Report 10: The Rays of Deepening Gloom.* .

Varzi, Roxanne. 2006. *Warring Souls: Youth, Media, and Martyrdom in Post-Revolutionary Iran.* Durham, N.C.: Duke University Press.

Vines, Alex. 1991. *RENAMO: From Terrorism to Democracy in Mozambique?* Amsterdam: CSAS, James Currey and EMS.

Virgili, Fabrice. 2002. *Shorn Women: Gender and Punishment in Liberation France.* Trans. John Flower. Oxford: Berg.

Wakeman, Frederic. 2000. Hanjian (Traitor)! Collaboration and Retribution in Wartime Shanghai. In *Becoming Chinese: Passages to Modernity and Beyond,* ed. Wen-hsin Yeh, 298–341. Berkeley: University of California Press.

Walker, Margaret. 2006. *Moral Repair: Reconstructing Moral Relations After Wrongdoing.* New York: Cambridge University Press.

Walton, Chris. 2004. Furtwängler the Apolitical? *Musical Times* 9 (Winter).

Wedeen, Lisa. 1999. *Ambiguities of Domination: Politics, Rhetoric, and Symbols in Contemporary Syria.* Chicago: University of Chicago Press.

————. 2003. Seeing like a Citizen, Acting like a State: Exemplary Events in a Unified Yemen. *Comparative Studies in Society and History* 45 (4): 680–713.

West, Harry G. and Scott Kloeck-Jenson. 1999. Betwixt and Between: "Traditional Authority" and Democratic Decentralization in Post-War Mozambique. *African Affairs* 98: 455–84.

West, Rebecca. 1985. *The Meaning of Treason.* New York: Penguin.

Western, John. 1996. *Outcast Cape Town.* Berkeley: University of California Press.

Whelpton, John. 2005. *A History of Nepal.* Cambridge: Cambridge University Press.

Whitaker, Ben et al. [1972] 1982. *Biharis in Bangladesh.* 4th rev. ed. Minority Rights Group 11. London: Minority Rights Group.

White, Luise. 1997. The Traffic in Heads: Bodies, Borders and the Articulation of Regional Histories. *Journal of Southern African Studies* 23 (2): 325–38.

Whitecross, Richard W. 2002. "The Zhabdrung's Legacy: State Transformation, Law and Social Values in Contemporary Bhutan." Ph.D. Dissertation, University of Edinburgh.

————. 2009. Migrants, Settlers and Refugees: Law and the Contestation of "Citizenship" in Bhutan. In *Spatialising Law: An Anthropological Geography of Law in Society,* ed. Franz Benda Beckman, Keebet Benda Beckman, and Anne Griffiths. Aldershot: Ashgate.

Williams, Bernard. 1985. *Ethics and the Limits of Philosophy.* Cambridge, Mass.: Harvard University Press.

————. 1986. Reply to Simon Blackburn. *Philosophical Books* 27 (4): 203–8.

————. 1993. *Shame and Necessity.* Berkeley: University of California Press.

————. 1996. Truth in Ethics. In *Truth in Ethics,* ed. Brad Hooker, 1–8. Oxford: Blackwell.

————. 2001. What Was Wrong with Minos? Thucydides and Historical Time. *Representations* 74 (1): 1–18.

————. 2002. *Truth and Truthfulness: An Essay in Genealogy.* Princeton, N.J.: Princeton University Press.

Yang, Kuisong. 2006. Mao Zedong yu "zhenya fangeming" yundong (Mao Zedong and the "Campaign to Suppress Counterrevolutionaries"). In *Liang'an Fentu: Lengzhan chuqude zhhengjing fazhan* (Separation of the Straits: Political and Economic Development at the Outset of the Cold War), ed. Chen Yongfa. Taipei: Zhongyang yanjiuyuan Jinshi yanjiusuo.

Zhang,Yanxian and Shuyuan Gao. 1998. *Luku shibian yanjiu diaocha* (Investigation and Research on the Luku Incident), Taibei County: Wenhua Zhongxin.

Žižek, Slavoj. 1989. *The Sublime Object of Ideology.* London: Verso.

———. 1990. Eastern Europe's Republics of Gilead. *New Left Review* 1 (183): 50–62.

———. 1992. Eastern Europe's Republics of Gilead. In *Dimensions of Radical Democracy*, ed Chantal Mouffe, 193–207. London: Verso.

———. 1997. *Plague of Fantasies.* London: Verso.

Contributors

Lars Buur is a Senior Researcher at the Danish Institute for International Studies, Copenhagen. He is co-editor of *The Security-Development Nexus: Expressions of Sovereignty and Securitization in Southern Africa* and *State Recognition and Democratization in Sub-Saharan Africa: A New Dawn for Chiefs?*

Stephan Feuchtwang is Director of the MSc Programme on China in Comparative Perspective, Department of Anthropology, London School of Economics. Among many other publications, he is author of *Popular Religion in China: The Imperial Metaphor* and *Grassroots Charisma in China*.

Steffen Jensen is a Senior Researcher at the Rehabilitation and Research Centre for Torture Victims, Copenhagen. He is co-editor of *The Security-Development Nexus: Expressions of Sovereignty and Securitization in Southern Africa* and *State Violence and Human Rights: State Officials in the South*, and author of *Gangs, Politics and Dignity in Cape Town*.

Tobias Kelly is a Senior Lecturer in the School of Social and Political Science, University of Edinburgh. He is author of *Law, Violence and Sovereignty Among West Bank Palestinians* and co-editor of *Paths to International Justice: Social and Legal Perspectives*.

Nayanika Mookherjee is a Lecturer in the Department of Sociology, Lancaster University. Apart from various peer-reviewed journal publications, she is author of *The Spectral Wound: Sexual Violence, Public Memories and the Bangladesh War of 1971*.

Kamran Rastegar teaches Arabic Literature and Culture at Tufts University. His recent publications include "Trauma and Maturation in Women's War Narratives: The Eye of the Mirror and Cracking India" in *Journal of Middle Eastern Women's Studies*, and a monograph, *Literary Modernity Between Middle East and Europe*.

István Rév is Director of the Open Society Archives, Department of History, Central European University. Most recently, he is author of *Retroactive Justice, Prehistories of Postcommunism.*

Julia C. Strauss is a Senior Lecturer in the Department of Politics and International Studies, SOAS. She is the author of *Strong Institutions in Weak Polities: State Building in Republican China, 1927–1940* and editor of *China Quarterly.*

Sharika Thiranagama teaches in the Department of Anthropology, New School for Social Research, New York. She is currently completing a monograph I*n My Mother's House: The Intimacy of War of Sri Lanka,* based on her fieldwork in Sri Lanka on issues of war, displacement, kinship, home, and memory.

Simon Turner is a Senior Researcher at the Danish Institute for International Studies. He is the author of numerous articles on the contemporary politics of Burundi.

Richard W. Whitecross is Honorary Fellow in Social Anthropology, University of Edinburgh, and an Associate Member of CNRS (Paris). Among other articles, he is author of " 'Keeping the Stream of Justice Pure': The Buddhicisation of Bhutanese Law?" in *The Power of Law in a Transnational World: Anthropological Enquiries,* ed. Franz von Benda-Beckmann, Keebel von Benda Beckmann, and Anne Griffiths.

Index

Acknowledgments

We would like to thank the British Academy for the generous assistance that made it possible to hold the original workshop upon which this volume is based. The workshop also benefited greatly from the participation of David Anderson, Andrew Jefferson, Henricke Donner, Heonik Kwon, Joost Fontein, Laura Jeffery, and Jacob Dlamini. We must especially thank Julie Hartley for helping ensure that the three days in Edinburgh ran smoothly. We wish to thank Social Anthropology at the University of Edinburgh for their financial support for the editing of this volume. Thanks are also due to Ana María Ulloa at the New School of Social Research who kindly gave up her time for the index. Thomas Blom Hansen gave typically constructive comments on the introduction. Peter Agree has been the most encouraging and supportive editor, and Ashley Nelson and Alison Anderson and University of Pennsylvania Press have ensured that the editorial process run exceptionally smoothly. Above all thanks must go to Faye, Thomas, and Laerke for their loyalty and support, and more recently Matilda and Mirak, for helping us see where our priorities lie.